ERNEST LAPOINTE
Mackenzie King's Great Quebec Lieutenant

Also by Lita-Rose Betcherman

The Swastika and the Maple Leaf: Fascist Movements in Canada in the Thirties

The Little Band: The Clashes between the Communists and the Political and Legal Establishment in Canada, 1928–1932

Ernest Lapointe

Mackenzie King's Great Quebec Lieutenant

LITA-ROSE BETCHERMAN

UNIVERSITY OF TORONTO PRESS
Toronto Buffalo London

ISBN 0-8020-3575-2 (cloth)

Printed on acid-free paper

National Library of Canada Cataloguing in Publication Data

Betcherman, Lita-Rose, 1927–
  Ernest Lapointe : Mackenzie King's great Quebec lieutenant

  Includes bibliographic references and index.
  ISBN 0-8020-3575-2

  1. Lapointe, Ernest, 1876–1941.   2. Canada – Politics and government –
  1921–1930.   3. Canada – Politics and government – 1930–1935.   4. Canada –
  Politics and government – 1935–1948.   5. Cabinet ministers – Canada –
  Biography.   6. Canada. Parliament. House of Commons – Biography.
  I. Title.

  FC581.L36B48 2002   971.063′2′092   C2001-903683-3
  F1034.3.L36B49 2002

University of Toronto Press acknowledges the financial assistance to its
publishing program of the Canada Council for the Arts and the Ontario
Arts Council.

This book has been published with the help of a grant from the Humanities
and Social Sciences Federation of Canada, using funds provided by the
Social Sciences and Humanities Research Council of Canada.

University of Toronto Press acknowledges the financial support for its
publishing activities of the Government of Canada through the Book
Publishing Industry Development Program (BPIDP).

To my husband, Irving Betcherman

Contents

Illustrations follow page 212

Preface

When Ernest Lapointe lay on his deathbed, Mackenzie King told him, 'But for you, I would never have been Prime Minister, nor would I have been able to hold the office, as I have held it through the years.'[1] These were not just soothing words to console a dying man. Canada's durable prime minister spoke no less than the truth. King was dependent on Quebec. He was elected time after time because Quebec as a bloc voted for him. Yet he understood neither the province nor its language. He left that to Ernest Lapointe, his minister of justice, 'as a kind of local governor, almost autonomous in his powers.'[2]

King was able to preserve national unity, and incidentally stay in power so long, because of Lapointe's ability to 'deliver' Quebec. The mass of French Canadians trusted Lapointe more than any other federal politician, not excepting Laurier or St Laurent. He shared the views of his people and was their spokesman at Ottawa. A loyal Quebecker, yes, but Lapointe envisioned Quebec only within the larger context of the Canadian nation. His lifelong task was to help construct a Canada broad enough to embrace French and English viewpoints.

The King-Lapointe partnership can be compared with that of Baldwin and Lafontaine or Macdonald and Cartier. Throughout the 1920s and 1930s and into the first years of the Second World War, Lapointe was King's highly effective Quebec lieutenant. But he was much more than that – he was the prime minister's closest associate. Reconciling his loyalty to Quebec with devotion to national unity was not an easy road for Lapointe; there were obstacles all along the way. The inevitability of war in the late 1930s confronted him with a challenge of epic proportions. Quebec wanted to remain neutral while the rest of Canada was resolved to join the Allies' fight against Hitler. Lapointe won Quebec's support for the declaration of war, and Canada entered the world conflict united. For his unifying role a national magazine saluted him as Canada's 'Number One Statesman.'[3]

In August 1940, a year before Lapointe died, Mackenzie King acknowledged their long partnership and what it had meant to him:

> To have been side by side during the past 21 years with the change in the party's fortunes which has come about within that time is an achievement which I feel we are entitled rightly to share with pride.
>
> How much all of this is owing to your loyal cooperation in the leadership of the party through every month and week and day of that time, you and I alone know but, I imagine, I know even better than you. For your never-failing devoted friendship, I cannot be too grateful.[4]

Acknowledgments

I want to take this opportunity to pay a special tribute to the archivists and librarians whose unstinting help smoothed my five-year journey through the source material for this book. My thanks also to my efficient research assistant, Martin Betcherman.

As well, I want to express my gratitude to the editors at the University of Toronto Press, in particular Siobhan McMenemy, who took charge of the manuscript with all the enthusiasm and helpfulness a writer could wish for, and Frances Mundy, who piloted the manuscript into print.

ERNEST LAPOINTE
Mackenzie King's Great Quebec Lieutenant

CHAPTER ONE

National Attention

On a bitterly cold night in February 1916 the Parliament Buildings on the bluff above the Ottawa River were gutted by fire; whether the cause was an overheated furnace or wartime sabotage no one knew. The homeless parliamentarians were transferred to makeshift quarters in the Victoria Natural History Museum, a barracklike structure outside the capital's downtown. (As the joke ran, the fossils were moved out and a new batch moved in.) The Department of Public Works did its best to create some semblance of the grandeur and dignity of the green and red chambers, but it had little to work with. A bare exhibition hall across from the museum entrance became the new House of Commons. A platform behind the Speaker's chair, serving as an improvised gallery for visitors and the press, was so low that one reporter quipped he could lean over and pat the Speaker's bald head if he felt so inclined. As if to highlight the nomadic nature of this Parliament, an enormous Union Jack was draped tentlike on the wall above the gallery.[1]

Ranged on either side of the room were the desks of the two parties: the Conservative government benches to the Speaker's right, the Liberal opposition to his left. The two commanding figures were Sir Robert Borden, his centre-parted hair resembling an oversize handlebar moustache, sitting bolt upright as befitted a wartime prime minister, and the elegant leader of the opposition, Sir Wilfrid Laurier, whose plumes of white hair and beaked nose gave him the appearance of a rare bird – as, indeed, he was in that company of old grey men.

H.F. Gadsby, *Maclean's* parliamentary correspondent and something of a humourist, described the changes wrought by the move. Much of the mystery and glamour of Parliament disappeared as behind-the-scenes activity became visible. The museum's wings had been partitioned off into offices, and according to Gadsby reporters could peak over the papier mâché partitions and watch the august leaders preparing for their entrance into the Commons chamber – 'the Speaker struggling with his high white cravat; or the Sergeant-at-Arms putting on the official trousers; or the Black Rod polishing his ebony wand; or Premier Borden gargling before he plunged into argument; or Sir Wilfrid snoozing while he waited for the bell.'[2]

Among the greybeards, Ernest Lapointe at forty was regarded as a young man. A head of thick black curls and his very size – he was over six feet tall and burly – lent him an appearance of youthful virility. Lapointe was the Liberal member for the Quebec riding of Kamouraska, a farming community on the south shore of the St Lawrence east of Quebec City. Unlike most of the Quebec members sitting around him, he did not come from the French-Canadian elite. He was bred of *le petit peuple*, the son of a farming couple from St Eloi, a village not far from Rivière-du-Loup. Ernest Lapointe's rise would be the French-Canadian version of the Horatio Alger success story.

As so often happened among the habitant families, Ernest's convent-educated mother was a cut above her husband. A contemporary described her as a woman of 'ardent faith and remarkable erudition.'[3] She was the guiding influence in her son's early years, making sure that he was kept out of the barn and the fields long enough to do his studies. Observing that he was intelligent and anxious to learn, the local curé took an interest in the boy and, perhaps hoping to make a priest of him, arranged for his tuition at the classical college in Rimouski. During Lapointe's time at the college his mother died. Indicative of his feelings for her, he kept her letters, full of piety and good advice, which many years later he showed to his daughter. Young Lapointe lived up to his mother's expectations, winning the Prince of Wales scholarship, the top award for rhetoric in the province's classical colleges,[4] which enabled him to study law at Laval University. In 1895 he applied to the Quebec City law firm of Lemieux and Lane. He was aiming high. The senior partner, François-Xavier Lemieux, was famous as the defender of Louis Riel. The eminent lawyer, later chief justice of Quebec, took Lapointe on as a law clerk with the caveat that he would have to learn some stenography and procedure before he could be useful enough to warrant a salary.[5] In the summer of 1898 Lapointe was admitted to the Quebec bar, and in partnership with Adolphe Stein (a thorough French Canadian despite a German grandfather) he opened a law practice in Rivière-du-Loup. To make their careers thrive, young lawyers had to cultivate political connections, and Lapointe and Stein, Liberals by conviction, became hard workers for the party. Lapointe had already worked for the local Liberal candidate in the 1896 election that first elected Wilfrid Laurier.[6]

In 1904 Lapointe married and was elected to the House of Commons. He met his wife through amateur theatricals. Emma ('Mimy') Pratte was considered a good match for a habitant's son. Her father was the station master at Rivière-du-Loup, no mean position in an important railway terminal town.[7] It was H.G. Carroll, then Laurier's solicitor general, who launched Lapointe into politics the same year. Carroll was the Member of Parliament for the county of Kamouraska. In 1904 he was appointed to the bench, and, looking around for someone to succeed him as MP, he remembered the young lawyer Ernest Lapointe. As crown prosecutor some years before, Carroll had come to know Lapointe as a very competent defence counsel who presented the vital points of a case swiftly and surely. Still, he might never have thought of him as his parliamentary successor if it had not been for a marvellous speech Lapointe delivered at a dinner two years earlier in Carroll's honour. Freed from the constraints of the courtroom, Lapointe had spoken with a passion that revealed him as a natural-born orator. On Carroll's recommendation Lapointe was nominated and elected to Parliament.[8] Thus it was Lapointe's oratorical skill that gave him his start. French Canadians loved rousing oratory, and they demanded it of their politicians. The saying was that Quebec produced orators while English Canada produced businessmen. A silver tongue was Laurier's greatest political asset. It would prove to be Ernest Lapointe's as well.

People remembered that Lapointe came to Ottawa with scarcely a word of English. He had been educated entirely in French, and clerking at a Quebec City law firm and practising law in Rivière-du-Loup had provided no opportunity for becoming bilingual. During his first decade in Parliament, the big country lawyer from Quebec's south shore was simply a likeable government backbencher, 'the picture of smiling good nature' sporting a dark-blue beret on his curly head. He spoke rarely and, when he did, he spoke in French. Moving across to the opposition backbenches after the Liberal defeat in 1911, Lapointe denounced the Tory alliance with Quebec nationalists that had led to Borden's victory and condemned the spoils system that saw the Liberal-appointed civil service dismissed by the new government. Stung by the anglophone members' lack of attention, according to one report he would at times become almost inarticulate with submerged rage.[9]

Years later, Lapointe liked to recall that Laurier encouraged him to learn English, recommending that he read Macaulay's English history aloud. But it was really Jacques Bureau, the member for Trois-Rivières, who took him in hand. Under Bureau's tutelage, Lapointe laboured long and hard to become proficient in English. Considerably older than Lapointe, Bureau had been postmaster general under Laurier. In the large, good-natured Lapointe, with his innate oratorical skills, Bureau believed he saw the successor to Laurier, but first that speaking ability had to be translated into facility in English. Unless he could master English, Bureau impressed upon Lapointe, he had no future on the national scene. Bureau was fluently bilingual, having spent time in Saskatchewan in his youth and, later, in the American Midwest, where he picked up the tricks and trade of machine politics. He began to coach Lapointe in English in a jovial but merciless fashion.

During the parliamentary session both men were in Ottawa without their wives. From 1912, when it opened its doors, they stayed at the baronial Chateau Laurier, whose copper-clad turrets and gables added elegance to the skyline of the capital. Lapointe was an omniverous newspaper reader, and in the morning Bureau would slyly slip the English-language Ottawa papers under his door, making sure that he never got his hands on *Le Droit*, the French daily. He would underline the difficult words and test Lapointe on their meaning and pronunciation. The lessons went on everywhere – in the Grill Room, in the men's lounge off the lobby, even in the barber shop. Amazed hotel guests overheard Bureau saying, 'No, Ernest. Not "dee-ficult." Say it like this, "diff-i-cult." No. No. No. It's difficult, difficult, difficult,' his voice rising in a crescendo. Bureau also forced Lapointe, who was essentially of a retiring nature, to socialize more – not with the Quebec MPs but with the English ones. As one journalist noted in amusement, the jaunty Bureau segregated Lapointe from his own kind 'as though every Frenchman had the plague.' They dined with anglophones and had their after-dinner cigar with them. As field work, Bureau had Lapointe ask a few questions in English in the House. Under Bureau's 'tough love' tactics, Lapointe gradually became proficient in English.[10] Still, if he had something important to say, he spoke French.

In 1912 he objected to increases in the defence budget, and in 1913 he opposed Borden's naval bill (a gift of $30 million to the British navy) for committing Canada to Britain's foreign policy. Hearkening back to Laurier's defeated naval bill of 1911, Lapointe declared that Canada was a nation – only its belittlers called it a colony – and should have its own navy for defence and trade. With his two speeches on the naval bill, he showed his colours as a Canadian autonomist strongly opposed to imperial centralization. In 1915 he championed bilingualism, calling for war stamps in French as well as English.[11]

In January 1916 Lapointe ventured his first major speech in English. He began by dissociating his province from the anti-British and anti-war statements of a Quebec senator. He declared that Quebec was doing its full share for the war, and he expressed his own support for 'all measures that would help the Mother Country.' But in his opinion the government's target of half a million Canadian troops was 'rather large and would be very difficult to reach.' He blasted wartime profiteering and accused the Borden government of trying to avoid an investigation on the ground of security. His eloquence left Laurier 'simply amazed.' 'I thought I knew his talent,' the old gentleman wrote Mimy Lapointe, 'but I knew it only imperfectly. As proof, I am sending you a clipping from the Conservative Evening Journal ... You can judge how proud we who are his friends are of him.'[12]

Although he had sat in the House of Commons since 1904, Lapointe was unknown outside Quebec. That changed in May 1916, when he gained national attention with the introduction of a controversial resolution dealing with French instruction in Ontario separate schools. The bilingual schools question, which periodically tore apart English and French Canada, made him first-page news along with the war. Many people were incensed that the question of bilingual schools should be raised when the country was at war. 'CRIME TO FAN RACE HATRED' blazed a *Toronto Daily Star* headline.

The war news in 1916 made sombre reading. Newspapers across the country were full of casualty lists and photographs of local boys listed as wounded, missing, or killed in action. Canada had three divisions overseas, and the loss of life was staggering. Over 6,000 Canadian soldiers had died at the battle of Ypres in 1915, and the most recent engagement in the Ypres salient had reaped some 1,400 dead. Replacements for the fallen were imperative, but with the harsh realities of trench warfare apparent there were no more line-ups at recruitment offices. Enlistment was perceived to be especially low in Quebec. A brigadier general in the Senate presented statistics that purported to show that French Canadians accounted for only 4.5 per cent of the recruits.[13] Stirred up by jingoists and Orangemen, anti-French sentiment was rampant in English Canada. It was in this atmosphere that

Lapointe introduced a resolution whose purpose was to protect the use of French in Ontario schools.

The British North America Act of 1867 made provision for Roman Catholic separate schools in Ontario, but it said nothing about French instruction in these schools. Nevertheless, since the 1880s Franco-Ontarian children had been taught almost exclusively in their own language in the so-called bilingual schools.[14] From the turn of the century the French population in Ontario grew rapidly and by 1912 numbered a quarter of a million people. The powerful Orange Order, rabidly anti-French and anti-Catholic, raised the alarm. For them Canada was a British country and English should be its only language. Many Orangemen believed that the French, spilling over from Quebec, meant to force French on Ontario children. In 1912 the Ontario Department of Education brought in Regulation 17, which severely restricted French instruction and was ultimately intended to eliminate bilingual schools in the province. (Lapointe had condemned Regulation 17 as anti-Catholic in one of his rare speeches in the House.) More rigorously administered in 1915–16, the regulation was seen by Franco-Ontarians as forced assimilation. The provincial minister of education, Howard Ferguson, a staunch Orangeman, defended Regulation 17 as the only way to force Franco-Ontarian children to learn English. As an example of politics making strange bedfellows, the province's Irish Catholics were as opposed to French in the separate schools as were the Orangemen, their traditional enemy.[15] Ottawa had the power to disallow provincial acts or to pass remedial legislation. Prime Minister Borden, owing little to the French vote, which was solidly Liberal, refused to touch Regulation 17.

This put Laurier in a difficult situation. It was his firm belief that the Dominion government should never override provincial legislation in the interests of a French minority because such a precedent could boomerang against the French majority in Quebec. As prime minister in 1896 he had chosen not to interfere with provincial rights when Manitoba abolished bilingual schooling. An even more compelling reason for staying out of the Regulation 17 controversy was the unalterable opposition of his western supporters to bilingual schools, and indeed to anything that smacked of concessions to the French. Then, also, Newton Rowell, the leader of the Liberal party in Ontario, was on record as favouring Regulation 17.[16] On the other hand, in his home province Laurier was being denounced by Henri Bourassa and the nationalists for his lack of action on behalf of the Franco-Ontarians.

Henri Bourassa was the grandson of Louis Papineau, the legendary leader of the 1837 rebellion in Lower Canada. Bourassa had sat in the Commons as a Liberal until 1899, when he broke with Laurier over Canadian participation in the Boer War. Bourassa had undoubtedly inherited the rebel blood of his grandfather. Years ahead of his time, he fought against Canada's colonial status in his lectures and in his newspaper, *Le Devoir*. His vision was of an independent Canada within the British Empire. Bourassa was never a separatist – just as Canada should be equal within the empire, he believed French and English should be equal within Canada. Although initially supporting the First World War, he now opposed Canada's war policy as excessive and wasteful. Bourassa was branded a traitor in English Canada, but in Quebec his influence was growing rapidly at Laurier's expense. People fell under his spell, as they had with Laurier. Like his rival, he had an old-world courtesy that enhanced his keen intelligence and articulateness. Bourassa and his nationalists took up the cause of the Franco-Ontarians. Indeed, they linked participation in the war with the 'persecution' of the French in Ontario. Bourassa's disciple, Armand Lavergne, loudly demanded to know why French Canadians should fight for a country that would not honour their fundamental rights: they must fight the *Boches* of Ontario, he told cheering crowds in Quebec, before fighting the *Boches* in France. No statements were too extreme for him. 'Every French Canadian who enlists fails to do his duty,' he told a banquet crowd in January 1916.[17]

The Quebec nationalists, with their hostility to the war and their aggressive demands for bilingualism, were a thorn in Laurier's side, weakening his popularity in Quebec and turning the rest of the country against him as a French Canadian. Although leader of the opposition, Laurier feared his putative opponent, Borden – the reasonable prime minister sitting across the aisle from him – less than he did the editor of *Le Devoir*. Even harder to put up with than Bourassa was Lavergne with his demagoguery. Laurier was hounded by the unquenchable rumour that Armand Lavergne was his son by his long-time friend, Emilie Lavergne. Lavergne himself emphasized the faint resemblance by combing his hair like Laurier. Whether an Oedipal impulse was involved, Armand Lavergne certainly caused Laurier a good deal of aggravation. Quebec's outrage over Ontario's intolerance went far beyond the nationalists. Regulation 17 was denounced from the pulpit and condemned by politicians who pointed out that the English minority in Quebec had their own Protestant schools. A monster petition with 600,000 signatures asking for disallowance of Regulation 17 had been presented to the Borden government.[18]

Finally, Laurier decided to bring Regulation 17 before the House, hoping that his manifest support for the war – from his 'Ready, aye ready' speech in 1914 to his present recruitment efforts in Quebec – would help him retain the goodwill of English Canadians. Given the attitude of his western supporters, it was not politic for him to move the resolution himself. Indeed, Liberals from the three prairie provinces announced that they would not support their party's resolution and attempted to nip it in the bud by maintaining that the House had no business discussing the Ontario schools question because education was strictly a provincial matter.[19] After looking in vain for a suitable anglophone proposer, Laurier assigned the task to Lapointe, who had helped draft the motion. Lapointe was Laurier's most dependable man in the Lower St Lawrence region and, session by session, was rising in the old chief's estimation.

The *Toronto Star* found it 'curious' that Lapointe presented his bilingual schools resolution in English. The truth was that Quebec MPs knew that if they spoke in their own language it would be wasted breath in the predominantly anglophone assembly. (The official translation did not come out for at least two weeks.) A reporter who covered the House for seven years said he never heard Laurier speak in French. Indeed, Laurier often said that he blessed his father for sending him to English school at the age of eleven.

On 9 May 1916 the floor of the House and the gallery were filled in anticipation of Lapointe's resolution on Regulation 17. Lapointe had an attractive voice, rich with habitant inflections, and he spoke in an unhurried and dignified fashion. The resolution when it came bore all the hallmarks of Laurier's conciliatory style; indeed, it was crafted largely by Liberalism's high priest, and Lapointe was still by way of being an acolyte. The Lapointe resolution did not ask the Borden government for remedial legislation, nor did it ask the Ontario government to repeal Regulation 17; it freely granted the need for French children to be given a thorough English education. It simply asked the House to 'suggest' to the Ontario legislature the 'wisdom' of not interfering with the 'privilege' of children of French parentage being taught in their mother tongue. It sounded bland enough, but as the journalist Grant Dexter would say twenty-five years later, it was dynamite.

Speaking in support of his motion, the acolyte moved a little away from the conciliatory tone of the resolution: 'The advocates of Regulation 17 claim that they do not want to stop the teaching of French, but to improve the conditions under which it is taught. But the wolf would always find a justification for eating the lamb.' There was not the slightest doubt in his mind, Lapointe told the House, that the regulation would insidiously strangle the French tongue in Ontario.[20]

His resolution was seconded by an English Liberal, but the real seconder was Laurier himself, who delivered one of his unforgettable parliamentary addresses. Yet even this could not sway the House. Laurier had freed his caucus to vote as their conscience dictated, and when the vote was taken on the morning of 12 May the resolution was defeated 107 to 60. Despite its defeat, Lapointe had caught the public's eye with his resolution on Regulation 17. He had appeared as Laurier's spokesman on an issue of prime importance for Anglo-French relations. Banner headlines unfurled his name. English Canada was beginning to hear of Ernest Lapointe.

Meanwhile, Lapointe's law practice in Rivière-du-Loup was thriving. For his family of four – a daughter, Odette, was born in 1910 and a son, Hugues, in 1911 – Lapointe rented one of the finest houses in town, next door to the presbytery of the principal church. Like most lawyers, he sometimes thought of going to the bench – this ambition crops up more than once in his career – and in 1908, while Laurier was still prime minister, Lapointe had asked for a judgeship. The reply was a rather blunt turndown. If he granted judgeships to all those who asked for them, Laurier told his backbencher, there would not be a single lawyer left in the Quebec caucus.[21] (Perhaps as a consolation prize, Lapointe received his KC that year.) With the Liberals out of office in 1911, an appointment to the higher courts was out of the question; but by that time Lapointe was a rising man in party ranks. His political career both helped and hindered his law practice. It took up a lot of his time, but it made him a big man in Quebec with a network of connections. Moreover, though Lapointe could not deliver federal patronage while the Liberals were in opposition, his law partner, Adolphe Stein, represented the district in the provincial legislature and had considerable influence in Quebec City.

Kamouraska county was their bailiwick, and when Sir Lomer Gouin, the Quebec premier, interfered in local affairs they did not hesitate to confront him. One such run-in had occurred in April 1914 when Gouin let it be known that he was appointing someone other than their choice to the legislative council for their county. Lapointe dashed off an angry letter to Quebec City:

For the love of God, do not impose on me and on our division John Hall Kelly as Legislative Councillor. That is an affront to us. People who know me well know that I am *faithful* and *loyal* and they know what it would cost me to take the attitude that you are forcing me to take.

I cannot, will not accept Kelly, and you cannot, will not want to impose him on us. In the name of my services to the party for eighteen years, and those I can render, I ask you not to inflict on me this humiliation in my own county and district.[22]

Lapointe would not have been pleased to hear Stein's account of a meeting in Gouin's office, where the premier and his favourite minister, Louis-Alexandre Taschereau, dismissed any need to consult with Lapointe. Stein added his own protests to Lapointe's, but Kelly was duly appointed. This and similar incidents rankled with these country lawyers, all the more so since Gouin and Taschereau were members of the Quebec elite and hand in glove with the English financiers of St James Street.

In October 1916 Lapointe's law practice took him to London to argue two cases before the Judicial Committee of the Privy Council. Exemplifying Canada's colonial status, the country's highest court was not within its own boundaries but in England. While overseas Lapointe hoped to have an opportunity of visiting Canadian troops at the Front. He approached Prime Minister Borden, who told him that his request might be difficult to grant and gave him a rather half-hearted letter of introduction to the acting high commissioner in London, Sir George Perley. Less than satisfied, Lapointe discussed the matter with his own chief. Laurier was anxious for Lapointe to observe and report on the situation at the Front. A fourth division had just gone to France, and accounts of the horrible conditions in which Canadian troops were fighting were drifting back to Canada. Laurier gave Lapointe a letter to take to the secretary of state for war, David Lloyd George, asking him to arrange a visit to the Front for 'my friend, Mr. Ernest Lapointe,' and assuring him that the bearer was 'the very soul of honour and absolutely trustworthy.'[23] Although Lapointe crossed over to France, he did not get to the Front. Civilians were prohibited from doing so by regulations, though in some cases these were waived. A few months earlier, the Ontario Liberal leader, Newton Rowell, who was a strong proponent of total mobilization, had been given a thorough tour of the Ypres salient.[24] However, in the autumn of 1916 the Somme offensive was underway, and Lloyd George would have been no more anxious than

Borden to have Lapointe go home and report to Laurier on Canadian boys slogging through knee-deep mud and going over the top to be mowed down by enemy fire.

Over 24,000 Canadians were either killed or wounded in the battle of the Somme. Those who survived were sent back into action as soon as they could be patched up. There was an outcry at home for reinforcements. The Borden administration had promised there would be no conscription, but the demand from English Canada was intensifying. Recruitment drives were failures: the volunteer supply (a large proportion of whom were British immigrants) had already been exhausted. The mood was ugly. Respectable women stood on street corners waving the white feather at men of military age in civilian garb. 'Call up the slackers,' was the general hue and cry. Liberal papers such as the *Toronto Daily Star* and the *Manitoba Free Press* were demanding conscription. Pressure on the government was coming from the mother country too. Borden was in England during the assault on Vimy Ridge in April 1917. The four divisions of the Canadian Corps were the heroes of the bloody victory at Vimy, yet the Canadian contribution was still not enough to satisfy the British. Borden came home convinced that Canada must send more troops.

CHAPTER TWO

Conscription

Although the United States entered the war in April 1917, the Americans could not be mobilized quickly enough to reinforce the dwindling Allied troops. On 18 May Prime Minister Borden announced to a divided country that he intended to introduce conscription for overseas service – something he had assured Canadians would never happen. In the hope that conscription would be viewed as a non-partisan policy, Borden tried to induce Laurier to enter into a coalition. The prospect of conscription, however, was creating near hysteria in Quebec, where mobs, raised to fury by nationalist tirades, were breaking the windows of newspapers such as *La Patrie* and *La Presse* in Montreal that seemed ready to accept it. Henri Bourassa was hardly exaggerating when he wrote in *Le Devoir* that two million French Canadians were opposed en masse to conscription. Laurier told Borden he would consult with his advisers.[1]

Whenever he needed a reading on Quebec opinion, Laurier turned to Rodolphe Lemieux 'to call the turn.' Lemieux had enjoyed a distinguished career in the Laurier regime as cabinet minister, diplomat, and chief strategist on French Canada. In opposition, he continued to be Laurier's Quebec adjutant. In the present crisis his advice to Laurier was to resign rather than join a coalition government.[2] On 6 June Laurier refused Borden's offer. If he accepted conscription, he told the prime minister, he would be handing over the province to the extremists. On 11 June Borden introduced conscription with the Military Service bill. Laurier moved an amendment calling for a referendum.

Ernest Lapointe did not rave and rant as many speakers did in the heated and emotional conscription debate, but he was nevertheless one of the bill's most forceful opponents. Conscription, he told the House on 20 June, 'is a direct violation of all the pledges given by this Government, this Parliament, and all the public men of this country to the Canadian people.' The bill with its 'selective conscription' was the very opposite of democracy. Appointed boards would decide whose son would go overseas and give his life for his country and whose son would remain comfortably at home. Favouritism and patronage would be rife.

Lapointe defended the French-Canadian record in the war. It was well established, he said, that French Canadians had been kept out of the militia for years, and when the First Canadian Contingent was organized French-Canadian officers who offered their services were not accepted. Out of fifty-three commanding officers, only one was a French Canadian. A great obstacle to recruiting in Quebec was the 'slanderous campaign carried on by one influential section of the Ontario press against the people of our province.' 'It is a wonder that enlistment had been so large in spite of what seems to have been a deliberate effort to stop it,' he declared.

Lapointe questioned the accuracy of the ministry of militia's figures of the number of recruits of French descent. One just had to look at the casualty lists to see the many French-Canadian names: 'Are we to infer that French Canadians are always put in the places of danger?' His speech made a great impression – even on the Conservative *Ottawa Journal*, which called it 'thoughtful, well reasoned and wonderfully moderate in tone.' While 'firm in his convictions,' the paper stated, Mr Lapointe remained 'courteous and conciliatory to his opponents.' An added compliment was that 'his diction is that of a scholarly man with a delightful French accent in English which is attractive.'[3]

Laurier's referendum amendment was soundly defeated, and the conscription law was passed. Laurier's refusal to enter into a coalition or to agree to prolong the life of the current Parliament (it had already sat one year beyond the five-year term) left the Borden government with no alternative but to call an election. The introduction of the Wartime Elections Act, disenfranchising those naturalized citizens who were from enemy countries and giving the vote to female relatives of servicemen, stacked the deck in the government's favour.

The author of the Wartime Elections Act was the secretary of state, Arthur Meighen. An austere individual admired by some but detested by more, Meighen did the dirty work of the Borden administration. It was he who piloted conscription through Parliament, ramming it through at the end by invoking closure. In the case of the Wartime

Elections Act, he made no attempt to disguise its purpose. On 14 September, when the bill was in its final stage, Lapointe launched a personal attack on Meighen:

> The Secretary of State who has been given credit for this undemocratic legislation, after having already been the recognized father of the closure rules and other narrow Tory enactments, was more frank in his cynical admission that he expected the Conservative Party to get the votes of such as are given the franchise by this Bill, and the Liberal Party to lose the votes of those whose rights are taken away.

While he admired Meighen's talent, Lapointe said, 'a man whose ethics would permit him to consider as justifiable the tampering with the election law of the country on the eve of a general election in order to secure the return of his party, cannot be morally fit to occupy a prominent position amongst the rulers of this country.' Lapointe specifically objected to the provision in the bill granting the vote to female relatives of soldiers. 'I am not a partisan of women suffrage as many gentlemen in this House seem to be,' he announced. 'In the province from which I come this new move does not get the general approval of public opinion.' He may simply have taken this stand for home consumption, and not out of conviction, because only a few months earlier he fervently opposed a motion put forward by a French-Canadian Conservative to bar women from the federal civil service.[4]

The Wartime Elections Act passed easily and was followed by the Military Voters' Act, which allowed the government to use the soldiers' vote to weight the conscription side in any riding. The Tories could easily have won an election on their own, but Borden wanted a unified home front, and on 12 October he announced a coalition cabinet. His two French-Canadian ministers stayed on ('Their names can no longer be spoken in public,' Lapointe would declaim at election rallies), but not a single French-Canadian Liberal could be enlisted. Nine anglophone Liberals in all joined the Unionists, among them Newton Rowell and William Stevens Fielding, Laurier's former finance minister. Fielding's 'desertion,' Laurier wrote Lapointe, had been 'particularly cruel.'[5]

The Liberal party was reduced to a Quebec rump. Fearing annihilation at the polls, some of Laurier's oldest colleagues suggested he should resign the party leadership. (Laurier himself had reached the conclusion that a French Canadian should never be prime minister.) Lapointe was outraged. It was unbelievable to him that Liberals could forsake their great leader. 'Have these people lost their heads? You are the only possible man at this time to be leader of the Liberal party,' he wrote his chief. 'I would prefer to go down to defeat with you than to win with anybody else.'[6] As time would show, fidelity to his chosen leader was Ernest Lapointe's guiding principle.

The 'khaki election,' as it became known, was announced for 17 December 1917. It was in effect a referendum on conscription and the campaign was dirty from the beginning. Headlines in the English-language press screamed that a vote for Laurier was a vote for the Kaiser. In Quebec several Unionist candidates were threatened with bodily harm if they dared to mount the podium. Lapointe devoted all his time to campaigning. The Liberal party organ, *Le Soleil*, dubbed him Laurier's *premier soldat* in Quebec. His influence went beyond the Lower St Lawrence. The nomination for Liberal standard-bearer in Quebec South was being contested by a well-known politician, Arthur Lachance, and a young newcomer, Lieutenant Charles Power, affectionately known as Chubby to his legion of friends. Recently invalided home with a crippled arm from a German bullet in Picardy, Power had jumped into the election campaign. Politics was in his blood; his father had been the Liberal MP for Quebec West as long as anyone could remember, and his brother was mayor of a town in Kamouraska county. Lapointe threw his weight behind Power and, with some arm-twisting, got Arthur Lachance to step aside. Complaints reached Laurier's ears that this was a pay-off to the Power family, to whom Lapointe was indebted for political support. The tale-bearers were dismissed peremptorily: 'What you're saying about Ernest Lapointe is absolutely false and unjust to him,' Laurier retorted, as loyal to his follower as his follower was to him.[7]

Campaigning in the Quebec winter was an endurance test. The roads, many little better than tracks, were blocked by snow as high as a man. Many a day found Lapointe battling the elements to reach some town or village for a rousing *assemblée contradictoire* – a political debate peculiar to the province where audiences were entertained with pyrotechnical oratory and dirty tricks against the opposing speakers. At one small town 10,000 people turned out to hear Lapointe, Armand Lavergne, and other stars of the circuit.[8] On the stump Lapointe took aim against the war profiteers. As he wrote Laurier on 27 December, 'I think that our most formidable weapon is to present the fight as one against the sharks of high finance, identifying Unionism with Flavellism, Siftonism, Max Aitkenism ... All these war profiteers are on the government's side, and it's important to give evidence of this fact.'[9]

Lapointe's advice to take on the capitalists differed sharply from Rodolphe Lemieux's election strategy. A law partner of Sir Lomer Gouin, Lemieux was close to the business interests in Montreal. He would have cautioned strongly against alienating campaign donors. A man who stood on ceremony and was very set up with himself (the caustic reporter J.K. Munro called him 'a politician after a fashion and the same kind of an orator; but he spoils both by trying to look like a statesman'), Lemieux and the populist Lapointe were decidedly not *sympathique*. There is even a hint that Lemieux absented himself from Laurier's big election rally in Quebec City when he heard that Lapointe was also to be on the platform.[10]

On 17 December 1917, as expected, the Unionists swept to victory. In a macabre development, the conscriptionist party was helped by the carnage of the battle of Passchendaele, which left 16,000 Canadians dead or wounded in Flanders fields. It was this battle which moved Borden to write to Lloyd George, the new British prime minister, that if ever there was a repetition, 'not a Canadian soldier will leave the shore of Canada so long as the Canadian people entrust the Government of their country to my hands.'[11] The election divided Canada surgically along French-English lines. Conscription had killed the Conservatives in Quebec, and Laurier's Liberals were barely breathing in the rest of the country. In his own riding of Kamouraska Lapointe enjoyed a landslide victory with a majority of 3,000 votes – previously he had never won by more than a few hundred. Chubby Power was also elected, in the long-term giving Lapointe one of his staunchest supporters. Still, Lapointe was dreadfully disappointed that Laurier had been deprived of his 'rightful' post as prime minister. Laurier was fatalistic. 'After the defection of our old Liberal friends who became Tories, we couldn't hope for victory,' he wrote Lapointe just before Christmas. And in the same letter: 'Our front benches are a little empty, the young will have to go to work.'[12]

On 18 March 1918, when the House reconvened, Ernest Lapointe and Jacques Bureau moved up to the front benches directly behind Laurier. The two men were inseparable friends and always spoken of in the same breath. Despite their close friendship, they were very different. Bureau was a heavy drinker who was only too delighted to be known as 'the Playboy of Parliament.' His 'humorous sallies, exploding like joyous firecrackers on the floor,' made him extremely popular in the House, and he used humour to make the French and English MPs see one another's point of view.[13] Lapointe had the same sunny personality – he said of himself that he had a smile in his heart – but he was strait-laced in his private life and more reserved in the House, where his wit took the form of irony rather than farce. Chubby Power and the other novice Quebec MPs turned to these two for guidance on how to be effective in opposition.

Laurier was now seventy-seven, and to Frederick Griffin of the *Toronto Star* the spirit seemed to have gone out of him: 'For the most part, he sat, a sad and tired wraith, seldom rising to speak, while around him lesser men wrangled.'[14] There were flashes of the old brilliance, but the talk in the corridors of the Victoria Museum was of a possible successor. J.K. Munro, who was covering Parliament for the *Toronto Telegram* as well as *Maclean's*, cast his eye over the sparse Liberal benches and found 'nothing in the way of leadership timber.' Lemieux struck him as pompous and prosy. D.D. McKenzie from Cape Breton and Charles Murphy, both Laurier loyalists, he marked off the list without a second thought. Next he considered 'the two jolly Frenchmen of more than ordinary ability – Ernest Lapointe of Kamouraska and Hon. Jacques Bureau of Three Rivers,' but he decided 'they'd hardly do for leaders even if they didn't come from Quebec.'[15] It was the general consensus that the next prime minister would be English – there was too much bitterness in the country against the French for perceived slacking in the war.

Seated beside Laurier, Lemieux remained the unchallenged Quebec lieutenant. Indeed, Lapointe had recently shown that he could not yet 'call the turn' in Quebec nearly as well. In January he had assured Laurier that there would be no violence in Quebec over the implementation of the conscription law. The session was hardly underway when riots over conscription broke out in Quebec City. The trouble began during Easter week when the military police arrested a young man named Mercier. On producing his exemption papers he was released, but by that time an angry mob had set fire to the police station. An English-speaking troop from Toronto was called in, and the result was a small-scale repetition of what was going on at the Front: sniper fire returned by infantry, a cavalry charge with drawn swords and fixed bayonets, which ended with four civilians dead and five soldiers wounded. In the House Borden's official version of the riots omitted any reference to the harshness and indignities with which conscription was being pursued in Quebec. Nor did he mention the provocation of anti-French sentiment in English Canada. The *Orange Sentinel* was not the only newspaper calling for 'one flag, one

school and one official language from coast to coast.' Sombrely listen-
ing to the debate, Lapointe spoke for his fellow French Canadians:
'We have not any friends, Mr. Speaker, outside the province of
Quebec.'[16]

As it happened, few of the conscripts saw action. By the summer of
1918 the American doughboys were 'over there' in full force. Nevertheless, the war-weathered Canadian Corps was in the vanguard in the
Allied breakthrough that began in August 1918. Among the best and
bravest was the Royal 22nd regiment from Quebec – the famous Van
Doos. After heavy fighting (which among thousands of others took the
son of Rodolphe Lemieux) the Armistice was signed on 11 November
1918.

The war over, Laurier immediately summoned his high command to
a meeting at the Windsor Hotel in Montreal. In his invitation to Lapointe
he mentioned that he was limiting the number to those who would be
his counsellors during the coming session. Laurier's top priority was to
reconstruct the party by healing the wounds that conscription had
inflicted, and he was making overtures to former colleagues who had
deserted him. Lapointe was not vindictive, but some Liberal loyalists,
such as Laurier's old secretary of state, Charlie Murphy, refused to sit
down with the 'traitors.'[17]

In Quebec too there were those who wanted to settle scores now that
the war was over. Lapointe would not cooperate with them. A journalist from *La Patrie* who felt he had been vilified by *Le Devoir*'s Georges
Pelletier asked Lapointe to dig up some dirt about Pelletier's father,
who had gone bankrupt in Rivière-du-Loup many years before. Lapointe
had ample reason to complain of his own treatment by the nationalist
organ. Nevertheless, he refused out of hand to lend himself to such an
inquiry: 'In the first place, in my own fights I have never employed
arms of this type and I would hardly want to furnish them for other
people's battles. But my principal reason is that I know personally that
Georges Pelletier imposed very great sacrifices on himself to pay off
debts he did not have to. If there is a man who does not merit being
attacked on a question of this nature it is he. We are adversaries in
political life, but loyalty obliges me to render him this witness.' The
man from *La Patrie* replied that he hoped Lapointe would never suffer
for his generosity.[18]

Lapointe's prestige had grown immensely during the war. A backbencher at the beginning, he emerged from it an influential member of
Laurier's shadow cabinet. Though not yet touting him as a possible

successor to Laurier, J.K. Munro called him 'one of the ablest debaters on the Opposition side [with] a command of the English language that puts most Anglo-Canadians to shame.' Munro's articles in *Maclean's* did much to further Lapointe's reputation. Years later in Geneva, Lapointe would thank J.B. Maclean, the publisher, for making him a national figure during the war. 'Don't thank me,' Maclean replied, 'the credit goes to J.K. Munro who had a very high opinion of you.' None of this praise went to Lapointe's head. Unlike Rodolphe Lemieux, he had no pretensions and remained a modest, even diffident, person.[19]

In the middle of February 1919 Lapointe was in Ottawa for the opening of the parliamentary session. The Union government was falling apart; the Liberal ministers were either retiring or moving back to their party. A most welcome prodigal son was W.S. Fielding. Nevertheless, Laurier had no intention of forcing an election. He was not even anxious for a by-election. When Lapointe raised the matter of several vacant seats in the Commons, the old chief remarked that an election campaign would unleash more anti-French sentiment: 'The cry "Down with Quebec" is always there and can be dangerous,' he instructed his disciple. 'The government will not call an election at this time, having lost so much ground, but we have not won it.'[20] In fact, Prime Minister Borden was out of the country at the Paris Peace Conference insisting on Canada's right, earned by the sacrifice of 60,000 of its young men, to sign the peace treaty on its own and not as part of the British Empire. He would not be back in Canada when Parliament convened on 20 February.

On 16 February came the shocking news that Sir Wilfrid had had a paralytic stroke. The next day he was dead, lying in state in the Victoria Museum before being moved to the Notre Dame basilica for the funeral. Fifty thousand people braved the cold to watch the funeral procession plod its way through Ottawa's snow-banked streets. In the House of Commons the acting prime minister, Sir Thomas White, and Rodolphe Lemieux for the opposition pronounced the eulogies. A few months later, in the House of Commons, Lapointe expressed his own debt to the leader: 'We who have had the privilege of learning our political doctrines under the guidance of the great statesman whose loss we mourn, shall endeavour to remain true to his teaching and inspiration. From the grave where he has been laid, Sir Wilfrid Laurier still leads us. We shall never forget his great lessons of tolerance, moderation and equal justice for all. "Live and let live" ought to be the standard principle of Canadians.'[21]

With Laurier's passing, Ernest Lapointe's tutelage ended. He had thoroughly learned the lesson of the Great Conciliator, that compromise was essential to reconcile Canada's two founding peoples. The war, the bilingual schools controversy, and conscription had left Canada much as Lord Durham had found it in 1838: two nations warring in the bosom of a single state. As a federal politician from Quebec, Lapointe would have to reconcile his loyalty to 'my dear old province,' as he called it fondly, with his legacy from Laurier – a passionate devotion to national unity.

CHAPTER THREE

King-Maker

The convention to choose Laurier's successor opened on Tuesday, 5 August 1919, in the Howick Building in Ottawa's Exhibition Grounds. There were over a thousand voting delegates, a radical departure from the past, when leaders had been chosen by the parliamentary caucus. As a prominent member of the planning committee, Ernest Lapointe was quoted in the press as saying that 'Sir Wilfrid Laurier had been leader of a democratic party and it was therefore fitting that his successor should be chosen not by a coterie of politicians but by a great democratic convention.'[1] It was a sorely divided gathering: eastern Liberals versus western, rural interests versus urban, protectionists versus free traders. Above all, conscription had left a French-English schism. The one thing agreed upon by the Laurier loyalists and the Liberal Unionists who had returned to the fold was that the new leader would have to be an anglophone. It was English Canada's turn. Underlining the dual nature of the party, the joint chairmen were Premier George Murray of Nova Scotia and the Quebec premier, Sir Lomer Gouin.

Gouin ruled his province with an iron hand and was expected by many to dominate the French-Canadian delegation. When he walked into the Chateau Laurier lobby, thick with the cigar smoke of the delegates, a 'welcoming roar' went up. Someone was heard to observe, 'No matter who is elected, there's the real leader of the Liberal party.'[2] Gouin was far from an imposing figure. Short and dark, with a face like a mastiff, he was taciturn by nature. A businessman as well as a politician, he was one of a handful of French Canadians sitting on the boards of banks and large corporations. During his fifteen years as premier, Gouin ran the government for the benefit of his friends on St James

Street. A by-product was a businesslike and fairly efficient administration. While his high-tariff protectionist views would seem to have made him a natural Tory, over the summer he had resisted all Borden's blandishments to join the Union government.

In fact, Sir Lomer had made it abundantly clear to Sir Robert that Toryism was about as popular in Quebec as the new Bolshevism. After declining on his own account, he referred Borden to Lemieux, Bureau, and Lapointe. Lapointe duly received a letter from Borden telling him that the prime minister was taking a cruise on the St Lawrence and hoped to visit him in Rivière-du-Loup. Lapointe replied that it would be a privilege to greet Sir Robert in his home town. Madame Lapointe, an excellent political wife, would have helped her husband to graciously entertain the prime minister. When Borden broached the possibility of some French Canadians entering the Union government now that conscription was a dead issue, Lapointe informed him that no Quebec politician would ever get elected if he lined up with the conscriptionists. The prime minister met the same response when he stopped at Trois-Rivières to see Bureau and at Murray Bay to see Lemieux. At least his trip was not a total loss – he had a very pleasant golf game at Murray Bay with Sir Lomer Gouin and the former U.S. president, William Howard Taft, who had a summer place there.[3]

In contrast to Gouin, Lapointe was a low-tariff man and no friend to big business. He came to the convention with the reputation of a reformer who spoke for the little people – the farmers and industrial workers. In recent speeches in the House he had opposed the protective tariff as an unfair method of raising revenue and criticized 'the reactionary Tories' for refusing to discuss changes in tariff policy. During the Winnipeg General Strike in May, he had earned the gratitude of the labour movement for his support of collective bargaining. In a hard-hitting speech critical of the government's handling of the strike, he suggested that the conspicuous consumption of war profiteers was an incitement to unrest and maintained that industrial unionism was inevitable as the counterpoise to massive organization of capital. Lapointe was an outspoken critic of 'the interests,' charging that they used the fear of Bolshevism to discredit reformers: 'Profiteers, monopolists, trust magnates, the protected interests, have always tried to associate reform and progressiveness with revolution and crime.'[4] He objected to titles and was fully in favour of banning them. Long known as a liberal committed to civil rights, in his address on the throne speech in March Lapointe had urged the government to immediately lift press censorship: 'Certain restrictions were justifiable during the war, but the condition of war no longer exists.'[5]

As a spokesman for rural Quebec, Lapointe had struck up an informal alliance in Parliament with T.A. Crerar, the head of the United Grain Growers, a forthright man, lanky as a cowboy with a shock of red hair and a weather-beaten face. In June Crerar had resigned as minister of agriculture in the Union government and, unaligned with either party, sat in the Commons as the representative of the western farmers. The farmers were a political force to be reckoned with since the war. They demanded low tariffs, if not virtual free trade, and challenged the eastern protectionists in both traditional parties. In the throne speech debate, Lapointe had assured the West 'that the rural interests of eastern Canada – and they constitute the great majority of the people – are prepared and willing to work with the western farmers to obtain a lowering of the tariff.'[6]

Although Lapointe had a genuine concern for the working classes, it was really a misnomer to call him a social reformer. Reflecting Quebec's hostility to social legislation, he was no champion of old age pensions or unemployment insurance. Indeed, he opposed anything that would lead to state control. Speaking in the House of Commons on 25 April 1919, he set out his political philosophy: 'Liberalism stands for liberty – liberty of the subject, liberty of speech, liberty of action, liberty of commerce. Liberalism stands for freedom and competition in all lines and spheres.' This placed him on the same side as Gouin in the dispute then raging on nationalization of the railways, but not for the same reason. Lapointe viewed nationalization as an unjustifiable restraint on private enterprise while Gouin was simply defending the interests of his associates in the privately owned Canadian Pacific Railway.

Lapointe's laissez-faire liberalism resulted in a skirmish in the House with Newton Rowell. A firm advocate of conscription, the Ontario Liberal leader had left provincial politics in 1917 to join the Union government as president of the Privy Council and had remained in the Borden administration after the war. Rowell was a pioneer advocate of the welfare state – and was hated for it by the old guard, both Liberals and Tories. In a debate on the railway issue in April, Rowell had not hesitated to tell Lapointe that his brand of liberalism was fifty years out of date. 'Progressive liberalism,' he instructed the member for Kamouraska, 'has felt compelled not to increase personal liberty but to restrict the power of the strong for the protection of the weak.'[7] Some of Rowell's views on state interventionism had crossed the floor and found their way into the Liberal party platform to be put before the convention. With the veterans demanding a better deal and the Winnipeg General Strike a recent memory, it was no time to trot out the old shibboleths. The program was decidedly reformist, calling for welfare measures and industrial relations legislation, a freeing up of trade, and continuation of wartime income taxes.

The candidate to beat at the leadership convention was the Honourable W.S. Fielding, former minister of finance in the Laurier administration. This bearded septuagenarian was the incarnation of elderly sagacity, the perfect model of the old grey men who had run pre-war Canada. Convinced that conscription was necessary, Fielding had joined the Unionists, but when war ended he moved back to the Liberal side of the House. He was extremely conservative, with a colonial mentality, and made no bones about his intention of scrapping the progressive elements of the party program if chosen leader. Sir Lomer Gouin was vigorously supporting this fossil. So were the seven other Liberal provincial premiers and their political machines. However, the Quebec delegates and certain anglophone Laurier loyalists were unforgiving of those Liberals who had joined the Union government. They would not accept Fielding even though Sir Wilfrid had welcomed him back with open arms and, according to Lady Laurier, had designated him as his successor.[8]

Also in the running were D.D. McKenzie, a scripture-quoting Scot from Cape Breton, and George Graham from Ontario, a newspaper publisher as well as a politician. In April when the Liberals named McKenzie interim House leader, the press gallery (according to J.K. Munro) 'looked on him as a sort of serious joke' and had burst out laughing; but either he had grown in the job, or the aura of power had subtly transformed him, because he was now being seriously considered as a successor to the great Laurier. Graham, as genial a jester in the House as Jacques Bureau, was thought to be too lacking in *gravitas* for the top job. As the journalist H.F. Gadsby once said, 'The only charge against him is that he lends a spice of humor to the dreary declamation of the Green Chamber.'[9]

The younger generation was represented by William Lyon Mackenzie King, an industrial relations specialist with a gift for impressing the right people. It was King who had drafted the welfare and labour planks in the new party platform. At forty-four he was young for politicians of the time, and with his boyishness and bouncing manner he looked even less of a leader than Graham. But among all the old war horses he had the advantage of being a fresh face. He had run and lost in the elections of 1911 and 1917 and consequently had been mercifully absent from the wearying politics of the war years. In presenting himself as a reformer, he traded upon the fact that he was the grandson of William Lyon Mackenzie, the leader of the 1837 rebellion in Upper Canada. Unlike his grandfather, he did not take up arms but spent the war years working for John D. Rockefeller, whose Colorado mines were plagued by strikes. In running for leader of the Liberal party in 1919 King had in effect come home. In 1907 Laurier had chosen him to set up a department of labour, and shortly before the Liberals' defeat in 1911 King had succeeded Rodolphe Lemieux as minister. While his war record worked against him with English Liberals, his support of Laurier on the conscription issue made him acceptable to the Quebec delegates. Indeed, he claimed to be Laurier's heir apparent. With all his credentials, King was not regarded as a likely winner (except by himself). The pre-convention newspaper coverage did not give him much of a chance. According to *Maclean's* pundit J.K. Munro, 'rude laughter greeted his claims to the vacant leadership.'[10]

The big question in the corridors of the Chateau Laurier and down the street at the Rideau Club was how damaging Fielding's association with the Unionist government would be to his campaign. Certainly the three distinguished elderly gentlemen lunching at the Rideau Club the Sunday before the convention were dead set against him. Sir Allen Aylesworth, Laurier's former minister of justice, Sydney Fisher, a Quebec member and former minister of agriculture, and the patrician Senator Raoul Dandurand were all Laurier loyalists. With a snort of derision, Sir Allen Aylesworth announced to his dining companions that if Fielding was chosen he himself would join the farmers' party. This was as likely as the socialist J.S. Woodsworth joining the Tories, but it indicated the opposition to Fielding among some influential anglophones. Sir Allen suggested sounding out the delegates on behalf of Fisher if it appeared that King could not carry the convention. Fisher unenthusiastically agreed to let his name stand.[11]

The convention was quite different in tone from American conventions. There were no brass bands playing 'Happy Days Are Here Again' and no rousing speeches for favourite sons. There would be no roll call by province; each delegate would vote by secret ballot as he (or she) chose (another post-war innovation was the presence of a handful of female delegates). The candidates campaigned discreetly by speaking to the various resolutions. King did himself much good with a placatory and uncontroversial address on labour, which he wound up with a deep reverential bow to Laurier's enormous portrait above the stage.[12]

Confident of his power to control the Quebec caucus, Sir Lomer Gouin issued orders: vote Fielding, Fielding, and no one else but Fielding. However, he failed to take into account how unpopular the conscriptionist Fielding was with the Quebec delegation. And he completely underestimated the influence on the caucus of Lapointe and Bureau, who made no secret of their opposition to Fielding. At a meeting of the Quebec caucus early in the convention Sir Lomer met with open revolt. The delegates made it clear that they would have no truck with Fielding. There was a strong suspicion that the foxy Gouin had anticipated just such an eventuality and had prepared a contingency plan. To everyone's surprise, Athanase David, one of Gouin's bright young men in the provincial legislature, suddenly introduced a motion that the Quebec delegation abstain from voting for the leadership. No French Canadian was in the running, and he argued that it would only increase anglophone hostility if the Quebec vote should decide the leadership. Quebec should stand aloof and let the English provinces elect whom they pleased. If this motion passed, Fielding would be unbeatable.

The caucus was in an uproar, and in the confusion it looked as if the motion might pass. Then Lapointe took the floor. In a speech that presaged many others he would deliver to keep Quebec in the Canadian mainstream, he convinced the delegates that it would be utter stupidity for French Canadians to isolate themselves still further from the rest of Canada. Rodolphe Lemieux, the caucus chairman, upheld Lapointe's position against the David motion, and the motion was defeated almost unanimously. Lapointe was the hero of the hour.[13]

Speaking from the podium the next day, Lapointe continued his crusade to unify the party. He began by castigating the Conservatives for fomenting divisions in the country. The Liberals must work for a united Canada, he told his audience. Let racial and religious prejudices disappear and they would destroy the Tories. He then made a comment that brought the convention to its feet and was to become a classic in the party: 'A Liberal is a Liberal because he likes something or somebody; a Tory is a Tory because he hates something or somebody.'[14] When he sat down, Lapointe received a table-thumping, standing ovation. 'Lapointe is the coming man,' shouted a triumphant Bureau above all the noise.

At this juncture Lapointe was more anti-Fielding than pro-King. He opposed Fielding not only because he had deserted the old chief but because he was a reactionary. In his speech Lapointe had declared himself for reform: 'Young Liberals, and I flatter myself to still be among them, want aggressive and courageous politics.' The only reformer among the anti-conscriptionist candidates was Mackenzie King. Perhaps for lack of a better candidate, Lapointe and Bureau came out for him. According to Chubby Power who was there, 'King had no prestige and no great reputation' and the delegates took him on faith because Lapointe and Bureau supported him.[15]

Nevertheless, the King supporters had not yet won the battle. As Senator Dandurand observed to his friends at lunch at the Rideau Club on the day of the vote, Quebec could not elect a candidate by itself. They would have to consolidate the Fisher and King supporters to defeat Fielding. Fisher was only too happy to step aside. Over lunch he told his friends that he would nominate King and he was going to ask Lapointe to second the nomination. Dandurand did not think Lapointe was a good choice. They had to bear in mind that the English provinces would be prejudiced against any candidate chosen by Quebec. He convinced Fisher that Aylesworth should be the seconder instead of Lapointe. Aylesworth was deaf as a post. Dandurand, not wanting to shout out their private business in the crowded dining room, wrote a note asking if he would second King's nomination and passed it across the table to Aylesworth. It came back with one word – Yes.[16] The consolidation of the Fisher and King forces brought Rodolphe Lemieux on side. Lemieux had flitted from one candidate to another at the convention. He had come intending to fall in line behind his friend Sir Lomer Gouin and vote for Fielding. Later, he was reported to be supporting a western candidate. Then when Dandurand and Fisher threw their support behind King, Lemieux followed suit.[17]

King led the first ballot with 344 votes to Fielding's 297. Graham and McKenzie tied with 153 each. On the second ballot King pulled ahead with 411 votes to Fielding's 344. Graham received 124 votes and McKenzie trailed with 60. The last two candidates then withdrew. Graham freed his supporters, but McKenzie threw his Maritimers behind King. For the final ballot all eyes were on the finalists sitting on the platform. King was poker-faced, absently fingering his chin. The stifling heat alone did not account for the perspiration dripping down his round, smooth face and wilting his collar. The frail grey-bearded man opposite him was inscrutable. Even when the announcement came that King had won and the packed hall exploded with cheers, Fielding did not so much as move a muscle. As soon as the noise died down, he went to the front of the platform, and in a voice that trembled slightly as a result of a minor stroke, he moved that King's election be made unanimous.[18] It was a tight squeeze, as Aylesworth put it. The final vote was 476 for King to 438 for Fielding. Aylesworth disputed the newspaper tally that gave Fielding 70 of Quebec's 297 votes: 'Fielding got 25 or 30 votes from Quebec – all of them Englishmen – and not more than 30 all told – whatever the poor old fool Globe may say.'[19] The consensus was that Quebec had voted almost as a bloc for King. And it was Ernest Lapointe who had stopped Quebec from withdrawing from the convention.

No one knew better than King that Lapointe had turned the tide in his favour. Describing the convention in his diary when it was all over, King wrote: 'The Quebec members had a caucus on the second day of the convention and thrashed out the situation. Senator David's son read a long paper and spoke eloquently on Quebec abstaining from voting. This, Ernest Lapointe in a smashing speech destroyed completely, only the mover and seconder supporting the motion. Then the caucus put the "protectionist" group to the wall and declared open revolt against the Quebec leaders Gouin et al. The province almost solidly agreed to stand by me.'[20] The new Liberal leader was not yet a Member of Parliament when Prime Minister Borden called a special session in September to approve the peace treaty and protocols signed at Versailles on 28 June 1919. In the first week of the session Borden took ill, leaving Newton Rowell to pilot the treaty through the House. D.D. McKenzie, still the Liberal House leader, was patently unequal to the debate, and Ernest Lapointe responded for the opposition with a hard-hitting critique of Borden's role in the peace negotiations.

Through assiduous study the country lawyer from Rivière-du-Loup had turned himself into a debater on constitutional issues that made him a match for Rowell the legal scholar. Even Bourassa's *Le Devoir* sang the praises of 'this man who delights in high policy and can dissert with Mr. Rowell the Czechoslovakian problems, the deliberations of the Imperial Conference of 1907, or the different definitions of collective security, without losing an inch of his height or a hair on his head.'[21] Actually, there was little substantive disagreement between the two men, or between their parties for that matter. All but the most died-in-the-wool imperialists believed that after Canada's immense contribution to the war effort its colonial status had to be changed. But changed to what? Should the self-governing Dominions – Canada, Australia, New Zealand, South Africa – take their places around the table at an imperial cabinet in London, or should they conduct their external affairs as independent nations still within the empire but in no way subordinate to the United Kingdom? Lapointe espoused the latter view.

Citing the fact that Prime Minister Borden and one of his ministers had signed the Treaty of Versailles, Rowell proclaimed that Canada had advanced to nationhood. Lapointe disagreed. Waiving his copy of the treaty, he pointed out that the signatories for the Dominions were not among the twenty-seven specified parties to the treaty – their names appeared merely as representatives of their countries. He maintained that British plenipotentiaries had signed for the entire empire: 'The Treaty is made between the British Empire and the other powers, and whether we approve of it or not, it binds the whole of the British Empire, including the Dominion of Canada.' His complaint, he told the House, was that 'our representatives were not there on a basis of perfect equality with those of the Mother Country.' He moved on to question Canada's role in the League of Nations, the international body created by the Treaty of Versailles to keep world peace. Canada had not become a member on its own volition, Lapointe declared. Rather, it had been 'contracted in' as part of the British Empire. He dryly observed that India, which was not even a Dominion, was also a member of the League.

Rowell was hard put to answer Lapointe as to what exactly Canada's status had been at the peace conference. He attempted to square the circle. 'Canada had her own representatives and she was entitled to share in the Empire representation as well.' Glancing over at Lapointe, Rowell commented, 'My honorable friend looks incredulous.' 'Very much so,' was Lapointe's response. What he would like to see, Lapointe concluded, was 'an amendment or reservation clearly stating that our approval of the Treaty shall in no way impair or take away the rights and privileges of the Parliament of Canada.' Above all, 'it must be made perfectly clear that no Canadian soldiers can ever be ordered to fight any where except by the authority of this Parliament.'[22]

From his listening post in the gallery, Mackenzie King thought it 'a splendid debate.' Lapointe had spoken 'exceedingly well,' and so had Rowell – 'It is a pity he is on the Conservative side.' Frankly, King felt that Rowell had made a good case that Canada had already achieved national status as a result of Borden's negotiations. The following day King held a caucus where it was decided to move an amendment to the peace treaty resolution exactly as Lapointe had recommended. Fielding handled it, however, and he managed to make the call for Canadian autonomy sound like 'a colonial speech.' 'The old men are out of joint with our times,' King scribbled in his diary.[23]

Lapointe's speech in the peace treaty debate and his victory over Gouin at the Liberal leadership convention enhanced his growing reputation. Parliamentarians were beginning to say that here was Laurier's successor.[24] On 20 October 1919 Laurier's actual successor was elected by acclamation in a safe seat so that he could take his place in the House of Commons. A by-election had also been called in Laurier's old riding of Quebec East. At the time of Laurier's death, King had hoped to represent that hallowed ground,[25] but after the leadership convention the party was anxious to play down King's dependence on Quebec. In any event, Quebec Liberals wanted to reserve Laurier's riding for a French Canadian.

Armand Lavergne, the rabid Quebec nationalist, anxious to be recognized as Sir Wilfrid's true heir in a more meaningful way than by a slight physical resemblance, was making a bid for the Quebec East nomination. Because of Lavergne's venomous tongue, other candidates were afraid to contest the nomination. King discussed the situation with Lapointe, D.D. McKenzie, and Jim Robb, the party whip. They all agreed that on no account should Lavergne be allowed to run as the Liberal candidate. Lapointe said he would run himself rather than have Sir Wilfrid's constituency represented by a nationalist. King left it up to Lapointe but told him not to risk his own chances 'as he would be wanted in any Liberal government formed.'[26] Jacques Bureau was urging his friend to take the plunge. Bureau regarded the vacancy in Quebec East as a heaven-sent opportunity to establish Lapointe as head of the anti-Gouin faction and at the same time to deliver a blow to the nationalists.[27]

Lapointe was hesitant. He had a loyal riding that regularly re-elected him. Why should he risk his political future? He had his family to provide for: Mimy and the two children, nine-year-old Odette and eight-year-old Hugues, whom they still called Baby. He was very happy in his marriage. Mimy Lapointe was a handsome, reserved woman whose life revolved around her husband's career and her children. While Ernest was in Ottawa for the parliamentary sessions she remained in their large rented house in Rivière-du-Loup. Sir Wilfrid and Lady Laurier had often urged Lapointe to bring her to Ottawa: 'We haven't seen her for a long time here,' the suave old gentleman had written Lapointe in 1915. 'Her friends have not forgotten her. You know

I'm one of her admirers.' In her quiet way, Mimy looked after her absent husband's political interests. She 'stood guard over his constituency,' writing him daily to keep him informed.[28] Ernest knew that she would not like moving to Quebec City. She had her family in Rivière-du-Loup – her brother was the manager of the local Banque Provinciale. But he also knew that his wife would never stand in his way.

No, the reluctance was all on his part. Though politics was his great love, Ernest Lapointe lacked the ambition that powered men like Mackenzie King, Arthur Meighen, and the rising Conservative R.B. Bennett. An insightful journalist commented at this time that Lapointe had 'no hankerings for leadership': 'It is the figurative kick from behind that up to the present has been an essential part of the development of Ernest Lapointe. He is reticent and prone to hang back and depreciate his own ability. He perhaps has not the ambition nor as yet the feeling of obligation, either of which may drive a man into active politics. He needs the forward urge, but when he has consented to do a thing he goes into it with a will. He has a fighting heart.'[29]

It was Jacques Bureau who delivered that kick from behind. Bureau told his friend and protégé that he had to run in Quebec East. Laurier had fought the nationalists all his life. How could they let a nationalist, and in particular Lavergne, step into Laurier's shoes? Lavergne was no longer trying for the Liberal nomination because the committee had made loyalty to Mackenzie King an unacceptable condition for him.[30] Instead, he was running as an independent nationalist. He was a dangerous opponent. His anti-war stand had made him a hero with many Quebeckers, and with his skill in oratory he could be expected to demolish Arthur Lachance, the official Liberal candidate, at the *assemblées contradictoires*.

Lapointe finally agreed to stand as a candidate, and Bureau hurried down ahead to arrange matters. Essentially this meant inducing Arthur Lachance to withdraw his candidacy. Poor Lachance – he had stepped aside for Chubby Power in Quebec South in 1917, and now he had to cede his place to Lapointe. (His party loyalty was later rewarded with a judgeship.)[31] On 8 October Lapointe arrived at Quebec City, supposedly to chair the nomination meeting. To no surprise of the insiders, he himself was nominated by Lachance. Two days later, before a large crowd at the skating rink in the district of St Roch, Lapointe accepted the nomination in Quebec East. It was a sign of Lapointe's prestige and popularity that Lavergne, anticipating defeat, dropped out of the race.[32] On 14 October 1919 Lapointe stood up in the House of Commons and announced his resignation as the member for Kamouraska. (He was not just flattering his former constitutents at Rivière-du-Loup when he said that it was the most difficult decision he had ever made.) On 27 October he won the by-election over a couple of independent candidates by a huge majority, and on 5 November he was introduced by Mackenzie King as the member for Quebec East.

Upgraded to Laurier's seat, Lapointe had to replace himself in the Kamouraska riding. This by-election was of key importance to the party. The United Farmers of Ontario had just defeated the entrenched Tory government in a provincial election. Farmer candidates were winning by-elections all over the West. 'At the moment, the dangers of the farmers' movement is uppermost in our people's minds,' King recorded in his diary.[33] Quebec could also fall victim to 'the farmer epidemic.' The Kamouraska by-election was the first in a Quebec rural constituency since the success of the agrarian movement. The Liberals had to field a strong candidate to ward off a possible contender representing the farmers. In Lapointe's opinion, his law partner, Adolphe Stein, was 'overwhelmingly the strongest man in the riding,' and he prevailed upon him to accept the nomination.[34] Stein resigned his seat in the Quebec Legislative Assembly and was duly elected Member of Parliament for Kamouraska.

How did Lapointe really feel about the grass-roots farmer movement? He and Tom Crerar, the leading light of the movement, had become real friends. Lapointe's *entente* with Crerar was apparent to Parliament-watchers such as J.K. Munro. The political winds were 'blowing the Hon. T.A. Crerar and Ernest Lapointe closer together every day,' he informed *Maclean's* readers.[35] Clearly, Lapointe saw an alliance with the western agrarian movement as a counterweight to the influence of the Montreal oligarchy in the Liberal party.

King was thinking along the same lines. He confided to his diary that he was 'delighted with the political earthquake' caused by the farmers' movement. He wanted to form 'a really progressive party,' and he felt the best way was through a Liberal-Farmer alliance. If he could reach an alliance with the more moderate agrarian element represented by Tom Crerar, he would be able to override the protectionist element in the Liberal party. During the Christmas recess he sent the new party secretary, Andrew Haydon, to Winnipeg to talk to Crerar. 'I believe he may be able to link up Crerar with Lapointe and myself,' King wrote in his diary. 'If the three of us ever get together on the one platform we will be able to sweep the country.'[36]

CHAPTER FOUR

Cabinet Minister

The parliamentary session opened on 26 February 1920 in the rebuilt Parliament Buildings, much grander than before the fire and destined to be truly magnificent when the Peace Tower – a national memorial to the war dead – was completed. Borden was down south for his health, and Sir George Foster was acting prime minister. Neither Foster nor Mackenzie King excited as much press comment as T.A. Crerar, who headed up the new Progressive party, an amalgamation of the eastern and western farmer MPs. Ranged along the cross benches the Progressives sat in judgment on government and opposition.

The Liberal party under its neophyte leader was in serious disarray. The Quebec delegation itself was split on the tariff question, half being for protection, the other half against it. It was common knowledge around Parliament Hill (according to *Manitoba Free Press* reporter Grant Dexter) that 'a contest was going on in the French Liberal party between Lapointe who represents the Rouge tradition and Lemieux who is pretty tender to "the interests," and that Lemieux realizes that he is going to be dislodged from his position of leadership.'[1] Though Lemieux continued to have pride of place in the front row beside the leader, it was to Lapointe and Bureau (who had modestly elected to sit in the second row) that King more often turned for advice on Quebec.

King was pushing for a dissolution, and on 9 March Lapointe backed him up in a forceful speech. No wonder the government would not grant a dissolution, he said, it was a single-purpose government, elected to carry on the war, and it had no mandate to exist any longer. Why, in the 1919 by-election in Quebec East that returned him to Parliament, the Union government did not get a single vote! For the absent Borden to try to hang on to power was 'a challenge to democracy.' By contrast, the Liberal party was the party of national unity:

> The Liberal party holds the middle course between dangerous and violent changes that would bring disaster to our institutions, and obstinate resistance to progress and the spirit of the time. Between capital and labour, between individualism and corporations, between the big interests and the plain citizen like you and me, Mr. Speaker, between the Canadian Manufacturing Association and the Canadian Council of Agriculture.
>
> Since we are denounced as dangerous free traders and protectionists in disguise, I take it we are discharging the true and normal functions of Liberalism holding the sane and safe middle course.

It was a splendid speech in King's opinion, and indeed it coincided with his own view that finding a common ground among divers interests and groups was the only way to run the country.

Jacques Bureau's efforts to turn Lapointe into a good English-language speaker had succeeded beyond his wildest hopes. Lapointe's speeches were a highlight in the unending drone of the House. When word went round that 'Lapointe is up,' the almost empty benches would soon fill. His appearance was an asset in itself. 'Standing well over six feet, heavy of shoulder, with kindly face and prominent brow,' as a journalist described him in 1920, 'his very presence gains the attention of the crowd.' And he knew how to hold his audience: 'He takes his hearers with him, by easy paths that they can follow, and lifts them with a mighty flame of passionate utterance.'[2]

In July Sir Robert Borden announced his resignation, and Arthur Meighen succeeded him as prime minister. King greeted the announcement in the privacy of his diary as 'too good to be true.' His acquaintance with Meighen went back to their university days, and he knew him to be too extreme and patently ambitious, narrow, and inflexible. He was not a man for the times (King was Providence's answer to that). Moreover, Meighen was the author of the conscription bill, which should damn him eternally in Quebec. This happy development quite took King's mind off the divisions within his own party. For his part, Lapointe heartily disliked the new prime minister, and not only for his politics. Meighen's unbending, humourless personality did not sit well with the Gallic *joie de vivre* of the French-Canadian members. Lapointe remarked to Chubby Power that Canada was 'too damn good a country to let Arthur Meighen run it.'[3]

Sir Lomer Gouin also stepped down as premier of Quebec in July, leaving his chosen successor, Louis-Alexandre Taschereau, with a strong Liberal majority in the provincial legislature. (At the banquet honouring Taschereau, Lapointe gave an eloquent testimonial. The new premier returned the compliment by dubbing Lapointe 'a professor of amiability.') Gouin was not retiring from politics. In fact, he was heading for Ottawa. This had become apparent some months earlier when Gouin's old friend, Senator Raoul Dandurand, called upon Mackenzie King to urge him to ask Sir Lomer to run in an upcoming Montreal by-election. Wishing to talk to Lapointe and Bureau first, King was noncommittal. Dandurand had then asked if King would authorize *him* to speak to Sir Lomer. King had put him off and the Liberal party had fielded another candidate, but it was obvious that this was just the opening thrust. 'The big interests want their representative in Ottawa,' King recorded in his diary.[4]

Lapointe had opened a law office in Quebec City in order to service his constituency. For his wife's sake he maintained the family home in Rivière-du-Loup, but now with the children older and in boarding schools, Mimy was able to join Ernest in Ottawa during the session and from time to time in Quebec City. Lapointe's move from a rural to an urban constituency paralleled the change in post-war Quebec. For the first time, more Quebeckers were living in the cities than in the villages and countryside. Montreal, with over 680,000 inhabitants, was Canada's largest city. Quebec City had grown significantly too in the past decade. As well as the seat of government, it had become a manufacturing centre second only to Montreal in the province. Boot and shoe manufacturing, one of Quebec's major and most protected industries, was largely located in Lapointe's riding of Quebec East. This posed a problem for him. Was the friend of the farmers to become a high-tariff spokesman? Not unexpectedly, the question was put to him in the House. Would moving from Kamouraska to Quebec East change his views on fiscal policy?

Lapointe was ready with his answer: 'I challenge the member for Brantford to quote one word of mine in support of absolute free trade. I have always stated we must have a tariff, and more today because of the war debt. I was in favour of a policy that would reduce the price of ploughs to the farmers when I was in Kamouraska, and I am in favour of that policy today when I represent Quebec East. But I was and am in favour of a lower tariff.'[5] What 'a lower tariff' meant in actual terms could be shelved for the time being. In opposition the Liberals were not responsible for tariff policies. Lapointe remained a populist, a friend of the anti-protectionist farmers, and a soulmate for Mackenzie King. 'As between Gouin and the interests and Lapointe and the people, I am with the latter,' King told his diary in 1920.[6]

The new leader of the Liberal party was quite unknown to the public. To introduce himself to the country before the next election, Mackenzie King was touring coast to coast. In January Lapointe had accompanied him on a speaking tour of the Maritimes, and in the summer they had shared Ontario platforms. Now King was planning an extensive tour of the West for September and wanted Lapointe to accompany him. Lapointe's initial response was that it would entail a sacrifice for him to be away from his new law practice for more than a few weeks in the fall. King took him at his word. In the latter part of August Lapointe received a letter from King. The tour was going to last some six to eight weeks, and bearing in mind what Lapointe had told him, King had arranged with Dr Henri Béland to take over part of the tour. Béland would accompany King through British Columbia ('his war service will be a help there') while Lapointe would join King in Edmonton and they would work their way eastward through the prairies ('the farmers are particularly anxious to hear you'). The letter closed: 'Of course if you would prefer to come on at the start, do not hesitate for a moment to say so.'[7]

Henri Béland was a French-Canadian war hero and as such was very popular with English-Canadian audiences. He had been in Belgium with his Belgian wife when Germany invaded and had at once volunteered his services as a surgeon to the Belgian forces defending Liège and Antwerp. When British marines arrived to help besieged Antwerp he was able to contact Canada and was commissioned as a major in the Canadian Army Medical Corps. Badly wounded in the bombardment of Antwerp, he had refused to leave his post when the British force evacuated the city. Under the German occupation Béland managed to spirit out some letters in which he described the suffering and heroism of the Belgian people, the trains of wounded soldiers, and the closed trains of the dead ones. These letters served as effective war propaganda in Canada and may have had something to do with his being taken to a prisoner of war camp in Germany, where he remained until the end of the war. While he was in Germany, his wife, who had turned her villa at Ostend into a hospital and had been working tirelessly as a nurse, was killed by a shell. In 1918 Béland returned to Canada, his health much damaged by his wartime experiences. Before the war he had been a junior minister under Laurier, and on his return he resumed his seat as a Liberal Member of Parliament.[8]

Béland had an easy relationship with Lapointe, and on the first of September he sent him a breezy note. He had agreed to take on British Columbia because King was so insistent, he said. Wouldn't it be *magnifique* to travel to Edmonton together? They could then take a compartment for two; the CPR had five or six on each trans-Canada train. Lapointe did not answer. A week later Béland wrote again: 'Are you dead or alive?'[9] It seems that Lapointe was hurt to find himself so easily replaced. King must have realized this because Béland did not go west and plans were finalized for Lapointe to join King in Victoria. 'I am looking forward with great delight to our meeting together by the waters of the Pacific,' King soothed Lapointe. 'We will remain together till the western schedule is completed.'[10]

Lapointe made the trip west with Andrew Haydon, the party's well-liked national organizer, W.C. Kennedy from Ontario, and a Maritimer named Duff. A federal politician spent a good portion of his life on the train, travelling to and from Ottawa, to speaking engagements, to election campaigns, to testimonial banquets. Time aboard was not wasted. Many a back-scratching deal was hatched in the smoking car, or over a tasty plate of Winnipeg gold-eye in the diner. The quartet of politicians travelling across the country in September 1920 had five full days to discuss matters of mutual interest, such as the odds for victory in the election that could not be far off. They did not have the luxury of a compartment, however; when Béland inquired he was told that these were all booked until the end of the month. So after an evening of talking, smoking, and imbibing, they would have lurched down the swaying aisle to curtained upper or lower berths in the sleeping car.

Their hectic schedule began in Victoria with a visit to the wharfs and docks, the military hospital, and the naval college. Then lunch with a cabinet minister at the magnificent Empress Hotel where they were staying, tea at Government House, and back to the hotel for a reception with Liberal workers. In the evening, a public meeting at the arena with a turnout of no less than three thousand. Lapointe spoke extremely well but a little too long, in King's opinion, because by the time he himself took the podium people were leaving in droves. King attributed it to the hour, but he admitted in his diary that he was 'a little disappointed at not having been in better form.'

The next day, they paid a courtesy call on Premier Oliver and his cabinet and had a tour of the legislature. After lunch the visitors took the ferry to Vancouver where they were met at the wharf by a group of enthusiastic young Liberals. Their late arrival gave them little time to change for a large reception of Liberal supporters at the Vancouver Hotel, where they were graciously welcomed by the mayor. Lapointe and King replied in kind. The handshaking went on until eleven in the evening. Next day a Liberal committee took them on a tour of the harbour and city, then on to the arena for the evening's public meeting. King graded Kennedy's and Lapointe's speeches only 'fair.' His own speech, for once, satisfied him perfectly. The next morning they motored to New Westminster for a tour of the Fall Exhibition where they admired the livestock and kissed the babies.

Up the coast to Prince Rupert. After beautiful Victoria and big-cityish Vancouver, the town with its crudely built wooden stores and houses hugging a rocky shoreline revealed a different western Canada. With no railway connection, the local people told them they felt quite 'sidetracked.' Taken by launch across the harbour, the visitors got a better impression: docks piled high with coal and lumber, dry docks, shipyards, and fish processing plants indicated the unlimited resources of the region. In the evening the town's one theatre was filled to capacity to hear the easterners. Local hospitality saved them from reliance on the Chinese café near the hotel.

Back to Vancouver where they entrained for Alberta, making whistle stops along the way. (King, at least, enjoyed the comfort of a compartment.) At Edmonton they were met by a large crowd and escorted to the Macdonald Hotel. That evening the visitors drew such a huge audience that a nearby church had to be opened for the overflow. Lapointe spoke first and was in top form. King did not speak 'with the effect I would have liked.' Still, everyone, including Premier Stewart, seemed well satisfied. Then back on the train and more whistle stops to Calgary. Although the train steamed into the station at seven in the morning, the mayor and the local committee were there in their stetsons to greet them. Another grand railway hotel – the Palliser – where the obligatory reception was held for the faithful before the public meeting.[11]

They were at Cranbrooke at the southern tip of British Columbia when Lapointe received terrible news: his son was dangerously ill and he must return at once. Lapointe was in shock. His first thought was of his wife – it would kill her, he told his friends. Later, a wire arrived from Jacques Bureau indicating that the boy was still alive but seriously ill. When they reached Lethbridge Lapointe caught the first train for home.[12] Lapointe's son had developed pleural pneumonia. Thanks to a friend of Mimy's who had dropped in to see the child at his boarding school, it had been discovered just in time. This lady had found 'Baby' in the infirmary gravely ill. The nuns had failed to recognize pneumonia. The child was now in the care of the best physician in the province, but it was touch and go whether he would survive.[13] On 3 November Lapointe was able to write to Adolphe Stein that 'our little sick one is better, and out of danger, all the same his convalescence will be long.'[14] They were taking him with them to Ottawa for the session.

By the beginning of December his son had still not fully recovered, but Lapointe resumed his duties. One duty he would not undertake was to attend the testimonial banquet for Sir Lomer Gouin. On his return from a most gratifying European tour, which had included luncheon with King George and Queen Mary, Sir Lomer was being honoured for his long service as premier of the province of Quebec. 'I am absolutely of your opinion about the Sir Lomer banquet,' wrote Joseph Archambault, a Lapointe follower and one of the more left-wing Liberals in the Commons. 'Either one is *rouge* or one is not.'[15] Naturally, Lapointe used his son's illness as an excuse. 'I would love to have seen you at our beautiful family affair,' Gouin wrote back smoothly, 'but I understand the reasons for your absence. I know how much anxiety the illness of your dear son must cause you.'[16] The rivals understood each other perfectly.

For Lapointe, Gouin was an unregenerate Tory in the guise of a Liberal. An anecdote he often repeated in the bosom of his family was how after one of his speeches, in which he expounded on Liberalism as the protector of the people against special interests, Gouin had sneered, 'You don't believe *that*, do you?'[17] Lapointe would not have been surprised to see the letter Gouin received from one industrialist when he retired as premier: 'I wish there was some manner in which the business interests of the Province could show their appreciation to you for the assistance that your Government rendered them, because I believe it would be the popular desire of them all to show not only those who come after you in the government but in all Governments that a wise and steadfast adherence to business principles still has its place under the sun.'[18]

Gouin would have been quite unapologetic if this letter had been leaked to Lapointe. As he had told Mackenzie King when the latter visited him in Quebec City, a party needed more than speeches to win elections; it needed financial contributions, and these could only come from business. There was undoubtedly a personal element in Lapointe's antipathy to Gouin. Taschereau was as much a friend of big business as

Gouin, but Lapointe did not boycott *his* testimonial dinner. The hard feelings went back to Lapointe's days as MP for Kamouraska when Gouin had ignored him in doling out patronage. Now in the 1920s, even with Lapointe's great prestige in the province, Gouin still regarded him as 'un grand petit gars' – a large Little Man – and perhaps did not hide his feelings. Nevertheless, when the time came, Lapointe favoured bringing Gouin into the King administration.

In September 1921 the election was just a few months away, and campaigning had begun in earnest. King had heard rumbles of a conspiracy to replace him with Gouin. He was told that once he was out of the way, Gouin and the protectionist Liberals would make an alliance with the Tories. This would extinguish the 'Prairie Fire' that threatened to engulf the industrialized East. With the Progressives isolated, the tariff could be raised as high as Ontario and Quebec manufacturers liked.

Although it was true that some Conservatives were counselling Meighen to make a deal with Gouin, it was never a practical possibility. Meighen was the driving force behind nationalization of the railways and in fact had all but completed the Canadian National Railways system with the acquisition of the insolvent Grand Trunk Railway. Gouin was the political front for the CPR, which was privately owned, and its allied corporate interests in Montreal. Gouin could not have been considering a coalition when he announced publicly that 'if the Meighen policy continues we will certainly have a national disaster.'[19] Nevertheless, there was more than smoke to the rumours.

King believed that Rodolphe Lemieux had started the 'Gouin boom' in concert with Lord Atholston, the publisher of the *Montreal Star*. Since Quebec was the bedrock of King's support, to counter the right wing he needed to marshal the Lapointe and Bureau wing solidly behind him. Early in September King encountered Lapointe on the train to Montreal. Comfortably ensconced on the upholstered swivel armchairs of the club car, they chatted like old friends. In this congenial atmosphere King cemented Lapointe's loyalty to him. 'If I am returned,' he told Lapointe, 'you can have whatever portfolio you wish, and I will look first to you in all my negotiations.'[20] King was delighted to find Lapointe 'most friendly.'

It was the defining moment for both of them. They had sealed an alliance based on personal empathy, similarity of views, and mutual benefit. They agreed that the way to withstand a protectionist coalition was to work out a Liberal-Farmer alliance. Lapointe's good relationship with T.A. Crerar would be of great assistance. They then discussed the composition of a future cabinet. Speaking as King's Quebec lieutenant-elect, Lapointe was firm that Quebec should have three French ministers and the solicitor general post. It was when they moved on to discuss individuals that Lapointe told King (as the latter recorded in his diary) that he 'thought Gouin would be a strength and should be encouraged to come in.' He assured King that he could speak for Bureau as well.

Obviously Lapointe and Bureau were not confident enough of their strength in Quebec to declare war on Gouin and his Montreal friends. It was a time to put aside their personal feelings and help Sir Lomer to a cabinet post. Gouin would bring with him the support of the CPR, the Bank of Montreal, and other financial interests. If it meant getting the necessary campaign contributions, Lapointe said, King could tell Gouin that he and Bureau welcomed him in the federal arena. At a banquet in Quebec City honouring Lemieux on his twenty-five years in Parliament, King sounded out Sir Lomer Gouin. Sir Lomer indicated he was not anxious to run for Parliament; what he really wanted was a Senate appointment. King said he could promise him that, but the boys would like him to contest a constituency. He passed on the information that Lapointe was glad to know he was coming into the fight.[21] On 6 October Gouin accepted the nomination in a Montreal riding.

In the following weeks all kinds of tales reached King about 'the protectionist conspiracy.' From a confidential source he heard that the prime movers were the Montreal plutocrats, several Conservative senators, and in the shadows Gouin himself. According to this source, at a meeting in a Montreal lawyer's office these men had decided that 'Gouin would continue to fight on the Liberal platform, Meighen on the Conservative and after elections would join together, Gouin to be called on as Premier.' King was told that Lemieux had been in on the conspiracy from the start. A mutual friend claimed to have heard Lemieux, 'with his own ears,' telling people that if the Liberals won the election the governor general would not call on Mackenzie King because he had not served in the war.[22]

King did not tax Lemieux immediately with his 'treachery.' He continued to invite him to lunch at the Rideau Club and the Country Club, and he left no doubt that Lemieux would be invited into cabinet. The wily King intended to make good use in the campaign of Lemieux's powerful connections in Quebec and his oratorical skills. The moment of reckoning came, however, on 19 October when King was returning from the Maritimes and Lemieux, who had been campaigning in his Gaspé riding, boarded the train. Taking him aside, King charged him with trying to engineer a Gouin leadership. Though Lemieux did not deny the plot, he attempted to exculpate himself; however, the red flush that suffused his face when confronted with his derogatory remarks about King's war record was as good as an admission. Smoothly, King turned the conversation to more pleasant subjects.

As the campaign neared its end, King was proved right about Meighen. Meighen had no idea how to appeal to voters. A veritable Don Quixote of unpopular causes, he defended conscription in Quebec and championed high tariffs in the West. King enunciated few policies of his own and simply criticized the government's record. A post-war depression also told against the government. While Meighen ventured fearlessly into Quebec, King left the province completely to Lapointe, Béland, and Lemieux.

On 6 December 1921 the Liberals were returned with 117 seats, one short of a majority. The Progressives gained 64 seats to the Conservatives' 50. A handful of seats went to independents and labour candidates. Liberal strength was all in the East; the West had voted for the Progressives. The Liberals took all 65 Quebec seats. A few months later, an outspoken Liberal MP from Quebec would tell King that he could not last a week without the French-Canadian representation.[23] It was true. Quebec had elected him.

The clean sweep in Quebec was a triumph for Lapointe, who had campaigned across the length and breadth of the province. At the Rimouski seminary they were bursting with pride over their distinguished alumnus. 'Congratulations for yourself but above all for the considerable success of the troops you command with such distinction in the lower Quebec region,' wrote the head of the college, reminding Lapointe that the year before he had predicted he would be a cabinet minister. A former cabinet minister, William Pugsley, now lieutenant-governor of New Brunswick, congratulated Lapointe, attributing the Liberals' total victory in Quebec to him: 'You ought to be very proud.' Lapointe was greatly admired by the large Montreal Jewish community for his broad-mindedness, and a community leader expressed his pleasure in fulsome terms: 'Your splendid endowments have gained for you a nationwide reputation, and I feel that I can, without presumption, hazard the opinion that your success in the political affairs of our country is only beginning. Mr. King will be well advised to include men of your sterling character and ability in his cabinet.'[24]

Two days after the election, Lapointe received a telegram from the new prime minister summoning him to Ottawa. At 10:30 on the morning of 10 December Lapointe arrived at Mackenzie King's rooms in the Roxborough apartments. It was a portentous occasion. Seating Lapointe beneath the lamplit portrait of his dead mother, King told him, 'I regard you as nearest to me and will give you my confidence in full now and always ... I regard you as the real leader in Quebec and I sent for you first as I promised.'[25] Which portfolio did Lapointe want? King asked.

Lapointe replied he would like the justice department. It would give him a chance to study his beloved legal authorities and would also give him the prestige he needed in his province. King assured him in all sincerity that he would be minister of justice. ('He is *worthy* of Justice, is just and honorable at heart – a beautiful Christian character – he shall have it,' King vowed in his diary.) Later in the morning King waxed biblical. In every twelve there was one Judas and one Peter, also one beloved disciple. Lapointe was the latter, he said, and they must beware of the other two. Lapointe understood him to refer to Lemieux and Gouin. He expressed some concern that he had been sent for before them.

The soulmates discussed possible cabinet ministers (excepting Justice) and planned their strategy. To counter the protectionists in the party, some form of alliance with the Progressives was necessary. Despite his need for their support, King dismissed any idea of coalition. Here too he and Lapointe were of one mind. Lapointe had been opposed to a formal Liberal-Progressive administration from the beginning. The plan was to bring several of the farmers into the cabinet as Liberals. Lapointe volunteered to contact Crerar and E.C. Drury, the United Farmer premier of Ontario.

On 13 December King entertained the newly elected Sir Lomer Gouin at dinner at the Rideau Club. Over oysters on the half shell, Gouin affably set out his wishes. He wanted Justice or the presidency of the Privy Council and later to go to the Senate. King told him he had promised Lapointe whatever he wished, but subject to that he would agree to any portfolio. Gouin turned his nose up when King suggested Marine and Fisheries and said to give that to Lapointe. By the third week of December none of the Progressives had been lured into the Liberal cabinet, and it was clear to King that he would need the protectionists. Sir Lomer had to be conciliated. On 22 December King wrote in his diary: 'I began to urge Lapointe to take Marine and Fisheries, on the ground that Justice would lose him to political power in the province ["too young" was crossed out], he would become secluded in books and cases and cease to be a creature of the people.' The next day King spoke to Lapointe again about giving up Justice and taking Marine and Fisheries. This time he argued that if Lapointe was to lead in Quebec he must get the goodwill of Montreal and be available for 'outside' work. Justice would tend to isolate him.

Lapointe finally gave in under this pressure. With great dignity he said that he would do anything for the sake of the party and to help King form a government. Gouin could have Justice. He could not avoid a tiny flash of anger when he thought of Jacques Bureau's disappointment. His friend and mentor from his earliest days in politics had been so anxious to see him get the justice portfolio. 'Bureau will be exasperated,' he told King. Then wearily, 'but he will fall in line.'[26]

Indeed, it was the prospect of Bureau's disappointment that was uppermost in Lapointe's mind as he left King's office. Once again it was Bureau's 'kick from behind' that had made him ask for Justice. As for himself, he was not anxious for a senior portfolio. Two days after the election he had called upon his good friend, Mr Justice Louis Brodeur of the Supreme Court, and had shocked the old gentleman by saying that he did not want an important portfolio. Brodeur, a sincere admirer of the up-and-coming young politician, had continued his persuasion by mail: 'You deserve an important portfolio. Justice would be the best. Don't hesitate to take it. Your natural modesty left me under the impression the other day when you came to see me that you did not want an important portfolio.'[27] Other people were expecting him to be minister of justice as well. The chief justice of Quebec, François Lemieux, thought he had the appointment. In a letter dated 29 December, His Lordship expressed the pride he felt in seeing his former clerk in the federal ministry. He was convinced, he wrote, that Lapointe would follow the old traditions, respect justice, and give the country good judges. 'Providence reserves for you a great destiny.'[28]

Even wringing this concession out of Lapointe did not satisfy Sir Lomer. That evening King invited Gouin and his friend, Senator Dandurand, to dinner at the Rideau Club to break the good news. But it appeared that Gouin would not take the justice portfolio after all. King found himself under pressure from these two powerful personalities to make Gouin president of the Privy Council. All through the meal Dandurand kept shoving a paper across the table to King on which he had written, 'Give our friend the Presidency of the Privy Council.' It was clear to King that the Montreal group hoped to control the administration by placing Gouin in a post where he would be a rival to the prime minister. King intended to keep this post for himself, and certainly by the dessert course he had so informed his guests.[29]

Lemieux was another problem. He was bitterly jealous of Lapointe. It all poured out during a talk King had with him in the sequence of endless discussions about the new cabinet. Lemieux complained that Lapointe received greater recognition than himself and that he was being passed over. He especially resented King's calling Lapointe in first after the election. He could not tolerate a King-Lapointe ministry, he said. He himself had only one leader and that was King. He accused Lapointe and Bureau of conspiring against him while he was in Europe. After this tirade King formed the opinion that his own friendship with Lapointe was at the bottom of Lemieux's attempt to supplant him with Gouin. To name Lemieux to the cabinet would be asking for trouble. Nevertheless, Lemieux had played a leading role in the campaign and was still the putative Quebec lieutenant – he could not be ignored. There was a further complication. King still had a faint hope of bringing Tom Crerar into cabinet, and the agrarian leader was strongly opposed to both Gouin and Lemieux. Fortunately, it turned out that Lemieux did not want a cabinet post; he put in his bid for the speakership of the House of Commons. King sighed with relief. Lemieux possessed the necessary prestige and dignity to make an excellent Speaker. It was an ideal solution all around.[30]

At the last moment Gouin gave in and agreed to accept the justice portfolio, on condition that they find him a bright lawyer from English Canada to handle common law matters. On 29 December 1921 the new governor general, Lord Byng of Vimy, swore in Mackenzie King and his cabinet. The senior ministries of finance and justice went respectively to William Fielding and Sir Lomer Gouin. Ernest Lapointe became minister of marine and fisheries. (Though not his first choice, it was 'not to be disdained,' as his old patron, Judge Carroll, wrote him.)[31] Jacques Bureau's hopes for a Senate appointment were disappointed, but as minister of customs and excise he had the satisfaction of knowing that his $10,000 salary was $4,000 higher than Lemieux would earn as Speaker. Dr Henri Béland was appropriately named minister of soldiers' civil re-establishment and health. No longer a neophyte politician, King had done a masterful job of conciliating the diverse factions within the Liberal party.

Immediately after the ceremony, King and Lapointe went to Notre Dame cemetery to lay flowers on Sir Wilfrid Laurier's grave. It was a deeply moving occasion for both men. Here they were, Laurier's chief English and French disciples, symbolizing, as it were, the national unity to which their mentor had devoted his career. 'Would it not be nice if Sir Wilfrid could see us together here,' Lapointe said. King replied emphatically, 'But he does see us. He is right here with us. I am sure of that.'[32]

CHAPTER FIVE

Diplomat

On 22 August 1922 Ernest Lapointe, accompanied by his wife, sailed for Europe on the *Empress of Scotland*, one of the CPR's luxurious steamships. Lapointe and the minister of finance, William Fielding, were bound for Geneva to represent Canada at the third Assembly of the League of Nations. Canada had made its debut on the international stage two years earlier, when the Meighen government sent a delegation to the first session of the League Assembly. The purpose of the League was to ensure that the Great War would be the war to end all wars. Although Woodrow Wilson had fathered the idea of an international body to preserve world peace, in the end the United States had not joined the League. Strangely enough, Canada was held partly to blame for America's isolationism. The Americans claimed that allowing the Dominions and India separate representation at the League Assembly would give Britain five extra votes. In the eyes of the United States, Canada and the others were just part of the British Empire.

Nationhood was the reward England bestowed upon the Dominions for participating in the First World War, but Canada had to be on constant alert not to slip back into colonial status. While Britain gave lip service to more autonomy for the overseas Dominions, it had not digested the change and imperial centralists were undeterred. Even assuming eventual acceptance of its voice in imperial foreign policy, Canada's position was anomolous in the event of Anglo-American disagreement. This had already emerged at the Imperial Conference of 1921. Britain wanted to commit the empire to a renewal of the Anglo-Japanese naval treaty. Meighen, however, knowing that the United States opposed the treaty as unfriendly to its interests in the Pacific, took a stand against renewal. Eventually England yielded to American pressure. Had it not, Canada would have found itself in opposition to the mother country or else a signatory to a treaty strongly opposed by its powerful neighbour.

Lapointe vigorously espoused the post-war view of Canada's equal status within the empire, but he was fully aware of the dilemma this posed in the area of foreign affairs. At the founding of the League in 1919 he had put the question to Newton Rowell: Would Canada have full and separate membership in the League or be 'a mere addition to the voting power of the British Empire?'[1] Lapointe set out for Geneva firmly intending to promote Canada's independent role in foreign affairs. Not so his colleague. Fielding's views harkened back to pre-war days when Canada left its foreign affairs entirely in Britain's hands. As he often said with a chuckle, he was perfectly happy to belong to the firm of 'John Bull & Sons.'[2] Consistent with his colonial attitude, Fielding was opposed to separate Canadian representation at Washington, then under discussion in cabinet. The prime minister had indeed dispatched an odd couple to Geneva.

Lapointe carried letters of introduction from Mackenzie King to Prime Minister Lloyd George, First Lord of the Admiralty L.S. Amery, the Canadian-born under-secretary of the Home Office, Sir Hamar Greenwood, Lord Gray of Fallodon, Lord Haldane, and the colonial secretary, Winston Churchill. All identical letters, they praised Lapointe to the skies. 'There is no member of our own parliament,' King had written, 'who enjoys more completely the confidence and good will of his fellow members than Mr. Lapointe does.'[3] Lapointe had not seen King before leaving the capital. The prime minister was at Kingsmere, his summer home near Ottawa, and Lapointe, according to his secretary, was diffident about going there without an invitation. The relationship between the two men remained formal and a little lopsided. Although King called him Ernest, Lapointe did not address the prime minister by his first name.[4] It was via a long-distance telephone call to Quebec City, followed by a letter,[5] that King gave last-minute instructions to his departing diplomat.

Among other matters, King's letter dealt with Canada's stand on the admission of Germany to the League of Nations. This was expected to be top of the agenda and was bound to pose a problem because France and England held different views. King wrote that the French consul general had called on him to say that he hoped Canada's representatives would not support Germany's immediate admission. His concern was that this would lead to German representation on the League

Council and would give Germany a voice in interpreting the Treaty of Versailles. The diplomat made no bones about the fact that the French view was in opposition to the British. Without actually issuing instructions to Lapointe ('I mention this only that you may turn it over in your own thoughts'), King indicated that it would be unwise to take a decided stand against Germany's admission. The 'happiest solution,' of course, would be if France and England would agree to postpone the matter.

King also informed Lapointe of a confidential cable from the colonial secretary, Winston Churchill, regarding a British embargo on Canadian cattle. Lapointe and Fielding were to try to get it lifted when they went to England after the League session. 'Don't fail to associate yourself with Fielding in the negotiations,' King wrote. Carefully choosing his words, he instructed Lapointe not to defer to his older and more experienced colleague. The fact was that King's minister of agriculture, W.R. Motherwell, and his minister of the interior, Charles Stewart, both westerners, did not trust Fielding to represent the prairie farmer – as King phrased it delicately in a subsequent letter, 'they hesitate to leave the matter to your colleague.'[6] They would be satisfied only if Lapointe handled the negotiations.

King also touched on the matter of a Quebec director for the Canadian National Railways Board. In 1919 the Borden government had taken over the vast network of insolvent railways and created a giant competitor for the privately owned CPR. In the late summer of 1922 the King government announced that a board of directors would be set up to administer the national railways system. The delay in appointing the board and chairman was drawing criticism in the press. King asked Lapointe to suggest the name of a Quebec director without fail before he sailed.

The night before he left, Lapointe wrote a hurried reply to his chief's letter. With regard to Germany's admission to the League he gave a balanced assessment: 'I have always maintained that all nations should be included in the membership. On the other hand, I am somewhat afraid the situation is so acute as to be one of extreme difficulty. If by accepting Germany it means the withdrawal of France do you not think that success of the League would be seriously compromised? That might be a great evil. I will acquaint you with developments.'[7]

Nearer to home, and frankly more important to Lapointe as a politician, was the naming of a Quebec City representative to the CNR board as well as someone from Montreal. The MPs in the Quebec district were under great pressure from local businessmen, and they looked to Lapointe to use his influence in cabinet. After discussions with King and W.C. Kennedy, the minister of railways, Lapointe had assured the MPs before leaving for Europe that Quebec City would have its own director. His choice was Philippe Paradis, the chief Liberal organizer in the province and an old comrade-in-arms. King had initially approved. Unfortunately, Paradis sold asbestos products, and when the *Globe* intimated that he had dealings with the railways, Kennedy refused to have him. Lapointe was upset. Nevertheless, while standing behind Paradis as the better man, he named a second choice in his letter to King. He impressed upon King that 'this position is of vital importance to us in this district.'

Fielding and Lapointe arrived at Geneva at the beginning of September. The anticipated problem over Germany did not materialize, as the powers-that-be postponed the issue. The real problem for the Canadian delegation was Article X of the League Covenant. Article X was the collective security clause, which stated categorically: 'Members of the League undertake to respect and preserve as against external aggression the territorial integrity and existing political independence of all Members of the League. In case of any such aggression, or in case of any threat or danger of such aggression, the Council shall advise upon the means by which this obligation shall be fulfilled.' This call for joint action if a member state was invaded was the sticking point of the Covenant's twenty-six articles. Even long-time advocates for the League, such as Lord Bryce, the former British ambassador to Washington, and President Lowell of Harvard, felt Article X went too far. The Paris Peace Conference had carved out new states and redrawn borders, in some cases with no reason but political expediency. Article X guaranteed these frontiers as well. Why should Canada, protected by a moat three thousand miles wide, send troops to defend the territorial integrity of any and all European states? The Borden government had protested against Article X at the Paris Peace Conference (though reluctantly defending it at home), and Meighen's delegates had tried to get it deleted at both preceding sessions of the League Assembly.[8] After the recent carnage, English Canada was as unready as Quebec to become embroiled in Europe's wars.

Fielding and Lapointe soon realized there was no possibility of striking out Article X. It was a non-negotiable item with France, the victim of two German invasions in forty-five years, and the smaller states also relied on its protection. Fielding wrote King that he and

Lapointe would have been quite content to do nothing, but Canada's motion for deletion was there on the order paper and had to be dealt with.[9] Throughout their mission Fielding had a habit of speaking for both men when, in reality, it was his own opinion only. Lapointe was far from satisfied to leave Article X as it stood. At a meeting of the Committee of Amendments, he moved that the following words be added to Article X – 'taking into account the political and geographic circumstances of each state.' This qualifying phrase would serve as an escape clause, allowing member states to avoid automatic military involvement. Distance alone would ensure Canada's non-intervention.

He went on to propose a second amendment. Prefaced by expressions of deference to the League Council's opinion and 'utmost endeavours' to conform to its conclusions, the operative part of his amendment was that 'no member shall be under the obligation to engage in any act of war without the consent of its Parliament, legislature or other representative body.'[10] Here Lapointe was restating what he had said during the parliamentary debate on the peace treaty in 1919 – that no Canadian soldiers should ever be ordered to fight anywhere except by the authority of Parliament. His proposed amendment to Article X was one of the earliest renditions abroad of 'Parliament Will Decide' – the King government's theme song.

Lapointe was a very strong speaker, and the committee was visibly impressed. The Canadian delegation was commended for its desire 'to remove all the obstacles which barred the League's progress.' But goodwill and good wishes were as far as the committee was prepared to go. As Lapointe and Fielding expected, no action was taken on the amendments.[11] Nevertheless, Lapointe had given a decent burial to the embarrassing deletion motion, replacing it with another Canadian initiative that, if acted upon, would water down the troublesome Article X. Lapointe was not just catering to the Canadian isolationism that was particularly strong in his home province. From the beginning, he had regarded Article X as wrong-headed and pernicious; in his view, disarmament, not militarism, was the way to abolish war. As he had told Parliament in 1919, the League did not display much confidence in itself for maintaining the peace of the world if Article X required member states to resort to warfare. He even coined a phrase that he used to good effect in his speeches: 'Great policies must be thought out rather than fought out.'[12]

Canada's Ernest Lapointe had started the process of extracting the teeth from Article X. But while Canada would not go to war at the call of the League of Nations, what if the mother country blew the bugle? Lapointe and Fielding were at Geneva less than two weeks when the Chanak crisis broke. The Turkish army under the nationalist leader Kemal Ataturk had launched a successful offensive against the Greeks in the Dardanelles and was advancing on the neutral zone at Chanak in Asia Minor, dangerously undermanned by a British force. Without consultation with the Canadian prime minister, Britain had issued a communiqué announcing its request for military aid from the Dominions. King immediately cabled Fielding and Lapointe for their opinion, instructing them to sound out the British delegation. Once again, Fielding gave his own opinion in both their names: 'We heartily approve attitude British Government respecting Constantinople. Would willingly have some statement made on behalf of our Government indicating readiness to participate if necessary, but send troops abroad at present without parliamentary authority very undesirable. Cannot something be said that will serve the purpose without actual sending of contingent.'[13]

In fact, Lapointe was strongly opposed to Britain's cavalier action and had tried, with some success, to soften the senior diplomat's 'Ready, aye ready' reponse. In a confidential coded cable to King, Lapointe corrected the misleading impression that he shared Fielding's opinion, and tendered completely contrary advice: 'Regarding our official cable, I was glad my colleague agreed to two essential conditions, necessity and consent of Parliament. Be governed by Canadian public opinion. Imperial authorities should not have made such request. French newspaper and part English press very critical. Would advise delaying answer and being non-committal. Doubtful if France will join and seems certain Italy will not.'[14]

Lapointe's confidential advice concurred with action King had already taken. After an all-day cabinet meeting on 18 September, King notified the British government through the governor general that 'public opinion in Canada would demand authorization on the part of Parliament as a necessary preliminary to the despatch of a contingent.'[15] As it happened, the crisis blew over with Lloyd George's resignation in October. But as King noted in his diary, the Chanak affair revealed that the British were still playing 'the imperial game, testing centralization vs. autonomy as regards European wars.'

The meeting with Churchill over the cattle embargo was set for 26 September. King must have intimated that it would be preferable if Fielding could be shunted aside because in a coded cable from Geneva

Lapointe replied that Fielding 'seems to rely on our going together to Paris and London. I suppose Motherwell would not object as Larkin and myself will be there.' Later from London, Lapointe gently teased King (whom he knew secretly resented the party's elder statesman), saying that the valetudinarian Fielding was in excellent health and good for many more budget speeches.[16]

On their arrival in London, Lapointe and Fielding were briefed by the Canadian high commissioner, Peter Larkin. He told them that for years British farmers had been stubbornly opposing the importation of Canadian cattle. Larkin had been dealing with different British ministers over the cattle embargo since he had arrived, and he left these meetings 'with the conviction that in their hearts they have the same feeling towards me that they would have towards a child.' The condescension of the British towards 'the Colonials' did not bother Fielding one whit, but it would have made negotiations very frustrating for the nationalistic Lapointe. (The British managed to put one over on the colonials after all. While Fielding and Lapointe achieved a partial lifting of the embargo, when they got home they found that it only applied to cattle for breeding purposes.)[17]

Early in October Lapointe learned that the CNR board had been announced and there was no representative from Quebec City. He was furious. Having a Montrealer represent the whole province was 'a deadly political blow.' He had counted on King; in turn, Lucien Cannon, Chubby Power, and the other Quebec district MPs had counted on him. If he could not deliver on his promises, he had little hope of replacing Gouin as leader of the Quebec bloc. On 11 October he cabled King from London: 'Believe appointment of representative for Quebec on National Railways Board most unfortunate both politically and for giving fair trial to Government ownership. Moreover Quebec district and Transcontinental [railway] cannot expect fair play from that gentleman. Can't another additional appointment be made? Important for you as much as for me.'[18]

For once King was not overly careful of Lapointe's feelings. The initial response to his announcement of the new CNR board had been gratifyingly favourable. For chairman he had obtained the services (at $50,000 per annum) of Sir Henry Thornton, who, as president of the Great Eastern Railway in England, had run an empire of trains, steamships, and hotels. The *Globe* praised the appointment, saluting Sir Henry as 'one of the ablest and most eminent railway executives of Great Britain.'[19] Board members had been selected to represent the different regions of the country. Quebec province's representative was Ernest Decary, a forty-five-year-old Montreal lawyer, formerly chairman of the Commission for the Administration of Montreal. That had been a Gouin appointment during Sir Lomer's premiership, and it was commonly assumed that his CNR appointment was too. Decary was a pillar of the Montreal Reform Club, which doled out Liberal patronage, and he was closely allied with the St James Street financiers whom Lapointe so abhorred.[20]

Premier Taschereau was almost as angry as Lapointe that there was no director from Quebec City. 'I will not hide from you,' he wrote Sir Lomer Gouin, 'that our friends are furious and that, not only the federal government, but I fear ourselves will suffer for it. Quebec is the terminus of the Transcontinental, and it seems to me that this would be a good reason for giving us the satisfaction of a representative. I repeat, the situation is excessively grave and revolt is in the air.'[21]

In announcing the CNR board King had stressed that 'members shall have no business dealings whatever as between their previous connections and the Government Railway system.' Decary had acted for the Canadian Northern Railway, the near-bankrupt line of the notorious promoters Mackenzie and Mann, which had been brought into the nationalized system.[22] Philippe Paradis, Lapointe's choice, had been eliminated on the ground of conflict of interest, yet it appeared to make no difference in Decary's case. Notwithstanding, Decary was certainly an asset to the board, which could not be said of most of the other appointees. Sir Henry Thornton would later complain that the board members were all political hacks.[23] Indeed, it was not too far-fetched to say that Frederick Dawson, a loyal British Columbia Liberal, earned his appointment by providing a delicious grouse dinner when King was in the culinary desert of Prince Rupert on his 1920 speaking tour.

Anticipating complaints from unrepresented parts of the country, King had left the door open to further appointments to the statutory limit of fifteen. On 13 October he attempted to placate Lapointe: 'It is understood that upon your return there will be further consideration of representation from Quebec. I have so informed members from Quebec District. Readjustment can best be arranged when Sir Henry Thornton returns. Would advise your seeing him while in London. He sailed from New York on the Olympic Saturday.'[24]

Lapointe's indignation was mild compared to the outrage expressed by Lucien Cannon, a firebrand MP from the Quebec district. A pale, dark, slight, clever-looking young lawyer, he was as sharp-tongued in the House as he was in conducting a cross-examination. Like his law partner Chubby Power, he had come into federal politics on the wave of young French-Canadian Liberals elected in 1917. Explosive and vitriolic, he was the scourge of those Liberals who had joined the Unionist government. His particular target was Newton Rowell – Cannon's abuse may well have been a factor in Rowell's decision to quit active politics in 1921. Now the aptly named Cannon turned his fire on Mackenzie King.

The appointment of the CNR board was most unsatisfactory, he chastised his leader. The Quebec deputation was greatly surprised, 'the more so since Lapointe had assured us we would have at least one director from our city.' He then launched into an attack, much of it personal – 'Your best friends are those who can tell you the truth.' King should know that his government subsisted only because of French-Canadian support. He should not forget that Quebec's confidence in the present government and its representatives could not be maintained unless the Liberals delivered on their promises. The Quebec members had offered their compatriots an era of equal justice and fair treatment, and he was sure that King would give it 'if sinister influences from men who betrayed the party' were removed from national policy-making. (The villains behind the scene were of course those Liberal Unionists who had returned to the party.) Quebec had elected 65 members to 25 from the Maritimes; yet the latter had more directors on the new board. It was not fair, especially as the board could be increased to fifteen. In a scarcely veiled threat, Cannon warned King that he had better deal with their well-founded grievances. A Quebec City man should be appointed to the CNR board without delay, he all but ordered the prime minister. It was not necessary to wait for Lapointe's return: 'I know his opinion perfectly well.'[25]

Blandly, King replied to this diatribe by thanking Cannon for his 'cordial note of co-operation.' He assured him that his confidence was not misplaced, and that as soon as Lapointe returned it would all be straightened out.[26] At the same time, from overseas Lapointe was urging King to make the appointment immediately. By the end of November it still had not been made. In the hope of expediting matters, Lapointe cabled Bureau to explain the Quebec situation to King, and to see if Paradis's appointment was possible.[27] It seemed that King would not name an additional Quebec board member without Sir Henry Thornton's approval, which was not obtained until his return from Europe in the middle of December. On 18 December King wired Lapointe the good news, informing him that he had asked the Quebec members to agree on a recommendation.[28]

Lapointe was anxious to return home, but Fielding would not let him go. The two were shuttling between London and Paris, where they were negotiating trade agreements with France, Italy, and Spain. From Paris Lapointe reported that they were facing many difficulties in their negotiations. The Canadian commissioner general in Paris, Philippe Roy, felt that Fielding was the problem; he was too intransigent. 'It's very important that you be in Paris with Fielding for this treaty,' he told Lapointe confidentially. If Canada would give some concessions to the French wine industry, the favour would be returned. *Entre nous*, he said, the French government wanted to negotiate with a French Canadian – Lapointe should whisper this in the prime minister's ear. A French-Canadian negotiator would also be a source of pride in Quebec.[29]

Still hoping to be home for Christmas, Lapointe booked passage for his wife and himself for early December. But as the sailing date approached, he saw that he could not get away. There was much business to be done in London, and Fielding wanted him to stay until the Paris negotiations were completed. Madame Lapointe sailed home alone. Meanwhile, King was missing Lapointe. 'As soon as the treaty with Spain and Italy is over, hurry back,' King cabled on 21 December. Among other matters requiring his presence, the Quebec district members were waiting for him to discuss the CNR appointment.

During his time in France Lapointe at last had his visit to the Front. The Canadian visitors were taken as the guests of the French government to view the Verdun battlefield. The site where France and Germany each lost 400,000 men in 1916 was burned into Lapointe's mind, strengthening his conviction that arming nations could only lead to a repetition of this horror. Indeed, disarmament was his message when shortly after his return he addressed the Canadian Club in Ottawa on the topic of the League of Nations. This assembly of prosperous businessmen, politicians, and senior civil servants held their monthly luncheon meetings at the Chateau Laurier (a CNR hotel since the takeover of the Grand Trunk Railway). Flanked by such head-table guests as the governor general, Lord Byng of Vimy, Prime Minister King, Sir Robert Borden, Sir Lomer Gouin, Sir George Foster, William Fielding, and Newton Rowell, Lapointe was introduced by Colonel C.M. Edwards, a lumber baron with a distinguished military record. 'Canada owes a debt of gratitude to the delegation,' the colonel stated, 'and especially to Mr. Lapointe for the delicate handling of the vexed question of the famous Article 10.'[30]

King heartily approved Lapointe's non-coercive interpretation of Article X. Though like Lapointe he praised the League of Nations publicly, Canada's prime minister was unwilling to accept any responsibility for collective security.[31] Anyway, it was Canada's relationship to Britain that was most on his mind these days. Even before the war Canada had negotiated and signed commercial treaties but always with Britain as co-signatory. This had been the case with the French and Italian treaties that Fielding and Lapointe had recently concluded in France. Fielding had no objection whatsoever to signing jointly with the British ambassador. For Lapointe, however, it was humiliating for a Canadian negotiator to be seen in tutelage to a British diplomat. As it happened, a commercial treaty was afoot in Lapointe's own ministry of marine and fisheries.

The United States and Canada had just negotiated a treaty to regulate halibut fishing off the Pacific coast. Mackenzie King made up his mind that there should be no British counter-signature to mar this piece of Canadian treaty-making.[32] It was a strictly bilateral treaty between Canada and the United States, so why shouldn't Lapointe sign the treaty without the British ambassador in Washington? Making its own treaties independently of Britain seemed to be the logical next step in Canada's march towards nationhood, and Lapointe concurred enthusiastically with King's plan. Though Lapointe gave the prime minister full credit for this 'new departure,'[33] the nature of the treaty and the timing suggest that he influenced King to take this step towards an independent foreign policy. In any event, he and King were of one mind that having Britain co-sign treaties where it was not involved in any way did not accord with Canada's new status. However, their attempt to substitute the words 'The Dominion of Canada' for the words 'Great Britain' in the title of the draft treaty was foiled by the British ambassador in Washington, Sir Auckland Geddes.[34] Geddes would prove to be a formidable enemy to their plan.

On 16 January Canada officially requested powers for Ernest Lapointe to sign the Halibut Treaty on behalf of Canada. The usual commission signed by King George V duly arrived giving 'full power to the Minister of Marine and Fisheries to conclude a treaty with the United States on the subject of the halibut fisheries in the Pacific Ocean.' Nothing was said to the British government about the plan to have Lapointe sign alone without the signature of the British ambassador. In early February King revealed his plan to the cabinet, and all except Fielding were in complete agreement – grumbling a little, even he acquiesced shortly thereafter. Apparently the first the governor general heard of the plan was at the Canadian Club luncheon on 17 February. Seated beside Byng, King referred to Sir Auckland Geddes's assumption that he would sign the treaty with Lapointe and said, 'We think our own minister is enough.' Perhaps concentrating on the halibut on his plate, His Excellency replied absently, 'Quite right.' On 20 February King advised the governor general that the proposed change had been approved by the cabinet, and when Lord Byng, alert now to the significance of the change, expressed some reservations, King threatened to open a Canadian legation in Washington. On 21 February, Lord Byng wired Sir Auckland that 'in my ministers' opinion the signature of Mr. Lapointe alone will be sufficient and that it will not be necessary for you to sign as well.'

Sir Auckland did not give up easily. On 23 February he replied to Lord Byng that 'I have been instructed by His Majesty's Government to sign the Treaty in association with Mr. Lapointe.' On the evening of 27 February he again wired Lord Byng informing him that the treaty had to be ratified before Congress adjourned on 4 March, and with superb arrogance inquired whether he could sign 'tomorrow on behalf of Canada.' If Canada preferred to have Lapointe sign with him, then Lapointe would have to be in Washington by the afternoon of the first of March. Either way Sir Auckland's name would be on the treaty. On 28 February Byng wired the colonial secretary that as the treaty did not affect the imperial interest, the Canadian government wished to have Lapointe sign alone, and he respectfully requested that Sir Auckland be so instructed. He added that Mr Lapointe was on his way to Washington.[35]

Time was of the essence. Lapointe was in Windsor, Ontario, on 28 February campaigning in a by-election. Late that evening he received a wire from Mackenzie King's secretary directing him to go at once to Washington. Lapointe caught the CPR train in Toronto, changed trains at Pennsylvania station in New York, and arrived in Washington on the morning of the first of March.[36] Although no one from the British embassy was at the station to meet him, he dined that evening with Sir Auckland. When he was leaving, the ambassador, grimly determined to override the Canadian declaration of independence, told Lapointe that he would pick him up the next day and take him to the signing. Lapointe firmly declined, saying he had made other arrangements.[37]

Geddes's doggedness indicates that he was prepared to ignore a telegram sent that day from the Foreign Office ordering him not to sign the treaty. King's threat to open a Canadian legation in Washington had proved sufficient leverage to force the British to back down.

The following afternoon, Lapointe took a taxi to meet the American secretary of state, Charles Evans Hughes, and after some strained moments signed the Halibut Treaty of 1923 for Canada without a British co-signatory. Before any recriminations could start, Lapointe left for New York and checked into the Vanderbilt Hotel. The first thing he did was to wire King advising him that the deed was done. There followed a telegram from King, who was clearly bubbling over with excitement: 'Please accept my hearty congratulations upon your successful negotiations of a treaty between the United States and Canada respecting the Halibut Fisheries, and upon the signing of the same on behalf of Canada by yourself.'[38]

It was not over yet. When the treaty came up for ratification in the United States Senate on 4 March 1923, the Americans had added Great Britain and the rest of the empire as parties. With obvious relish, Geddes reported this development to the Canadian governor general. This would have completely undone what King and Lapointe accomplished, and they refused to accept the change. Lapointe put up a spirited fight, and Geddes had to disabuse Secretary of State Hughes of his 'misapprehension' that the treaty was between the United States and Great Britain. In the end the Halibut Treaty was ratified by the American Senate just as Lapointe and Hughes had signed it.[39]

Lapointe and King could congratulate themselves. They had established a precedent. Canada had made a treaty independently of Britain. The next Imperial Conference would confirm this giant step for all the Dominions. Strange to say, neither King nor Lapointe boasted of their achievement at home. Signing a trade treaty without the British ambassador was regarded as a slap in the face to the mother country in many quarters of English Canada. It was not until Meighen secured an order of the House for the correspondence leading up to the Halibut Treaty that the Canadian public was fully informed of this important and controversial move towards independence.[40]

CHAPTER SIX

Relative Obscurity

In the words of J.K. Munro, Lapointe returned to Canada from Europe 'plump and lazy.' Formerly one of Lapointe's admirers, the influential *Maclean's* columnist rebuked him for deserting the cause of 'the newer Liberalism.' He 'would rather gather a few more millions to improve Quebec harbour' than attempt to reduce the nefarious influence of St James Street on the government. According to Munro, Lapointe's 'contribution to statesmanship of recent vintage' was merely to have a Quebec City resident appointed to the CNR board of directors.[1] As Munro's censure shows, Lapointe's career was in the doldrums despite his triumphs abroad.

After two years in power, King had done little or nothing to implement the reforms he and Lapointe had championed at the leadership convention in 1919. To hold his shaky minority government together, he had put aside his liberal leanings and deferred to Gouin and Fielding, who were Tories in all but name. Indeed, King had come to accept the political facts of life (as enunciated by Gouin) that it took more than oratory to win elections and by-elections; a political party had to have campaign funds from banks and corporations. Though Lapointe was extremely popular with the rank and file in Quebec, as Chubby Power said 'he had no connection whatsoever with the larger interests and was not at all amenable to influence from that quarter.'[2] Thus Lapointe had to take a back seat to Gouin.

Lapointe's lack of influence in cabinet came to the fore over the appointment of a Quebec City director to the CNR board. On his return to Canada, Lapointe continued his fight to get the post for Philippe Paradis. The 'kick from behind' in this instance was coming from the Quebec district MPs, particularly from Chubby Power. In a letter to

King impressing upon him that Paradis was the district's unanimous choice, Chubby Power tacitly acknowledged that Ernest Lapointe lacked the necessary influence in Ottawa to deliver patronage.[3]

When a Quebec City director was finally appointed to the railway board, Lapointe reaped no credit. Paradis was overlooked in favour of Onesiphore Talbot, a man who, according to *Le Devoir*, 'not five people in the city would have thought to recommend.' Only the *Quebec Chronicle* found something to praise: Colonel Talbot had helped the paper's proprietor, Sir William Price, raise a bilingual battalion in Quebec. Indeed, this may have been the reason for his appointment.[4]

While Lapointe must have agreed to the appointment, Talbot was far from his first choice. Nevertheless, as the cabinet minister representing the Quebec district, Lapointe bore the brunt of the criticism. 'We don't wish ill to the Minister,' commented the Quebec daily *L'Evénement*, 'but if the dubious use he has made of his authority draws embarrassment upon him in Quebec, we fear he won't find an increased prestige elsewhere to compensate him for what he lost with his fellow-townsmen.'[5]

The power to dole out government appointments and contracts was the stock in trade of a successful politician. It would seem that frustration over the CNR appointment spurred Lapointe to take on Gouin and stand up to King. On 28 March 1923 King noted in his diary: 'Lapointe wants Gouin out of the way in Quebec.' King acknowledged that getting rid of Gouin 'would make the party truly more liberal.' He contemplated elevating him to the Senate. But there was a danger that the resulting lack of a spokesman in cabinet would make St James Street turn to the Conservatives. As King told Tom Crerar around this time, Gouin's 'word with the big interests is helpful.'[6]

Lapointe's open opposition to Gouin in 1923 was a reversal of his earlier position. Before leaving for the League of Nations in August 1922, he had agreed with King that the time was not ripe to remove Gouin. At that moment he and King were once again trying to entice Tom Crerar into the cabinet. Crerar was amenable on condition that Gouin be removed first. Like many westerners, he feared an alliance between the manufacturing provinces of Ontario and Quebec against the agricultural West. This thinking, prevalent in Montreal business circles, was represented in the cabinet by Gouin. Hence Crerar's desire to get him out. Although their sympathies were with Crerar, King and Lapointe were fully in accord that they could not accept his condition. The night before he sailed, Lapointe had sent a note to his friend in

Winnipeg, urging him to come into cabinet but not to insist upon Gouin's withdrawal – 'Things will settle themselves with less friction and just as certainly.'[7]

Though their power struggle was more or less out in the open, Lapointe did not challenge Gouin in cabinet. King noted in his diary that Lapointe 'said practically nothing' as the stand-pat Fielding budget took shape.[8] No doubt whenever he considered speaking up against protectionism the member for Quebec East felt the boot of the shoe manufacturers on his behind. Gouin and the ultra-conservative Fielding dominated the cabinet of 1923. They resisted any move towards lower tariffs. In fact, Gouin threatened to resign if British preference was increased even marginally. King's own inclination was to free up trade just a little as a nod to the 1919 party platform, but fearful of antagonizing Gouin and Fielding he waited in vain for his low-tariff ministers to counter the protectionists.

While Lapointe's influence in domestic policy was at a low ebb, King took his advice to the letter in a foreign affairs matter that cropped up at this time. With the weakening of collective security as a result of the Canadian assault on Article X, the League of Nations was now promoting a regional security pact among Germany, France, Belgium, Italy, and Great Britain. As a League member state, Canada was asked for its view of this proposed Treaty of Mutual Guarantee. It appears that King did not give much thought to the matter because his under-secretary of state for external affairs, the about-to-retire Sir Joseph Pope, dashed off a brief letter expressing Canada's 'sympathy with the object sought to be attained.' When Lapointe learned of Pope's letter, he feared that Canada was committing itself to another collective security instrument like Article X. He advised King to have the letter withdrawn and replaced by one making it very clear that while Canada supported disarmament it would not support new military guarantees:

You might mention, however, that, as to a Treaty of Mutual Guarantee binding the nations to render assistance to a country which is attacked, our peculiar national conditions and geographical situation make it difficult for us to acquiesce without much consideration and without reservation. Such obligation is intended to be limited in principle to those countries situated in the same part of the Globe. Canada is a country situated in Northern America. She is also a nation forming part of the British Empire. It seems difficult to devise any scheme which would reconcile these two basic points. Furthermore, I do not think that our people would be prepared to ratify any agreement binding Canada to help other nations, under our present circumstances.

I would suggest that your letter should embody all these view points.

On King's instructions, Sir Joseph Pope rescinded his original letter in a second letter to the League's secretary general. In this letter rejecting Canadian participation in the Treaty of Mutual Guarantee, the under-secretary of state simply quoted Lapointe verbatim.[9] Once again Lapointe had struck a blow against collective security. King would see to it that Canada would pursue the same autonomous and isolationist policies at the upcoming session of the League of Nations.

In the autumn King took Sir Lomer Gouin with him to the Imperial Conference of 1923. Concurrently, Sir Lomer served as Canada's chief representative at the League of Nations Assembly. Laying aside his personal feelings towards Lapointe, Gouin took up the latter's 1922 proposal to amend Article X so as to make any military action voluntary. At the 1923 Assembly, Gouin introduced a resolution that did not require changing Article X but proposed an interpretation along the lines of Lapointe's amendment. Resolutions required unanimous consent – another of the League's problems – and the Canadian resolution failed to be adopted by one vote, that of Persia.[10] Nevertheless, the all-but-unanimous vote showed that the membership, including France and the smaller states, was satisfied to 'interpret' Article X in the voluntary way Lapointe had wished. From Geneva Gouin reported to King in London that henceforth Article X would be interpreted 'in the sense of the amendment proposed by our colleague, Mr. Lapointe.'[11] Though Lapointe had not foreseen it, his amendment did not abort but grew into the prevailing interpretation of Article X.

While King and Gouin were at the Imperial Conference in London, Lapointe made a speaking tour through the four western provinces. Friends of Sir Lomer suspected that Lapointe had been sent west by the prime minister to make an alliance with Crerar and the Progressives.[12] However, a handwritten note from Lapointe to King shows that Lapointe went on his own initiative, no doubt with the express purpose of building up the western alliance to supplant Gouin and the Montreal interests:

My dear King,

I have definitely decided to yield to pressure to go to the four western provinces. I receive requests for meetings every day. I have many departmental matters in British Columbia and my deputy minister will accompany me.

As you will be away in Europe, may I have the use of your [railway] car for the trip? I'll have to stop at so many places that it is necessary that I should get out. My wife and my secretary will accompany me.[13]

This note is strangely out of character for the modest Lapointe – almost as if he were crying out, 'Don't forget about me!' True, he was in demand in the West ever since his 1920 tour, when he had made 'a splendid impression upon the people of British Columbia,' but he obviously exaggerated when he claimed daily speaking requests. 'Phone Lapointe,' King instructed his secretary. 'I must arrange matters to his satisfaction.'[14] Whether Lapointe decided not to borrow King's private railway car or whether King found some excuse for not lending it, on 29 September Lapointe took the CNR direct to Vancouver accompanied only by his wife.

Vancouver was an economic miracle in a Canada just slowly pulling out of the post-war depression. Until 1921 barely a shipment of wheat passed over its docks; but in that year the prairies began shipping wheat by way of Vancouver and the Panama Canal as a cheaper alternative to the Great Lakes and St Lawrence route. A big advantage was that the port of Vancouver was open all year round. One of Lapointe's few triumphs in the 1923 parliamentary session was the unanimous passage of his motion to lend $5 million to the port of Vancouver. In fact, the Progressives were so delighted they had even suggested making the $5 million an outright gift.

Lapointe's first official duty was to open a new pier at the port of Vancouver. Later, he received a delegation of fishing vessel owners, who seized upon the presence of the minister of marine and fisheries to press for the lifting of limitations on the number of Japanese fishermen. No less prejudiced than their fellow British Columbians who passed legislation removing Orientals' civil rights, the boat owners were simply trying to maximize profits. As they told Lapointe, the Japanese worked harder and for less money than the white fishermen. After several speaking engagements in Vancouver, Ernest and Mimy moved on to Victoria and Prince Rupert. On their way back east, Lapointe addressed meetings in the main cities, liaising with western colleagues Charles Stewart, the minister of mines and interior, and W.R. Motherwell, the minister of agriculture. On 4 November they arrived in Winnipeg in time for Lapointe to speak at a banquet at the Fort Garry hotel in honour of E.J. McMurray, the recently appointed federal solicitor general. The next day he addressed the Canadian Club on the League of Nations. Tom Crerar attended and reported to their mutual friend Kirk Cameron in Montreal that Lapointe had made a very good speech.

Lapointe's three days in Winnipeg gave him the opportunity to renew his personal friendship with Crerar. He and Mimy were invited to lunch at the Crerars, and after lunch the men had a frank discussion. 'I find myself, as in the past, in very close agreement with him,' Crerar wrote Cameron. But he added that Lapointe seemed to lack the power to make his views felt in the cabinet. Crerar rightly sensed that Lapointe stood 'pretty much alone.' It was against Lapointe's principles to support the high-tariff policies of Gouin and Fielding, but he could not support the anti-protectionist views of the western ministers since he himself represented an industrial riding. In Crerar's opinion, Lapointe had made a great mistake in leaving his rural riding of Kamouraska. He even suspected that St James Street had had a hand in Lapointe's move to Quebec East in order to neutralize him as the spokesman for a more liberal trade policy. 'I fancy there was a little bit more in that move than merely having the mantle of Sir Wilfrid fall upon Ernest,' Crerar observed to Cameron.[15]

After talking to Crerar, Lapointe returned from his tour convinced that an alliance with the Progressives and the western farmers was feasible if the government would distance itself from the protectionist policy imposed by Gouin and his Montreal friends. Meanwhile, in England, Mackenzie King was changing his mind about keeping Gouin. Sir Lomer's big-business mentality was basically offensive to King's social conscience. Moreover, the two were completely at odds on the tariff. Gouin's veiled threats to resign no longer frightened King. The prime minister was determined to absorb the Progressives once and for all and thus liberate himself from the St James Street financiers. Rumours of dissension between King and Gouin floated back to Canada.

On 14 November 1923 the Montreal *Gazette* carried a news story that Sir Lomer Gouin was resigning as minister of justice for reasons of health to go into the Senate and would be replaced by Ernest Lapointe. According to the paper, Sir Lomer had been weakened by overwork at Geneva and had suffered violent indigestion causing cerebral congestion. Gouin's family expressed surprise. Paul Gouin told the press that he had just received a cable from his father saying that he was very well and was sailing home on the *Majestic*. He had simply had an attack of indigestion, which was understandable after all the banquets at London. 'That's the first I've heard of it,' Ernest Lapointe told reporters who brought the story to his attention. 'I'm certain Sir Lomer enjoys good enough health to stay at the head of his department.'

Gouin landed at New York on 21 November. Greeted by reporters, he categorically denied that he was resigning.[16] Yes, his health had left something to be desired at London, but he was better now and the sea voyage had proved very beneficial. No, there had been absolutely no friction between the prime minister and himself at London. He was almost gushing in his praise of Mackenzie King, declaring that the prime minister had made a 'magnificent impression' at the Imperial Conference. Over the next few weeks, while waiting for King to return, both Gouin and Lapointe tried to quash rumours of strain between them. On 25 November Gouin risked indigestion by attending a dinner at Montreal's Windsor Hotel in honour of his rival. In his address Lapointe graciously welcomed Sir Lomer home: 'We are happy to say that Sir Lomer Gouin enjoys excellent health, and represented us abroad with his customary fine character and great talent.'[17]

Montreal Liberals had planned a royal welcome for the prime minister on his return from London, hoping for a semblance of the enthusiastic demonstrations that marked Sir Wilfrid Laurier's appearances in the city. It was a windy, rainy December day, but a goodly crowd lined the streets to cheer the small figure of Mackenzie King in an open touring car followed by a motorcade of limousines, Fords, and trucks. The crowd was thickest around a platform on Craig Street, waiting to hear speeches by the prime minister, Premier Taschereau, Sir Lomer Gouin, and George Graham. It was Sir Lomer's moment (politicians are never so popular as when they are departing), and his remarks received thunderous applause. After describing how King had heroically resisted the imperialistic pressures at London, he congratulated his colleague Ernest Lapointe, sitting among the dignitaries on the platform, for minimizing Canadian obligations under the worrisome Article X.[18] The audience applauded when Gouin spoke of the need for a protective tariff.

The next day, after a cabinet meeting where King made clear his intention to conciliate the Progressives, perhaps even bringing in Crerar, Sir Lomer called on the prime minister in his office in the East Block. As King described the interview, Gouin told him that he had been warned by his physician that if he wanted to live he would have to give up public work. He had a heart problem and rheumatism from his early days. He then spoke of their discussions on the tariff and said it would be better if he were out of the cabinet. If Gouin expected an argument from King he was disappointed: 'I told him I had noted the change in his health and condition and could not press him to stay on under such circumstances, though I was sorry to lose his great and good support in the government.'[19]

According to King, the interview ended on a cordial note with a discussion of a possible Senate appointment, which Gouin leaped at, or a diplomatic posting to Washington, which Gouin said his wife would like. But a rumour was circulating on Parliament Hill that the two had parted in anger. According to some unnamed witnesses, Gouin had burst out of the prime minister's office shouting, 'You make me sick,' while from inside the office a voice wafted out, 'Sick enough to resign?'[20] The final straw came when King took Lapointe's recommendation for a Supreme Court appointment over that of the (still incumbent) minister of justice. The jurist recommended by Lapointe was Albert Malouin of the Quebec Superior Court. Malouin was a diabetic and accepted the appointment reluctantly. Some said that Lapointe had chosen him simply to block Gouin's candidate.[21]

On 2 January 1924 King received Gouin's letter of resignation 'for reasons of health.' The following day he handed the surprised and unhappy Sir Lomer a letter accepting his resignation. As he had told reporters when he landed at New York, Gouin had had no intention of resigning. Overvaluing his own importance in the administration, he used the threat of resignation to make King back off from the tariff reductions towards which he was leaning. At the same time, he underestimated Lapointe, who was standing in the wings. On learning that Ernest Lapointe had been named acting minister of justice, Gouin's cup of bitterness brimmed over. To save Gouin's face, his friend Senator Dandurand urged the prime minister to delay Lapointe's appointment, but King was adamant. He recorded in his diary: 'I feel a great load off to be rid of Gouin. He just represented the interests. He never moved to Ottawa. The real Liberals of Quebec are all pleased.'[22]

The most pleased, of course, was Lapointe. This time King agreed when Lapointe said that he favoured Crerar coming in even if it necessitated a break with the Montreal group. He and King were soulmates again. The loss of two Nova Scotia by-elections in December further decided King 'to take the bold course and link up with the farmers.'[23] A wire went off inviting Crerar to Ottawa for talks. Indeed, the old order had passed. In December the seemingly indestructible William Fielding was felled by a stroke.

As he had after the 1921 election, King turned to Lapointe as his principal adviser on appointments. Who should succeed Lapointe himself in the department of marine and fisheries? Who should take over Fielding's finance department on an interim basis? Louis Brodeur had died suddenly after only a month as Quebec's lieutenant-governor. Lapointe was to advise King who should get that plum after discussing the matter with Premier Taschereau. The train ride to Quebec for Brodeur's funeral provided a good opportunity for King and Lapointe to thrash out the business of the new appointments. Although, as King told his diary, 'Lapointe had never been too favourable to Lemieux, he seemed to realize he was the best man.' Lapointe agreed that Rodolphe Lemieux should have the right of refusal to the cabinet vacancy as well as to the lieutenant-governorship.

On the train back to Ottawa, King sounded out Lemieux, who rejected both posts out of hand. King may well have offered Lemieux the justice department without Lapointe's knowledge. Lemieux always claimed that he had been offered the post before Lapointe, and this was so important to his self-esteem that he included it in his biographical entry in the 1936 *Canadian Who's Who*: 'Declined offer of lieut.-govship. of P.Q., and later portfolio of min. of justice to succeed Hon. Sir Lomer Gouin, declining both 1924.' Certainly, King covered a range of possibilities with Lemieux on the train and in subsequent discussions. Knowing how Lemieux loved France, King suggested he succeed Philippe Roy as Canadian representative in Paris. 'Just a post office,' scoffed Lemieux.[24] Like Gouin and Bureau, Lemieux wanted to go to the Senate. Failing that, he would remain as Speaker of the House.

Having vanquished his rivals, Lapointe was seized by inertia. When King asked him who should fill the Quebec cabinet vacancy, he found him 'very indecisive, unwilling to take responsibility.' 'You're the boss,' was all he would say. In the privacy of his diary King almost sounded as if he were regretting the loss of Gouin. 'I can see we are without strength in Quebec,' he noted on 14 January 1924. 'Lapointe has no organizing capacity and is not in touch with the province. We will fare badly there.'

In the end, Bureau made up Lapointe's mind for him. He chose Arthur Cardin, a Sorel lawyer and the sitting member for Richelieu county near Montreal. An insignificant looking individual except for his deep-set eyes, Cardin was unsociable, even something of a loner; yet surprisingly he was one of the best platform speakers in Quebec.

Bureau had reason to be grateful for his campaigning skills. Cardin had helped Bureau hold his Trois-Rivières riding in 1921, and in the 1923 provincial election he had steadied the Bureau machine, which was being rocked by a rising Maurice Duplessis. When Lapointe was aspiring to Laurier's old riding in 1919, Cardin's speech in praise of the newcomer was so memorable that the Chateau Frontenac barbers were still quoting it. Cardin's name was being bruited in the Quebec press for the cabinet vacancy, but he was little known nationally since he rarely spoke in the House of Commons. As *Le Devoir* put it, he had 'persevered in his silence for thirteen years' and would now have to prove himself.[25] King might have hesitated making him minister of marine if he had known what the Quebec MPs knew, that Cardin was in the pocket of the Simard shipbuilding family at Sorel.

On 30 January 1924, at five o'clock in the afternoon, King escorted Lapointe and Cardin to Government House where the old soldier, Lord Byng, conducted the swearing-in ceremony. Fifteen minutes later, Cardin left the vice-regal residence as minister of marine and fisheries and Lapointe as minister of justice. *Le Devoir* summarized the rivalry between Lapointe and Sir Lomer Gouin and the former's victory:

> After remaining in obscurity for several years, M. Ernest Lapointe has suddenly moved into the top rank of his party ... In 1921 he all but became leader of the French-Canadian Liberals ... at a time when there was only Rodolphe Lemieux to contest his title and aspire to the same honour. Then M. Gouin appeared on the scene with his prestige and experience, supported by powerful forces, and he snatched the crown the Quebec City member was about to put on his own head. Lapointe had to be content as Liberal chief in Quebec district and the south bank of the St Lawrence while his redoubtable antagonist gave direction to ministerial politics.
>
> After Gouin's resignation, after Lemieux's refusal to succeed him, Ernest Lapointe finds himself without competition and becomes Minister of Justice.[26]

Comparing the two men, *Le Devoir* found that Gouin was the more fearless and decisive. Moreover, Lapointe would never be *persona grata* with the Montreal interests because of his leanings towards the Progressives. But he could compensate by gains in the West for losses his party would sustain in Quebec. The writer sounded a cautionary note. With almost half the province not yet under his influence, Lapointe would have considerable difficulty in becoming the uncontested chief of the Quebec Liberals.

Le Devoir's columnist concluded that while Lapointe's appointment could be criticized, 'there was no one in parliament who deserved the honour more.'

CHAPTER SEVEN

Minister of Justice

The post of justice minister carried with it material and social advantages for Ernest Lapointe. As a senior minister he had a salary of $10,000, plus an indemnity of $4,000 for expenses, at a time when the average family of four lived on $1,500 a year. Naturally he had to give up his law practice. He moved his family to Ottawa, leasing the spacious ground floor of a converted mansion on Chapel Street in the residential district of Sandy Hill. Whether by chance or design, it was half a block from Laurier House, the fine residence King had inherited from Sir Wilfrid's widow. Odette, now a charming fifteen-year-old, was a boarder at a local convent, and Hugues – whom everyone called Bobby, an evolution from his childhood name of Baby – lived at home and attended a Catholic high school. English colleagues had urged Lapointe to send his tall young son to the Royal Military College in Kingston, but Lapointe knew that this would not go down well in Quebec.[1] Mimy was an avid bridge player, which combined well with her social duties as a cabinet wife. Golf was Lapointe's great relaxation, and he was looking forward to a golfing vacation in the spring.

Meanwhile, Mackenzie King was re-evaluating his new appointee. An exceptional judge of men (women were not even considered), King was out to get the best cabinet material available. Cool-headed and objective, he was not swayed by the old-boy's network or friendship. Indeed, he did not permit himself to have real friends among his associates. Despite his extreme apparent friendliness, Chubby Power, for one, was 'never much impressed by his sincerity.' Understanding little of Quebec and nothing of its language, King had to have a French lieutenant.[2] Gouin had not filled the bill, partly because he and King had not been sympathetic. In Lapointe, King had someone who shared his essentially humanitarian views but like himself was always ready to practise the politic 'art of the possible.' If Lapointe could 'manage' Quebec in the interests of national unity he would be the undisputed Quebec lieutenant. King had some doubt whether this slow-moving, genial man of the people was sufficiently forceful or decisive.

Lapointe had a commanding presence and a natural authority, but behind that impressive facade King found him 'very timid' and 'indecisive.' Much as King liked him and appreciated his loyalty, he was very aware of these flaws in Lapointe's character. On the other side of the scale, Lapointe was one of the foremost parliamentary orators of the day, and above all there was his popularity in Quebec. As *Maclean's* pundit J.K. Munro said of him, the 'Hon. Ernest has an eloquence that rouses the enthusiasm of the habitant and causes him to vote as he should.'[3] Quebec craved a hero; it did not have one in King. Time would tell if Lapointe was the *chef* to follow in Laurier's footsteps. For the present, the astute King realized that the more he showed confidence in Lapointe, the greater Lapointe's prestige would be in his home province.

After two years on the sidelines, Lapointe was glad to move into the limelight. At the 1924 session of Parliament King made him his deskmate. And it was Lapointe who led off for the government in the throne speech debate. This gave him the opportunity of matching debating skills with Arthur Meighen. Having taunted the government through two parliamentary sessions for failing to keep its promise to reduce the tariff, Meighen had the rug pulled out from under him with the governor general's announcement that customs duties would be lowered on agricultural implements and other items. For the next two weeks the austere Meighen, looking the very personification of the Grim Reaper in a tight black coat and waistcoat and stiff high collar, presaged doom for the country as a result of freer trade and heaped destructive criticism upon all the government's initiatives. Lapointe's response was to paint an upbeat, optimistic picture of the country.

'With hesitant delivery, but with a native eloquence that lightly leaped the barrier of another tongue,' wrote the *Globe*, 'the Minister of Justice surveyed the whole political field covered by the Gubernatorial utterance.' Everything, in fact, but the tariff issue. Given Quebec's growing protectionism, Lapointe steered clear of that topic (although the opposition had spoken of little else), saying merely that he would 'follow precedent and not anticipate the Budget by being too specific.' Canada was coming back with vigour and courage, he told the House. Trade was increasing as never before: since the treaty with France exports of farm implements to that country had increased 100 per cent; exports had also expanded in automobiles, electrical apparatus, and aluminum ware. Public loans were oversubscribed; bankruptcies were down by 50 per cent. 'Why the gloom?' he inquired rhetorically of the opposite benches. Looking in the same direction he charged that it was 'the whisperers of death, the preachers of blue ruin' who were primarily responsible for the drain of Canadian manpower to the United States. The sound of Liberals and Progressives pounding their desks in approval was deafening.

Turning to the Progressives, he articulated the new orientation of his party. 'Though proud of the progress of industry in this country, we must not forget that agriculture is the basis of our national life.' The Progressives had voted as a bloc to accept the throne speech. Lapointe's declaration would help to keep them on side for the budget. To get it passed the Liberals had to have their support. The government was two short of a majority, and several Liberals from industrial ridings were poised to bolt.

The most rousing part of Lapointe's speech was his unquestionably heartfelt appeal for national unity. Attacking the sectionalism that divided the country, he declared: 'If Canada is to be a great country, Maritime rights, Western rights, Central Canada rights must be subordinated to the national duty of all Canadians: to build up an undivided and indivisible nation – the home of a big, united people. To the accomplishment of that task we will devote all our energies ... No Canadian, whether he lives in the West or in the East, should concentrate his vision and mould his opinion as if Canada ended at Lake Superior.' Laurier's true disciple, he told his listeners that compromise was necessary to achieve national unity. 'If we have to follow some middle course, I contend that the course is a national duty.' The speech made the front pages. 'WHY THIS GLOOM? ASKS MR. LAPOINTE OF SAD MR. MEIGHEN' was the headline in the *Globe*. The *Montreal Star*, a Conservative organ that nonetheless detested Meighen, dubbed it 'A Brilliant Oration,' taking obvious pleasure in adding that Lapointe saw Meighen as Canada's Evil Star.[4]

Public interest in the budget was running high. King was employing such ringing phrases as 'freer trade and freer living for the great mass of the people.' The business class saw it coming with foreboding. On 10 April 1924 the excitement in the House was palpable, both in the crowded galleries and on the floor. Sir Lomer Gouin was present for the first time that session, and so was Tom Crerar. Although Crerar had resigned as leader of the Progressives, he was sitting with them, sporting a new fedora at a rakish angle. Crerar had the eccentric habit of wearing a hat in the chamber, but he whisked it off when James Robb, the acting finance minister, rose to speak. Even the Tories acknowledged that substituting for the veteran Fielding was no easy task.

Robb began with the cheerful news that the government had reduced the national debt by $30 million and for the first time in years was operating with a surplus. (So much for Meighen's charges of over-spending.) After giving the encouraging trade figures Robb laid down the details of what he called a new National Policy. As expected there were reductions in customs duties on many items, but these were not as great as the Progressives had hoped for and the right wing (Liberals and Tories) had feared. Moreover, the cautious departure from protectionism was softened by the removal of sales tax on machinery and foodstuffs. There was tax relief for the consumer, with the general sales tax dropping from 6 to 5 per cent. The budget was passed with the support of the Progressives. However, the latter paid a price. A group of the more doctrinaire free-traders in their party had wanted deeper cuts in the tariff and broke away to form, with the two Labour members, what became known as the Ginger Group. The predicted discontent among the Quebec bloc did not materialize. Lapointe had proved a good manager of men.

Unfortunately, the modest move away from protectionism in the 1924 budget caused Lapointe problems with his constituents. A delegation of 160 boot and shoe manufacturers from Montreal and Quebec City descended upon Ottawa, irate about the preferential tariff on footwear imports from Britain. The spokesmen claimed that the home industry could not compete with cheap British imports when weekly wages in Canada were $23 compared with an equivalent $12 or $13 in England and the currency exchange was unfavourable to the Canadian dollar. King did not make it any easier for Lapointe. Regarding the boot and shoe manufacturers as 'very selfish' – indeed, living proof that 'the protective tariff was evil and a curse' – he replied to their demand for increased protection with the tart remark that the government had not heard from the much larger deputation of consumers who wanted reduced duties.[5] Lapointe tried to placate the boot and shoe manufacturers without much success. Soon the Quebec City daily L'Evénement was stirring up workers in the shoe factories, telling them they would lose their jobs thanks to Lapointe.

High on the list of priorities for King and his new minister of justice was Senate reform. The unelected upper chamber had taken to vetoing bills and sending them back to the Commons. In January 1924 King talked the cabinet into introducing legislation whereby a bill that passed the Commons three times and was twice defeated in the Senate would automatically become law. He reassured his colleagues that this was just following a British precedent. He and Lapointe also got cabinet to approve mandatory retirement for senators at seventy-five years of age. These changes required amendments to the British North America Act, and Lapointe instructed his law officers to draft appropriate resolutions. Neither measure got past the talking stage, largely because of opposition from Senator Dandurand and other Quebeckers.[6] In his unceasing promotion of constitutional reform, Lapointe was not speaking for Quebec, which was tradition-bound and afraid of change. But he was most definitely Quebec's spokesman when it came to pressing for French-Canadian rights at Ottawa.

French Canadians felt themselves discriminated against by the federal government not without reason. *Le Devoir* exposed example after example of discrimination in the federal civil service. Citing statistics from the auditor general's annual report of 1923, the nationalist paper reported that of the 229 income tax collectors in Montreal, 150 were English and only 79 French. Moreover, in the finance department, twenty-one English Canadians were in the top salary bracket ($2,000 to $5,000) compared with only three French Canadians. The paper complained that while French Canadians had traditionally enjoyed a monopoly on jobs at the King's Printer, now the King's Printer himself was English and only one department head was French. According to *Le Devoir*, barely half of government publications were translated into French. More printing in the French language was a constant demand from Quebec. *Le Devoir* held the Quebec MPs partially to blame for this situation. 'When we complain of the poor treatment of French civil servants, our Members of Parliament shrug and blame the Civil Service Commission.' As the representatives of three million French-speaking Canadians, *Le Devoir* scolded, the MPs should speak French in the House of Commons: no wonder there were not more French civil servants when French was so little used.[7]

Lapointe was the recipient of a steady stream of complaints from his fellow French Canadians. He attempted to satisfy them with varying success. One such complaint arose when word got out that the position of assistant Dominion statistician was to be abolished on the retirement of the francophone incumbent. Lapointe informed T.A. Low, the minister of trade and commerce, that this position had been created expressly to give representation to the French-speaking population at the statistics bureau. 'I have personally heard many complaints in the Province of Quebec with regard to what is looked upon as an unfair way of taking censuses and other statistical work.' Quebec groups had taken up this matter with him, he informed his English colleague, and 'your refusal to allow the French-speaking population to be represented at the head of the branch might be the cause of serious difficulties.'[8]

The job of Quebec lieutenant involved not only securing appointments for French Canadians but also ensuring that persons unacceptable to Quebec did not get appointed. Rightly or wrongly, Mr Justice Lyman Duff thought he had been denied the chief justiceship in 1924 because he was *persona non grata* in French Canada. On the death of the incumbent chief justice, the choice of a successor boiled down to Lyman Duff and another Supreme Court justice, Frank Anglin. King confided to his diary that he could not appoint Duff because 'he gets off on sprees for weeks at a time.' Unenthusiastically, he appointed the Roman Catholic, Jesuit-educated Anglin, whom he regarded as 'vain and narrow.'

The deeply disappointed Duff felt that it was not his drinking that disqualified him but Lapointe's opposition. As central appeals judge during the war, Duff had refused exemptions to French-Canadian seminarians, and he believed that Lapointe had turned thumbs down on him for this reason. In a letter to Lord Haldane, the British Lord Chancellor, a few months after Anglin's appointment, Duff delivered a strong indictment of the Quebec bloc and of King for toadying to it:

> The turn of the political wheel brought Quebec into power in the last election, and the machine there is pressing the spoils doctrine to the extreme limit, and the present Prime Minister, who owes his office to his attitude of sympathy with Quebec during the war, is willing to acquiesce in that policy so long as Quebec's support is essential to him.
>
> Unfortunately, the whole thing is unprincipled. With the Quebec machine, office is the *summum bonum*. Its ascendancy in Quebec Province is maintained largely by keeping alive the anti-conscription bitterness and by avoiding offence to the clergy; subject to that, any policy is acceptable which assures political support elsewhere.[9]

Lapointe was proving to be a stronger justice minister than King had expected. Perhaps 'kicked from behind' by his deputy minister J.W. Edwards, he immediately set about reorganizing his department. The RCMP now reported to Lapointe, and he was diligently retrieving functions that had been allowed to slip over to the solicitor general's department. The solicitor general's duties, Lapointe told King, were simply to assist the minister of justice when asked to do so. One piece of legislation that Lapointe retrieved from the solicitor general's department was the Ticket-of-Leave Act, providing discretionary leave for prisoners. Lapointe asked King to approach the solicitor general, E.J. McMurray, and King was happy to report that McMurray was 'wholly agreeable' to the transfer of the Act.[10]

McMurray was not in a good position to defend his department against Lapointe's depredations. His position in the cabinet was tenuous. His Winnipeg law firm had borrowed some $30,000 from the failed Home Bank, and this would come out at the inquiry into the bank's failure. In front of Lapointe and several others, King threatened McMurray with dismissal from the cabinet unless the debt was paid. King further humiliated his solicitor general by repeating his threat at a cabinet meeting the next day. The devious King had another reason for wanting to get rid of McMurray. The top criminal lawyer in Manitoba, McMurray took on many left-wing clients – he had helped defend the strikers in the Winnipeg General Strike. He was a maverick in King's essentially conservative cabinet. King had only appointed him because he could not get Crerar. But McMurray was unpopular with the Progressives, and his days as a cabinet minister were numbered.[11]

That the minister of justice and the solicitor general were at odds was most apparent when it came to capital punishment. Under the Criminal Code, convicted murderers were sentenced to be hanged. There were many private bills to abolish capital punishment, including one introduced in 1924 by William Irvine, a Labour MP. The seven-hour debate on the Irvine bill cut across party lines. Most governmment members, among them King and Lapointe, joined the Conservatives in opposing the bill. However, McMurray supported it, arguing that capital punishment was not a deterrent. He was convinced that many innocent men had been executed. He also maintained that murderers were walking the streets because juries were reluctant to convict them because of the death penalty.

Lapointe claimed that the death penalty was a deterrent. 'By temperament and instinct,' he said, he favoured the bill, but 'from a high sense of duty as Minister' he could not support it: 'If I could convince myself that life imprisonment would be an effective substitute for capital punishment in Canada, and would afford the Canadian people the same degree of protection, it would be my duty to suggest it. But because I do not believe that it would I can only oppose the bill.' Lapointe buttressed his case with statistics bound to appeal to the prevailing xenophobia. He informed the House that 45 per cent of murders in Canada were committed by foreigners. The bill was rejected by a vote of 92 to 29.[12]

Justice ministers were faced with the agonizing decision whether to recommend to cabinet that a death sentence be carried out or commuted to life imprisonment. Even the granite-like Gouin could hardly stand the strain. A cabinet colleague once found Sir Lomer sunk in misery in his office on the day a condemned murderess, whose sentence he had refused to commute, was hanged.[13] Lapointe saw it as his duty to uphold the courts when they imposed the death penalty. A sensational case in 1924 involved a gang of bank robbers who killed a messenger while making their getaway. Four of the gang were captured and sentenced to be hanged. Lapointe refused clemency although it was not known which of the gang had pulled the trigger. The *Ottawa Journal* heartily approved: 'It should be widely known that in Canada conspirators to a crime are held as guilty as the actual perpetrators.'

Another 1924 case involved a young American convicted of murdering a man in Valleyfield, Quebec, during a quarrel over hunting dogs. Lapointe refused clemency despite a spate of appeals from Americans, including Secretary of State Hughes. No one could call Lapointe weak or irresolute when it came to hanging. Indeed, cabinet more than once reversed his recommendation of the death penalty, and on one occasion King cast the deciding vote in favour of commutation.[14] In contrast with Lapointe, McMurray was considered to be soft on criminals. Detesting corporal as well as capital punishment, McMurray remitted the sentence of the lash for a convicted bank robber whose case was under appeal. This brought down upon him the wrath of the trial judge and the criticism of the *Montreal Star* for McMurray's 'astoundingly swift intervention on behalf of a convicted bank robber.'[15]

Lapointe was also responsible for the federal penitentiaries holding some 2,500 inmates. Brigadier General W.S. Hughes, the superintendent of penitentiaries, commanded a sizeable force of inspectors, guards, wardens, and parole officers. These jobs were sought after by war veterans, who under a 1921 statute were to receive preference in government employment.[16] The government-appointed watchdog for the ex-servicemen was Colonel J.L. Ralston of Nova Scotia, a decorated veteran himself. In the summer of 1924 Ralston was incensed over the case of Lieutenant Colonel Eric McDonald of Halifax. McDonald had applied for the post of inspector of penitentiaries for Nova Scotia. He had headed the list in the civil service competition, and his appointment had been announced in the newspapers. Then his appointment was suddenly rescinded. Ralston had not the slightest doubt that Lapointe and his senior officials had interfered. It was known that Lapointe's department favoured a candidate named Jackson who apparently had not even sat for the civil service examination.

On 20 October Ralston dispatched a highly critical letter to Lapointe about Lieutenant Colonel McDonald's treatment. This gallant young soldier, Ralston wrote, had commanded a battalion in the field and was entitled to veteran's preference. Moreover, he had come first in the civil service competition and merited the post. The irate Ralston warned that he would make the matter public. 'No department should run roughshod over a statutory provision,' he declared.[17] King was drawn into the controversy. The Liberal premier of Nova Scotia, E.H. Armstrong, implored the prime minister to correct 'the raw deal' handled out to McDonald. A Liberal MLA warned King that 'the failure to recognize McDonald's legal and moral claim will seriously affect the prospects of the Liberal candidate in this part of Nova Scotia.' King promised 'to take up the question with Mr. Lapointe,' but, in fact, he steered clear of it.[18]

Lapointe set out his side of the dispute in a letter to Premier Veniot of New Brunswick. Lapointe complained that the Civil Service Commission had refused to appoint the only man he and his department officials considered qualified. Instead, the commission had appointed a veteran who lacked the necessary qualifications. Lapointe added that he realized the situation was 'rather awkward' because the veterans' associations were backing the soldier. Finally Lapointe conceded that the law giving preference to veterans 'cannot very well be modified or removed.'[19]

While Lapointe was moving up to second-in-command in the King administration, Arthur Cardin had emerged from obscurity to become an important minister. 'He is very active, full of fight and generally speaking, gains strength by way of contrast with what we have been accustomed to in the past,' the Montreal businessman and backroom Liberal Kirk Cameron informed Tom Crerar. He added that 'Cardin and Ernest are on the very best of terms and are working into each other's hands with considerable success.'[20]

At this time the two French ministers were making a concerted effort to secure a large grant for the port of Quebec. In his day, Laurier had promised to 'aggrandize' the harbour. Hopes had run high with the return of the Liberals in 1921, but in four years no major grant had yet materialized. This had been a source of constant frustration for Lapointe when he was minister of marine and fisheries, but he was helpless because Quebec harbour came under the department of public works. Meanwhile, he had to explain the government's inaction to the Quebec district MPs, which was no easy job in the face of grants for the ports of Toronto, Vancouver, and Montreal. Lapointe decided that the best course was to get the matter transferred to Marine and Fisheries where Cardin would be in a position to push for funds. Though Cardin represented Montreal, it would enhance his reputation throughout the province if he could present Quebec City with several million dollars to improve its harbour.

In August Lapointe and Cardin managed to convince the minister of public works, Dr J.H. King, that Quebec harbour should be transferred from his department to Cardin's. Several factors could have accounted for Dr King's ready cooperation. He may have been tired of pressure from his Quebec colleagues. Or he may have wanted to conciliate Lapointe because at this time they were having a rather unpleasant argument about patronage. In any event Dr King agreed, and Lapointe assured the prime minister that the transfer was perfectly legal.[21] Apparently King gave his qualified approval because Lapointe went ahead and pledged the government to a multimillion dollar grant for the port of Quebec – prematurely as it turned out.

Right after the meeting with Dr King, Lapointe and Cardin left for Quebec to take charge of two crucial by-elections. The prime minister was very worried about the outcome. 'I am greatly afraid of the Rimouski by-election and not sure of St. Antoine,' he confided to his diary on 11 August. 'I cannot believe we can carry the latter and greatly fear for the former.' The Liberal incumbent in the Montreal riding of St Antoine had resigned over tariff reductions in the budget; his constituents were thought to be just as protectionist, and Cardin would have his work cut out for him to hold the riding with a new candidate. Lapointe's equally daunting task was to win the by-election in Rimouski with General Sir Eugène Fiset, who had been deputy minister of militia and defence during the 1917 conscription crisis. Having been on the receiving end of the Liberals' vicious smear campaigns in Quebec for bringing in conscription, the Conservatives were playing up the general's wartime role for all it was worth. Not only were the Liberals on the defensive with their candidate, but Lapointe found the county 'flooded with Tory money [while] we are destitute.' His response was to roll out the pork barrel. At a public meeting he promised that if the Liberal candidate was elected a railway tunnel would be constructed at St Fabien, thus providing jobs for the county. And he made Fiset state publicly that he would resign if the government did not keep its promise.[22]

There was a second patronage issue in the Rimouski by-election. For this Lapointe needed the cooperation of his cabinet colleague, Dr King, and he felt very strongly that the doctor was undermining him. A dredging contract was being let in connection with the building of a bridge in Rimouski county, and Lapointe had assured an old friend and supporter, Louis Letourneau, that his company would get it. Letourneau had been the Liberal MLA for Quebec East since 1908, and he was devoted to his federal counterpart. He had campaigned door to door for Lapointe in 1919, and it was to Letourneau's house on St François Street that Lapointe had been carried in triumph for the victory celebration. So there were personal as well as party reasons why Lapointe was anxious for Letourneau to get the contract.

But Dr King's department of public works insisted on putting the dredging job out to tender. The matter had come up at a cabinet meeting and an order-in-council was passed calling for tenders, 'failing agreement on some other arrangement' between Dr King and Lapointe. When the two ministers continued to wrangle, Mackenzie King signed the order-in-council.[23] Letourneau was furious to have his deposit returned by the department of public works. He wrote a violent letter to Dr King and a contemptuous one to Lapointe, 'thanking me for my trouble in this matter, and stating that he will not annoy me any more.'

A distressed Lapointe was utterly humiliated by his inability to provide patronage for his faithful provincial lieutenant. 'I am simply discouraged,' Lapointe wrote King. 'I cannot help feeling that I have not received the help and consideration from some of my colleagues that I thought I was entitled to.' He threatened to resign. He would 'put up the best battle he could' in the by-election, but when it was over he and King would have to have 'the fullest and frankest discussion': 'I will submit to you the advisability of having someone else replace me as the leader of the Quebec district. A general becomes worthless when his lieutenants and soldiers have no longer confidence in him and believe his authority and prestige are gone.'[24] No doubt soothed by King, Lapointe calmed down sufficiently to propose that nothing be done about the contract until after election day at least. The prime minister wired Dr King to defer the order-in-council.

Lapointe was extremely well liked by his colleagues. He had great wit and charm. Towards the end of his life, a political opponent would say, 'You owe a great deal of your success to that God-given gift of "personality." You charm everyone.'[25] But his hearty, friendly manner camouflaged his darker side. If Dr King abided by the rules on tendering contracts, Lapointe took it as a personal affront; that Dr King had cooperated with him over Quebec harbour was forgotten. McMurray had yielded legislation to him just for the asking. Still, he felt that his colleagues were not giving him the consideration he was entitled to. When he felt let-down, he was apt to become overdramatic: even the smallest patronage issue became a matter of 'life or death.'

Mackenzie King recognized this characteristic in Lapointe and gave into him as much as possible. When he could not do so, he was all apologies. Figuratively wringing his hands, he told Lapointe that he had hated to sign the order-in-council putting the dredging job out to tender, but he had had no alternative since it had been passed at cabinet: it was 'a most unpleasant and trying duty,' he assured his Quebec lieutenant.[26] Lapointe certainly got special treatment. Some months earlier when McMurray wanted to avoid calling for tenders in regard to some timber concessions in Manitoba, King (to quote his own words) had 'jumped on him pretty hard.' 'I was very outspoken in my repudiation of the idea,' he wrote self-righteously in his diary.[27]

On election night Mackenzie King, surrounded by most of his cabinet, was waiting with bated breath at Laurier House. When the results came in he was almost speechless with delight. The Liberals had won both Quebec by-elections and had taken an Ontario seat from the Conservatives. He was particularly gratified by the victory in the urbanized riding of St Antoine, as the issue had been the lower tariff; he exulted that it was a 'knockout blow to the Tories.' And he had worried for nothing about running General Fiset in Rimouski. It seemed that Quebec had recovered from its resentment over conscription since it had elected a man who helped put it into force. King kept this thought between the covers of his diary. In between champagne toasts, the prime minister dispatched ecstatic telegrams to Lapointe and Cardin. A day or so later he was still elated, writing to Lapointe that he was 'delighted beyond words ... he had not experienced a comparable degree of happiness since he had entered public affairs.'[28]

Fiset, however, gave credit not to Lapointe but to Lucien Cannon, calling him 'a talented, brilliant speaker who had contributed more than anyone else to the victory.' In the aftermath of the election the general had even less cause to thank the minister of justice. Lapointe had made him promise to resign if the railway tunnel at St Fabien was not built that year, and now Sir Henry Thornton refused to authorize the tunnel, informing Lapointe that the CNR did not have the funds to do so. General Fiset wrote an anguished letter to George Graham, minister of railways. In light of Sir Henry's decision he had no option but to resign his seat.[29] (In the end Fiset's constituents did not hold him to his promise and sent him back to Parliament as long as he cared to run.)

Lapointe also had his problems about unkept promises. Mackenzie King's delay in making a decision about the grant for Quebec harbour was, Lapointe lamented, 'poisoning my life continuously.' The matter dragged on for months; the stumbling block seemed to be the amount of the grant. On 15 May 1925 Lapointe made a desperate appeal to King: 'Your hesitation when I mentioned to you the amount for the Quebec Harbour is giving me much anxiety. I have been miserable for over a year ... and I beseech you not to prolong the agony. The matter is no longer a debatable one as far as I am concerned; I am pledged, I have pledged the government.'[30] Then he got down to hard bargaining. 'Our friends' in Quebec district were asking for $10 million; however, he and Cardin agreed that the government should offer $5 million. He would try to have it accepted, and Taschereau would help him. He assured King that offering anything less would be useless. The price was now right. Within a few days King announced the grant. Lapointe received congratulations from a Quebec friend: 'The five million for Quebec port has rejoiced hearts and warmed up feeling for the Liberals.'[31] The friend recommended an election as soon as possible.

CHAPTER EIGHT

Leader of the House

It was the dog days of August. The ministers reluctantly left their summer homes for a cabinet meeting in Ottawa, but that did not account for the glum faces around the cabinet table. The government was entering its fifth year. It would soon have to call an election, and its prospects were not good. The Liberal regimes in Nova Scotia and New Brunswick had been toppled due in no small part to King's neglect of the East while catering to the West. The only remaining Liberal strongholds were Saskatchewan, which Charles Dunning had swept in a June election, and Quebec. The prime minister was so gloomy that Lapointe remarked 'it was like attending our own funeral.'[1]

Not the least of King's worries was Jacques Bureau. Bureau had returned from a long rest cure in the United States only to go off on another drunken spree. His department of customs and excise was becoming a national disgrace. Prohibition in the United States had spawned a gigantic smuggling operation. Bootleggers were picking up liquor and beer in hidden coves along the St Lawrence and the Great Lakes and smuggling them into the United States. Perhaps the most notorious overland stretch was the 130 miles between Rock Island, Quebec, and Cornwall, Ontario, where sixty unguarded roads crossed the international border. While this traffic breached American prohibition legislation, it was the return traffic that broke Canadian law. Ready-to-wear clothing, silk, jewellery, radios, prison-made denim overalls, and cigarettes in egg cases were slipping into Canada free of duty. Even Canadian liquor found its way back thus avoiding excise taxes. The government was losing millions in revenue, and there were loud complaints from Canadian manufacturers.

Everyone knew smuggling was going on under the eyes of the customs officials. As long ago as the previous August a delegation of clothing manufacturers had complained to a cabinet committee that cheaper contraband goods would run them out of business. In the face of government inaction, they had formed the Commercial Protective Association to investigate smuggling. In a letter to King dated 26 February 1925, the association's chairman, R.P. Sparks, set out their findings of graft and corruption in the customs department. Bureau's response to the smuggling problem ranged from a stupefying lack of concern to downright collusion. He defended his worthless officials, including R.R. Farrow, his deputy minister, another hard drinker. Probably on Farrow's advice, Bureau promoted J.E. Bisaillon to chief preventive officer for Montreal despite his reputation as a crook and bootlegger.

Sparks wrote King that he had shown Bureau evidence of Bisaillon's illegal activities. Bureau had inquired whether these incidents had occurred after Bisaillon's promotion. Told that they had happened while Bisaillon was a regular customs officer, Bureau replied that he would only consider matters that had occurred since Bisaillon was promoted. The logic of this understandably escaped Sparks. Questioned in the House in February 1925 on what his department was doing about the smuggling, Bureau answered, 'I don't believe any human force can stop it.'[2]

The RCMP tried, but they were repeatedly stymied. One of Bureau's first acts as minister of customs and excise was to ban the Mounties from patrolling the Quebec border. Any narcotics or other contraband goods they seized in Montreal harbour were to be turned over to Bisaillon's customs officers.[3] Although the turf wars were fought mainly in Quebec where the federal police in their stetsons and red jackets were highly unpopular, the RCMP and the customs department also clashed in British Columbia. In the opinion of a British Columbia senator, the failure to catch smugglers on the west coast was the result of friction between the customs officers and the Mounties.

The notorious Barge Tremblay affair indicated the extent of corruption in the customs department. A boatload of liquor was transferred in the St Lawrence from a Belgian schooner to the barge. Bootleggers planned to secretly unload the liquor in Canada and then smuggle it into the United States. The liquor was seized on the river and subsequently fell into the hands of Bisaillon's customs officers and the smugglers were allowed to escape. Bisaillon testified at the ensuing trial, and among other things his cross-examination revealed that he had deposited customs duties into his own bank account.[4]

King and Lapointe had been aware for a year that Bisaillon was a tool of the bootleggers and that Bureau was protecting him. King was anxious to clean up 'the rotten situation.' Jim Robb threatened to resign if nothing was done. Privately, King blamed Lapointe and Cardin. He consoled himself with the thought that he was trying to get action, but 'the determination of the Quebec men to do as Bureau wished prevented it.' It was no secret that King and Robb wanted to 'let in the light.' Insiders heard rumours of 'civil war in the cabinet because the Prime Minister could not control and discipline Hon. Jacques Bureau and certain other colleagues who were "sympathetic" in their attitude toward the smuggling conspiracy.'[5]

Skirmishes between the RCMP and customs led to a 'row' between Lapointe and Bureau – probably the first and only one they ever had. Bureau insisted that the Mounties be called off and stop interfering with customs matters. Clearly, Lapointe wanted to apprehend the smugglers, but in the end the friendship between the two prevailed. The Mounties were not given the resources to be truly effective. For example, in Vancouver in April 1925, some opium smugglers escaped because the RCMP officers had no car and were forced to take the streetcar to carry out the sting operation.[6] The inescapable conclusion is that Lapointe did not give a high priority to the anti-smuggling work of the Mounted Police. In 1925 the Customs Act was amended to provide for jail sentences in addition to fines, but the justice department launched no major prosecutions under the revised legislation. RCMP reports on known smugglers gathered dust in the department.[7]

Despite his close friendship with Bureau, Lapointe was regarded as personally incorruptible. According to one reporter, when a pair of convicted bootleggers from Rock Island, Quebec, made the mistake of asking Lapointe to mitigate their sentences, he responded, 'Gentlemen, you took a gambling chance and you lost. You cannot expect any sympathy from me or from my department. I advise you to take your medicine.'[8] Such was Lapointe's reputation, although this conversation may have been apocryphal.

When King polled his perspiring cabinet on 17 August 1925 he found opinion split between a fall or spring election. Lapointe and Cardin were for going to the country as soon as possible. King decided to call the election for the end of October. The timing, as he acknowledged in his diary, had more than a little to do with Bureau. Hoping to have the election over before the customs scandal broke, the wily King nonetheless protected himself with a burst of belated activity against the smugglers. King's secretary jogged Lapointe to start enforcing Canada's anti-smuggling treaties with the United States,[9] and the RCMP was taken off the leash.

On the first of September King summoned a few of his inner circle to Laurier House to discuss who should be appointed to the Senate before the election and what new cabinet ministers they should recruit. Afterwards, King wrote in his diary that it was 'one of the most trying evenings' he ever had. It was even worse for Lapointe. A painful discussion about Jacques Bureau took place. The problem had to be faced, King told his men. The customs department – he did not hesitate to call it 'a sink of iniquity' – needed house-cleaning, and Bureau was not the one to do it. Lapointe held out doggedly for keeping Bureau in cabinet. No doubt he reminded King of the 1919 Liberal convention where he and Bureau had effectively secured King's election. Later in the evening Cardin arrived. What he had to say clinched the argument. He had left Bureau in a state of intoxication, he informed his colleagues. He had to agree with the prime minister that poor Jacques was too far gone to be kept in his ministry any longer. Reluctantly, Lapointe gave in: Bureau would retire from Customs and go to the Senate. King wanted to drop him completely, but Lapointe and Cardin would not hear of it.

As for new cabinet ministers from Quebec, Lapointe's choice was Lucien Cannon, while Cardin favoured George Boivin, a youngish MP from the Eastern Townships. Boivin was highly regarded by both parties – in 1921 Meighen had tried to enlist him as his Quebec lieutenant. King was enthusiastic about Boivin but hesitant about Cannon because Lucien was a drinker. To relieve King's mind, Lapointe said Cannon could go to the bench after the campaign. Like the Senate, the judiciary had its uses as a sanitarium for alcoholic politicians.

The net result of this disagreeable meeting at Laurier House was that Bureau was appointed to the Senate. Boivin succeeded him as minister of customs and excise, although the more experienced Cardin was to administer the department until after the election. Cannon was to be solicitor general, but the department had been so cut back by Lapointe that King had downgraded it to non-cabinet status; he had even thought of abolishing it. At the insistence of Lapointe and the other Quebec ministers, King agreed to promote Cannon to cabinet rank.[10]

Bureau's 'exile' to the Senate was a wrenching experience for Lapointe. Bureau was his best friend. Without Bureau's mentoring it was more than likely that he would not be where he was. Lapointe had watched

Bureau deteriorate in the past year or two. It was not only his drinking. Bureau had a serious heart condition. While his old friend was in the southern United States trying to regain his health, Lapointe did what he could to help. In April 1925 Bureau was worried about his parliamentary indemnity. 'I can't afford to lose it in toto,' he wrote. 'Sickness does not enrich you.' Lapointe immediately replied with a kind and reassuring letter: 'I am very happy to hear you are better but do not hesitate to take a complete rest in the United States. There will be no difficulty with your indemnity. At the end of the session we always vote a sum for those who are absent because of sickness. I will look after it myself.'[11]

The election campaign in Quebec was notable for the absence of both national party leaders. King left the province to Lapointe, Cardin, and Cannon and campaigned out west. Meighen was banned from Quebec by his own party. In his place, the Tories presented E.L. Patenaude, who was popular in Quebec because he had resigned from Borden's government over conscription. Patenaude repudiated Meighen in his campaign and promised an independent, pro-Quebec policy in Ottawa. In this way the Conservatives hoped to revive the Tory alliance with Bourassa's nationalists, which had defeated Laurier in 1911. Armand Lavergne agreed to run as a Conservative on the understanding that if the Tories got in they would persuade Howard Ferguson to repeal Regulation 17, but Bourassa could not be won over. After twenty years out of Parliament he was standing for election, but as an independent: his paper Le Devoir opposed Patenaude.

The Quebec Liberals conducted what could only be called a slanderous campaign. Meighen was vilified as a monster, the murderer of Quebec's youth. A cartoon in the Liberal paper Le Soleil portrayed him as 'The Trafficker in Human Flesh,' though in fact not a single conscript was killed in battle. At the assemblées contradictoires Liberal orators reminded the audience of Meighen's own 'Ready, aye ready' at the time of Chanak and warned that he would have their sons' 'entrails scattered on the streets of Constantinople.'[12] Though Quebec voted solidly for the Liberals, the election results on 29 October 1925 were as bad as King had feared in his gloomiest moments. The Conservatives elected 116 members to the Liberals' 101. The Progressives too dropped substantially; they were now down to 24 seats. Bourassa and two independent Labourites had been elected. The one ray of hope for the Liberals was that Meighen was seven seats short of a majority. The much reduced Progressive party would hold the balance of power.

Lapointe won his seat but not as handily as in 1921. He had spent little time in his riding, having been called upon to campaign in the rest of the province and outside. His opponent gained a large share of the workers' vote by claiming that the government's policy of British preference was ruining the Canadian shoe industry. King lost his seat, as had eight of his ministers. His initial reaction was to resign. But when he hinted to Lapointe what he had in mind, he could see that the French Canadians would be strongly opposed. When cabinet met, King found the English ministers full of good reasons why he should not resign either.[13] Politicians would not willingly abandon the trough to their political opponents. King needed no further encouragement. On 4 November he informed the governor general that he would stay on and let Parliament decide the government's fate, and the next day he issued a statement to that effect. Fatigued by the election, Lapointe went off to Atlantic City with Jim Robb to rest up and play some golf. On his return to Ottawa he found that there was a plot afoot to dump King and that the plotters were depending on him to wield the axe.

Neither the East nor the West saw King as representing their regional interests. The 1925 budget had not followed up on the tariff reductions of 1924, and the western Liberals, as well as Crerar and the Progressives, felt neglected. The Montreal power brokers were equally disaffected to the King administration with Gouin gone. Indeed, King's policy of compromise for the sake of national unity meant that he had no committed followers in either camp; in the face of the poor election results the troops were ready to desert. Coordinators for the western and eastern dissidents were Tom Crerar in Winnipeg and A.K. Cameron in Montreal. President of a manufacturing company and sidekick of the mining promoter Noah Timmins, Kirk Cameron was the self-appointed eyes and ears of the Liberal party in English Montreal. Somewhat incongruously, this urbanist and Tom Crerar, the voice of the prairie farmers, found common ground and carried on a voluminous correspondence. In this instance, they saw eye to eye on the necessity of getting rid of King. The best the Montreal cabal could come up with was the has-been Nova Scotia politician George Murray, who had retired from the premiership some years earlier because of his age and poor health. According to this plan, King had to agree to retire and, as Cameron reported to Winnipeg, the Montreal group felt that 'Lapointe and Cardin were the men who must put this up to him.'

Lapointe was also the key figure in the Winnipeg group's scheme. Crerar and his friends wanted to replace King with Charles Dunning, the very successful Saskatchewan premier whom King himself was wooing for his cabinet, and to pair him with Ernest Lapointe in a de facto Baldwin-Lafontaine type of joint leadership. (When Dunning was sounded out he was cautiously interested but told his interrogator that they should 'leave [the plotting] entirely to the Frenchmen.')[14] The alliance was doomed from the start. The Western plotters retorted that Murray was out of the question, and the Montreal business interests would not accept Farmer Dunning – a pioneer in the western co-op movement who reportedly wore tan shoes with a morning coat.

Impractical as the plot was, it became impossible when Lapointe refused to have anything to do with it. He proved himself as loyal to King as he had been to Laurier. On 21 November the *Montreal Daily Star* carried an announcement from Ernest Lapointe that he was remaining loyal to his leader despite King's personal defeat in the recent election. King followed up two days later with a statement to the press denying any intention of retiring and blaming the Tory party for spreading the rumour.[15]

King decided not to wait until he got a Commons seat but to convene Parliament as early as possible and then, if the government could get a vote of confidence, to adjourn the House so that he could repair his devastated cabinet. At first he intended to have Robb act as House leader, but ultimately he settled on Lapointe, although the latter was far from eager to take on the task. The pundits at *Le Devoir* felt that King had no other choice. He had to count on the Quebec MPs and Lapointe was their chief. But his Quebec followers were not blind to Lapointe's weaknesses. 'One of the best observers confides in us,' *Le Devoir* reported, 'that he is weak outside the House but on the floor he is in his element. He's a parliamentarian and you'll see, he'll be able to conduct the manoeuvre.'[16] Besides, Cardin would help him, the columnist added. The consensus was that Cardin served as a buttress for the more popular, but less decisive, Lapointe.

As House leader of a minority party whose premier had been defeated, Lapointe was confronted with an unprecedented situation. To combat the Conservatives' superior numbers, he would have to win over the Progressives, the independents, and the two Labour members – J.S. Woodsworth had been joined by A.A. Heaps, who had defeated E.J. McMurray in North Winnipeg. Ten years had wrought big changes in Lapointe's appearance since he had come to the forefront in the House of Commons with his resolution on Regulation 17. Gone were the black curls – his head was almost bald – and the walrus moustache had contracted to a little brush. Only his height and thick, black-rimmed glasses set him apart from the other grey men of the Parliament.

As soon as the Commons trooped back to their own chamber after listening to Lord Byng read the throne speech, Lapointe moved a resolution declaring that the government was justified in summoning Parliament and retaining office unless defeated by a vote of non-confidence. Meighen was taken by surprise. He had intended to make the opening thrust by asserting that the government had no right to stay in office without a prime minister in Parliament and with fewer seats than the Conservatives. Aware of Meighen's intention, Lapointe had made a pre-emptive strike. Meighen now had to present his motion in the form of an amendment to Lapointe's resolution. The Meighen amendment was in effect a motion of non-confidence in the government.

Caged in his office and 'regretful at not having the right to take a seat in the House of Commons,' King had mixed feelings when his MPs raved about Lapointe's reply to Meighen's amendment. Lapointe's speech was indeed masterful. He pointed out that the British precedents for resignation cited by Meighen only held true when the opposition had a clear majority: otherwise the government met the House to let Parliament decide who should govern. He reminded Meighen that he had created a vacancy for himself in 1921 by appointing an incumbent Conservative to public office. His own leader, Lapointe informed the House, had honourably refrained from making appointments to public office until Parliament decided which party should constitute the government. A vote for or against the Meighen amendment would decide the issue: 'This government does not want to remain in office one day or one hour, unless the parliament of Canada approves of it.'[17] The rest of his speech was a subliminal appeal to the self-interest of the Progressives and the two Labour members. The Members of Parliament were still paying off election costs, and if they did not sit for a minimum fifty days they would forfeit their indemnities. Voting for the Meighen amendment meant that they would be in the midst of another election.

A long-time Liberal provided Lapointe with the view from the gallery: 'Congratulations and thanks for your great speech in most trying circumstances. It was worthy of the best traditions of the old Liberal party in which you and I were brought up and still belong. The way in which you dealt lightly with the Prime Minister's absence emphasized Meighen's great mistake in labouring it. The impression grew of the fierce personal nature of his attack.'[18] After days of rancorous debate the vote was taken at midnight on 15 January. Meighen's amendment was narrowly defeated, 123 to 120. Lapointe had managed to keep his party in office while holding fewer seats than the opposition.

Telegrams of congratulations poured in upon him. Many were from English Canada, but the greater number came from French Canadians bursting with pride in their *chef*. 'They ought to leave you in this premier post,' one Quebec politician wired him.[19] His admirers ranged from Premier Taschereau and Pamphile Du Tremblay, the powerful publisher of *La Presse*, to a grocer from Limoilou in his riding. On first-name terms with Lapointe, the grocer reported that the group around his cracker barrel all agreed that Ernest Lapointe was the heart of the government.

Lapointe's triumph was a little too much for King. Confined to bed with a cold, he wrote disparagingly in his diary that both Meighen's and Lapointe's speeches in the debate on the throne speech 'were far from being up to the mark ... In these days when I am beginning to doubt my own capacity to lead as I ought, there is some consolation in knowing I can equal these standards at least.'[20] It was possibly pique rather than his cold that made him decline the Lapointes' invitation to dinner at the Country Club for Philippe Roy, home from Paris for a visit. (Lapointe was one of the few French members of the snobbish Country Club.) However, when King entertained for Lord and Lady Willingdon a few days later, he included Ernest and Mimy.

Meanwhile, the Progressives and the splinter groups had to be kept on side. Lapointe made a special effort with Agnes Macphail, the only woman MP and a leading member of the small but vocal Ginger Group. King disliked her ('Parliament is no place for her,' he once confided to his diary)[21] and was happy to leave her wooing to Lapointe. He himself was occupied with Woodsworth and Heaps. The two Labour MPs were using their bargaining power to force the Liberals to bring in old age pensions and unemployment insurance. While King regarded the latter as a provincial responsibility, he was personally in favour of a pension scheme. Up till now he had been restrained from introducing one because of resistance from the Quebec bloc. Quebec politicians took a strong provincial rights position. Since pensions would be federally administered, they were against them as leading to greater centralization. Much of the opposition to social legislation in Quebec emanated from the Catholic Church jealously guarding its control over welfare and education. Lapointe opposed pension legislation. Nevertheless, with the party's survival at stake he gave in. On 26 January King had the cabinet meet with Woodsworth and Heaps in his office. Silencing his own objections, Lapointe joined in the consensus to introduce an old age pensions bill. It fell to him as minister of justice to inform the House of the intended legislation.[22]

On the first of February Lapointe successfully piloted the government through another crucial vote. Meighen had moved a second non-confidence amendment to the throne speech, which was defeated 125 to 115 thanks to all the Progressives, Labour, and independents voting with the government. The prime minister was in Saskatchewan, contesting the by-election that was to give him a seat in the Commons, when he received Lapointe's telegram. It was 'a great triumph,' he had to admit. The next step was to have some breathing space so that he could reconstruct his cabinet. He wired Lapointe to seek an adjournment of at least six weeks.[23]

On 2 February Lapointe moved that the House adjourn until the middle of March once the debate on the throne speech was over. He did not give any explanation. Taking their cue from the House leader, other Liberals remained silent. The Conservatives tore into the government. 'The ghastliest feature,' Meighen thundered, 'is that the government convened parliament supposedly for the despatch of the country's business, and before any business is despatched suggests that we go to our homes for six weeks because it is not in a position to carry on, and then refuses to give any single reason to parliament for not carrying on.'[24] As the Conservatives railed on throughout the evening, Lapointe sat motionless as an owl, staring at the House through his thick round lenses. He was determined to get his adjournment even if they sat all night. But the Tories were equally determined that he should not.

At midnight, H.H. Stevens, the Conservative member for Vancouver Centre, awakened the dozing members with a thunderbolt. He had been gathering evidence of corruption in the customs department for months and had no intention of allowing the Liberals to have an adjournment until he was assured of a full parliamentary investigation. Exempting the ministers of finance, militia, interior, and agriculture (all English), he related a tale of heinous misdeeds committed by the government: of Bureau, his deputy minister, and two civil service commissioners accepting cases of illegal liquor; of Bureau removing nine filing cabinets of damning evidence, which he destroyed at Trois-Rivières; of Bureau promoting the crooked Bisaillon to take charge of customs in Montreal in full knowledge of his key role in the smuggling ring. Stevens estimated that the illegal traffic in drugs and goods had defrauded the treasury of as much as $200 million. He accused the prime minister and his French ministers of knowing for at least a year that 'the grossest violations of the customs laws were being perpetrated in this country.' Stevens spoke with the authority of a fifteen-year veteran of the House:

> I want to say here, on my responsibility as a member of this House, that there is the most flagrant, organized, persistent, wholesale smuggling in the border towns along the province of Quebec and the American boundary, and again I say, so that the members from Quebec will not think I am picking on their province, that the same thing, perhaps in a lesser degree, exists along the boundary in other places. But here we have it erected into a legalized traffic, a regular occupation, or vocation, and with the individuals practising it known to the government.

He charged that the department of justice was concealing papers he had requested concerning certain cases. At this Lapointe rose to object: 'I have inquired from the officers of the Department of Justice and they say there is nothing in the department concerning those cases.' Stevens was unimpressed:

> The Royal Canadian Mounted Police have investigated some of these things; they have reported, and the reports are in his department. I do not know whether he has seen them or not, but they are there. In that case, one of two things is true; Either the minister has deliberately neglected his duties, or he is too innocent to occupy the exalted position of Minister of Justice.[25]

At four in the morning the members straggled out. The next day the puritanical Progressives had to swallow their disgust and vote with the tainted government in order to keep out the protectionist Tories. But Lapointe was forced to agree to Stevens's demand for a parliamentary committee to investigate the smuggling before he could get his adjournment motion passed.

King was in Prince Albert when he heard that the customs scandal had been raised in the House. 'I am glad our Quebec friends had to face it alone,' he told his diary with evident malice. They had refused to jettison Bureau when he had wanted them to. This would be 'a lesson' to them. He was glad that a full parliamentary inquiry into the 'unsavory business' had been promised. Travelling east two days later, he read

Hansard's reporting of Stevens's smuggling charges. He took grim satisfaction in Lapointe's ordeal during the late-night session: 'The debate revealed what I had surmised, namely that Lapointe had not been quick in speaking at the outset on reasons for an adjournment and that others hesitated as a consequence.' At North Bay on 6 February he was 'not sorry that Lapointe had had the anxiety he had – and has found the difficulty of leadership.' Now he would better understand 'my' problems.[26] Lapointe would have been astounded had he been able to peek into King's diary. He assumed that King had the same loyalty to him that he had for King. The diary reveals that in these early years when King felt vulnerable, he secretly harboured jealous feelings towards his soulmate.

To delay the adjournment, the Tories kept the House debating the throne speech for weeks. Under Lapointe's skilful management the government squeaked through eight non-confidence votes. At last, on 2 March he ended the filibuster by imposing closure. The Progressives gazed heavenward for forgiveness and voted with the government to accept the throne speech. Finally, Lapointe's gruelling test as House leader was over. Against all odds, he had saved the government, outnumbered by the opposition and battered by the customs scandal, from going down to defeat. He had got the adjournment (albeit only twelve days) that King needed to reorganize his cabinet.

On the surface Lapointe had sailed through it all with imperturbability, at times lightening the proceedings with shafts of humour. The minister of national defence, E.M. MacDonald, who had seconded Lapointe's crucial motion after the throne speech, admired 'the consummate ability' with which Lapointe handled the House under such 'trying and difficult conditions.'[27] But the 'moderation, patience and smiling tolerance,'[28] for which the press praised Lapointe, masqued internal turmoil. Lapointe's stomach was in revolt. While the others enjoyed the lavish (and subsidized) meals in the parliamentary restaurant, he stuck to a rigorous diet. Still, it had no appreciable effect on his imposing bulk. The chief justice of Quebec, François Lemieux, with whom he had articled in 1896, dropped him a droll, if somewhat class-conscious, note shortly after the adjournment. 'Congratulations from your old boss. You have proved that a habitant's son can be a very distinguished party chief, capable of wearing the tunic of Sir Wilfrid.'[29] But, he added playfully, he was speaking figuratively since the tunic would be too tight.

At the next cabinet meeting Lapointe's colleagues presented him with a gold watch in recognition of his services as interim leader. Indeed, Lapointe had done so well as the temporary party leader that many of the Liberal MPs wanted to see him take on the post permanently. According to Chubby Power, a group approached Lapointe about getting rid of King and becoming prime minister himself. 'They were thrown out on their ears,' Power said. 'Lapointe would not listen to any thought of that kind at all.'[30]

Later in March, the Lapointes attended a function at Government House. Mackenzie King took Madame Lapointe into dinner, and while holding his arm she recounted a remarkable prediction. A year or so earlier, she said, Ernest had gone to a fortune-teller who had predicted that something would happen to the prime minister and he would be called upon to be the leader.[31] King put a great deal of stock in clairvoyants – all through these difficult days he was consulting his mother and Sir Wilfrid through a medium named Mrs Bleaney. Indeed, Mrs Bleaney was invited to Laurier House to tell King's fortune just before the election.[32] No doubt the thought crossed his mind that, in the wake of the October 1925 election debacle, Lapointe could have displaced him. But King did not have to worry. Lapointe did not want to be prime minister; he was quite content to remain the undisputed leader of the Quebec bloc.

CHAPTER NINE

The Bilingual Schools Issue

On 15 March 1926 the House of Commons reconvened after its brief adjournment. Following tradition, the new member for Prince Albert, Saskatchewan, had to ask for his right to take his seat, so Ernest Lapointe escorted the prime minister up to the Speaker's chair and solemnly introduced him to the Speaker. Standing no higher than Lapointe's chin, King looked pale but pleased. The cheering Liberals were all sporting red carnations in their buttonholes, as were many of the opposition and the press. This note of gaiety, it was hoped, would forecast a less acrimonious House than before the adjournment. King had managed some reconstruction of his decimated cabinet; Tom Crerar had again refused, but King had achieved a real coup by bringing in Charles Dunning as minister of railways.

As the business of the House resumed, the Progressives consistently supported the government in return for the promise of lower tariffs, old age pensions, rural credits, and new railway lines. Meighen sarcastically asked the prime minister if he could estimate the cost of all this legislation, 'say within a hundred million dollars?' 'It is common knowledge,' Gratton O'Leary wrote in the March *Maclean's*, 'that the government does not take a step without getting leave from the Progressives.' As part of their price for supporting King, the Progressives had obtained his promise that the resource-rich public lands, retained by the Dominion government when Alberta was created a province in 1905, would be transferred to the province. Ottawa had kept vast areas of all three prairie provinces to provide land for railways and free homesteads, compensating the provinces with subsidies. No longer satisfied with subsidies alone, the provinces wanted to control their own natural resources. King had been promising to hand over the western lands since 1922.[1]

Desperately anxious to keep their Progressive allies, King and Lapointe negotiated an agreement for the transfer of the retained lands with the premier of Alberta, John Brownlee. On 9 January 1926 Lapointe and Charles Stewart, minister of mines and the interior, signed a memorandum of agreement with Premier Brownlee. The agreement was to be the basis for concurrent legislation in the Alberta legislature, and a few days later the Alberta Natural Resources bill was tabled in the House. Everything went smoothly until Henri Bourassa pointed out that the agreement did not guarantee the continuance of separate schools and threatened to raise the matter in the Commons.[2]

During Ottawa's custodianship of the western lands, a percentage of the proceeds from land sales were statutorily reserved for financing education. A portion of this was earmarked for separate schools. Although Section 17 of the Alberta Act of 1905 stipulated that 'Nothing shall prejudicially affect any right or privilege with regard to separate schools which any class of persons have at the date of the passing of this Act,' the school clause was so watered down that teaching in the new province's separate schools was in English except for one hour of French at the end of the schoolday.[3] Without some guarantee, bilingual separate schools would disappear when the Dominion government handed over the retained lands.

Lapointe was caught unawares. He had signed the federal-provincial agreement without realizing that it might remove the safeguard for existing bilingual separate schools. As King wrote in his diary, Lapointe 'has wakened up to what it is likely to involve so far as he is concerned if Bourassa, as he has indicated, brings the matter up.' It would do unforeseeable harm in Quebec if Bourassa drew attention to the fact that the French lieutenant had signed away the right to bilingual separate schools on the prairies. King thought that Lapointe was as frightened of Bourassa as Laurier had been.

On 29 January Bourassa made good his threat. He told the House that when the provinces of Alberta and Saskatchewan were created in 1905, the Laurier government (implying Laurier himself) had secretly guaranteed the 'school rights of the Catholic and French minorities' in the territory the federal government retained. Obviously savouring the moment, he informed his audience that he had been present at the secret meeting, and as the sole surviving witness he would be remiss in his duty if he did not ensure that these 'solemn moral obligations' were honoured. (A disgusted Tory commented that Bourassa had a tendency to quote those who were dead and could not defend themselves.)[4]

Lapointe was on the spot. It would be disastrous for him in Quebec if he did not carry out the revered French-Canadian leader's commitment from the other side of the grave. Lapointe insisted that the agreement with Alberta be amended to include a clause guaranteeing the French-Catholic population their own schools. After consulting with Bourassa and with Judge W.F.A. Turgeon of the Saskatchewan bench who had raised similar concerns, Lapointe drafted a clause and sent it to both men for their approval. In essence, Lapointe's clause provided for an educational system in accordance with Section 17 of the Alberta Act, thus guaranteeing bilingual separate schools in the territory to be transferred to the province. 'I believe paragraph A of section 2 is entirely what you wish,' he wrote Bourassa.[5] Over a propitiatory dinner at Laurier House, Bourassa assured King he was pleased with the bill as it now stood.

Initially, Premier Brownlee was amenable to the change, and he reintroduced the bill in the provincial legislature with Lapointe's amendment. Then an article appeared in the *Orange Sentinel* full of dire warnings that the bill would preserve French-Catholic schools in the West for all time. An Alberta election was looming. Well aware of the strong anti-French feeling in the province, Brownlee reneged. He informed Ottawa that the school clause would have to be amended again to read 'in accordance with the law of the province' instead of 'in accordance with the provisions of section 17 of the Alberta Act.'[6] Brownlee's new language would eliminate publicly funded bilingual schools in the transferred territory.

Lapointe was beside himself. He informed Brownlee that 'to suggest a change in the wording of the clause, now that it has been published, would reopen the 1905 dispute with a vengeance and was quite unnecessary.'[7] When Brownlee came to Ottawa in May he told King confidentially that 'he would not be afraid once the election was over and he had a few years ahead to take chances on the issue.' For public consumption, however, he criticized Lapointe in the press, and on 25 May the Alberta legislature passed the bill, substituting Brownlee's language for Lapointe's. Lapointe, who was just back at his desk following a bout of illness diagnosed as liver trouble, was grimly determined to keep the clause as he had drafted it. On 26 May he explained to caucus that the government's position was to continue the existing non-discriminatory schools policy mandated by Section 17 of the Alberta Act. From the 'vigorous' discussion, King saw how easily the whole matter could degenerate into a bitter controversy between the French and English.

Privately, he blamed Lapointe. It was Lapointe's fear of Bourassa in the first instance that had got them 'into this tangle over the Alberta Resources matter.'[8]

After caucus King met with Lapointe, Stewart, and Dunning. They all agreed that the only solution was to seek an opinion from the Supreme Court and ultimately from the Privy Council on the constitutionality of Section 17 of the 1905 Alberta Act. If it was declared valid, bilingual schools would continue by right; otherwise they would exist, if at all, by the grace and favour of the provincial government. King wanted to proceed by way of a joint reference with Alberta, but Lapointe convinced his colleagues to go ahead with a reference to the Supreme Court unilaterally – 'off our own bat,' as he put it.[9] On the first of June Lapointe announced the government's intention of submitting the question to the Supreme Court.

Catering to Bourassa over the schools issue had delayed the long-overdue transfer of the western lands. *Saturday Night* expressed disgust that 'the bromidic Mr Bourassa was enabled to hold up and alter a measure so vitally important to both the Progressives and Liberals of the West as the Alberta Resources bill.' Even the *Manitoba Free Press*, a Liberal paper, condemned the government for 'the stupidest performance that any political party was ever guilty of.'[10] At first the Progressives agreed that the transfer of the Alberta lands could be postponed until the Supreme Court decision came down. But by the middle of June they were restless, complaining that the government had broken its promise and demanding legislation during the present session. King thought it might well be this issue that would bring down the government.[11] However, a far greater threat emerged when the customs probe committee reported on 18 June.

The Special Parliamentary Committee investigating the administration of the department of customs and excise – otherwise known as the Stevens inquiry – verified widespread corruption and concluded that the department had been 'slowly degenerating in efficiency and that the process was greatly accelerated in the last few years.' With considerable understatement in light of the facts, it found that Jacques Bureau 'failed to appreciate and properly discharge the responsibilities of his office, and as a result there was a lack of efficient continuous and vigorous control of subordinates by the headquarters staff at Ottawa.' The committee report disgraced not only Bureau but George Boivin, the present minister. It revealed that Boivin had interfered with the course of justice by staying the jail sentence of a convicted smuggler named

Moses Aziz so that he could help a Liberal candidate in New Brunswick in the 1926 election. The report stopped just short of censuring Boivin.[12]

King had seen this coming and had suggested to Boivin that he resign and run in a by-election to be vindicated. Boivin was willing. But when word of his possible resignation reached the French-Canadian members, they let King know in caucus that they would not stand for Boivin being 'sacrificed.' It had been the same a month earlier when King had broached the subject of Bureau resigning. Lapointe and Cardin would not hear of it. Indeed, Cardin justified Bureau's conduct by saying that he had just tried to help his friends. 'It did not seem to matter that he had permitted criminal acts,' King mused in his diary. 'The French Canadian has a different view of these matters than the Anglo Saxon.' The way they stood by their own was chivalrous, but from the standpoint of morality King found it highly questionable.[13]

The Stevens inquiry's recommendations slashed through the ranks of government, officialdom, and business. The report called for the dismissal of high-placed officers in the customs department, including the 'retirement' of Farrow, the deputy minister. Calling for the complete reorganization of the customs preventive service, it strongly recommended using the RCMP for border patrol work with full powers of customs officers. Moreover, the minister should no longer be able to interfere in administrative decisions. Another recommendation was that Bisaillon's self-incriminating evidence regarding his bank account ($69,000 on a $2,500 salary) be turned over to the Quebec attorney general. The committee urged the government to proceed against the twenty-five firms named in the report for unpaid duty and sales tax and to order an audit of all distilleries. The final recommendation was to amend the law to prohibit clearances to vessels laden with liquor for the United States.[14]

As damning as the report was, it still left the Liberals in place. At the first opportunity, H.H. Stevens moved an amendment calling for a vote of censure on the government in general and on Boivin in particular for 'unjustifiable' conduct in the Aziz case. If passed, the Stevens amendment would bring down the government. It was J.S. Woodsworth who came to King's rescue. Fearing that all his hard-bargained-for social legislation would go into oblivion with the Liberals if there were an election (the Senate had just rejected the Old Age Pensions bill and the Commons would have to send it up again), he introduced a subamendment proposing a judicial inquiry into the customs affair. This would effectively avert the motion of censure and an imminent election. An indignant Progressive member jumped up and accused Woodsworth of trying to 'whitewash the whole filthy business.' For the highly moral Woodsworth, who even looked like a saint with his narrow, bearded face, this was as agonizing as lying on a bed of nails – particularly as it was true. To salve his conscience, he lashed out at the government for appointing Bureau to the Senate. Swallowing the criticism, King gratefully supported the Woodsworth subamendment.[15]

Whereas King had been almost maudlin in a rambling defence of poor, sick Bureau, Meighen, quietly and pitilessly, took the House through the bare, unvarnished facts. It was the performance of a superb prosecutor. All eyes turned to Lapointe. As King's second-in-command and one of the best debaters in the House, he was expected to respond to Meighen. Instead, Lucien Cannon shot off the government's volley without scoring a hit on the cold, contemptuous figure on the opposite benches. In fact, as Meighen's biographer has noted, Lapointe 'remained strangely silent throughout the debate on the customs scandal.'[16] The Woodsworth subamendment was defeated by two votes. Considering Lapointe's prestige in the Progressive camp, he might have swayed a few waverers had he spoken up.

Lapointe was working behind the scenes. After the failure of the Woodsworth subamendment, the Liberals' next ploy was to try to get the House adjourned. The Progressives had slipped the ropes of party discipline and were voting according to their conscience. Lapointe and King met with one of the swing votes – an Alberta MP named Coote. If Coote and his friends would support an adjournment, they promised to put through the Alberta Natural Resources bill as originally drafted and tranfer the land to the province without delay, leaving aside the separate schools question until the court decision. Exhausted from all-night sessions – Coote was a farmer, used to going to bed and getting up with the sun – he agreed reluctantly. Nevertheless, the motion to adjourn was defeated by one vote. King and Lapointe canvassed other possibilities, seeking an opinion from the noted constitutional lawyer Aimé Geoffrion of Montreal, but the best they could do was to get a weekend adjournment.[17]

King spent the weekend pleading with the governor general to dissolve Parliament. Not only would this head off the inevitable vote of censure, but the Liberals would go into the election with all the advantages of the government party, notably the dispensing of patronage. Byng adamantly refused to grant a dissolution. Instead, he called on Meighen to form a ministry. The aristocratic general was acting by the rules of the playing fields of Eton rather than modern constitutional theory, which required the king's representative to follow the advice of his prime minister. As Byng saw it, it was Meighen's innings.[18]

On Monday King informed the House that he had been refused a dissolution and consequently was resigning. He was haggard and there were tears in his eyes.[19] Meighen accepted the prime ministership with alacrity, but with only 116 seats out of 245, he was unable to form a cabinet in the conventional way. According to parliamentary rules of the day, when an MP was appointed to the cabinet he had to resign and be re-elected. No more than a formality, it nonetheless meant that with five or six members out of the House Meighen's government could be outvoted on the first division. To keep them in the House, Meighen devised the expedient of a cabinet of 'acting ministers.' He alone was sworn in and vacated his seat – a prime minister out in the corridors was becoming a parliamentary tradition. Under Sir Henry Drayton as acting House leader, the Conservative government called the vote on Stevens's motion of censure. Most of the Progressives voted for it and the motion passed. The two Labour members and Henri Bourassa stuck by the Liberals. Indeed, Bourassa sided with King throughout the constitutional crisis of June 1926.

On the first of July, while Canadians were celebrating Dominion Day, the MPs were at their desks in anticipation of winding up the session. The Conservative House leader was taken by surprise when Ernest Lapointe rose to his feet and, striking his characteristic pose with hands thrust in his pants pockets, thumbs out, tore to shreds Meighen's contention that his 'acting' ministry was legally constituted. He was followed by Jim Robb, the former minister of finance, who cleverly phrased a non-confidence motion: either Meighen's appointees were ministers, in which case they had to resign and be re-elected, or they were not ministers and had no right exercising ministerial duties in the House. While the finest mind on the government side paced the corridors in frustration, the constitutional argument raged in the green chamber. At two in the morning the Robb motion was carried by one vote. The Meighen government was defeated.[20]

Though Byng had refused King a dissolution, when Meighen asked for one the governor general granted it. This was the nub of the famous King-Byng crisis. King claimed that the Crown's representative had acted like a colonial governor instead of a constitutional figurehead. It gave King his election issue, allowing him to divert attention from the customs scandal. Lord Byng's term was nearly up, and the commander of the Canadian forces at the battle of Vimy Ridge returned to England under a cloud.

The myth grew that Mackenzie King, with machiavellian cleverness, had planned the entire episode to save his own political skin. King's reactive behaviour belies such forethought. According to Bruce Hutchison, many people at the time supposed that Lapointe had guided King through the constitutional crisis.[21] In any event, Lapointe's prestige had never been higher. A few days after the dissolution a group of Liberals decided to set up a fund of $100,000 for him.[22]

Gifts from political parties to their leaders went back as far as Sir John A. Macdonald. Sir Clifford Sifton had nudged his fellow millionaires into buying Laurier an Ottawa mansion. And as well as giving King $40,000 to renovate Laurier House when he inherited it, Peter Larkin would raise some $250,000 for King before he was done. This was squirrelled away in a Boston bank. King did not care if people knew a fund had been set up for him by the party; he just did not want them to know how immense it was. Fielding had also received $125,000 from a grateful Liberal party.

Lapointe was not a rich man. He had given up his law practice, and if the Liberals lost the 1926 election (as many expected because of the customs scandal) he would have a hard time getting by on an MP's salary. Even the Tory organ *L'Evénement* approved of the Lapointe fund, declaring, 'We have often expressed the opinion that he would have been a more acceptable leader than Mr. King.'[23] But Lapointe did not actually receive any money until 1929. The protracted money-raising indicates that Lapointe had no 'fairy godfather' – as King called Larkin in his diary.[24]

CHAPTER TEN

The *Margaret* Affair

The week following the dissolution of Parliament on 4 July 1926 was exhausting for Lapointe, who was in poor health. There were long meetings in King's office, telephone discussions, a working dinner at Laurier House. King was building an election issue out of the governor general's refusal to grant him a dissolution while giving one to Meighen, and Lapointe had to draft statements to the press involving elaborate constitutional and legal arguments. Eventually King noticed how tired Lapointe was. 'The truth is,' he wrote in his diary, 'that like the rest of us he is done out after the strain of the year.'[1] Much as he hated to desert King at this time, Lapointe decided he must have a short vacation before starting to campaign for the election Meighen had announced for 14 September. He took a ten-day lakeside holiday in upper New York State.[2]

Whatever good his holiday did for him was quickly undone. He returned to face the most shocking charges: Ernest Lapointe, the respectable family man, was publicly accused of participating in an orgy of wine, women, and song. His accuser was A.J. Doucet, a Conservative MP who had served on the Stevens customs inquiry. On 24 July, with Meighen on the same platform, Doucet told a large audience in Saint John, New Brunswick, that Ernest Lapointe and Jacques Bureau had treated themselves to a scandalous cruise aboard the coast guard steamer *Margaret*. He alleged that in the summer of 1923, while minister of customs, Bureau had diverted the vessel from patrolling the Atlantic coast in search of rum-runners, and used it for a six-week pleasure cruise on the St Lawrence and the Saguenay River. With Bureau and his friends aboard, he said, the *Margaret* picked up hundreds of cases of confiscated whisky and beer from the customs house in Montreal, a jazz band at Trois-Rivières, and loose women at Quebec City. According to Doucet, the ship's log showed that Lapointe and his party had boarded at Quebec City. What went on on that cruise was 'such filth,' Doucet told his gaping audience, that it was not fit to print in the parliamentary report – 'It could not be uttered even before an audience of men!'[3] The *Margaret* affair was spread across the nation's newspapers.

Shocked and hurt, Lapointe fired off a telegram to Meighen denying Doucet's story: 'As it relates to me it is utterly untrue. I have never travelled on the Margaret. You and I have been colleagues in Parliament for twenty years. In all our controversies I believe I have always fought fairly and honorably. I ask you to repudiate a statement which constitutes an unequivocal calumny, uttered in your presence.'[4] Meighen must have chided Doucet because in his next speech 'the lusty little Acadian campaigner,' as *Saturday Night* dubbed him, made a retraction of sorts. He had assumed, he said, that since the logbook showed they picked up 'Mr. Lapointe and party' at Quebec, 'it was a case of Mr. Bureau wanting to give a good time to his colleague.' With tongue in cheek, he said he was ready to concede that it might not have been the Mr Lapointe who was the former minister of justice.[5] The retraction was as bad as the original accusation.

Chubby Power jumped in to defend his friends. At a Quebec election rally, he declared that there had been no Liberal binge as described by the Tory Doucet; Bureau had simply taken his wife and his daughter's family on the *Margaret's* regular patrol duty. Power made light of the whole affair, using his own reputation as a hard drinker to raise a laugh: 'I can assure you that if it was that kind of a party, in prospect or in deed, my good friend, the Honorable Jacques Bureau would not have invited Ernest Lapointe to take part in it. I would have been his special guest.'[6]

Though the newspapers played up the so-called joy sail for all it was worth, by and large Doucet's charges were dismissed as mud-slinging. Lapointe was one of the few Quebec political figures well thought of in English Canada. Unlike Bureau, Cardin, and Boivin, he had come through the customs scandal virtually unscathed. In French Canada, the customs inquiry was regarded as nothing more than an attempt to besmirch Quebec. Campaigning in and around Quebec City, Chubby Power found that people were totally in support of Lapointe and even sympathetic to Bureau. On 30 July Chubby wrote Jacques: 'In this District, at any rate, the Customs Inquiry is proving a boomerang for the Tories, and it will pay us to talk about it as much as possible. Ernest has become a national "martyr" and incidentally a hero, and you too, if the cards are played right, may join the ranks of the Saints and Angels together with the Powers and the Cherubims.'[7]

The day before Doucet's sensational charges, King had launched the Liberal campaign in Ottawa's hockey auditorium with Lapointe by his side. Piped into the arena by a kilted band, King and Lapointe were pleased to see every seat filled as if it were hockey night. About a thousand people from Hull on the Quebec side of the Ottawa River had come over to hear their compatriot. The building was stifling hot and airless, yet speaking first in French and then in English Lapointe put the audience in a good mood for one of King's interminable addresses. For two hours and ten minutes King delivered a legalistic speech that was far above the heads of his sweating listeners. Quoting and citing, he made the case that the governor general's action threatened Canada's right to self-government. He hastened to add that it was Meighen's fault for giving the governor general bad advice, thus deflecting the blame on to his political opponent. King's speech served notice that the Liberal campaign would be fought on Byng's questionable actions. Boring as it may have been for that audience, the address put the scandal-racked Liberals on the offensive and provided a manual for Liberal candidates faced with unfriendly questions. Thousands of voters across the country heard King's and Lapointe's speeches. From a studio on the top floor of the Chateau Laurier the CNR's two-year-old radio station broadcast them nationwide.

His leader's confidence in him did not waver, but Lapointe could not rest until his name was cleared. The 'usually complacent Ernest Lapointe,' wrote an unfriendly columnist in *Saturday Night*, 'has been keeping the wires hot with demands on Mr Meighen for a repudiation of Mr Doucet's suggestion that the former Minister was associated with the famous cruise of the revenue cutter *Margaret*.' The columnist turned the screw. 'Perhaps' Mr Doucet had done an injustice to Mr Lapointe, but the latter's determination to disassociate himself from the incident indicated that 'it was no Sunday School excursion.'[8]

Lapointe had to put an end to such innuendo and to the rumours in circulation: there was even a story going the rounds that he was in trouble with his wife. At a Liberal gathering in Quebec he lashed out at Meighen, calling him 'a coward' for not repudiating Doucet's 'infamous story.' Before this friendly audience, Lapointe expressed his burning anger in strong language: 'Despicable individuals have repeated this vile calumny with the same pleasure ill-breeding insects take in spreading a plague. But I am free to walk bolt upright and to look anyone and all straight in the eye. The only wealth I have to leave my children is a name I hold honorable and a reputation I feel is worthy.'[9]

Since Prime Minister Meighen would not repudiate Doucet, Lapointe dispatched another wire to him, demanding an inquiry into Doucet's charges. Meighen could have left the two former Liberal ministers mired in the *Margaret* affair throughout the election campaign. Instead, in an unusual example of fair play in the heat of an election, he ordered an immediate investigation. The Tory government referred the charges against Bureau and Lapointe to a one-man royal commission set up 'to continue and complete' the parliamentary customs inquiry. The sole commissioner was the chief justice of Quebec, Sir François Lemieux, Lapointe's 'old boss' and well-wisher.[10] Indeed, Lapointe had named him to head the royal commission before the Liberals went out of power. He could not have found a better-disposed judge. The government counsel was R.L. Calder, a bilingual Montreal lawyer who had served as counsel for the Stevens inquiry. The commission's counsel was W.F. O'Connor, whom Borden had appointed to investigate wartime profiteering. The two lawyers were strong Conservatives. Bureau was represented by the eminent Quebec lawyer N.K. LaFlamme. Lapointe had chosen Lucien Cannon – a loyal friend as well as a brilliant litigator. The hearing began on 5 August in Quebec City. There was no press, Mr Justice Lemieux having ruled that the hearing would be conducted in camera.

Seated beside Bureau, Lapointe could not help but reflect sadly on what the years had done to the jolly, playful Jacques of their Chateau Laurier days. Dropping in on Bureau a few weeks earlier, Mackenzie King had found him 'anxious and worn.' Bureau had confided to King that he had just taken a sister to the asylum; she had been driven out of her mind by his disgrace.[11] Lapointe was aware that his friend's heart condition had reached a serious stage. Living on nitroglycerine pills, Bureau no doubt swallowed one whenever he glanced at Calder. He had told King that it was because of Calder's personal dislike that he had avoided testifying before the Stevens inquiry.

Both families were present in the hearing room; Madame Lapointe with her teenage son and daughter, and Madame Bureau flanked by her daughter and son-in-law. With what emotion they would have heard the 'grave accusation' that 'the Honourable Ernest Lapointe and the Honourable Jacques Bureau, while ministers in 1923, had made an excursion or cruise, that was discreditable, immoral, and contrary to the dignity of public men, aboard the steamer Margaret, a coast guard vessel of the Department of Customs.'

They need not have worried. In his opening statement, Calder, the government lawyer, announced that there was not an atom of proof to support the Doucet accusation. Switching to English, he was even more emphatic: 'I wish to declare categorically, publicly, that Mr. O'Connor, Mr. Duncan and myself have examined every bit of relevant evidence; the files, the crew, etc., and we wish to declare publicly, and to that extent make a measure of reparation, that there is not any evidence supporting the statements made.' At this, Chief Justice Lemieux declared the incident closed but for some reason thought it 'more prudent' to examine several witnesses.

Lapointe was the first witness. He testified that he had never taken a cruise on the *Margaret* as alleged, and had only once stepped foot on the vessel. That was in the summer of 1923 when he was on his way back from Pictou, Nova Scotia, after representing the federal government at an official celebration. He had stopped at Charlottetown where the *Margaret* was docked, and had gone aboard to visit Monsieur and Madame Bureau who were travelling with their daughter and her two children. He had stayed just long enough to take a cup of tea.

Bureau then took the stand. In his capacity as minister of customs, he said, he had made several inspection trips on the *Margaret*. In the summer of 1923 he was accompanied by his family, his law partner, his doctor, and a cousin or two. He dismissed as ridiculous the allegation that he had commandeered 3,600 bottles of beer and 20 cases of wine from the customs house in Montreal; there was only enough brandy and spirits for his guests and himself. He vigorously denied that 'a hostess of a certain establishment in Montreal' had been among his guests. He produced photographs of his wife, his daughter, and his grandchildren with Captain Legouvée of the *Margaret*.

Captain Legouvée corroborated Lapointe's and Bureau's testimony, stating that there had been no expedition with wine and women. The next witness was Walter Duncan, a former detective inspector from Toronto whom George Boivin had hired soon after becoming minister of customs. Known as 'a fearless and incorruptible investigator, a bloodhound on the trail of crime,' Duncan had written the report that supplied most of the evidence for the Stevens inquiry. An impressive witness, he testified that he had gone into Doucet's allegations thoroughly and had found 'absolutely nothing' to support them.

Doucet was not present, and the key piece of evidence, on which he 'rested his case' – the *Margaret*'s logbook – was missing at the hearing. Calder told the judge that through a misunderstanding it had been left in Ottawa. The hearing was adjourned for two days to give him time to produce the ship's log.[12] When the hearing reconvened on 7 August, the logbook was there and so were Doucet and his lawyers. Doucet asked for an adjournment to allow his lawyers to examine the log and call witnesses, but the judge refused his request. The inquiry before Lemieux was limited to whether Lapointe and Bureau had made 'yes or no, an immoral excursion on the Margaret in 1923.' Judge Lemieux decided that the answer was 'no.' He refused to consider whether the *Margaret* had been illegally diverted from its regular work as a coast guard ship. This, he said, would be decided at a future hearing.

Lapointe and Bureau were cleared. Even the sceptical *Saturday Night* was 'glad to see Hon. Ernest Lapointe, a man for whom it has a high respect, exonerated.' Nevertheless, it left no doubt that in its opinion the hearing was a cover-up: 'For some reason best known to those in charge the evidence was taken in camera in Quebec, and the lawyers employed by the Government undertook to satisfy public curiosity by proclaiming that nothing had occurred in connection with the Margaret that reflected on anybody's character. Their statement conveyed the impression that Mr Bureau's trip was nothing more than a family affair and that he and his guests merely combined public services with pleasure, the cruise being ostensibly for the purpose of departmental inspection.'[13]

There is no doubt that Doucet was not given the opportunity to prove his charges. On the first day of hearing, without the crucial logbook, without cross-examination of witnesses, indeed with neither Doucet nor his lawyers present, Mr Justice Lemieux declared the charges baseless. His decision was immediately made public and blazoned across the newspapers. Understandably, Doucet's lawyer, the Honourable L.G. Belley, KC, issued a statement claiming that the probe was incomplete. He also posed the question, 'Why were there so many lawyers, all on the same side?'[14]

Why did the Tory government's lawyers, Calder and O'Connor, stifle a proper inquiry? The truth was that Bureau had done no more than his Tory counterparts. Coast guard steamers were widely used by the government in power for entertaining and electioneering. These ships all had comfortable guest quarters and a dining room well appointed with fine china and silverware. In 1923 Lapointe took the *Lady Grey* to

Pictou, Nova Scotia, to entertain the VIPs attending the highlanders' centenary. He also used it for party business. During the 1925 election campaign, while touring the province with the chief party organizer, Philippe Paradis, Ernest wired Mimy: 'Will probably go to Chicoutimi Saturday with Paradis on the Druid. Would you and children come. I believe Mme. Paradis would come. Will telephone from Quebec.'[15] Indeed, a summer cruise for the families of cabinet ministers was, as Charlie Bowman of the *Ottawa Citizen* put it, 'a perquisite of public office like a private car.'

Though Bureau used the *Margaret* for a summer cruise, it was not the infamous 'joy sail' described so luridly by Doucet. In a letter to Chubby Power just before the Lemieux inquiry, Bureau swore that 'every word uttered by Doucet as to misconduct on the "Margaret" is false ... There never was a finer set of people on board than those that accompanied me and every man of the crew will so state. I never got the "Margaret" out of her course one mile.'[16] Jacques Bureau had no reason to lie to the unshockable Chubby Power. Moreover, Lapointe's testimony that he visited the Bureaus on board at Charlottetown in mid-July places the *Margaret* just where it should have been for patrolling the Northumberland Straits in search of rum-runners. Still, calling this an inspection trip merits the satirical response it evoked from Doucet's lawyer. In his press statement Belley inquired rhetorically: 'Was it necessary for Mr. Bureau in 1923, to inspect the foreign ports: Rivière-du-Loup, Rimouski, Gaspé, Port Daniel, Dalhousie and Charlottetown? And in order that the inspection might be effective, he had at his side his wife, his daughter, his son-in-law, his two young sons and two of his cousins.'[17]

There was an ironic postscript to the *Margaret* affair that would have given Lapointe and Bureau some satisfaction. In late August the *Toronto Star* revealed that at the very time Doucet was making his charges, Meighen was using the *Margaret* to take him from place to place in his Maritimes campaign. He even made speeches from its deck. Lapointe received the clipping from a friend who scrawled on it, 'You might call it immanent justice or the vengeance of the Margaret.'[18] Lapointe emerged from the *Margaret* affair with his reputation intact. The Liberal press castigated Meighen, as in this *Ottawa Citizen* editorial by Charles Bowman: 'Mr. Meighen knew Mr. Lapointe. He knew that Mr. Lapointe is an honorable man, the devoted husband of a talented woman. Mr. Meighen knew without any evidence that the story so far as Mr. Lapointe was concerned was untrue. Notwithstanding, Mr. Meighen, prime minister of Canada, uttered no protest. Night after night he sat on the platform and heard his follower slander away the reputation and destroy the happiness of an honorable gentleman ... Mr. Meighen can never make reparation to Mr. Lapointe for the injury done to him.'[19]

On 7 August 1926, the very day that the *Margaret* inquiry cleared Lapointe and Bureau, George Boivin, the former minister of customs, died in a Philadelphia hospital, reportedly of a ruptured appendix. The death of this still-young Liberal politician aroused widespread sympathy. The Liberal press intimated that he had been hounded to death by H.H. Stevens over the Moses Aziz affair. It was true that in June, with a vote of censure hanging over his head, Boivin had sounded despondent, telling the House that the cares of office had forced him 'to renounce my private affairs and abandon my family life.'[20] The Tory campaign was based almost exclusively on the customs scandal, and Boivin had been a special target. His tragic death took the wind out of the Tory sails. In his diary King somewhat shamefacedly repeated the cynical remark of an English visitor – 'Through death to life for the Liberal party.'[21]

In that same diary entry King expressed concern about Lapointe's health. In spite of continual discomfort Lapointe fought a vigorous campaign. One week found him speaking in Ontario, the next in northern New Brunswick. But for the most part he was in Quebec City working to recoup the votes he had lost in 1925. As Chubby Power had predicted, the false charges against Lapointe made a martyr and a hero of him and greatly enhanced his popularity. On the hustings, Lapointe did not hesitate to angle for a sympathy vote with his references to 'certain calumnies directed against my reputation by unworthy opponents.'

In parish halls and hockey rinks Lapointe presented King's constitutional issue. It was going over very well with Quebeckers. According to Chubby Power, they were proud of the fact that 'a leader of a political party had not only talked back to a representative of the imperial government but had defied him and was actually campaigning against the power and strength of the imperial government.'[22] Lapointe put the King-Byng question in terms that the average voter could understand. Was it just, he asked the voters of Limoilou, for the governor general to refuse dissolution to a prime minister of five years and grant one to a prime minister of three days? British preference was also less of an election issue than in 1925 due to the recovery of Quebec's boot and shoe industry. 'You will recall,' Lapointe told a working-class audience, 'that they fought me on the shoe question last year, saying that the preferential tariff would ruin our shoe industry. They don't speak of it this year because the tariff has done no harm and foreign-made shoes are no longer coming in.'[23]

Hoping to harness Sir Lomer Gouin's great prestige in the province, Lapointe solicited his help in the campaign. At the beginning of September he invited Gouin to join him on the platform at a women's meeting in Quebec City. Sir Lomer declined gracefully. 'I am very touched by the compliment of your invitation,' he wrote Lapointe, 'but I have just made a long trip to Percé and I have to listen to my doctors and cannot have the pleasure of addressing crowds.'[24] His trip to the Gaspé to campaign for their mutual friend Rodolphe Lemieux was all he could do in the present campaign. Cardin got no further with Gouin when he asked him to address a rally on the constitutional question. Nevertheless, Gouin was still a staunch Liberal. In July he had turned down Meighen's offer of a choice of portfolios if he would run as a Conservative with the terse remark that he believed in parties and intended to stay in his.[25] He had not cooperated in the Liberal campaign because he was angry that a promised Senate appointment had not come through. He blamed Lapointe and Cardin for this.

Gouin had agreed to run in the 1921 election because he had been promised that the House of Commons would be a way station en route to the Senate. In 1924, when he retired as minister of justice, it was a foregone conclusion that he would be appointed to the upper chamber. However, his only appointment came from Premier Taschereau – the chairmanship of a provincial committee. Again in May 1926, with King still in office, his old friend Senator Dandurand assured Gouin that he would get a Senate seat. Hearing nothing after some weeks, Gouin asked Dandurand why he had not been appointed. Dandurand explained that Lapointe and Cardin wanted to wait until after the session. Gouin did not credit this explanation because in the meantime another Montrealer, Dr W.L. McDougald, had been nominated for the Senate. At the next Bank of Montreal board meeting, Dandurand gently scolded his old friend for not helping in the election. Gouin did not beat around the bush: 'Why should I since I haven't got the Senate seat.'[26]

The Liberals sailed to victory in Quebec without Gouin's help. Lapointe was pleased to garner a hundred more votes than the year before. Above all, he could rejoice that the Liberal party was back in power. In a letter congratulating Lapointe, the astute Kirk Cameron commented that 'Doucet and Nicholson [another Tory mud-slinger] must have been worth tens of thousands of votes for the Liberal party.

We ought to be grateful to them.' On the other hand, Mr Justice H.G. Carroll expressed surprise at the happy outcome for Lapointe: 'Frankly, I believed the business of the customs was going to kill you.'[27]

Meighen lost his seat along with five of his acting ministers, four of whom were French. Doucet was also defeated. To the end of the campaign Meighen had believed that an unsophisticated electorate would be horrified over the customs scandal, and he had scoffed at King's esoteric constitutional issue. The election result seemed to Meighen to fly in the face of logic. But in Kirk Cameron's opinion, Meighen's blunders were the main reason why he lost. 'As a political Blunderer,' Cameron told Charles Dunning, 'Meighen is the most outstanding success of our time.' It was true that Meighen displayed a peculiar incapacity for judging public sentiment. He had even made the 'fatal error,' King told his diary, of attacking poor Boivin lying in his grave.[28]

Once again Lapointe was the first person summoned to Laurier House. When King asked him what portfolio he wanted, he said he would like to continue as minister of justice. Yet King had the feeling that for reasons of health Lapointe would not want to stay long in the ministry, and that what he really wanted was to retire to the Supreme Court. King suspected that Lapointe had even 'given Cannon to understand that if he measured up' he could succeed him as justice minister. Was King disturbed at the thought of losing his loyal Quebec lieutenant who, as interim leader, had kept the government afloat while he himself fretted in the corridors, and who once again had delivered Quebec? Assuming he was honest in his diary, King was not the least upset. 'This to my mind is all right,' he wrote. 'Cannon comes from a line of distinguished jurists and I think might be a very effective Minister of Justice.'[29]

However, Lapointe said nothing about resigning, and the two men proceeded to discuss the new cabinet. In place of the reluctant Crerar, they decided to bring in Robert Forke, his successor as leader of the now shattered Progressive party. King had already convinced J.L. Ralston to enter the cabinet as minister of national defence by appealing to his concern for the war veterans. King's and Lapointe's primary concern was to find a top-notch person for the customs department. While insisting that Quebec maintain the same number of ministers it had had in the last cabinet, Lapointe agreed with King that Customs should go to Ontario. Removing the Customs portfolio from Quebec was, in fact, the consensus of all Lapointe's correspondents. Speaking from experience as a former Quebec politician, Judge Carroll was blunt: 'Don't you think in the party's interest the next Customs Minister should be from another province? He would escape the pressure that the Quebec bloc exerts on a Quebec minister.'[30]

Kirk Cameron asked Lapointe to use his influence with King to have Customs filled by a first-class businessman. 'Nothing the new government can do will be more appreciated by business.' He suggested the Ontario MP William Euler. At the same time, Cameron strongly urged taking S.W. Jacobs into cabinet as a minister without portfolio. The only Jewish member of the House, Jacobs had represented a Montreal riding for years; he was a willing party worker and excelled in debate. Cameron (questionably) estimated that there were twenty or more constituencies where the Jewish vote 'pretty well' determined the result. The quarter of a million Jews in Canada, Cameron said, ought to be given some recognition. Lapointe replied that he had been pleased to pass on Cameron's suggestion regarding Euler to 'the Chief.' He had been thinking of Euler himself, he said.[31] He made no mention of Cameron's other suggestion about S.W. Jacobs.

King would have liked to appoint Newton Rowell to the Customs post. A figure of uncompromising rectitude, Rowell would lend substance to King's promise to clean up the department. Since leaving politics, Rowell, an outstanding constitutional lawyer, had written several opinion papers for the King administration. One, entirely to King's satisfaction, was on the unconstitutionality of Lord Byng's actions. Unfortunately, Rowell was still as disliked in Quebec as he had been in 1919 when the French MPs threatened to leave the chamber if he were permitted to pay a tribute to Laurier. Not only had he deserted Laurier over conscription, but he was regarded as anti-Catholic and, almost as bad, he was a Prohibitionist. Despite Quebec opinion, Lapointe 'heartily approved' of bringing Rowell into the government but not necessarily as minister of customs. When Cardin heard that Rowell was being considered for Customs, he raised the objection that he would be too 'zealous.' With some asperity King replied that in collecting revenue there was no occasion for leniency. 'It is apparent that the French-Canadian point of view on the Customs matter is different to that in the other Provinces,' he wrote in his diary. 'Clearly it was a mistake ever to let Customs go to Quebec, and it should never be done again.'[32]

William Euler of Kitchener, Ontario, was made minister of customs and excise. Publisher of Kitchener's daily paper, a director of several insurance companies, and a past president of the local Board of Trade, Euler had the requisite business mentality. A few months into his ministry, he was asking Kirk Cameron to get him in on the ground floor of a mining company stock flotation.[33] As compensation for the Customs portfolio, Newton Rowell was offered the position of counsel to the royal commission investigating the customs department. King gladly accepted Rowell's conditions that there be no political interference and that the commission be enlarged by the appointment of two high court judges. Obviously viewing the judicial reinforcement as a reflection on his impartiality, Sir François Lemieux stepped off the commission and was replaced by another Quebec judge.[34]

Lapointe did not advise bringing Chubby Power into the cabinet. It may have been because of Power's drinking (though Lucien Cannon was just as poor a risk in that respect). More likely, with Cannon and himself in cabinet there was no room for a third minister from the district of Quebec. That was what he told the Quebec Reform Club, which was lobbying hard for the popular Power. 'You know the links of friendship that unite me to Mr. Power,' he wrote the club secretary, 'but you also know it is impossible to have more than two ministers from Quebec [district].'[35]

Senate appointments posed as many difficulties as picking a cabinet. There were said to be sixty-five candidates beating on the doors of the red chamber. One seat was reserved for Donat Raymond, a wealthy and generous party bagman. In spite of Senator Dandurand's supplications, Sir Lomer Gouin did not get the other Quebec vacancy. Evidently Lapointe and Cardin had reported Gouin's lack of cooperation, for King asked Dandurand, 'What did Sir Lomer do for us during this campaign?' Dandurand cited his long service to the Liberal cause and mentioned how humiliated Sir Lomer had been when Bureau was appointed to the Senate ahead of him. Lapointe said little during the discussion, but Cardin 'was strong' that Sir Lomer's appointment would be unpopular in Quebec. In view of their eagerness to have Gouin campaign, this was unlikely but was enough to persuade King.[36]

For months Dandurand could not bring himself to tell Gouin the bad news. He and Rodolphe Lemieux continued to keep up Gouin's hopes for several months. But dining with Sir Lomer and Lady Gouin at their Peel Street mansion early in December, Dandurand forewarned his host that there were a lot of candidates for the Senate, including Donat Raymond to whom the party was very indebted. Shortly afterwards, at a bank board meeting, Dandurand broke the news that Raymond was to be appointed to the Senate the next day. Why was *he* not appointed,

Gouin wanted to know. Dandurand had to tell him that the French-Canadian ministers were against his appointment.[37]

Meanwhile, Lapointe was inundated with requests (more accurately, demands) to fill a Senate vacancy with a Franco-Ontarian. The vacancy had been created by the death of an Irish Catholic senator from Ontario. This still left four Irish Catholics, and Senator Napoleon Belcourt, the only French senator from Ontario, urged Lapointe to get the nomination for Samuel Genest, the feisty chairman of the Ottawa Separate School Board who, with Belcourt, fought unceasingly for the abolition of Regulation 17. The Catholic hierarchy, from Cardinal Begin down, wrote Lapointe recommending Genest. Despite all this, William McGuire, an Irish Catholic lawyer from Toronto and a founder of the Men's Liberal Association in that city, was appointed. Angry letters poured in from disappointed Franco-Ontarians and Quebeckers. Senator Dandurand, who had supported Genest, informed Lapointe that the government's action was being strongly criticized in Quebec. He reminded Lapointe that he had told him how important it was to name a second French senator for 'Upper Canada.' At the same time, he said, he had to admire Lapointe's ability to stay cool: in this he was like Laurier 'who always surprised me by his inalterable calm.'[38] 'I'm not indifferent to the criticism that the nomination of the Ontario senator has occasioned,' Lapointe replied. But he reminded Dandurand that Genest had been campaigning against King for months. How could King put Genest 'on a pedestal'? Lapointe's loyalty to his leader was paramount.

Lapointe had had some wins and some losses in this latest round of appointments. Genest may not have received a senatorship, but then neither had Gouin. Customs had gone to Ontario with his blessing. Lapointe and Cardin had been able to maintain the French quota in cabinet with Fernand Rinfret as secretary of state, P.J. Veniot, the former New Brunswick premier, as postmaster general, and Lucien Cannon as solicitor general. Happily for King and Lapointe, the Imperial Conference of 1926 provided some respite from cabinet-making and filling Senate vacancies.

CHAPTER ELEVEN

The Imperial Conference of 1926

On 9 October 1926 the White Star liner *Megantic* left Quebec City for Liverpool. It made smooth passage down the St Lawrence, and the passengers, lounging in deck chairs, watched the glorious autumn colour unroll along the shores. When the ship reached the open sea, however, rough water caused most passengers to retire to their staterooms.

The Canadians on shipboard bound for the Imperial Conference in London formed an exclusive coterie. There was the small, rotund prime minister and his benefactor Peter Larkin, the Canadian high commissioner in London, who during his home leave had cajoled Bank of Montreal directors into contributing $25,000 to the Laurier House fund.[1] There was Vincent Massey (another generous Liberal) who was going over to have his appointment as the first Canadian minister to Washington ratified by the British government. The chief of staff, the very pukka General MacBrien, lent a military note to the delegation. Also aboard were a number of civil servants, notably Dr O.D. Skelton, the under-secretary of state for external affairs, and Skelton's newest recruit to his fledgling department, Jean Désy. Next to King, the leading delegate was Lapointe (indeed, Skelton referred to both of them as 'my chiefs'). As usual Mimy accompanied Ernest, and this time they had brought Odette: she was now sixteen and her mother was taking her to Paris to enrol her in an elite finishing school. Also travelling in Lapointe's party was his new private secretary, Philippe Picard, a young lawyer from an upper-class Quebec family. Once over his seasickness, Lapointe, in tweeds and a cloth cap, took his daily constitutional around the deck chatting with Picard and Désy.

The *Megantic* group was joined in London by the rest of the delegation, which had sailed on the *Baltic*. Their British hosts treated them royally. The Canadian delegation was installed at the Ritz, and King and Lapointe were each assigned a chauffeured limousine. After showing off the impressive new Canadian High Commission, Larkin took King and Lapointe to pay courtesy calls at the various palaces and Number 10 Downing Street. The talk everywhere was of the General Strike that spring and of the continuing coal miners' strike.[2]

Henri Bourassa was also staying at the Ritz. Returning to the hotel after the Empire Press Union banquet at the Savoy, Lapointe and King had a satisfying discussion with him. Bourassa was no longer the fearsome Quebec nationalist of the war years. In fact he was out of sympathy with the French-Canadian nationalists of the twenties who, influenced by the teachings of the historian Abbé Groulx, were talking of a separate Quebec state.[3] As strong a Canadian nationalist as ever, Bourassa applauded each step towards autonomy that King and Lapointe were taking. He suggested that they join forces with the other pro-autonomy delegations, the South Africans and the Irish. On one thing only was there disagreement during their talk at the Ritz. Bourassa, an ardent Roman Catholic, wanted to have a Canadian representative at the Vatican – something King would not even contemplate.[4]

Like the previous conferences in 1921 and 1923, the Imperial Conference of 1926 had to grapple with the problem of the post-war status of the self-governing Dominions: Canada, Australia, New Zealand, South Africa, and the Irish Free State. The 1923 conference had revealed a breach among the Dominions. Australia and New Zealand, still looking to the British navy to defend them, were loath to loosen the ties of empire and were content to have Britain speak for them. King, who wanted no more marching orders after Chanak, had strongly opposed a common imperial foreign policy and had locked horns more than once with the Australian prime minister, Stanley Bruce. Throughout the conference, King had refused to commit himself to anything that smacked of centralized diplomacy, insisting that Canada must have 'a foreign policy on our own.'[5] To his surprise the British gracefully accepted the precedent of the Halibut Treaty and drafted a resolution allowing the Dominions to make bilateral treaties with foreign countries without a British co-signer. Significantly, Australia and New Zealand had dissociated themselves from King's innovation, prompting the customarily tactful prime minister to ask the New Zealand prime minister if New Zealand was 'a crown colony or a self-governing Dominion.'[6]

Satisfied that he had won the battle for Canadian autonomy at the 1923 conference, King was not anxious to rock the constitutional boat in 1926. On his arrival in London, he was told unofficially by the under-secretary of the Dominions Office (the old Colonial Office was renamed in 1925) that Britain would accede to virtually any demand for autonomy so long as the Dominions remained in the empire. The only outstanding issue, as far as King was concerned, was to change the status of the governor general.[7]

Lapointe was less sanguine than King that Britain had given up the fight to speak for all the Dominions under the umbrella of the 'British Empire.' Even before the Great War Lapointe had supported the concept of a commonwealth of sovereign nations that would make up their own minds if and when to go to war. His proposal to amend Article X in 1922 had been made with that objective in mind. In 1923 he had deflected the British attempt to have Canada sign the Treaty of Mutual Guarantee that would have obligated Canada to defend western European borders. Now the same thing had cropped up in the guise of the Locarno Treaty, a diplomatic initiative promoted by Britain to guarantee the Belgian and French frontiers with Germany. Though the Dominions were not bound by the treaty unless they chose to be, Lapointe feared that Britain would exert less than subtle pressure on Canada to sign on. In a dispatch dated 8 January 1926, Canada had already notified the Dominions Office that it was not prepared to sign the Locarno Treaty, but in his typical conciliatory fashion King left it open to discuss the matter at the conference.[8]

Meanwhile, Dr Skelton was determined to keep his 'chiefs' from making any compromises at the conference.[9] O.D. Skelton was a Canadian nationalist to the core. Formerly dean of arts at Queen's University and the author of a biography of Laurier, Skelton had been plucked from academia by King after the latter had heard him deliver a strongly anti-imperialist lecture.[10] He had acted as King's special adviser at the 1923 conference and on their return accepted appointment as undersecretary of state for external affairs. Skelton was the prototype of the faceless bureaucrat. Unimpressive in appearance and distant in manner, he studiously faded into the background leaving the stage to his political masters, King and Lapointe.[11] But behind the scenes he spurred them on to demand greater independence from Great Britain. In his view, the British Empire meant no more than Britain and its remaining colonies. Understandably, the British ministers and officials, remembering him from 1923, regarded Skelton 'with intense suspicion.'[12] His intention in 1926, as in 1923, was to 'stiffen Mackenzie King's back-bone.'[13] He was less concerned with Lapointe backsliding in view of anti-imperialist sentiment in Quebec.

The first thing Skelton did was to arrange for the Irish delegates, Fitzgerald and Costello, to meet with King and Lapointe. The Irish Free State, created in 1921, had decidedly republican tendencies, but its leaders, still shaky from the civil war, were not ready to declare independence from Great Britain. In the meantime, the Irish delegates planned to press for removal of 'anomalies' such as British control over merchant shipping, appeals to the Privy Council, and the role of the governor general as an agent of the British government. This pragmatic approach appealed much more to King and Lapointe than the incipiently pro-independence position of South Africa.[14] This was General Jacob Hertzog's first Imperial Conference. An ultra-nationalist Afrikaner, in 1924 he had been elected prime minister in place of the more moderate General Smuts. He had already served notice on the colonial secretary, Leo Amery, that he would demand a public statement from the conference informing the world of the Dominions' independent status within the empire – otherwise South Africa would declare its independence.[15] Australia and New Zealand were happy with the status quo, and there would be no support for autonomy from them: Skelton thought Stanley Bruce 'as much an imperialist and tom-tom beater as ever.'[16]

On 19 October the conference opened with a solemn ceremony at Westminster Abbey where the Prince of Wales unveiled a memorial to the empire's One Million Dead. The delegates then strolled over to Downing Street. For Ernest Lapointe, the son of a poor Quebec farmer, participating in these councils would have been an occasion for self-congratulation. Seated beside Mackenzie King, he looked across the table at such pillars of empire as Prime Minister Baldwin, Lord Balfour, Sir Austen Chamberlain, and Winston Churchill. On the Canadians' side of the table were the delegates of the other Dominions. An Indian maharaja presided over one end of the table while the famous lawyer-politician, Lord Birkenhead, then secretary of state for India, presided over the other.[17]

At meetings at the Foreign Office, King and Lapointe worked out the specifics for a new Dominion status. After his tug of war with Byng, King's main concern was to win endorsement for his view of the governor general's role as a viceroy representing the Crown only and having no relationship to the British government of the day. Skelton and Lapointe 'both cordially approved the idea,' and King put it forward 'as coming from Canada.'[18] Just as King George acted on the advice of his ministers, so should the governor general act on the advice of the Canadian ministers. If Sir Austen Chamberlain and Lord Balfour wished to have a representative in Canada, King suggested they appoint a high commissioner as Canada had done in England. The Canadian proposal found no favour with the New Zealand and Australian delegates, who warned against doing 'anything to diminish the dignity or the status of the Governor-General.'[19]

Hertzog's demand for a public statement on the independent status of the Dominions had alarmed the British, and under the chairmanship of Lord Balfour a committee of prime ministers was struck to deal with this sensitive issue. The in camera sessions opened with Hertzog's draft, which described the Dominions as independent nations. Predictably, Balfour finessed Hertzog by presenting a draft of his own, which purported to be merely a revision. However, although declaring the equal status of the Dominions, Balfour's draft introduced references to imperial unity. When Skelton saw the draft, he wrote his wife that Balfour 'tried to turn the declaration into a pledge of one Empire and one Crown interdependence, and pretty well carried W.L.M.K. with him. I wish Lapointe was on that committee.'[20] Though Lapointe stated publicly that the principle of equality had been generally accepted at the Prime Ministers' Committee,[21] he agreed with Skelton that Balfour's definition held dangerous implications for a unified imperial foreign policy.[22] 'We've had a dickens of a job,' Skelton wrote his wife on 4 November, 'to prevent that being adopted, so far with success, but without assurance there won't be a compromise eventually.'

Meanwhile, the prime minister was glorying in the social life laid on for him, and, in Skelton's opinion, did not give enough time to conference questions. 'The Irish and Mr Lapointe are our only sure-fire reliables,' Skelton wrote his wife.[23] The conference was not all work and no play for Lapointe either. At a state banquet at Buckingham Palace, Queen Mary honoured him with a few minutes of private conversation, which she graciously offered to conduct in French.[24] (On the several occasions when he met the dashing Prince of Wales, that professionally charming young royal invariably spoke to him in French.) There were unforgettable moments of pomp and ceremony, as when Lapointe and Charlie Bowman attended the naval review off Portland in the admiral's flagship, the HMS *Repulse*.[25] At other times Lapointe just enjoyed being in London. Mimy and Odette had gone to Paris, but Lapointe found a pleasant companion in young Jean Désy. Years later Désy recalled their times together in London during the conference of 1926, 'the sessions of the legal committee, our walks and our evenings at the theatre.' Ernest Lapointe became Jean Désy's role model. 'Each time I worked under your direction,' Désy would write Lapointe in 1939 when he received his first ambassadorial appointment, 'I appreciated the clarity of your conceptions, the breadth of your views, the sure rapidity of your judgment, your smiling cordiality ... Your teachings and example made their mark on my training.'[26]

Lapointe was playing a prominent part at the conference. It was quite a feather in Canada's cap when its minister of justice was appointed chairman of a subcommittee to consider the question of treaty procedure. Lapointe would later tell the House of Commons that it was 'a very important committee, indeed, and its work was a difficult one, but I am pleased to say that a solution was found which was acceptable to all members of the committee.'[27] The hard-won solution ultimately arrived at was to regularize the precedent he himself had set in signing the Halibut Treaty in Washington without the British ambassador. Actually, King had won this concession in 1923. It should have been simply a case of approving the draft resolution from the last conference, but it soon became evident at the meetings of the subcommittee that the British would not give up easily on a unified foreign policy. Sir Cecil Hurst, a constitutional lawyer at the Foreign Office, defended the use of a 'central panel' whereby Britain would sign for the empire. An alarmed Skelton shot back: 'The whole system of the central panel seems to me to be quite inconsistent with the idea of any equal status, either in the League or elsewhere.' Hertzog weighed in in his blunt fashion: 'The Central Panel must go.'[28]

Lapointe made it clear that Canada would exercise its right to act independently on foreign treaties. Midway through the conference, on 4 November, Lord Balfour asked Lapointe to state Canada's position on the Locarno Treaty. Following the general lines of the January 1926 dispatch to the Dominions Office, Lapointe told Lord Balfour that Locarno was strictly a European treaty and was of no direct concern to Canada. 'This view is consistent with our previous attitude on Article 10 of the Covenant ... of which Locarno has been called the posthumous child.' He added rather snidely that Canada's position was 'in apparent harmony' with Britain's refusal to guarantee the Polish corridor on Germany's eastern boundary because it was outside its area of concern. Reflecting the isolationism current in Canada, Lapointe stated that undertaking any fresh burdens for continental Europe's security would endanger national unity. Moreover, he said, 'Our neighbours to the south have not assumed even those which we already have in the League.'[29]

King chimed in. Because of the United States, the Canadian government was in a difficult position. Furthermore, he was afraid it would be impossible to induce the Canadian Parliament to adhere to the agreement. Although Canada would not sign and consequently was not bound by the Locarno Treaty, 'if the situation arose,' King stated, 'Canada would do her part.' Nor did Lapointe rule out military action: Canada was fully aware of 'our obligations as a member of the British Commonwealth and of the League of Nations,' he told the conference.[30] Australia and New Zealand were willing to sign the Locarno Treaty, but Sir Cecil Hurst opined that it should be all the Dominions or none. In the end only Britain signed the treaty.

Throughout the conference, the Canadians, the Irish, and the South Africans had steadfastly rejected imperial centralization. By the time it wound up, a common imperial policy was dead and buried. In reaching an acceptable definition of the empire/Commonwealth, King had played an important mediatory role by convincing Hertzog to give up the word 'independence' for 'equal in status.' The Balfour report, which was adopted by the conference, acknowledged Canada and the other Dominions to be 'autonomous communities within the British Empire, equal in status, and in no way subordinate to one another in any respect of their domestic or external affairs, though united by a common allegiance to the Crown and freely associated as members of the British Commonwealth of Nations.'

They had got much more than Lapointe ever expected. He saw the report as the basis for complete autonomy and a declaration that the old order had gone.[31] The nomenclature signalled the momentous change. In international affairs, Canada would no longer be an anonymous part of 'the British Empire' but would henceforth become 'His Majesty's Government in Canada.' It was now official that the Dominion governments could sign bilateral treaties. British legislation affecting the Dominions would only apply with the consent of the Dominion concerned: a legal committee was set up to work out the ways and means. King's harping on the issue of the governor general gained him what he wanted; his victory over Byng was complete. Byng's successors would take their instructions from the Dominion government rather than from the British cabinet and would inform the Crown directly. Sir Cecil Hurst had put up a last-ditch fight, citing instances when the British ministers would have to offer advice to the monarch regarding a Dominion – for example, in the appointment of a new governor general. Everyone wanted to go home, and a loophole was quickly inserted into the report.[32]

The umbilical chord with the mother country was not completely severed. Canada still was unable to amend its constitution – the British North America Act remained an Act of the British Parliament. And although any Dominion could now abolish appeals to the Judicial Committee of the Privy Council, Canada was not ready to do so. Lapointe himself was still undecided about abolishing appeals, although, as he told the House in his speech on the conference, he was 'leaning in that direction.' Some other powers were reserved to the British Parliament, but these were not invoked and would be removed by the Statute of Westminster in 1931.

When the editor of the *Ottawa Citizen*, Charles Bowman, read the Balfour report (Lapointe handed him one of the original copies) he hailed King and Lapointe as 'the structural architects' of the new Commonwealth. Skelton too appropriated much of the credit for the Canadians: the declaration was 'an epoch-making document, the most important pronouncement on the subject ever made,' and it was 'mainly thanks to the pertinacity of the Irish and ourselves.'[33] Skelton was pleased with his 'chiefs.' He told J.W. Dafoe after the conference that 'Mr. King and Mr. Lapointe stood firm, though occupying to some extent a middle ground.' While the Canadians were instrumental in formulating the new concept of Dominion autonomy, it was Hertzog and the Irish Free State delegates who were the cutting edge at the conference, mainly because of their underlying threat of independence.

Before leaving for Canada, Lapointe went to Paris to say goodbye to Mimy and Odette. The privileges he had enjoyed in London followed him across the Channel, the French ambassador in London writing ahead to make sure that Monsieur Lapointe did not run into any annoyance at customs. He continued in the lap of luxury to the end of the trip, travelling first-class to New York on the *Majestic*, the White Star's flagship: at 56,551 tons it was the largest ship afloat and was certainly one of the most luxurious with its Italian and English Renaissance decor, a choice of dining rooms, a 'swimming bath,' smoking rooms, and suites with two bathrooms.

Mackenzie King was on board, but it is uncertain that Lapointe saw much of him. King spent all his time with Senator McDougald, avoiding the Canadian delegation and taking his meals as McDougald's guest in an exclusive restaurant on a different deck from the dining saloon. A lobbyist and influence-peddler, McDougald assiduously cultivated King's friendship. He had not been a delegate to the conference; in retrospect, at the time of the Beauharnois scandal, Charlie Bowman (one of the passengers King was avoiding) suspected that McDougald had 'purposely booked on the same liner to pave the way for a hydro-electric power deal.'[34]

Lapointe returned home in poorish health but buoyed up by the results of the conference. He and King had helped change the face of empire. Skelton felt that Lapointe pushed harder for autonomy than King, but in fact Lapointe, no more than King, contemplated independence as the Irish and Hertzog did.[35] Vincent Massey, who as a delegate worked closely with Lapointe at the conference (and was to be his host at the Washington embassy numerous times in the late 1920s), has written that Lapointe 'represented Canadian statesmanship in the best sense – with a quiet and distinguished assertion of the principle of nationality, tempered by a deep sense of tradition and belief in the blessings of the British connection.' Indeed, Sir Lomer Gouin remarked sardonically in his diary that Lapointe had returned from London 'conquered by the English.'[36]

On 9 December King convened Parliament; with a clear majority, he was no longer dependent on the likes of Agnes Macphail and J.S. Woodsworth. Moreover, Meighen had resigned, and the acting leader of the opposition, Hugh Guthrie, was no more than a caretaker. The Old Age Pensions bill was reintroduced and easily passed the House. King and Lapointe looked forward with confidence to 1927 and the celebration of Canada's Diamond Jubilee.

Then from Toronto, the heartland of British Canada, came carping criticism of their role at the Imperial Conference. The traditional and deeply conservative *Toronto Telegram* and the *Mail and Empire* accused them of undermining the empire. Even the Liberal *Globe* was censorious, complaining that they stressed the equality of the Dominions at the expense of the British partnership. In early January an address to the Canadian Club by the Australian prime minister, Stanley Bruce, afforded the *Telegram* an opportunity to compare Bruce's 'broad-visioned, generous, Empire-strengthening nationalism' with the 'narrow, suspicious, selfish, Empire-weakening nationalism' of King and Lapointe.[37]

No longer boasting of his triumph at London, the prime minister quickly backtracked. He decided to hold a huge dinner meeting in

Toronto to reassure British Canadians that imperial relations had not been jeopardized. On 3 February 1927 King's entire cabinet (with the exception of Cardin and Dr J.H. King) stepped off the train in Toronto's Union Station, lining up three rows deep for the *Toronto Star*'s photographer – a phalanx of substantial-looking gentlemen in homburgs or bowlers. (Like King, Lapointe belonged to the bowler brigade.) At the banquet that evening at the King Edward Hotel, at least five hundred people had to be turned away because the ballroom could accommodate no more than fourteen hundred. The Union Jack was everywhere: each table had its own miniature flag.

In an after-dinner speech lasting two and a half hours, King 'declared unequivocally' that nothing had been done at the conference to mar the unity of the empire: the British North America Act remained untouched; the rights of minorities, by which his audience understood him to mean French Canadians, were not put in jeopardy by the Balfour Report. His long speech was well received. However, it was Ernest Lapointe who 'captivated the great audience,' according to the *Toronto Daily Star*. Despite the lateness of the hour, he had his audience with him from the outset, laughing at his jibes at the Tories, but then settling into an attentive hush when he began his serious discourse.

The main achievement of the conference, he said, was the 'clear and official adherence to the doctrine of equality of status.' He stressed that this simply recognized Canada as it existed in the present. Far from tending towards republicanism, he told his monarchist audience, the king more than ever would be the keystone of the structure of the empire since each Dominion owed allegiance to him. Those 'timid souls' who were afraid of freedom and equality of status within the Commonwealth had 'the inferiority complex, the subordinate state of mind.'

As the spokesman for his people, he demolished the argument being played up by the Conservatives to curry favour in Quebec that autonomy would leave the French-Canadian minority at the mercy of the majority: 'Let me tell you the men of my race have been in the very forefront of the battle for responsible government in this country; that they believe in self-government, freedom and national status within the British empire and under the British throne, and they do not believe that a condition of subordination and colonial inferiority is essential to the preservation of their sacred rights.'[38] Evidently still smarting from the *Margaret* affair, Lapointe took advantage of the occasion to complain of the besmirching of men in public life.

The praises heaped on each other by King and Lapointe were a clear announcement of their partnership. In a 'stirring tribute,' King acknowledged Lapointe's invaluable aid during the Imperial Conference and his leadership of the government 'during one of the tensest periods in parliamentary history.' The prime minister left his listeners in no doubt that he regarded Lapointe as his closest associate of all the cabinet members seated at the head table. Lapointe, in turn, proudly referred to the fact that he had stood by King as his leader since the death of Sir Wilfrid Laurier: 'We have defended the same causes. We have displayed with feelings of pride and affection the great banner of Liberalism.' Declaring that King well deserved the testimony rendered to him that evening, Lapointe saluted him as 'a great figure in Canada today.'[39] A few weeks later, King confirmed Lapointe's position by naming him acting prime minister in his absence. Moreover, King had decided to give Lapointe a large 'perk' – a trip to Australia.[40]

Canberra, the new capital of Australia, was to be officially opened by the Duke and Duchess of York on 9 May 1927, and King deputized Lapointe to represent Canada. 'I might have taken this trip,' King told his diary, 'and it means quite a little to lose his help, but I believe it is all for the best for him, to be off for a time and get really rested.'[41] Lapointe's private secretary, the indispensable Philippe Picard, was going with him and so was Lapointe's young son, Bobby.

Anxious to oblige the powerful minister of justice, the CPR offered to make travel arrangements to Australia for Lapointe's party. Lapointe would have nothing to do with the private railway: 'Don't reply,' he instructed Picard. On 31 March they took the CNR to Vancouver where they boarded a ship of the Canadian Australian line. Naturally, the manager of the line directed that 'every possible facility aboard ship' be afforded to these travellers. The ship put in at Honolulu, and Lapointe must have thought that he was getting more VIP treatment when the head waiter at the Royal Hawaiian Hotel greeted him effusively by name. It turned out that the man had previously worked at the Chateau Frontenac.[42]

Towards the end of the voyage, Lapointe received the good news that the Supreme Court of Canada had unanimously affirmed the validity of Section 17 of the Alberta Act. The first legal battle to ensure French-language separate schools in the West had been won. Lapointe cabled Lucien Cannon, acting minister of justice in his absence, to proceed immediately to the Judicial Committee of the Privy Council for a final and definitive decision.[43]

Eighty miles inland in the state of New South Wales, Canberra was situated in a natural amphitheatre. Plans had been drawn up by an American town planner. At this early stage, however, there was little visible evidence of a capital city other than the long, white, temporary Parliament Building, which was officially opened by the Duke of York. It had been arranged that after the opening ceremonies and festivities, Lapointe would go on to Geneva to represent Canada at the Naval Disarmament Conference. Accordingly, with his son and secretary, Lapointe made a world tour of it, travelling west across the Indian Ocean and through the Suez Canal to Cairo (commemorated by a photograph of the three, wearing topees, on camels in front of the Sphinx). Pleasure travel ended for Lapointe at Geneva, though not for his travelling companions. Madame Lapointe and Odette had joined them from Paris, and while Lapointe was busy with official duties, Philippe Picard rented a car and took Mimy and the children touring. There was not much fun to be had in Geneva for young people such as Odette and Bobby. Odette could not get over how strait-laced the Swiss were. Not only were men and women separated at church but even on the beach.[44]

From the moment the conference opened, it was clear to Lapointe that Canada could be caught in the middle of a battle royal between its two best friends. The purpose of the Naval Disarmament Conference was to set the number of vessels to be constructed by Britain, the United States, and Japan. The Washington Treaty of 1922 had established parity between the British and American navies, but it covered only battleships and battle cruisers; utilizing this loophole, Britain had been building a fleet of light cruisers to maintain supply lines with her far-flung empire. The Americans were furious, claiming that the British action violated the spirit of the Washington Treaty and destablized the agreed-upon parity between their respective navies.

To steer between these shoals, Lapointe realized that he would have to exercise the autonomy he and King had won for Canada at the Imperial Conference the previous year. Lapointe insisted that the delegates from the Dominions be registered as representing their own country, not the British Empire, and that their right to attend all committee meetings be fully recognized. A concession was that all Commonwealth delegates would not attend the same sessions, as they would swamp the American and Japanese delegations.[45]

The conference soon reached an impasse. The British proposals were unacceptable to the Americans, and the American counter-proposals were rejected by the British. After six weeks of 'vituperation, lies and turmoil,' the conference ended in failure. On 5 August the final session took place in the ballroom of the Hôtel des Bergues. The first lord of the admiralty, Lord Bridgeman, set out the British case in a long statement, liberally sprinkled with references to the British Empire, which ended by saying that the Dominions' delegates agreed with him. Lapointe felt it was time to run up the flag for Canadian autonomy. He proposed adding a sentence to clearly indicate that Bridgeman represented only Great Britain and that each of the enumerated Dominions spoke for itself. Lapointe's proposal met no opposition. He immediately dashed off a triumphant coded cable to O.D. Skelton, confident his initiative would please both the under-secretary of state and King.[46]

Lapointe was indeed proud of himself. Stopping off in Paris on the way home to deliver an address at the Cercle Inter-allié, he actually boasted. At the Geneva conference on naval disarmament, he told his distinguished audience, 'Great Britain spoke for itself, its territories and colonies. I am the only one who had the right and the authority to speak in the name of Canada, and whose signature could obligate her.'[47] But Bridgeman had an unpleasant surprise in store for Canada's spokesman. No doubt regarding Lapointe's initiative as colonial cheek, in a statement to the press he totally omitted any reference to Canada. The Conservative *Ottawa Journal* seized upon this slap in the face: 'Because Mr. Bridgeman, British First Lord of the Admiralty, has stated that at Geneva he spoke for Britain, Australia, New Zealand, and South Africa, people persist in asking "What about Canada?"'

Entitled 'Our Casual Foreign Policy,' the *Journal* editorial roundly denounced Lapointe's entire role at the disarmament conference: 'Canada, through Mr. Lapointe, spoke for herself. But what did he say? Was he for the United States levelling up or Britain levelling down? Did he agree with Lord Bridgeman that Britain must build more cruisers to protect her colonies including Canada?' The editorial concluded that Lapointe had contributed nothing of substance; worse than that, it declared that he was totally inadequate to the task: 'Did Mr. Lapointe who dropped in casually on his way home from Australia know anything about such things? If not, who advised him? What experts did Canada have to match minds with British or Americans? Or, incredible as that must seem, was he there as a tourist diplomat without any information at all?' The editorial writer enjoined Parliament to 'serve notice upon the government that, hereafter, when it is sending delegates to those European conferences it must send men who are properly equipped with knowledge of the subjects discussed.'[48]

Lapointe did not learn about the fallout from the conference until he was sailing home on the *Empress of France*. A coded cable arrived from an obviously disturbed under-secretary of state:[49] 'Bridgeman statement sent out from Geneva omitted Canada. Ottawa Journal editorial brings it to attention and also misleads by saying no technical adviser.' Skelton asked Lapointe to give an interview to correct this bad impression as soon as he landed.[49] Lapointe would have been intensely angry over the editorial. He had expressed his indignation at personal attacks during the parliamentary debate on the Imperial Conference. At that time he had told the House that if Canadian public men must face 'that kind of warfare,' they might well conclude that they should not attend these conferences.[50]

However, ignoring the criticism, Lapointe's next move was to insist that Canada should stand for election to the League of Nations Council. This was a major step towards international recognition of Canadian nationhood, and in taking this position Lapointe was far in advance of Mackenzie King. The League of Nations Council was composed of five permanent members (including Germany, which had joined the League in 1926) and four non-permanent members. Three of the latter positions were up for election in the summer of 1927. From Geneva, Lapointe strongly recommended that Canada contest a seat. Mackenzie King was against it. He was afraid that it could involve Canada in European matters, and if Canada found itself running counter to England or France there would be political reverberations at home.[51]

On his return from Geneva, Lapointe pressed King on the matter. Indeed, he was unusually determined to have his way and not give in to King. 'This is the only time you and I have differed,' he told his soulmate. King tried to temporize. Why not wait until cabinet met? Lapointe shrugged this off, saying that cabinet would do what King wished, not what he wished. 'Well, go ahead,' said King. Later King recorded in his diary that he thought it was a mistake, 'but a cleavage with Lapointe on a matter on which he feels deeply would be more unfortunate in the long run.'[52]

The next day, King sent word to Dr Skelton in Geneva that after conferring with Mr Lapointe he hereby authorized Canada to seek a seat on the Council. In a rather amusing report to King, Skelton described what happened when Senator Dandurand 'sprang the news' at a meeting at the Hôtel Beau Rivage. Sir Austen Chamberlain, the British secretary for foreign affairs, was visibly 'taken aback' and tried to postpone the evil hour. 'Would it not be better to wait another year?' he asked Canada's representative to the League. He emphasized how embarrassing it would be for him if Canada were elected and took a different attitude on the Council from his own. But seeing that Dandurand was determined, Sir Austen announced that he would support Canada's candidacy. The other Dominions also promised their support. Five candidates in all were running.

Skelton assessed Canada's chances for King. The bilingualism of the Canadian diplomats would help, and so would Senator Dandurand's personal popularity. Then too Canada was admired for taking independent positions in the League and for its 'pioneering' in the empire. On the other hand, Canada's negative attitude towards Article X was unpopular among a good many states that wanted the League to take a strong position on collective security. When the ballots were counted, Canada had got in 'by the skin of our teeth,' as Skelton put it, coming third after Cuba and Finland.[53] The British Empire had stood solidly behind its sister nation.

The election result was extremely gratifying to Lapointe. At his next public appearance, he declared that 'Canada has grown into full nationhood and now takes her place in the international Council of Nations while still proud to retain her position as an autonomous community within the British Empire.'[54] Henri Bourassa, once Lapointe's nemesis, was full of praise for his aggressive stance on Canadian autonomy. 'At Geneva, at London, at Washington, everywhere he has represented Canada,' wrote the editor of Le Devoir, 'Mr. Lapointe has done the work of a good Canadian.'[55]

In King's opinion, French Canadians were far keener than their English counterparts to have Canada recognized as 'a country by itself.'[56] The prime minister was only partially correct. The truth was that self-interest pulled French Canadians in opposite directions. On the one hand, they welcomed King and Lapointe's initiatives for more independence from Great Britain in that they had no desire to become embroiled in European wars. On the other hand, depending on Britain to protect them against the Anglo-Canadian majority, they resisted any move to end judicial appeals to the Privy Council or to alter the British Parliament's sole power to amend the British North America Act.

CHAPTER TWELVE

The Dominion-Provincial Conference of 1927

In 1927 Canada celebrated its Diamond Jubilee. At the time of the Golden Jubilee there had been no thought of celebration because the country was at war. Now, sixty years after Confederation, Canadians were in a party mood. From Halifax to Vancouver, downtown buildings were festooned with red, white, and blue bunting, while a forest of flagpoles flying the Union Jack sprouted in residential districts. On the first of July, every village, no matter how small, mustered a band concert, a militia march past (or at least a Boy Scouts parade), and a picnic in the park. Such an occasion called for a royal visit, and at the end of June the Prince of Wales, accompanied by his brother, the Duke of York, and the British prime minister, Stanley Baldwin, arrived at Quebec City on the *Empress of Australia*. In Ottawa the prince dedicated the beautiful Memorial Chamber in the Peace Tower containing the Book of Remembrance with the names of the 60,000 Canadians who died in the Great War and unveiled a statue of Sir Wilfrid Laurier on Parliament Hill. Later, before a crowd of a quarter of a million, he dedicated the International Peace Bridge spanning the Niagara River between Fort Erie, Ontario, and Buffalo, New York. As if a fairy-tale prince was not enough for Canada's birthday, a hero descended from the clouds when Charles Lindbergh, the handsome young aviator who had just made the first solo flight across the Atlantic, flew in.[1]

Lapointe was abroad for the July celebrations, but he, as much as King, was the moving spirit behind the culminating event of the Diamond Jubilee – the Dominion-Provincial Conference of 1927, heralded as the most important intergovernmental gathering since Confederation. Before leaving for Australia, Lapointe had announced a conference on Senate reform. He was responding to popular indignation, largely sparked by editorial outrage. The upper chamber was regarded as a luxurious private club for old politicians who had no business interfering with legislation passed by the elected Commons. Editorial writers also condemned it as a convenience for the government of the day, which passed progressive legislation in the Commons knowing that the Senate would reject it. King had been promising Senate reform since 1925.

While Lapointe was away the scope of the conference widened to include various provincial concerns such as jurisdiction over waterpower, return of the West's natural resources, and federal subsidies. During his travels, Lapointe himself had come to the conclusion that Senate reform was just the tip of the iceberg of necessary constitutional change for Canada. In the international circles in which he moved it was undoubtedly an embarrassment that Canada alone among the self-governing Dominions could not amend its own constitution. Indeed, at the Imperial Conference in 1926 he had been rather hard-pressed to explain the anomaly of a self-governing Dominion that had to ask England before it could change its constitution. The British North America Act had no amending clause, and as a British statute it could be amended only by an Act of the British Parliament. Until this time, Lapointe had agreed with King that Canada did not need the formal right to amend the BNA Act because the Parliament at Westminster simply rubber-stamped the few amendments the Canadian government had requested since Confederation. In 1924 and again in 1926, J.S. Woodsworth had proposed resolutions calling for the amending power to be transferred from Westminster to Ottawa. Lapointe had vigorously opposed the Woodsworth resolutions, asserting that the limitation did not make Canada subordinate to Britain because it continued to exist with Canadian agreement.

By the 1927 Dominion-Provincial Conference, however, Lapointe was ready to advocate patriating the amending process. Canadian status in the eyes of the world was more important to Lapointe than it was to King. When it came to Canada's contesting a seat on the League of Nations Council he had shown King the way; now he was prepared to take nationalism a step further than the prime minister. King's lack of interest was apparent at a cabinet meeting on the eve of the conference. When Lapointe argued that 'our self-respect as a nation demands our right to amend the constitution ourselves,' only Euler seconded him. All the rest agreed with King when he said that 'we in fact had the right and there was no use raising the issue.'[2] Nevertheless, Lapointe insisted that constitutional amendment had to be on the conference agenda. Assisted by a brief prepared by Norman Rogers, a young university professor temporarily employed as one of King's secretaries, Lapointe was to present the case for patriation of the amending process, but King would shed no tears if the provinces turned thumbs down.

On 3 November 1927 nine premiers, attended by their cabinet ministers and bureaucrats, assembled in the Parliament Buildings' arcaded Hall of Fame. Heavy rains did not dampen their spirits. With the country enjoying prosperity, the premiers were brimming with confidence, none more so than Ontario's premier, Howard Ferguson, who (noted a *Globe* staff writer) was 'all smiles.' The most powerful premier, Ferguson was also the most popular, glad-handing and backslapping his way through the hall. His smile was particularly welcoming when Premier Taschereau arrived and greeted him in French.[3]

The premiers of the two central provinces had formed a united front to fight the federal government on the waterpower question. Waterpower exemplified the problem that dogged Canada – the division of powers between the provinces and the federal government. According to Lapointe and his law officers, Ottawa's constitutional jurisdiction over navigation gave it the right to develop hydroelectric power on all waterways including the mighty St Lawrence. Taschereau and Ferguson disputed this vigorously, claiming that the federal government was entitled to only enough power to operate navigation locks: any surplus power belonged to the provinces by virtue of provincial jurisdiction over river beds and banks.[4] Until very recently King and Lapointe had taken comfort in the fact that Regulation 17 – the anti-French policy in the Ontario school system – ruled out a league between Quebec's premier and the Orangeman Howard Ferguson, who had led the campaign for English-only in the schools. But in September this last barrier was removed when Ferguson accepted a report that in effect nullified the obnoxious Regulation 17. This was precisely what Lapointe had asked of Ontario in his famous 1916 resolution. He took no joy in it now. He and King knew that Ferguson had made the concession to Franco-Ontarians so that Taschereau would join him in ganging up on Ottawa.[5]

The *bonne entente* between the Liberal Taschereau and the Conservative Ferguson was apparent from the moment the conference got down to business in the Railway Committee Room. Senate reform was the topic of discussion at the afternoon session. Like a law school professor, Lapointe gave a learned overview of possible reforms, such as an elective Senate or an age limit (one sitting senator was 100), but he offered no government policy or recommendations. King did not participate at all in the two-hour discussion. Obviously, he had no strong desire to reform the upper house. Like all his predecessors, he appreciated the patronage opportunities afforded by an appointed Senate. Enthusiasm for Senate reform was singularly lacking among the delegates as well. Although Ferguson criticized Lapointe for his noncommittal presentation, he made it clear that Ontario would not have countenanced change anyway. Taschereau seconded Ferguson, contending that Senate reform would open up a Pandora's box of unnecessary changes in a constitution that had worked well for sixty years.[6] Despite the centenarian senator, he saw no reason for an age limit.

The Ferguson-Taschereau alliance was similarly in evidence the following day when Lapointe turned to constitutional amendment. Here Lapointe was genuinely committed and 'argued the case with his usual brilliance.' He spoke of the autonomy Canada had won at the recent Imperial Conference and of her growing importance internationally. It would be consistent with her new status, he told the delegates, to have the amending power on this side of the Atlantic instead of going through the cumbersome procedure of applying to Westminster or Downing Street. Lapointe emphasized that, under his proposal, amendments involving provincial and minority rights would require the unanimous consent of all the provinces, thus in effect giving each a veto. Ferguson jumped in. Was Mr Lapointe speaking for himself alone or did his proposal represent the official government view? Lapointe held a whispered consultation with King. What should he say to this? King told him to reply that the government was just taking a theoretical position since it had no particular amendments in mind. Theoretical or not, Ferguson roundly denounced Lapointe's proposal. Amending its own constitution would be Canada's first step towards separation from Britain, he declared: appeals to the Privy Council would be dropped and the governor general would be the next to go.

Taschereau was even more opposed. In fact, he had 'a very spirited clash' with Lapointe. Asserting that the British Parliament was an independent tribunal whose fairness the French minority could trust, Taschereau said he feared discrimination if constitutional decisions were left to the Anglo-Canadian majority. At the very least, it would allow the centralizing government in Ottawa to make inroads into provincial rights. The delegations split along east-west lines, the Maritimes lining up with Ontario and Quebec and the western provinces supporting Lapointe's proposal. Lapointe closed the discussion with the King-like statement that the government would carefully consider all the opinions both pro and con.[7] Ferguson and Taschereau had killed constitutional reform for the time being.

The conference moved on to issues raised by the provinces. Taschereau and Ferguson were determined to have a 'showdown' with the federal government over the waterpower question. It was a pity, declared the Quebec premier, that after sixty years the question of who controlled waterpower had not been decided. He and Ferguson urged the federal government to refer the matter to the courts. Lapointe announced that he was opposed to any such reference; but King realized, even if Lapointe did not, that the dispute would have to be adjudicated. Within a few months the federal government would submit the question to the Supreme Court.[8]

Lapointe's insistence that Ottawa had the right to waterpower generated on navigable rivers and streams revealed how far he had travelled from his traditional Quebec position as defender of provincial rights. Indeed, some of his past pronouncements opposing pensions and other centralizing policies were thrown back at him by the premiers. Yet his amendment proposal requiring approval from the provinces was actually an important concession to provincial rights in that under the existing procedure Parliament took its proposed amendments to Westminster without consulting the provinces. Only once in the years from Confederation to 1927 had the provinces been consulted.[9]

Lapointe was a declared adherent of the pact theory of Confederation, which in effect favoured provincial rights. Speaking in the House in 1924, he described the BNA Act as 'a treaty between various colonies,' which fixed the respective powers of the central Parliament and the provinces that succeeded the colonies. He went on to say that 'this treaty could not be changed ... and I think it is only fair that no change should be accepted, without the consent of all those who were parties to it.'[10] As recently as the previous March he had reiterated that the constitution could not be changed without the consent of all the provinces. As his speech to the conference indicates, he had moved away somewhat from this position. Now he was saying that only amendments which touched upon minority rights or other fundamental rights would require unanimity; ordinary amendments would just require agreement from a majority of the provinces. However, he did not depart from his oft-repeated conviction that in their own constitutional jurisdiction, the provinces were supreme and the federal government should not step over the line. The question, of course, was where to draw the line. Waterpower was just one example.

Through his alliance with Ferguson, Taschereau had defeated all Lapointe's proposals. Presiding at the evening session on 9 November, Lapointe appeared to take his defeat gracefully. 'Conflict between the provinces and the federal government cannot be avoided,' he told the delegates, 'but it should be settled in a spirit of compromise.'[11] Under his calm exterior, however, Lapointe was burning with anger at Taschereau. This surfaced when he took the waterpower issue to the Supreme Court after failing to talk King out of it. Instead of a joint reference with Ontario and Quebec, which was the logical procedure, Lapointe submitted the questions to the court on behalf of the federal government alone. Taschereau voiced his exasperation to King: 'As Federal or Provincial rights are involved, I think it would have been more satisfactory if the questions had been prepared jointly by the Governments concerned.' The brewing feud between the two French-Canadian politicians made Mackenzie King feel as if he were caught up in a family quarrel. He wrote Taschereau: 'May I hasten to say to you very confidentially that personally I greatly deplore what on occasions has appeared to me to be a lack of whole-hearted confidence, and, to some extent, a degree of estrangement between some of my Quebec colleagues and yourself. Just what the reasons of this may be, I am at a loss to understand, and I hope that anything of the kind, if it exists, will not be permitted to continue.' With obvious reference to Lapointe, Taschereau replied, 'Unfortunately some of our friends at Ottawa sometimes take it as a personal attack against them when we do not share their views on these important matters.'[12]

Though Lapointe's proposal that Canada should have the right to amend its own constitution had been turned down by the conference delegates, his initiative was lauded elsewhere. Bourassa lavishly praised him in *Le Devoir*, deriding Taschereau's claim that 'England is the protector of our rights.' Reminding the Quebec premier of the recent Labrador boundary decision, which favoured Newfoundland over Quebec, Bourassa declared that 'the foot of the Throne was a chilly spot for French Canadians.'[13] The *Manitoba Free Press*, whose editor John Dafoe was as much of a Canadian nationalist as Bourassa, applauded Lapointe's bid for greater autonomy. But it was on the young that Lapointe made the greatest impression. At universities and law schools across the country, students debated the justice minister's proposal, which some welcomed as the initial step towards patriation of the constitution. His speech on Canadian status and constitutional reform at the Cercle Universitaire in Montreal (repeated before Quebec's association of young lawyers) was printed in several legal journals and in pamphlet form by *Le Devoir*.[14]

The Jubilee year of 1927 had added considerably to Lapointe's reputation as a progressive politician and champion of constitutional reform. It also marked a milestone in his life. In October Lapointe's father died at the age of eighty-four. Syfroid Lapointe had remained in his native village of St Eloi. Cared for by a daughter, the old man had become stone deaf. Lapointe and his family saw little of him throughout the years.[15] Returning to St Eloi for the funeral would have called up a store of memories. The little, white, habitant-style family home, the barn, and the strip of meadow sloping towards the line of hills looked just as they had when Lapointe's mother was alive. Indeed, the village with its wooden church and verandaed houses had not changed since the turn of the century and still numbered no more than a thousand inhabitants. After the church service, the funeral party crossed the road to the cemetery where Syfroid Lapointe was laid to rest beside Adèle Lavoie, the wife he had survived by thirty years. Not long afterwards, Lapointe received a letter from the curé, enclosing a photograph of the Lapointe home and a picture spread on St Eloi from a recent issue of *L'Action Catholique*. Although it was a funeral that brought Lapointe home, the curé was clearly delighted by the visit from St Eloi's most famous native son. In his letter of thanks, Lapointe slipped in a modest donation for the church.[16]

On his return from Europe and Australia, Lapointe had been surprised to find that Lucien Cannon, who had stood in for him as acting minister of justice, had ignored his instructions to refer the Supreme Court judgment on the Alberta schools question to the Privy Council. Cannon explained that it was on the advice of the department's law officers that he had not proceeded with the reference. Because the federal government had won its case at the Supreme Court and Alberta refused to 'mix into the appeal,' the legal opinion was that the Privy Council would not hear it. Cannon also mentioned that Henri Bourassa felt they should not run the risk of appeal, seeing that they had been victorious at the Supreme Court.

Lapointe was annoyed. It was Bourassa who had insisted on written guarantees for bilingual separate schools as a condition for handing over the retained land to Alberta, and now he was running scared.

Nevertheless, Lapointe was determined to have the favourable Supreme Court decision confirmed by the final authority. 'I believe the best policy is to get the Privy Council to decide the issue,' he told Bourassa. 'In not proceeding further, we give Orangemen, and all those who are against separate schools, the opportunity to be able to say that the question is not definitively settled.'[17] The government lawyers were proved right, however. The Judicial Committee of the Privy Council took the position that without Alberta's participation the Dominion government could not justify an appeal. It was back to the negotiating table.

Early in 1928 talks were resumed with Manitoba and Alberta. Manitoba's Premier Bracken was agreeable to bilingual separate schools, but he did not want any reference to them in the transfer agreement. The first draft was silent on the controversial issue. This, of course, was unacceptable to Lapointe. King complained in his diary that Lapointe 'was still wishing to hold back and do nothing, to postpone the whole matter.'[18] In the privacy of his diary King was often highly critical of Lapointe's tendency to put off unpleasant decisions. Not long before he had given vent to his exasperation: 'Lapointe is just slow as usual, he is very difficult to keep up to the mark, is very timid, always wanting to postpone.'[19] This was ironic coming from King, for whom procrastination (particularly through the use of royal commissions) was a favoured strategy. From King's Anglo-Canadian perspective, he seems not to have noticed that Lapointe's timidity was usually related to events or policies that could have repercussions in French Canada. That was certainly why Lapointe impeded the transfer of the western lands. Quebeckers were very concerned over the linguistic rights of their brethren in the Canadian diaspora.

In July a tentative agreement was reached with Manitoba that more or less satisfied Lapointe. To divert public attention from the school question, the canny King appointed a royal commission to advise on compensation to the province for lost revenue from land sales. The Manitoba agreement broke the impasse. Before the end of 1928, Alberta was mulling over a new offer, with a school clause proposed by Lapointe, which King thought would be accepted. With patent relief he wrote in his diary, 'Lapointe seemed pleased with the outcome.'[20]

CHAPTER THIRTEEN

The 'Persons' Case

The close collaboration between Lapointe and King worked well and was a source of satisfaction to both. Lapointe never disputed that King was 'the boss.' Still, King rarely took a step unless he could bring Lapointe on side. When it came to Quebec King deferred almost entirely to Lapointe, though not always in good grace – 'I agreed under protest and only at the unanimous wish of Quebec colleagues,' was his reaction on one occasion.[1] Quebec's constant monetary demands, funnelled through Lapointe, worried the thrifty prime minister. The $5 million for Quebec harbour in 1925 was just the beginning; within a few years the subsidy totalled some fifteen million. Next came a demand for $3 million for an arsenal in Quebec: King hoped against hope that Lapointe would not hold out for the full amount. After approving a further $8.5 million for the French province in March 1928, King resigned himself to the situation: 'Quebec is an all-important part of Canada and always will be.'[2]

Lapointe's advocacy on behalf of his people did not stop at the Quebec border. In 1928 there was still only one French senator of the twenty-six senators allotted to Ontario. Considering that Franco-Ontarians traditionally supported the Liberal party, they were not getting their share of Senate appointments. Lapointe had complained of this before, but now he was being jogged by a prominent Windsor physician named Gustave Lacasse. Dr Lacasse set out the case for a Franco-Ontarian senator (preferably from the Windsor area) in strong terms. He warned the minister that if the Liberals did not give the Franco-Ontarians their due, the party would lose their support in the next election. He claimed that they had actually received more recognition from Tory governments. Now with Premier Ferguson's conciliatory attitude on the separate schools question, Dr Lacasse had no doubt that 'Liberalism's star was paling more and more in the Ontario political firmament.' He appealed to Lapointe: 'We ask you respectfully, Mr. Minister, to put your precious influence at the service of your own people – whom you have the honour to represent in your country's government – and to bring pressure to bear on the prime minister so that he will finally recognize the existence of those who contribute so greatly to bring and maintain him in power and who moreover represent almost a third of the total Canadian population.'

Lapointe sent Dr Lacasse's letter on to King. 'There is no doubt in my mind,' he told the prime minister, 'that the government will have to give additional representation to the French Canadians of Ontario in the Senate. Why not do it gracefully at this time?'[3] King agreed that a French-Canadian senator should be appointed from Ontario – but not yet. He was planning to fill the three Ontario vacancies with anglophones when his French ministers delivered an ultimatum. If he did not appoint a Franco-Ontarian, they would boycott Ontario – no speeches, no campaigning. King gave in. Dr Lacasse, Lapointe's choice, was named to the Senate.[4]

Meanwhile, Lapointe remained unalterably opposed to a Senate seat for Sir Lomer Gouin. Apparently, he could not forget those first two years of the King administration when he had been forced to accept comparative obscurity to make way for Gouin. Although he had ultimately won the struggle for power, he was not prepared to show generosity to his vanquished rival. Knowing Lapointe's intense dislike for Sir Lomer, King had done nothing to reward his former minister of justice for a lifetime of service to the Liberal party. Speaking in Quebec City in November 1927, out of deference to Lapointe King had not so much as referred to Quebec's long-time premier. 'I should have done it and will always regret I did not,' he confessed to his diary. He had a sleepless night on the train back to Ottawa because of it.[5]

King hoped to salve his conscience by giving Gouin the Senate seat he had so long desired. A Senate vacancy for Quebec was in the offing, and Raoul Dandurand was urging his colleagues to let Gouin have it. The English cabinet members were all in favour. But glancing around the table, King could see that Lapointe, Cardin, and Rinfret were 'dead against it.'[6] He would not override them. A distraught Dandurand almost broke down pleading in vain for Gouin's appointment. When Sir Lomer heard of this latest rebuff he called his sons together and told them not to turn against the Liberal party 'to which I have given my life' because of two or three spiteful people. 'Lapointe remains *le gros petit homme* that he always was and will always be,' Gouin observed bitterly.[7]

With the Catholic Church dictating ultra-conservative social and educational values in Quebec, it was dangerous politically for Lapointe to be too progressive at the national level. This is not to say that he did not share many of the conservative views of his compatriots. Divorce was a good example. In Quebec divorce was illegal under the Civil Code, but as with citizens of Ontario and Prince Edward Island, Quebeckers could get a divorce through a private petition to Parliament. When J.S. Woodsworth proposed a bill to establish divorce tribunals in Ontario like those that existed in six other provinces, Lapointe declared that he opposed divorce on principle, and he killed the Woodsworth bill. Anything to legitimize divorce was anathema to him. He set out his strongly held views in notes for a speech:

> Divorce is a contempt of children ... an anti-social plague. It encourages a rather vile and mean action, namely by a courtesan wishing to supplant the wife who has spent a life of duty by appealing to the evil in the human heart.
>
> The usurper invades the house, she expels, she steals. Shame replaces honour and virtue. Divorce is detrimental to the public good and instead of making it easier, we should endeavour to suppress it. The possibility of divorce is itself a cause of divorce.[8]

'It is astonishing how afraid the Catholics are of their Church,' King commented in his diary. It was not just fear of the church, however; Lapointe was well aware of the political consequences of supporting divorce legislation. In March 1930 when Woodsworth reintroduced his bill, Lapointe told King that any Quebec member who was not in the House to vote against the bill would not dare to be a candidate again. 'Hardly conceivable,' King sputtered in his diary. Yet forewarned by Lapointe of Quebec's attitude, King thought it prudent 'not to be present to vote one way or the other' on the Woodsworth bill.[9] (On second reading King manfully appeared and voted in favour of the bill, which finally created an Ontario divorce court.)

When it came to women's political rights, however, Lapointe departed from the traditional Quebec position. His thinking had evolved from the war years, when he had opposed female suffrage. He now regarded the fact that women could not vote in Quebec elections as an anachronism and he sympathized with the struggle of Thérèse Casgrain and the other suffragists. This put him at odds with the leaders of church and state in his home province. At a dinner party at Premier Taschereau's house, he was the only one in favour of giving women the vote. When the male chauvinists around the table were expressing hilarity at the prospect of women in the Legislative Assembly, Lapointe silenced them by declaring that he had known as many clever women as stupid men.[10]

Lapointe could not open the doors of the Quebec legislature to women, but the Canadian Parliament was a different matter. Although Agnes Macphail had been sitting in the House of Commons since 1921, women were still barred from the Senate on the ground that they were not 'qualified persons' within the meaning of Section 24 of the British North America Act. For years women's organizations had been pressing the government to seek an amendment; first Meighen and later King had made vague promises. Tired of waiting for the government to act, in 1927 five leading Alberta women invoked a section of the Supreme Court Act that allowed them to petition the minister of justice to refer the eligibility question to the Supreme Court.[11] Lapointe agreed to request a reference on the question and undertook to pay the petitioners' legal costs, but his department would uphold the status quo. In October 1927 an order-in-council was issued:

> The Minister of Justice states that the law officers of the Crown who have considered this question on more than one occasion have expressed the view that male persons only may be summoned to the Senate under the provisions of the British North America Act.
>
> The Minister, however, while not disposed to question that view, considers it would be an act of justice to the women of Canada to obtain the opinion of the Supreme Court of Canada upon that point.

On 14 March 1928 five scarlet-robed male justices considered the question: 'Does the word "Persons" in section 24 of the British North America Act, 1867, include female persons?' There was Chief Justice Anglin, narrow-minded, Jesuit-educated, so self-important that in his diary King called him 'a laughing-stock and an ass.'[12] Then there was Mr Justice Duff, who also took a narrow reading of the law, and whose drinking problem did not always leave him sober on the bench. Their brother justices would take their lead from these two.

The solicitor general, Lucien Cannon, and the distinguished lawyer Eugene Lafleur argued the government's case on historical grounds. The British North America Act did not contemplate summoning women to the Senate. It would take an amendment to make them eligible, and this would introduce 'a revolutionary change, contrary to the intent of the Act.' Taschereau sent his deputy attorney general to intervene on behalf of Cannon and Lafleur. (The Quebec legislature had again vetoed women members.) The five Alberta women had chosen as their counsel Newton Rowell, a long-time advocate of female suffrage. He was also representing the province of Alberta, which supported the women's cause. Rowell took an evolutionary approach, maintaining that the term 'persons' should be interpreted according to its plain meaning in contemporary society and was therefore equally applicable to women.[13]

In a crowded courtroom on 24 April 1928, the Supreme Court handed down a unanimous judgment that women were not 'persons' eligible for the Senate. Chief Justice Anglin, who wrote the decision, more or less accepted the government's argument. In 1867 women were under the same legal incapacity as children and imbeciles and could not hold public office, and there was no doubt that the Fathers of Confederation did not envisage women sitting in the Senate; therefore, when the British North America Act spoke of 'qualified persons' it did not mean women. The chief justice traced female incapacity back to Roman times. Women did not fight in the Roman legions, so they could not govern in civil society. His lordship found support for his view in the 'significant fact' that 'never from 1867 to the present time has any woman sat in the Senate.' (Women were barred from sitting in the Senate because they had never done so, and they had never done so because they were barred. Anglin, after all, had studied scholastic philosophy.) He concluded that it would take explicit language to make them eligible for appointment.[14]

Lapointe was in the House when he learned of the Supreme Court's decision. Rising from his seat beside the prime minister, he passed on the information to the members: 'I understand that the basis for the judgment is that the act must be interpreted in the meaning it had when it was adopted in 1867, and that at that time the expression "fit and qualified persons" as it appears in the act could not apply to women as they were then disqualified for appointment to public offices.' Lapointe had become completely converted to the women's cause. Shocked by the antediluvian decision, with his desk-mate's approval he made a large promise that would prove difficult to keep:

> In view of this judgment, and in view of the fact that women in this country now have an equal franchise with men, and in view of the further fact that one of the seats in this house is occupied by a woman, the government have decided that they should have the equal right to sit in the other chamber, and means will be taken to secure an amendment to the British North America Act in that respect.[15]

His promise to seek a constitutional amendment was greeted with joy by the five Alberta women and generally approved by the English-language press. Most scathing in its criticism of the Supreme Court judgment was the *Ottawa Journal*. The judges made a shameful decision, the editor declared, and then blamed it on the dead Fathers of Confederation.[16] But in French Canada only Thérèse Casgrain and her small cohort of suffragists welcomed the justice minister's intention to amend the BNA Act. *Le Droit*, the Ottawa daily owned by a Catholic order, called it one more 'false step.' Female suffrage and access to the House of Commons were other steps in the wrong direction for which the present government was not responsible, 'but it does more than approve them since it wishes to crown the stupidities of its predecessors.' The editor then pontificated on women's place: it was not at the ballot box, nor in the House of Commons, nor in the Senate. It was elsewhere, in the home, in the education of children, in charitable works and social uplift. 'The government, guardian of order, should not ignore this.'[17]

As it turned out, Lapointe did not follow through on his promise to secure a constitutional amendment. Quebec was the impediment. It was not so much that he was intimidated by the Catholic hierarchy but that he knew he would never get the Taschereau government to agree to such an amendment. At the Dominion-Provincial Conference Lapointe had come out in favour of the compact theory of Confederation, which held that the BNA Act was a treaty between the Dominion and the provinces, and the consent of the provinces was obligatory for major amendments. He could hardly move ahead without at least consulting Quebec. 'There would be no end of wrangling,' the *Ottawa Journal* predicted. The constitutional amendment to permit women to sit in the upper house was put on hold. When the 1928 session ended without the proposed amendment going forward, the five Alberta women decided to appeal the Supreme Court decision to the Privy Council. This time the federal government would not oppose the women, and Lapointe again offered to foot the bill.[18]

There was speculation at this time that Lapointe would go to the Supreme Court. One of the two Quebec justices would be retiring in 1929. *Saturday Night* magazine conjectured that Lapointe might want to leave politics for the judiciary out of frustration with Taschereau and Ferguson:

> The Minister of Justice has been Mr King's chief abettor in the undertaking of improving the national status and for the last couple of years he has been a leading exponent of the idea that in order to properly assert herself this country should abandon the practice of applying to Westminster for amendments to the British North America Act. He has supported those western women who are seeking for their sex the right to seats in the Senate and is a leading champion of all constitutional reform.

'But the prospects of achievement were not very bright,' the writer continued, owing to the unsympathetic attitude of Ontario and Quebec: 'Mr Lapointe perhaps has concluded that he could better serve his country on the Supreme Court bench than in laboring for years as a cabinet minister while awaiting for opportunity to improve the constitution and the national status.'[19]

Whether or not he wanted to go to the bench was a moot point because King had no intention of letting him go. A few years earlier King had felt no qualms about replacing his Quebec lieutenant with Lucien Cannon. He was no longer so sanguine. At fifty-two, Lapointe was recognized as 'one of the strong men of the government,' 'a chief pillar in the King administration.' In the House he showed none of the timidity that King complained of in his diary. He was a superb orator who could sway the House as King could seldom do. ('He has a very happy way of expressing himself,' King observed somewhat wistfully.) As a rule calm and judicial in manner, if Lapointe deemed it expedient he would 'adopt the role of the indignant partisan.' As one columnist put it, 'He is a kindly man but can become aggressive at the drop of a hat.' His fighting reply to opposition critics of the 1928 budget brought the backbenchers to their feet, applauding thunderously. The *Ottawa Journal* commented on that occasion: 'Mr. Lapointe's marked French accent seems to give sting to his sarcasm, and this weapon with a good deal of appeal to the prejudices of his backbenchers, he used quite effectively.'[20]

Lapointe was the undisputed leader of the Quebec MPs. Although Cardin shared the responsibility of the federal organization in Quebec, he had little personal following and would not be acceptable on his own. Moreover, King knew that the cabinet would be cool to Lucien Cannon's appointment as justice minister. Indeed, Cannon was proving to be a nuisance. He was aggressive and demanding. Not content with presenting the important 'Persons' case for the government, he claimed the right to handle all references to the Supreme Court and the Privy Council. On 18 April 1928 he wrote King in a most peremptory tone complaining that he was being manoeuvred out of his 'legitimate' mandate by officials in the department of justice. He absolved Lapointe from any blame: 'May I add that my relations with the Honorable Ernest Lapointe have been most pleasant during the last two years.'[21]

Hardly anyone had a bad word to say about Lapointe. He was even popular with the members of the opposition. The new Conservative leader, R.B. Bennett, obviously liked him, and their frequent verbal jousts were a feature attraction in the House. A self-made millionaire, Bennett had been born in the Maritimes but had made his mark as a corporate lawyer in Calgary. Like King, he was a bachelor. For both Lapointe and King, Bennett was a welcome change from the detested Meighen, who had retired to private life. Though Bennett was the living image of the cartoon capitalist, from his top hat to his spats, Lapointe praised him in the House as 'a fine leader, a man of courage and strong convictions, and well able to express those convictions. He is an excellent type of Canadian manhood.'[22]

When Parliament was not in session, Lapointe always made sure that he had a week or so of golf. During the Easter adjournment in 1928 he went off with his golfing cronies, Jack Elliott and Charles Stewart – ministers respectively of Public Works and the Interior – to a resort not far from New York City. They unwittingly caused Mackenzie King acute embarrassment. King had sanctimoniously announced to the press that he would be spending the recess at Kingsmere, working. The truth was that he was taking his dearest friend, Joan Patteson, and her husband, Godfrey, on vacation to the mountains in his private railway car. It was all hush-hush. King took care that his railway car was next to the engine in the hope that it would not be noticed. At the end of their holiday they went to New York City for some shopping. King and Joan were strolling down Fifth Avenue when whom should they run into but Ernest Lapointe! (They also encountered Fernand Rinfret in an elevator in Macy's.) 'It shows how little one can get away unobserved anywhere,' King grumbled in his diary. But he put the best face on it, inviting 'the three golfers' to breakfast at his hotel and sharing his private car with them for the return trip.[23]

In September 1928 King went to Geneva to attend the League of Nations Assembly, leaving Lapointe acting prime minister. King had little interest in the League and had gone at Lapointe's urging.[24] Lapointe was known as a strong supporter of the international peace-keeping organization, and when a League of Nations Society was formed in Canada in the winter of 1928 he was the keynote speaker at the inaugural banquet at the Chateau Laurier. Nevertheless, Lapointe was no advocate of collective security. Consent, not coercion, was the answer, he told his audience of five hundred: 'The only way of securing peace is by what is usually called moral disarmament, and that can be obtained only when a strong public opinion, the opinion in the shops, in the factories, on the farms, in the universities, in the schools, when opinion everywhere is deeply and intimately convinced that war is a calamity and the worst of all calamities.'[25]

Canadians in general shared Lapointe's naivety. In calling for support of Article X, the collective security provision of the League of Nations Covenant, John Dafoe, the editor of the *Manitoba Free Press*, was a voice in the wilderness. In 1928 nothing seemed less likely than another war. Those who thought about it at all believed that it was enough to simply outlaw war, which was the purport of the Kellogg-Briand Pact. Initiated by the United States and France, it substituted arbitration for sanctions. On his way to Geneva, King signed the pact at Paris.

Things had seldom been better at home. 'It is the most prosperous period in our history,' King exulted in his diary. The bull market in the United States had surged across the border. On the Montreal exchange, stocks were trading at all-time highs. Following Larkin's sage advice, King stuck to bonds, but his ministers were not immune to the stock market fever. When Kirk Cameron offered Robb and Lapointe the opportunity of buying shares in a paper company at the underwriters' price, well below that offered to the public, they jumped at it. Not so Cardin. He treated the offer as a bribe and curtly refused it.[26] (The minister of marine was not so scrupulous when it came to taking favours from the Simard shipbuilding company.) When a few months later paper stocks dropped, Cameron made sure that his cabinet friends did not have to take their losses. To their surprise Lapointe and Robb received cheques from the brokerage, which had underwritten the issue, fully reimbursing them for the amount they had paid for the shares.[27]

It was fortunate for Lapointe that he recovered the few thousand because he had heavy expenses in connection with Odette's coming-out party at the Country Club on 28 December 1928. The prime minister sent the debutante flowers and attended the dance. Somewhat shocked by the flappers, he nonetheless admitted in his diary that he had enjoyed dancing with them.[28]

CHAPTER FOURTEEN

Silver Anniversaries

For the first time since 1904, Ernest Lapointe missed the opening of Parliament. A few days before the opening on 7 February 1929, he had slipped on an icy step and sprained his knee.[1] Despite stormy weather with huge snow drifts, Mimy and Odette attended the gala event. Photographed by the *Ottawa Citizen*, Mimy Lapointe made a handsome, dignified figure in a gown of white chiffon with gold embroidery and the obligatory elbow-length white kid-gloves. Odette was a fashionable flapper in 'a picturesque frock of pale green moire, with bustle effect in the back and large bow at the shoulders, the streamers falling to the hem of the skirt.'[2] Seated in the members' gallery, they listened to Viscount Willingdon deliver the throne speech. The speech itself held no surprises. After giving thanks for King George V's recovery from pneumonia, His Excellency, reading the government's self-congratulatory text, dwelt upon the unprecedented prosperity throughout the Dominion.

Ernest's sprained knee kept him housebound for the next month. Meanwhile, Mimy kept up their social obligations, attending among other functions a dinner party at the prime minister's. At the annual reception held by the cabinet ministers' wives on 21 February, Madame Lapointe, as the wife of the senior cabinet minister, stood first in the receiving line. From the fashion note in the *Ottawa Citizen* she appears to have thriftily dressed up her white chiffon with an 'overskirt formed of flounces of black chiffon with touches of green.' Because of Ernest's injury, he and Mimy celebrated their twenty-fifth anniversary quietly at their home on Chapel Street in Ottawa with their children and some near relatives. Bobby, tall like his father but of a slighter build, was now a law student at the University of Ottawa. Mimy's sister and two sisters-in-law had come from Quebec, and the day before the anniversary Mimy entertained for them at tea.[3]

Having Lapointe laid up during the session was very inconvenient for King. Nevertheless, when J.W. Edwards reintroduced a motion calling for the return of the West's natural resources without further delay he was not sorry that his lieutenant was *hors de combat*. King was anxious to be done with this pesky business, which had been dragging on for three years thanks to Lapointe's dilatory tactics. The previous March Lapointe had choked off the Edwards motion on a technicality,[4] but the Ontario Tory had now placed an unimpeachable resolution on the order paper. Identical to the resolution passed at the Tory convention in Winnipeg in October 1927, it called for a school system 'according to the laws of the respective provinces, but in compliance with the letter and spirit of the constitution.'[5] The constitution referred to was the Alberta Act of 1905. Actually Lapointe approved of the language since it incorporated the separate school guarantee in Section 17 of the Act, but he did not want to allow the Tories the privilege of fathering the school clause in the transfer agreements. Indeed, he suggested a very similar clause in the government's negotiations with Alberta in December 1928.[6] The cabinet was in favour of delaying the Edwards motion until Lapointe's return, and Bennett chivalrously offered to postpone the debate, but King had decided to accept the resolution and insisted on going ahead whether 'Lapointe was there or not.'[7] On 18 February 1929 Edwards presented his motion, and the Speaker witnessed the strange phenomenon of the government voting for an opposition resolution.[8]

King would have given a good deal the next day to have Lapointe present when the troublesome Tory, T.C. Church, moved second reading of his amendment to the Navigation Act. The purpose of Church's bill was to require parliamentary approval for any plan to develop hydroelectric power on the St Lawrence River.[9] A former mayor of Toronto, Tommy Church had united all privately owned utility companies into the Toronto Hydro-Electric Power Commission.[10] Consistent with his belief in public ownership of waterpower, he was out to block a scheme put forward by the Beauharnois syndicate (whose chairman was King's generous friend Senator McDougald) for a giant hydroelectric generating plant on the Quebec section of the river. The promoters of this scheme had obtained a charter from the Taschereau government – always the patron of private utility companies – but because the federal government had jurisdiction over navigation they also needed approval from Ottawa. (The Supreme Court decision on the division of powers had just come down, vaguely on the side of the provinces. Written by Justice Duff, it did little more than muddy the waters.) Under the Beauharnois plan, thousands of feet of water would be diverted into a canal. Tommy Church claimed that diverting such vast quantities of water would 'ruin navigation on the river and kill forever the St Lawrence waterway.'

Deepening the St Lawrence to make it navigable up to the Great Lakes for ocean-going vessels had been under discussion with the United States for years. The American government was keen to move ahead, especially once the engineer Herbert Hoover was in the White House. But King could see little advantage so far as Canada was concerned. It would be an enormously expensive undertaking, and although some Ontario business interests were behind it, Canadians on the whole were indifferent. As usual there was the Quebec factor. The Taschereau government opposed the seaway, foreseeing that the port of Montreal would lose its predominant position if ocean shipping could go up to the Great Lakes.

Tommy Church made a strong case for parliamentary control, and he flayed the government for lending its ear to the lobbyists: 'What the present government needs is a chief bouncer to clear out of the parliament buildings these gentlemen who spend most of the year in the city of Ottawa trying to grab the public domain and the natural resources of the mines, the timber, the forest and water powers of Canada, this magnificent heritage, and divert it to private greed and gain over the head of parliament.'[11]

Cabinet had been batting around the Beauharnois application for months. The Quebec ministers were strongly in favour, and in fact the only holdout was the minister responsible, Jack Elliott, who leaned towards public ownership and insisted on a public hearing. Since the company would be operating completely in Quebec, Cardin thought it was none of Elliott's business: 'What do you think of the Minister of Public Works?' he asked Lapointe. 'It's our affair not his.'[12] King was initially doubtful about the scheme; in the privacy of his diary he wrote that the justice department's opinion 'looks like a bit of drafting to make possible granting of certain powers, not intended by the Navigation Act. We will consider further with care.'[13] However, he gave in when he was finally convinced that the Beauharnois project would not affect the Dominion government's navigation rights. Since he was planning to quietly approve the Beauharnois application by order-in-council, Church's bill was extremely unwelcome to the prime minister. Yet without a good rebuttal, it would look as if the government were trying to evade parliamentary control. The ministers in the House that day (and King himself, he had to admit) proved utterly inadequate in the waterpower debate. 'It was a case where Lapointe was greatly needed,' a humiliated King wrote in his diary.[14]

King also missed Lapointe's solid presence at the bargaining table with Premier Jimmy Gardiner, who had come to Ottawa to negotiate the transfer of Saskatchewan's natural resources. Gardiner was making new and unacceptable demands for compensation. Lapointe fumed as he read the briefs and drafts that King sent over daily. He expressed his frustration that he was unable to back up his chief at the conference with the Saskatchewan delegates. His main concern, of course, was the separate schools issue: 'As far as the school land and the school fund are concerned, there should be the same reservation as in the Alberta proposed agreement; the more so owing to the unanimous vote of Parliament over the Edwards resolution.'[15]

At last on 18 March Lapointe returned to the House. Limping noticeably as he walked to his desk, he was greeted by tumultuous non-partisan applause. Whenever King had to witness Lapointe's extreme popularity he experienced little pinpricks of jealousy. 'It is nice to have him back,' the diary entry began graciously, 'but I did not feel in too pleasant a mood and for a time the House seemed to be at sixes and sevens. Eventually we got onto the budget.' Tommy Church provided his own welcome back for Lapointe by withdrawing his proposed bill to defeat the Beauharnois power project.[16] Church gave no reasons, but undoubtedly Bennett and Premier Ferguson had put pressure on him. Ferguson had dropped his opposition to Beauharnois on Taschereau's assurance that the Quebec company would sell Ontario enormous amounts of power to ease the province's chronic power shortage.[17]

During the Easter recess, news arrived that Sir Lomer Gouin had suffered a fatal heart attack while exercising his duties as lieutenant-governor of Quebec – an office he had held for only three months. King was at Old Point Comfort in Virginia when he heard the news. He immediately left for New York where he planned to catch a train to Quebec City for the funeral. While staying overnight at the Harvard Club, he received a telegram from H.R.L. Henry, his secretary, informing him that Mr Lapointe did not think it necessary for him to attend the funeral. Mr Lapointe felt that it would be a pity for the prime minister to forgo his rest. Moreover, Henry reported, Mr Lapointe did not think it advisable to have Pierre Casgrain, the party whip, represent the prime minister 'as it might emphasize the political side unduly.' In Mr Lapointe's opinion, one of the prime minister's private secretaries would be sufficient.[18] To demean the late Liberal statesman in this way was out of the question. The next day King telephoned Lapointe to say he would most certainly attend the funeral. Lapointe quickly changed his tune, claiming to be pleased that the prime minister would be among the mourners.[19] Lapointe's malice would not have surprised Gouin. It was said on good authority that in a paper attached to his will, Gouin had predicted that the chicanery of Ernest Lapointe would shorten his life.[20]

The Lapointe-Gouin hostilities have a place in the long history of political rivalries. Gouin stood for everything that the populist Lapointe detested. He represented the domination of St James Street – the Montreal financiers whose influence Lapointe countered as best he could throughout his career. Indeed, the journalist Bruce Hutchison questioned 'how any government containing this encrusted Tory and high protectionist could be called Liberal by any known definition.'[21] These were Lapointe's sentiments exactly, and he ultimately got rid of Gouin. For his part Gouin, like his friend and successor in the Quebec premiership, Alexandre Taschereau, regarded Lapointe as a thoroughly impractical politician.[22] Diametrically opposed ideologically, Lapointe and Gouin had stood in each other's way for years. Gouin had shunted Lapointe aside in the early years of the King administration; Lapointe had evened the score by depriving Gouin of the senatorship he craved. Lapointe's reluctant agreement to Gouin's appointment as lieutenant-governor of Quebec had been a trade-off imposed by King.

Lapointe had no complaints about Gouin's replacement. On the train to Montreal after the funeral, King discussed various candidates with Taschereau, Lapointe, and Dandurand. They all agreed on H.G. Carroll.[23] Once the decision was taken over drinks in the club car, it was simply a matter of confirming the appointment at the next cabinet meeting. To have this plum go to his old patron – 'the one man to whom I owe my political life'[24] – was a matter of great satisfaction to Lapointe.

On 11 April 1929 Lapointe's colleagues held a special caucus to celebrate his twenty-five years in Parliament, which coincided with his silver wedding anniversary. He was presented with a sterling tea service and a chest of sterling flatwear. Pierre Casgrain, who organized the event, paid him an elegant tribute in French. Other speakers were Jim

Robb, the finance minister and Lapointe's sometime golfing companion, Senator Dandurand, and of course the prime minister. Lapointe's reply, in which he spoke with sincere affection of their friendship, moved King almost to tears. 'It is indeed a fortunate thing that I have so true & able a colleague from the province of Quebec,' King wrote in his diary.[25]

More substantial was a purse for $125,000 that was presented to Lapointe at a banquet in his honour at Quebec City. There had been talk of a fund for Lapointe for several years, but little had been done until Philippe Paradis took charge. (Paradis had received his own reward for twenty years' service as chief Liberal organizer in Quebec with a Senate seat in 1927.) Before contacting prospective benefactors, Paradis wanted to make sure that the fund met with King's approval: 'You will agree with me that it is most important for the future of our Party to keep our friend into active life and we have, sometimes, fears that on account of ill health he might be willing, one of these days, to retire. Now I know that by relieving him of some of the worries that are impairing his health – and money is one of them, he would continue to render our party invaluable services.'[26] Given the go-ahead by King, Paradis approached wealthy Quebec Liberals, among them Premier Taschereau and Senators Donat Raymond and Dr McDougald. They were all 'exceedingly pleased' to help reach the objective, none more so than Dr McDougald, the chairman of the Beauharnois Power Corporation. King was happy for Lapointe, but happier still that 'my own good fortune [amounting to no less than half a million by this time] is greater than his.'[27]

The perfect harmony between the soulmates was somewhat disturbed towards the end of the parliamentary session over the matter of bilingual stamps. Several commemorative issues had been printed for the Jubilee Year bearing the French 'postes' as well as the English 'postage.' When the postmaster general, P.J. Veniot, a French Catholic from New Brunswick, continued to issue bilingual stamps into 1928 and 1929, King advised him that it was 'a mistake politically to press this bilingual business too far.'[28] He said as much in cabinet and soon realized that Lapointe and Cardin were extremely offended. To help mollify them King enlisted the diplomatic Senator Dandurand.[29] Perhaps the prime minister had forgotten that Dandurand had suggested bilingual stamps to him in 1926 as a sure way of 'holding' the French Canadians. Despite King's warning of a backlash from English Canada, Veniot stuck to his guns.

King suspected that his remarks about bilingual stamps accounted for Lapointe and Cardin's 'antipathy' to a conference for improving trade within the empire. Actually, Lapointe's opposition had nothing to do with the touchy matter of bilingual stamps. As he told King, you never knew what could come out of such a conference.[30] Always mindful of the protectionist boot and shoe industry in Quebec East, Lapointe wanted at all cost to avoid an increase in preferential treatment of British footwear.

Lapointe was scheduled to go to England in the fall for a conference, and before he went abroad King was anxious to have him sign the agreement for the transfer of Manitoba's natural resources. However, there was no time to draw up the formal agreement and draft the necessary legislation before Lapointe left for England on 24 September.[31] King was so set on having Lapointe's signature on the federal-provincial agreements – the Alberta agreement was concluded in the autumn – that although the other signatories signed the agreements on 14 December 1929, Lapointe's signature was not affixed until he returned from England at the end of the month. 'The prime minister preferred that the agreements should be held for Mr. Lapointe's signature rather than some other minister's,' one of the lawyers involved informed Lapointe's deputy minister.[32]

Obviously King felt that Lapointe's signature on the transfer agreements would reassure Quebec that French language rights had been protected. But the federal government's catering to Quebec over separate schools did not play well in the West. In fact, it was partially responsible for the defeat of Jimmy Gardiner's Liberals in Saskatchewan in 1929. In the late 1920s, the Ku Klux Klan was going strong on the prairies and, together with the Orange Lodges, whipped up religious and ethnic prejudices. Gardiner's beleaguered attorney general wrote King in the heat of the provincial election that the Conservatives were fear-mongering with such slogans as 'Quebec dominates Canada and the Roman Catholic church dominates Quebec.'[33] The Tory leader, Dr J.T.M. Anderson, made good use of the bilingual issue to win the election.

Premier Anderson proved more difficult to deal with than the Liberal Jimmy Gardiner when it came to wrapping up the transfer of Saskatchewan's natural resources. King and Lapointe began negotiating with him right after the new year. On 17 February 1930 Anderson sent them a draft memorandum of agreement. Lapointe read it with horror. Under paragraph 7, school lands were to be administered 'in accordance with the law of the province.' They were right back to 1926! Lapointe drafted a telegram for King to send Anderson: 'Paragraph 7 would be a fundamental departure from both Alberta and Manitoba agreements and might virtually destroy the trust that has been created for purposes of education, and cannot be accepted.'[34]

Early in March 1930 Anderson came to Ottawa and ultimately agreed to the same school clause as the one in the Alberta and Manitoba agreements. To the end, the school clause was a bone of contention. Indeed, to get Anderson to sign on the dotted line King and Lapointe had to agree that the province could launch a constitutional challenge.[35] Anderson contended that the Dominion government did not have the right to retain the province's natural resources in the first place. King was confident that the province would lose; but Lapointe's fears had not been unfounded that the question of separate schools in the West would not be 'definitively settled' until the Judicial Committee of the Privy Council spoke.

CHAPTER FIFTEEN

The 1929 Conference on the Operation of Dominion Legislation

Ernest Lapointe arrived in London in October 1929 to head the Canadian delegation to the Conference on the Operation of Dominion Legislation (ODL). The Balfour report from the Imperial Conference of 1926 had recommended equal status with Britain for the self-governing Dominions, but it had not spelled out how this was to be achieved. Instead, it provided for a committee of legal experts to survey British statutes affecting the Dominions and to recommend which ones should be amended or repealed. The purpose of the present conference was to carry out this task before the next Imperial Conference in 1930.[1]

The British Parliament still had the power to reserve on Dominion legislation and to disallow it. A particularly obnoxious example of legal inferiority was the Colonial Laws Validity Act of 1865, which rendered null and void any Dominion statute that conflicted with imperial legislation. Moreover, Canada, like the other Dominions, had no extraterritorial jurisdiction: once outside Canadian territory a Canadian was (with few exceptions) free of Canadian law. As Lapointe was only too aware, the courts regularly invoked imperial statutes to override Canadian legislation regarding shipping and navigation. A subconference on merchant shipping had been set up to deal with the outmoded restrictions on Dominion ships. But the main example of Canada's legal subordination was the British North America Act itself, and here Lapointe's hands were tied. Ontario, Quebec, and the Maritimes had made it clear at the Dominion-Provincial Conference in 1927 that they did not want Canada to have the right to amend its own constitution.

This time the *Ottawa Journal* could not say, as it had in 1927 when Lapointe represented Canada at the Naval Disarmaments Conference, that he did not have advisers capable of matching minds with the British. Lapointe was accompanied by outstanding legal experts. There was John Read, who had just retired as dean of Dalhousie Law School to become legal adviser to the department of external affairs.[2] Also from Nova Scotia was Charles Burchell, whose expertise in marine law earned him the chairmanship of the sub-conference on merchant shipping legislation.[3] To help with the drafting, Lapointe had brought Maurice Ollivier, the law clerk of the House of Commons – a constitutional expert in his own right. Dr O.D. Skelton, the under-secretary of external affairs, was there advising Lapointe at every turn.

Skelton was planning to 'link up with the Irish again,' as he wrote his wife, and he wasted no time in arranging a luncheon for the Irish delegates in Lapointe's suite. Skelton felt that the informal discussion had been 'very successful in preparing the way for working together.'[4] A less political gathering took place in Lapointe's suite that evening. In honour of his birthday, the Canadians fêted him with a midnight supper and presented him with a fine leather golf bag. Genuinely pleased, Lapointe tendered a most graceful thank-you: 'I usually spend the day with my family,' he told them. 'But I am very pleased to spend it this time with my friends, for, as a French author has said, friends are relatives whom we have chosen ourselves.'[5]

Skelton and his legal experts were not expecting the conference to be clear sailing. In a forty-eight-page memorandum for Lapointe, John Read set out the difficulties he expected would arise from the fact that the Dominions were divided. At one extreme, the Irish Free State would accept nothing less than complete independence from Britain. South Africa under its Afrikaner leaders was not far behind. At the other extreme, Australia and New Zealand were still in a state of dependency on the mother country (and indeed would opt out of the legislative autonomy offered in the Statute of Westminster when the time came). A Maritimer, John Read used seafaring idiom to make his point. Canada could not safely agree to be 'put in the same boat' as New Zealand and Australia. 'Progress is slowed to the speed of the slowest ship in the squadron,' he warned Lapointe.[6]

By coincidence, Lapointe received a letter from Senator Dandurand along the same lines. Dandurand was in Paris, having just attended a meeting of the League of Nations Council in Geneva. 'I am happy to know that you are involved in a work which interests me greatly,' he wrote Lapointe, 'and I wish you success.' Dandurand predicted that resistance to removing the legal vestiges of colonialism would not come from London; it would come from Australia and New Zealand. If no general understanding was possible, he suggested that Canada might make individual accords with Great Britain.[7]

England had a new government since Lapointe's last visit. Stanley Baldwin's Conservatives had been replaced by the Labour party under Ramsay MacDonald. The change of guard meant that Lapointe dealt with new people, many of whom like the home secretary, J.R. Clynes, came from the working classes. On his first day in London Lapointe had lunch with Sir William Jowitt, a former Liberal who had switched parties to become the attorney general in the Labour government. The new secretary for the Dominions and colonies was Lord Passfield. The former Sidney Webb, he and his wife Beatrice were the foremost intellectuals of British socialism. No sooner had Lapointe arrived than he was invited by the Canada Club to 'support the toast' to the newly created Lord Passfield. Later in his stay he met both Webbs socially at Sir William Jowitt's home. A 'Political At Home' at Mrs Philip Snowden's – the socially ambitious wife of the chancellor of the exchequer – brought introductions to other members of MacDonald's cabinet.[8]

At the conference Lapointe was determined to give legal force to the equal status he and King had won in principle at the Imperial Conference three years earlier. But he was not prepared to go as far as Skelton and the Irish would have liked, and he rejected at least one memo the under-secretary prepared for him.[9] While Lapointe distrusted the British negotiators, he did not share Skelton's dislike of the British connection. In King's opinion, Skelton was 'at heart against the British empire.'

Lapointe soon saw that the British were using the division among the Dominions to try to maintain a position as first among equals. This was evident in Sir William Jowitt's remarks at the session on merchant shipping at the Foreign Office on 22 October. The war had shown the importance of national merchant shipping, Jowitt said, and faced with international competition 'British ships should stand together as a united whole.' In his learned opinion, the present system of classifying the merchant fleets of the Dominions as British ships should not be altered except by common consent of all concerned – certainly not at the will of any single part. 'I take it none of us would wish to do anything that would detract from the present position which the British ship occupies,' Sir William stated confidently.[10] The Australian and New Zealand delegates nodded in agreement.

Here was Britain up to its old centralizing tricks, Lapointe thought. The changeover to a Labour government had made no difference. If

Canadian ships were simply classified as British ships, how could Canada be regarded as a nation in its own right in the world's eyes? It was similar to the galling situation Canada faced at the League of Nations. In his letter Dandurand had recounted a recent incident at the League Council. During a discussion on ratification, the president omitted to say that Canada had ratified thirteen of the conventions. When Dandurand drew his attention to the omission, the president blandly remarked that neither Australia's nor Canada's names were in the list because they were comprised under the rubric of the British Empire. Dandurand told Lapointe that in his fury he had banged his fist on the table and actually shouted that 'we weren't under anybody's wing and Canada should appear like any other member.'[11]

Lapointe spoke out quietly but just as passionately at the Foreign Office. 'What we must have in Canada, as a fully self-governing community, is full and complete legislative authority over Canadian ships,' he told the British. Under the Merchant Shipping Act of 1894 Canada had no legal authority over British ships coming into its harbours or territorial waters. Moreover, British ships enjoyed the same rights to the Canadian coastal trade as Canadian ships. Lapointe declared that these restrictions on Canadian autonomy must be removed. All ships in Canadian waters must be subject to Canadian laws – and that included British ships. He suggested that instead of a piecemeal repeal of the Merchant Shipping Act, 'which derogate so completely from Canada as an autonomous community,' the Canadian Parliament should be given full power to repeal any existing imperial legislation regarding navigation and shipping that was repugnant to Canada's autonomous status. After this clearing of the decks, 'the Canadian Parliament would be free to enact legislation as it deemed advisable in the interest of Canada.' 'The legal situation in Canada is quite embarrassing and confusing and calls for immediate remedy,' Lapointe told the conference. Having delivered himself of this stern message, the head of the Canadian delegation remarked amiably that he and his colleagues would always be agreeable to sit around the table and work out model sections of the final report with other members of the Commonwealth.[12]

At the next session Lapointe set out to scuttle the offensive term 'British ship' as applying to all Dominion vessels. 'The British Commonwealth of Nations is an association not a federation nor a political unit,' he reminded the British statesmen sitting around the table. 'The idea of a single appellation for all ships is not in accordance with the present situation.' South Africa and the Irish Free State supported

Canada. Sir William Jowitt salvaged what he could: Would 'British ship, Canadian registry' meet Mr Lapointe's suggestion? Lapointe acknowledged that it would. The discussion concluded with general agreement that each part of the Commonwealth could legislate as it liked, and any uniformity would have to be secured through cooperation and voluntary agreements. Since that was what the Dominions seemed to prefer, Sir William stated, he would not stand in their way. Perhaps to twist the lion's tail, Dr Skelton gravely announced at the session on 25 October that Canada wanted to be at liberty to change the details of the Red Ensign, such as adding the Maple Leaf. 'Anything that admitted the right of the Admiralty to decide what should be the flag of Canada is objectionable,' Lapointe added.[13] This 'acrimonious' discussion rankled with Jowitt, and at the Lord Mayor's banquet he complained to Lapointe about Skelton, calling him the 'the most extreme nationalist in the whole conference.'[14]

Much of Lapointe's efforts were devoted to securing equal status with Britain in merchant shipping. As he told the conference, 'We want to make clear to the world that we are a self-governing nation in shipping as other [areas], at the same time indicate our association in the Commonwealth.'[15] (It is important to note that however independent he sounded, Lapointe did not consider severing the British connection; in fact, he took Canada's continued membership in the empire/Commonwealth as a given.) He and his experts believed they had secured their aim. Canada would no longer be bound by the colonial sections of the Merchant Shipping Act and the Admiralty Act. The final report also contained the recommendation that 'each part [of the Commonwealth] would have full power to deal with its own coasting trade.' However, as a concession Lapointe agreed 'for a limited number of years to continue the present position under which ships of any part of the commonwealth are free to engage in the coasting trade of any other part.'[16]

Opening its coastal trade to empire ships was like letting the camel in the tent. The voluntary arrangement that could be revoked at any time became hard and fast under the British Commonwealth Merchant Shipping Agreement of 1931. Canadian ships could not compete with the British for a number of reasons, and during the 1930s British shipping was to dominate Canada's coastal trade, and most Canadian ships preferred to sail under British registry. A naval historian has written that 'in undertaking not to close the coastal trade to Empire ships, the Canadian government surrendered one of the primary instruments employed by nations intent on fostering their merchant marine and shipbuilding industries.'[17] But this was later. For the moment, Lapointe and his experts were satisfied that, supported by South Africa and the Irish Free State, Canada had torpedoed the prevailing system of centralized control of merchant shipping.

Other imperial restrictions on Dominion autonomy sank without a ripple. The obnoxious Colonial Laws Validity Act, as it applied to the Dominions, went by the board. The conference recommended that henceforth no laws passed at Westminster should extend to any Dominion except at the request and with the consent of that country. Canada would have extraterritorial jurisdiction over its nationals, its ships, and airships. Indeed, the British were ready to go further than Canada required, offering legislation that would enable Canada to amend its own constitution.[18] Lapointe would have loved to take this step, but as he told Skelton, he felt he would have to bring the provinces on side first.[19]

On one ground the British stood firm, and Canada and the 'down under' Dominions lined up beside them. Any alteration touching the succession to the Throne and the royal style and titles would require the consent of all the Parliaments in the Commonwealth. Beyers of South Africa found even this unacceptable. In an angry letter to Lord Passfield he stated that to impose unanimity was to fall into the very error that had been so deliberately avoided at the Imperial Conference of 1926 – the laying down of a constitution for the British Empire.[20]

Just when it looked as if the delegates could pack up and go home, a series of last-minute crises reared up. The report had to be unanimous, and Moore of Australia, a hair-splitting professor of constitutional law, threatened to dissent. Lapointe and Jowitt laboured long and hard at a tedious session in Lapointe's suite to talk him out of it. At the same time Beyers, whom Skelton regarded as 'the most obstinate Dutchman in history,' refused to sign until he had heard from Prime Minister Hertzog. It took some five days to get clearance from Pretoria. Then came the largest obstacle: Lord Passfield suddenly reneged, fearing the wrath of anti-Irish Tories. At this, Lapointe showed his mettle. 'Mr. Lapointe, very pacific hitherto, put the fear of the Lord into Passfield and Harding [Passfield's under-secretary],' Skelton reported to King with obvious relish.[21]

It had been a cliffhanger. At last, on 4 December 1929, the report was signed. The principle of Dominion autonomy was translated into legislative recommendations. The 'Report of the Conference on the Operation of Dominion Legislation and Merchant Shipping Legislation' was to be submitted to the Dominions before being made public. After passage by the Commonwealth Parliaments, it would be put before the Imperial Conference of 1930. The next and final step would be enactment by the British Parliament. Maurice Ollivier observed that Lapointe really led the conference.[22] And Skelton would later report to King that 'the Canadian delegation was fortunate in having at its head the best-informed member of the Conference, through his participation in the 1926 discussion, as well as its outstanding personality.'[23]

As the official representative of the senior Dominion, Lapointe no doubt anticipated an audience with the king. King George was always hospitable to important visitors from the Commonwealth, but no invitation was forthcoming from Buckingham Palace. Through the home secretary it was arranged that Lapointe would have the opportunity, at least, to 'shake hands' with Queen Mary, who would descend briefly from her Daimler on her stately way to an official engagement. Even this was cancelled because of rain.[24] Meanwhile, Lapointe learned that General Smuts (who was in London, though not at the conference) had been invited by King George to stay at Sandringham. When Mackenzie King heard that the South African had been invited to the palace while Lapointe had been ignored, he 'spoke plainly' to the governor general about it. In due course the royal response came back through the same channel: His Majesty would see whom he pleased.[25] Lapointe's very success at the conference had probably denied him the royal invitation. King George deeply resented the loosening of the imperial ties.

While Lapointe was in England the law lords of the Judicial Committee of the Privy Council handed down their decision on the appeal in the 'Persons' case. The lord chancellor, Lord Sankey (whom Lapointe had met at the Garrick Club), totally demolished the unanimous judgment of Canada's Supreme Court. 'The exclusion of women from public office was a relic of days more barbarous than ours,' Lord Sankey declared, and figuratively slapped the Canadian judges on the wrist for turning to Roman law and early English decisions as an aid in interpreting the British North America Act. The British North America Act was not the fossil postulated by Chief Justice Anglin but 'a living tree capable of growth and expansion within its natural limits.' His lordship concluded that women were persons within the meaning of the constitution and therefore eligible for the Canadian Senate.[26]

At this time, cables were flying back and forth between Lapointe and King over the replacement of one of the Supreme Court justices who had concurred in Chief Justice Anglin's overturned decision. Justice Mignault, an authority on Quebec civil law, had reached the mandatory retirement age of seventy-five,[27] leaving only one sitting justice from Quebec. According to tradition, civil law cases required a panel with two Quebec justices. A civil law case was waiting to be heard, and early in October King sent a coded cablegram to Lapointe urging an immediate replacement for Mignault.

He was no doubt taken aback by the reply. This was not his senior colleague's usual cooperative attitude. The appointment was so important, Lapointe cabled his chief, that he would prefer leaving it until he returned. 'Vacancy occurring while I am away surely sufficient excuse for postponement.' If King was determined to go ahead without him (and he clearly disapproved this course), he recommended the Quebec City lawyer Louis St Laurent or, second best, Lucien Cannon's brother Arthur, a judge of the Quebec Court of King's Bench. In view of Lapointe's strong feelings, King held off on the appointment.[28]

Strengthening the Supreme Court was certainly important. Moreover, Lapointe was naturally concerned to have a sound interpreter of Quebec's Civil Code on the predominantly common law court. But his reason for delaying the judicial appointment until he was back in Canada may have been that he wanted it for himself. After all, he could and did propose names from abroad. His delaying tactics suggest there might have been something to the persistent speculation that he would quit politics and go to the bench. This becomes more probable in light of his cable to King a few weeks later. It reveals a Lapointe seriously disgruntled at this period of his career, dissatisfied with his cabinet post and with what he perceived as Quebec's diminishing influence in the King administration. These sentiments surfaced, oddly enough, over the cabinet appointment of his special friend, Tom Crerar.

In November Jim Robb died suddenly of pneumonia. His post of finance minister was immediately filled by Charles Dunning. This opened up the railways portfolio, and King offered it to Crerar, who accepted. King cabled Lapointe in London: 'Crerar prepared to enter cabinet if given railways. Have not broached matter to any Quebec colleague, intending to hold over possible rearrangement of portfolios pending your return. Little fearful if we delay Crerar may hold back later though ready to come into government at once.' Lapointe and King had been trying since 1921 to convince Crerar to come to Ottawa. After eight years Crerar had finally given in.

King had every reason to expect Lapointe to be as jubilant as he was.

Instead, he received this coded cable: 'Crerar would add great strength and personally welcome to me but foresee difficulties if he insists on Railways. Balance and proportion in allocation of departments would be considerably disturbed. Quebec losing heavily. After '21 had Marine, Justice, Customs, Trade and Commerce, plus Soldiers and Health. With Finance gone, Marine only important Department left. Justice honorific but without business influence or patronage. Secretary of State and Solicitor General valueless positions.'[29] The tone of the cable was so bleak that King wired back that he would try to postpone final negotiations with Crerar until Lapointe returned. Nevertheless, he slipped in that if deferred too long it might be impossible to keep Crerar favourable. King had no intention of letting the fish get off the hook. The writs were issued for a by-election in Brandon, Manitoba, and Crerar was assured that he would have Railways.

On 15 December Lapointe sailed home. It was a stormy passage and there was trouble with the ship's engines. Seasickness, combined with his poor state of health, made the crossing an ordeal.[30] Arriving a day late in New York, Lapointe was in no mood to find the publisher of *La Tribune de Sherbrooke* waiting for him, greatly disturbed over Crerar's appointment as minister of railways. Fortin and his paper had been plumping for Charles Howard, the MP for Sherbrooke in the Eastern Townships. Fortin claimed that Mackenzie King had promised not to do anything until Lapointe returned, and he called Crerar's appointment 'treason to our province.' He demanded that Howard be taken into the cabinet. Lapointe was cold. 'You don't get in the cabinet by forcing the door,' he told him.

Dissatisfied now with Lapointe as well as King, Fortin published an article highly critical of both of them over the Crerar nomination and sent a copy to Lapointe. In a handwritten reply, Lapointe called the article 'deplorable.' Fortin and Howard's other friends were 'rendering him bad service' by their persistence, he said. 'A prime minister would not deserve to be a chief if such tactics could influence him.' Unrepentant, Fortin responded with a diatribe: 'Quebec's situation in the cabinet could make you weep. Maple syrup served to us since we've had this supreme stupidity of giving our confidence to these exploiters. They will continue to mock us, exploit us and use our inexhaustible stupidity as a springboard for a spurious national policy that is neither just, nor national, nor intelligent. I'm beginning to think it's time to join the opposition. We've had enough, Mr. Lapointe.'[31]

It was as if Fortin had turned up the volume on Lapointe's own bitter cable to King from London. But if he felt a sneaking sympathy with Fortin's views, he did not show it. On 29 December Crerar arrived in Ottawa and went directly to Laurier House for lunch. King invited Lapointe to join them, and the three had a jovial reunion, making fun of Chief Justice Anglin's pretensions before getting down to serious business. King suggested that it would be better not to make an appointment from the Eastern Townships at present since he had to keep something open for Stewart, whose department was vanishing with the transfer of natural resources to the western provinces. Later in the day Lapointe contacted Cardin and they agreed not to insist on a Quebec appointment. Despite his complaints about losing Quebec cabinet posts, Lapointe had yielded up another when King asked him.[32]

He also gave in about going to the Supreme Court. Immediately on his return from England, he laid to rest the rumours that he was leaving politics. On 23 December a *Montreal Star* headline blared, 'Stays in Cabinet. Minister of Justice Not to Go to Supreme Court Bench.' In January 1930 Arthur Cannon was named to fill the vacancy.

CHAPTER SIXTEEN

Defeat

In the late summer of 1929, a young journalist named Wilfrid Eggleston was sent to Ottawa by the *Toronto Star*. To him 'everyone in Ottawa seemed to be playing the stock market. It was a fever. The brokers' offices were jammed to the doorway during the lunch hour. The gossip of the day ran to stories of killings made by lucky speculators.'[1] On 29 October 1929 the euphoria ended abruptly. Wall Street crashed, causing devastation on the Canadian stock exchanges. Lapointe probably invested some of his newly acquired capital of $125,000 in the stock market before the Crash since he was short of money in the early 1930s and, in fact, could not pay his full taxes in 1933 and 1934.[2] But in 1930, even with large paper losses, he was among the fortunate with $10,000 a year as minister of justice and a further $4,000 indemnity.

The business world ushered in 1930 with optimistic forecasts. However, Canada as a wheat-producing nation was especially vulnerable because of a sharp decline in the world price. Hoping for a better price, the wheat pools let the 1928 and 1929 crops pile up in the grain elevators, and without wheat to ship freight trains were grinding to a halt, as were the iron and steel mills that supplied rails and rolling stock. Pulp and paper mills were going bankrupt because of reduced demand for newsprint in the United States, which was already feeling the full effects of the worldwide depression. When Parliament opened on 20 February 1930 unemployment was a growing problem, but this went unrecognized in the throne speech. King and Lapointe regarded unemployment relief as a provincial and municipal responsibility, and King, if not Lapointe, was sanguine that the unemployment was simply seasonal and therefore 'normal.' On 25 February he actually predicted in the House that 'Canada might well find 1930 to be the most prosperous year of her whole history.' King was going to the country sometime during the year with complete confidence that his government would be returned.

Outside the rarified precincts of Parliament, the situation looked very different to the people on the ground. Towards the end of March Lapointe received a letter from a Manitoba high school principal who identified himself as 'a firm liberal friend' although unknown personally to the minister. The writer had heard rumours that the Liberals were going to call an election after the present session. They would be 'the most foolish people on earth' if they did, he warned Lapointe. Mackenzie King should hang on to office as long as possible, otherwise the Liberals in the West would get 'the worst licking they ever received.'

Unemployment was terrible in the West, the combined effect of low grain prices and a ruinous drought. In Saskatchewan, said the writer, there was province-wide antipathy to former premier Gardiner. He should be given some office at Ottawa so provincial Liberals could pick a new leader to bring the party back into power. As for Liberalism in Manitoba, the writer pronounced it 'simply dead.' He predicted which seats the Liberals would lose, conceding that Dunning's popularity might hold Regina. Religious bigotry was sweeping through the prairies, and according to the writer the Tories were catering to it. 'Mackenzie King is pictured as being in alliance with the *Pope*, and you with forcing *French* on the *Protestants* of Saskatchewan.' As an Irish Catholic the writer felt he could be blunt.[3] Lapointe took this letter from the unknown Liberal seriously enough to send a copy to King, who had it filed without comment.

As the election loomed, office seekers closed in upon Lapointe. A Quebec lawyer demanded to be appointed attorney for the revenue department. The president of Toronto's Liberal Association wanted his 'fair share' of government legal work in the city. An elderly doctor in King's riding of Prince Albert in Saskatchewan solicited the position of medical officer in the local penitentiary. Mackenzie King himself exerted pressure on Lapointe to fill vacancies at the Prince Albert penitentiary with loyal Liberals. A daughter of a long-time Liberal in Prince Edward Island wrote 'a pathetic little note' begging a judgeship for her father.[4] The cabinet was split on last-minute appointments to the bench; King gladly left it to Lapointe to do as 'you yourself deem best and will follow whatever course you suggest.'[5]

There were three Quebec vacancies in the Senate, and Lapointe and

Cardin convinced King that they should be filled before the election. One went to Rodolphe Lemieux – King would have liked to keep him on as Speaker of the House, but Lapointe and Cardin did not want him. King let them choose the other two Quebec senators as well, though he did not think much of their choices. George Parent, the publisher of *Le Soleil*, was 'a poor type,' but King assumed that Lapointe and Cardin felt a senatorship was necessary to hold his paper for the party; the other new senator was 'a buffoon,' but it seemed that Cardin was depending upon him to help him out of a difficult situation. 'It is useless to oppose the French colleagues,' King wrote in his diary. 'They know their problems and apparently this is the only way they can effectively meet them.'[6]

Meanwhile, the appointment of the first woman senator was generating a good deal of excitement. King had chosen a wealthy Ottawa housewife and mother of eight, Mrs Norman Wilson. His choice disappointed Thérèse Casgrain, who had hoped to see the honour go to one of the five western women who had 'opened the doors of the Senate to Canadian women,'[7] and it infuriated Mr Norman Wilson, who telephoned the governor general to say that he and his wife did not want the appointment. It turned out that he was speaking only for himself. Mrs Wilson told the prime minister that even if it meant a divorce she would accept the senatorship.[8] (She added that 'Norman would be alright,' and so he was after he recovered from the initial shock.) When Senator Cairine Wilson made her maiden speech on 25 February 1930, Ernest Lapointe was seated in a place of honour on the floor of the Senate in recognition of his role in facilitating this epoch-making event.[9] Though he had failed to keep his promise to have the BNA Act amended to enable women to sit in the Senate, he had funded the western women's appeals and this had given him a reputation as their sponsor.

Of far greater importance to Lapointe than a token woman in the Senate was getting Parliament to sanction the changes to British law recommended at the 1929 London conference. On 26 May he tabled the report on the Operation of Dominion Legislation and Merchant Shipping Legislation. Once approved by the House it would go to the Senate and then to London to be presented at the 1930 Imperial Conference. Displaying the 'fine legal mind and acute powers of analysis' that so impressed a visiting American reporter at this time, Lapointe explained the report's various recommendations, which amounted to no less than emancipation from the restrictive laws of the mother country. The leader of the opposition, a match for Lapointe in legal controversy, was scathing about the boasted autonomy. There could be no such thing as equal status, said R.B. Bennett, as long as Canada could not amend its own constitution. Though Lapointe privately shared Bennett's view, he was forced to defend the policy imposed upon the federal government by the provinces. Putting the best face on it, he argued that 'this condition exists solely by the will of the Canadian people, and not by reason of the control of a superior non-Canadian authority. Indeed, the British authorities would gladly relinquish the exercise of such functions.' How could this be considered a condition of subordination, he asked Bennett, 'when all restrictions rest upon our own will.'[10]

The difference between the King-Lapointe nationalism and Tory imperialism stood out starkly in this debate. The concept of autonomous communities within the Commonwealth was offensive to Bennett. 'What resentment did they harbour against the little islands in the North Sea?' he asked the Liberals.[11] Bennett favoured the unitary system of empire, whereby Great Britain and the Dominions spoke with a single voice. (Whose voice, of course, was a question he did not have to answer in opposition.) Bennett accused the government of breaking this proud empire into fragments. When Bennett's bombast had blown out its force, Lapointe's resolution calling for the approval of the ODL conference recommendations was carried.

As it happened there was a constitutional amendment to be dealt with the following day. The agreements for the transfer of natural resources had been ratified by the provincial legislatures and Parliament. This substantive change required an amendment to the BNA Act. On 27 May 1930 the House of Commons passed an Address to the King 'praying for the enactment by the Parliament of the United Kingdom of Great Britain and Northern Ireland of an Act confirming the Agreement between the Dominion and the Provinces of Manitoba, British Columbia, Alberta and Saskatchewan regarding the transfer of Natural Resources.' In spite of the archaic language and the subservient procedure, Mackenzie King insisted it was an example of Canada amending its own constitution. The Parliament at Westminster 'simply lends its good offices, so to speak,' he told the House. This method of proceeding in no way lessened the significance of it being 'our own amendment.' R.B. Bennett scoffed. In his opinion it was 'complete and absolute proof' that Canada did not have full autonomy.[12] Despite Bennett's cavils, the 1929 London conference giving legislative form to the Balfour Declaration of 1926 effectively marked the end of Canada's colonial status. Lapointe was understandably proud of the constitutional changes he and King had achieved, and he dwelt upon them in his campaign speeches. Chubby Power was closer to the grass roots, and he had his doubts that this was a good selling point.

The election was announced for 28 July, and as soon as the Parliamentary session ended the campaigning began. Chubby Power observed that the prime minister had lost the fire and vigour he had shown in 1926. Unemployment had overtaken King's agenda of a balanced budget and minimum government intervention. For the first time his finger was off the nation's pulse. He seemed insensitive to the plight of the unemployed. In fact, the overly cautious King, who usually weighed every word he spoke, had made an incredible blunder during the session. Provoked by Woodsworth and Heaps, he had bellowed that he would not give a five-cent piece for relief to any province with a Tory government. It was a gift to his opponents. The millionaire Bennett barnstormed the country, thundering that he would cure unemployment 'or perish in the attempt.' He would 'blast his way' into world markets, at the same time protecting Canadian manufacturers behind a tariff wall. He promised to hold an emergency session of Parliament right after his election.

King and Lapointe campaigned in tandem as they had not done since 1921. It was as if King needed Lapointe's oratorical fire to warm his own tepid performance. On 19 June they launched their campaign at an open-air meeting in Quebec City. Thousands of people mainly of the working classes had come out to hear them. Unfortunately the weather could not have been worse – steady rain sporadically turning to a torrential downpour. Invoking the famous Macdonald-Cartier and Baldwin-Lafontaine partnerships, the prime minister declared that the present government ought to be called the King-Lapointe ministry. 'Ernest Lapointe has been a leader in the full meaning of the word,' King told his audience. There had never been the least divergence of opinion between them. They were in perfect accord. 'We are inspired by Laurier and we count on continuing to apply to the administration of the affairs of this country the principles of the great chieftain.' The huge crowd standing stoically in the rain was unable to respond approvingly, being too occupied in holding up their umbrellas and trying not to dump water on their neighbours. The scarlet draperies garlanding a huge portrait of King were in sodden tatters and streams of dye ran down the smiling image like tears.

Still, the crowd remained to hear Lapointe. Introduced as the worthy successor to Laurier, Lapointe stressed Canada's progress in the economic, social, and international spheres. He accused the Tories of seeking to diminish Canada's importance in the eyes of the world. If the present government was re-elected, he would be one of those entrusted with the promotion of Canadian status abroad. Understanding full well the French-Canadian sense of grievance, he declared that the King government stood for equality of the races: 'No class has a monopoly on intelligence and patriotism, but all have the right to be represented in the administration of the public body, and the Liberal government is ready to give their representatives that to which they have the right.'[13] This went down very well with the crowd. The mass of French Canadians believed that Lapointe had always done his best for them at Ottawa. The audience found their hands and applauded him vigorously. But neither Lapointe nor King had given the sodden crowd anything to cheer about. Although not yet in the grip óf the Great Depression, Quebeckers were only too conscious of the hard times just across the border in the northern United States. Afterwards King wrote in his diary that Lapointe spoke well. He himself was in anguish because 'I did not do myself justice.'

Next came a whirlwind tour through the prairies, starting at Edmonton on 10 July. King and Lapointe relied on their past record, but westerners were hurting and they wanted to know what the government would do for them in the present hard times. At the Edmonton meeting a heckler interrupted King's flow. 'What about unemployment,' he called out. Incredibly, King replied, 'I believe there are people who are unemployed because they do not want to work.' Protests flared up across the room like wildfire. Someone cried out: 'Take back those words!' King's response was to charge the speaker with being one of those slackers.[14] By the time they reached Saskatoon, King had smartened up enough to express concern over unemployment, but neither he nor Lapointe really addressed the plight of the unemployed. Wherever Lapointe spoke he got a good hand; nevertheless balanced budgets and diplomatic triumphs were of limited interest to his listeners. Meanwhile, Bennett was being well received in Lapointe's own fiefdom of Rivière-du-Loup and Quebec City.[15]

When he was not with King, Lapointe stumped northern Ontario. Indeed, he had little time for his own riding, relying upon Senator Paradis to do the organizing as usual, and he opened his campaign at Quebec's St Roch market only four days before the election. Having spent so much time abroad since the last election, he was virtually a stranger to his constituents. Oscar Drouin, the MLA for Quebec East, had warned him some months earlier that he was losing touch and had urged him to come to Quebec to inaugurate the 'magnificent' new club rooms of the Club Mercier: 'It will give you a chance to meet the voters of St Roch and Jacques Cartier. You've been away a long time and I humbly advise you its time to renew contact with your voters in Quebec East.'[16]

Running against a Quebec nationalist, Lapointe met considerable opposition in his riding fuelled by the shoe manufacturers. By increasing British preference the Dunning budget had effectively lowered the tariff on imported footwear from Britain. The workers in the shoe factories were fearful for their jobs and unconvinced by Lapointe's argument that British imports did not compete because they differed in variety and price.[17] Moreover, Lapointe was having his usual problems with the politically insensitive Sir Henry Thornton. Thornton had just announced a major lay-off of CNR workers in and around Quebec City effective election day! Lapointe fired off a furious telegram to the CNR president:

Am informed that following short investigations that lasted but one hour or two in certain places a large number of men from nearly all stations in this district have been notified that their services would not be required any more for reasons of economy and that this order was to be effective morning of July 28th STOP I understand that changes might have to be made for reasons of economy but I think it is most unfair to effect such changes during an electoral campaign when enough issues are at stake without adding new problems and creating unrest among certain classes of the population STOP I would appreciate if such orders were suspended until I can see you and discuss this question.[18]

While Thornton may have postponed the lay-off in the Quebec district, he was deaf to Lapointe's pleas in the case of three railway conductors from Rivière-du-Loup who had been discharged for pocketing cash fares. Since this would leave them without their pensions, sympathy for the men was running high. Rivière-du-Loup was up in arms on their behalf. Lapointe was under severe pressure not only from public delegations but from Jean-François Pouliot, the MP for the district. It would be a personal favour, Lapointe wrote Thornton, if these employees could be reinstated, or at least if the one who was just a few months away from retirement could have his pension. Thornton replied that the men had the right to appeal to the Canadian Railway Board of

Adjustment but had chosen not to do so. As for himself, he could and would do nothing for them.[19]

When election day came around, Lapointe managed to hold his riding with a comfortable majority, but the Tories took twenty-four seats in the province. Chubby Power proved right that Quebec voters were not interested in the Balfour report and Canada's new status on the world stage. 'The authority and prestige of Lapointe in this campaign was lower than it was before or afterwards,' he wrote in his memoirs, 'and there was a consequent deterioration in the strength of his leadership in the Quebec district.'[20]

Liberal losses in Quebec contributed substantially to Bennett's victory. When the votes were counted, the Conservatives held 138 seats, the Liberals 90, and 17 seats were divided among farmers and labour. The result was 'a great surprise' to King. In an age before polls, a leader could be so out of touch with the electorate that on the eve of the election King was confident he would win with a good majority. Unlike the 1925 election, he held his seat, but there was widespread carnage among his cabinet. Dunning and Crerar lost their seats. Power held his, but Lucien Cannon was defeated. In New Brunswick, Veniot was the sole Liberal elected – 'He'll find out the new ministry will give short shrift to bilingual stamps,' King told his diary.[21] King convened his cabinet for the last time on 6 August. Emotions were held in check until the end of the meeting when Lapointe turned to King and said, 'We are all proud of our leader' and shook his hand. There was a general shaking of hands then and gulping back of tears.

The post-mortems began immediately. A Saskatchewan Liberal attributed his defeat in great part to Lapointe. This very unhappy man reminded King that 'before we came west, all the men from Saskatchewan decided absolutely against having a man from Quebec come to this province.' How did it happen that Lapointe came out here against all their wishes? Headquarters should have abided by them. 'We knew perfectly well what would be the effect since their [sic] was such a terrible cry against domination of Quebec.' It did not matter that there was no truth in it; the people believed it and that was enough. They all 'thought the world of Mr. Lapointe,' he said, but 'there is no doubt his visit did us a very great deal of harm. I am sure it did to me anyway.'[22]

King's reply was a heartfelt testimony to his decade-long partnership with Lapointe and his policy of sharing government with his French lieutenant: 'I am afraid I must take the larger share of responsibility for Lapointe's going to the West. I have, as you know, always endeavoured to have it appear and have him feel that there was no monopoly of leadership so far as I myself was concerned, but that the two of us working together as one was an evidence in itself of the unity which Liberalism seeks to create and which has found a place in the hearts of so many of its adherents.'[23] On a less exalted plane, King defended himself by pointing out that there were large French-Canadian pockets in a number of prairie constituencies. Nevertheless, he conceded that bringing Lapointe with him on the western campaign trail might have been ill-advised. Anti-French sentiment was so prevalent during the election that the Shredded Wheat company announced it was abolishing bilingual packaging in western Canada. It seems the president had received a letter from a Saskatchewan man telling him that French on their cereal boxes was an irritation to nearly 95 per cent of the people in the West.[24]

There can be no doubt that Lapointe was humiliated by the turn of events. It was his job to 'deliver' Quebec, and he must have known that his English colleagues were telling King that they were 'astonished' by the Quebec results.[25] The loss of office was a great shock not only to Lapointe but to his family. Odette had worked unceasingly during the election, canvassing door to door in Ottawa. A leading light among the young Liberals, she was co-chair of the Twentieth Century Club, a newly formed association of Liberals born in the present century, and it had been a proud moment for her when her father, together with Senator Cairine Wilson, addressed the inaugural dinner in Toronto in March. The day before the election Odette and her co-chairman had driven out to Kingsmere to wish the prime minister luck. King had taken the two young people for a walk through the summer woods and no doubt shared his optimism with them.[26]

After the election defeat, Odette sent King a note to which he replied with unusual candour. Sensing her great disappointment, he began by condoling with her – 'My dear Odette, I am sorrier on your account than on my own' – but he then gave way to self-pity: 'I have had so many lickings in my day, and am so used to hearing myself called by all sorts of unpleasant names that I fear I have become like the sinner who is beyond pardon.' As consolation for both of them he concluded by saying that it began to look as if the party's defeat was a blessing in disguise.[27]

Lapointe's health deteriorated alarmingly after the election. It was as if his chronic stomach problems gave him respite for the duration of the campaign and then returned with a vengeance. In December he decided to go to the famous Johns Hopkins clinic in Baltimore, Maryland. It was King's advice to go there for a thorough check-up: 'Our own people cannot be expected to have the highly specialised knowledge which is the cumulation of years of experience by exceptionally brilliant men such as Johns Hopkins provides.' At a Baltimore hotel the night before he was to report to the clinic, Lapointe was stricken with an acute attack of abdominal pain. He waited until dawn to call the desk and then was rushed to the hospital and operated on immediately to remove his gallbladder and appendix. His family was told that he had arrived in the nick of time. Mimy left immediately for Baltimore. For the next few days Lapointe was on the critical list.[28]

King was in great distress when he heard the news. He felt extremely sorry for the family, but he was also thinking of himself. One after another the leaders of the party were melting away – through defeat, retirement, and illness. With Lapointe's survival uncertain, King was awash in self-pity. 'I am now all but completely alone,' he wrote in his diary. Putting aside his selfish concerns, he dictated a warm, encouraging letter to the sick man, assuring him that he and Madame Lapointe were continuously in his thoughts and promising to keep in touch with Odette and Bobby.[29]

At New Year's Lapointe received another soothing letter from King. Genuinely believing that he was in the special care of Providence, King brought his soulmate under the same divine protection:

> I am sure we are both fortunate to be out of office at the present time. I am sure it was an all-wise, as well as an all-kind Providence which caused us to make the appeal to the electorate when we did, and not to wait another year. Just what it might have meant to you personally, in your critical condition, to have been so near the harbour, and to have come so safely in at the moment you did, I shudder to think. All is working out for the very best, and I am sure that there is for you, and also for our Party, a long lease of life ahead.[30]

By the third week in January, Lapointe was able to sit up in a chair and the first thing he did was to write King. He had had a narrow escape, he wrote, but according to his doctors 'this miserable appendix' was the cause of his troubles and he would be much healthier now. He was reading the newspapers again and 'watching the course of events with great interest.' He was pleased that Bennett had postponed the opening of Parliament and was looking forward with 'great satisfaction to be there to do my bit.'[31]

On 24 February Lapointe returned to Ottawa with his wife and was touched to find King at the station to meet them. King found Lapointe thinner and 'quite shaky,' but it was Madame Lapointe's appearance that shocked him: 'She looked as if she might have a breakdown yet,' he told his diary. Mimy had in fact been undergoing treatment of some sort in the hospital while Ernest was there. King drove them home in his new Cadillac. On entering the house he was surprised to see that, aside from his own flowers, there was only one other bouquet. 'Had we been in office,' he observed dryly in his diary, 'the house would have been full of them.'[32]

CHAPTER SEVENTEEN

Member of the Opposition

In the May 1931 issue of the women's magazine *Chatelaine*, Madame Lapointe was quoted as saying that 'when a man who follows politics is out of office he may profess to be glad, but he really feels like a fish out of water.'[1] Mimy certainly knew her husband's true feelings. How galling it was for him to see the Conservatives represent Canada at the Imperial Conference of 1930. Lapointe was like the actor who attends all the rehearsals then misses the performance. At the 1926 Imperial Conference he and Mackenzie King had established Dominion autonomy in principle. At the 1929 Conference on the Operation of Dominion Legislation (ODL), which recommended the legislative changes necessary to implement the principle, Lapointe had played a leading role. Had the Liberals stayed in power, he would have led the Canadian delegation to the 1930 Imperial Conference, where the ODL report was approved and its proposals embodied in the draft Statute of Westminster. As it was, he had to stand in the wings while Bennett and the new minister of justice, Hugh Guthrie, got all the limelight.

Before going to the British Parliament the proposed Statute of Westminster was returned to each Dominion for approval. There was no real debate on the motion in the Canadian House of Commons since all parties were in favour. Nevertheless, Lapointe was anxious to have the record show that 'every paragraph of the proposed statute, as embodied in this resolution, is based upon one of the recommendations of the conference of 1929' at which he had had 'the honour to represent the Dominion of Canada.'[2] Lapointe had a little fun at Bennett's expense over the fact that Canada would still not be able to amend its own constitution: 'If my right hon. friend believes now as he did before that there cannot be equality of status as long as that condition remains, it is his paramount duty to take steps in order that this obstacle should disappear.'[3]

Lapointe himself had declined Britain's offer at the ODL conference to hand over the constitutional amending process. The political reality was that Quebec and Ontario would not hear of it. But out of power Lapointe was an outspoken advocate for bringing home the amending process, and for the first time he was speaking out publicly for ending appeals to the Privy Council. 'I am of the opinion,' he told the House during the debate on the Statute of Westminster, that 'if Canadians are competent to make their own laws they should be competent to interpret them.' It was 'a reflection on the legal men of Canada and on our judiciary to say that our supreme court should lack the competence necessary to inspire confidence in Canadian litigants. If that is so, by all means action should be taken to improve that condition. By all means the best men should be sought and appointed to the bench.'[4] (Was he bidding for the bench himself?) Early in 1932 he wrote an article for a French-language legal journal in which he stated that he could 'not find a single reason justifying Canada's being the only country in the world of its rank, population and intelligence, to confess its incompetence to decide its own judicial disputes.'[5]

Being in opposition enabled Lapointe to return to his early ideals. Although never a socialist, his natural sympathies were with the labouring classes on the farm and in the cities. Sir Wilfrid Laurier had called him 'the last of the *rouges*' – the red Liberals. Chubby Power, who was close to Lapointe, said of him in the opposition years: 'In principle and theory, he is a philosophical and theoretical radical. His radicalism is not so pronounced when it comes to definite action. Under these circumstances, he is sometimes hard to move leftward. He prefers what he calls a middle course – what some people term standpatism.'[6]

Free of pressure for the time being from the boot and shoe manufacturers in Quebec East, Lapointe could return to the low-tariff views he had held while MP for the rural riding of Kamouraska. In a forceful speech in the House on 26 March 1931, he lashed out at Bennett's high-tariff policies, asserting that Canada's high unemployment was the best evidence that Bennett's protectionist policy was a failure. To a great extent Bennett was acting defensively since the United States, Canada's main trading partner, had raised a veritable Great Wall of China along the border to keep out Canadian products. Like a child rejected by its playmate, Bennett turned to the mother country. His idea was to bully Great Britain – a free-trading nation – into agreeing to a self-contained imperial trading bloc that would give preference to its members and exclude foreign goods. Lapointe condemned the Conservatives' plan out of hand: 'I do not believe in economic imperialism any more than I believe in any other kind of imperialism,' he told the House. 'I am opposed to an imperial economic unit as I am opposed to an imperial diplomatic unit, naval unit, or military unit as is the dream of so many imperialists and which I believe would be the natural consequence of an economic unit.' Lapointe's reconversion to liberalization of trade prompted Agnes Macphail (his admirer but not an uncritical one) to remark that she wished 'he were always the splendid liberal he is to-day.' 'Constitutionally,' she said, 'the ex-Minister of Justice has always been a liberal; economically, not always.'[7]

Although Lapointe made some notable speeches during the 1931 session, he was absent a great deal. 'He is but little in the House,' King complained in his diary. Moreover, in caucus he was often 'mum as an oyster.'[8] During the budget debate in June he could not be persuaded to speak, and when King gently remonstrated with him he said, 'My wife and daughter think I am speaking too much.' Mimy and Odette were probably worrying about him overtaxing his strength. The famous medical team at the Johns Hopkins clinic had not cured his chronic abdominal pain and he was visibly losing weight. But because Lapointe kept up some social obligations and speaking engagements, King had little sympathy for him. He was particularly irritated when Lapointe took time out from the House to go to Quebec City during the budget debate: 'He is able to go to speak at the arrival of the Empress of Britain at a Tory banquet & stay the week at Govt. House in Quebec, attending funeral of the Cardinal etc., but is not able to speak in the most important debate of the session.'[9]

A letter from Premier Taschereau made King a little more charitable. After expressing pleasure over Lapointe's visit, the premier went on to say that 'all our friends here thought that he had not completely recovered his health and it has been suggested to me, by Mr. Lapointe's best friends, that I should write to you and ask you to see that Mr. Lapointe's strength be not taxed too much during the course of the Session. I am told that his doctors advise him to take a complete rest for at least six months.'[10]

Typically, King managed to turn Lapointe's poor state of health to his own ends. Tom Crerar had written asking if Lapointe could be made available to speak at a banquet for the Manitoba Liberal party. King replied: 'Lapointe, unfortunately, is far from wholly recovered. He will have to take things very easily for some little time. His speaking at Quebec a few days ago was a severe strain and I do not think he is in any shape to take on a banquet address to say nothing of a journey to and from Winnipeg.'[11] 'In addition,' King wrote, 'any time which he can spare between now and the end of the session should be given to the House of Commons. Lapointe does not know that I am writing you in this strain, and it is just as well that he should not know that any of us are unduly concerned about his health.' King's eagerness to keep Crerar's invitation from Lapointe suggests that the 'additional' reason was the main one. This was neither the first nor the last time he deflected speaking engagements that would have taken Lapointe away from his parliamentary duties.

The former prime minister was feeling very alone and vulnerable these days. A scandal was brewing over the Beauharnois Power Corporation contract. Robert Gardiner, an upright Scot and one of the few Progressives still sitting in the House, had introduced a motion calling for an investigation of the lease that the Liberal government had approved by order-in-council in 1929. Not only were the promoters making millions out of it, but Gardiner charged that two Liberal senators, Dr McDougald and Andrew Haydon, had been bought by the syndicate to use their influence with King to get approval of the company's plans. The very day that King was urging Lapointe to speak on the budget, a parliamentary committee was struck to investigate the 'Beauharnois canal matter' – as King delicately referred to it. That summer he would need his soulmate's support as he had not done since the dark days of 1926.

Now King understood why McDougald had turned up everywhere he went, treating him to expensive dinners on the ship returning from London in 1926, paying his hotel bill on a Bermuda holiday, and the like. He was obviously trying to 'use' me, King agonized in his diary. Not the least of King's worries was that McDougald's $25,000 contribution to Laurier House would come to light. The situation turned into a nightmare for him when the parliamentary committee got hold of a voucher showing that McDougald had passed on King's Bermuda hotel bill to the Beauharnois Power Corporation. The newspapers had a field day – the headline in the Conservative *Toronto Telegram* read, 'Beauharnois pays Mackenzie King's expenses and jaunt to Bermuda with Senator McDougald.'[12]

More revelations were to come. When King arrived at the House of Commons on the evening of 17 July, Lapointe greeted him with the foreboding words, 'The lid is off!' It seemed that at the committee meeting that morning, R.O. Sweezey, the Beauharnois company president, had testified that in 1930 the company had donated $700,000 to the Liberal campaign chest. Lapointe was mainly concerned with protecting Senator Donat Raymond, the Liberals' chief bagman in Quebec. In King's opinion, Raymond was more to be blamed than Haydon. Moreover, from what he had heard, 'Cardin and others are not free from having profited indirectly.'

It looked for a while as if the Beauharnois scandal would not spare Lapointe. The parliamentary committee's report was tabled in the House at the end of July. On the night of the debate, Bennett took King aside and informed him that some of the Beauharnois money had gone into Lapointe's fund. Bennett said he understood that Lapointe had 'a fiery speech ready.' 'If he went on with it,' the prime minister told King, 'he would find he had made a mistake.' Knowing 'the frame of mind Lapointe was in,' King agreed with his political opponent and forbade Lapointe to speak.[13]

The Conservative government was as anxious as the Liberals to avoid further inquiry into campaign funds. The two parties in effect negotiated a settlement. With a sigh of relief King wrote in his diary, 'There was not a line in [the report] which reflects on the Govt ... nor a line on myself.' The only casualties were Haydon and McDougald, and they were left to the mercies of the Senate. (The result of the Senate inquiry was that McDougald was forced to resign and the disgrace killed Haydon.)[14]

The Beauharnois scandal hardly raised its head in the campaign leading up to the Quebec provincial election on 24 August 1931. If anything it backfired against the provincial Conservatives because many Quebeckers regarded the federal Conservatives' parliamentary inquiry as just another attempt to smear the province. This time the seigneurial Taschereau was opposed by Camillien Houde, Montreal's colourful mayor and the leader of the provincial Conservative party, who billed himself as 'le petit gars de Ste Marie' – a working-class district in Montreal. Physically resembling Benito Mussolini and, like him, a demagogue, Houde was drawing much larger crowds than the cold, personally unpopular premier. Chubby Power had taken over the job of Liberal campaign manager from the ailing Senator Paradis, and with only three weeks to go he felt that chances of defeating Houde were 'very poor.' He called on Ernest Lapointe to come to the rescue. A week before the election, Lapointe addressed an enormous public meeting in an arena in a working-class district of Quebec City. It had been a dirty campaign on both sides, and Power's 'enforcers' disarmed several paid trouble-makers who had come equipped with stink bombs. Ignoring all provincial issues, Lapointe lashed out at Bennett for his failure to cure unemployment and gave Houde, the man of the people, the kiss of death by linking him with the plutocrat in Ottawa.

In Power's opinion, Ernest's intervention was the 'turning-point' in the campaign. The Taschereau government swept back in with 79 seats to the Conservatives' 11. Houde lost in both ridings where he was running. His successor-in-waiting, Maurice Duplessis, was barely re-elected in Trois-Rivières. After the election Power wrote a long letter to King analysing the campaign. He was ecstatic in his praise for Lapointe: 'Ernest Lapointe held two of the most successful and enthusiastic meetings which it has ever been my privilege to attend. The sympathy and enthusiasm manifested made it quite clear that Ernest in the Province of Quebec has become the most popular figure which we have had since Laurier. His presence and his eloquent speeches, because I do not believe he has ever spoken better in his whole career, were a potent and decisive factor in the Election.'[15]

The resurgence of Lapointe's popularity coincided with the family's long-delayed move to Quebec City. Lapointe had arranged to join the Quebec City law firm of Pratte and Germain (Garon Pratte was Mimy's brother) as senior partner. Before they left Ottawa in September 1931, King invited Ernest, Mimy, and Odette to Kingsmere for lunch. Much of the pleasant discussion centred on the recent Quebec elections. Though Lapointe was delighted with his enthusiastic reception in Quebec City and 'full of heart and hope,' he was far from pleased at the prospect of moving there. His finances were tight (he had clearly been caught in the 1929 stock market crash), and he was worried about the expense of furnishing a house. King, for his part, thought it a very good idea to have Lapointe living in Quebec. As he wrote Chubby Power, it would put Lapointe 'in closer touch with the province which, in the end, will be as satisfying to him as to the people, and which is all that is needed to hold what has been gained by the recent provincial campaign.'[16]

In Quebec the Lapointes rented an attractive apartment on the top floor of the Claridge, a new apartment house. Lapointe joined the Royal Quebec Golf Club – a fine course on the bluff beside the Plains of Abraham, which in the not too distant past had been out of bounds to French golfers. Mimy was less satisfied than her husband with the move. As she said to Odette, here they ask, 'Who are these Lapointes?'

In her opinion, newcomers had to be related to the elite families to be thoroughly accepted.[17]

Business was slow in the depression and law firms were hungry for clients, so Lapointe was pleased to get a good paying client almost as soon as he hung out his shingle. The Quebec Power Company's lease with the provincial capital was about to expire, and there was considerable agitation to municipalize the utility. The power company was just one tentacle of the Holt octopus that controlled gas, electricity, and tramways in the province. (Even the Beauharnois company had fallen within Sir Herbert Holt's grasp.) Quebec City was petitioning the legislature to allow municipalization, and it retained Lapointe to argue its case before the private bills committee. Lapointe was opposed by Lucien Cannon and Louis St Laurent who were representing the company, which had filed a counter-petition. Lapointe's detestation of the trusts and their monopolistic power gave him a strong personal interest in the case.[18]

Because he was tied up at the hearings, he had to bow out at the last minute from a Laurier Revival evening in Trois-Rivières arranged by his old friend, Jacques Bureau. Bureau was a very sick man, and a disappointed one too. With his reputation lost over the customs scandal, Bureau had seen his Trois-Rivières fiefdom taken over by the Conservative Maurice Duplessis. Within the past six months his hand-picked candidates had been defeated in a federal by-election and in the provincial election by Duplessis. The Laurier Revival evening was more an attempt to revive Bureau's reputation than that of the never-to-be-forgotten Sir Wilfrid.

King was at Bureau's home when Lapointe's telegram arrived. It was not the only one. Last-minute regrets came in one after another from Rinfret, Cardin, and Cannon (who like Lapointe at least had a good excuse). King could see that the old man was heartbroken. 'He had gone to no end of trouble and expense, and it looked as if he & I wd. be alone,' King recorded afterwards. It was Lapointe's absence that most distressed Bureau. A call was put in to Quebec City, but Lapointe explained that he had to appear before the legislative committee that evening. Bureau's daughter-in-law, who was Maurice Duplessis's sister, saved the day. She rang her brother, and he, as acting leader of the opposition, took the unusual step of having the committee adjourned 'to let Lapointe off.' Lapointe arrived in Trois-Rivières just in time to wind up a successful evening. King thought it was no exaggeration to say that if Lapointe had not come, 'it might have lost Bureau his life with his heart what it was.'[19] Bureau died almost a year to the day after his big night. No doubt Lapointe was glad he had attended for old time's sake.

Lapointe did not win his case before the private bills committee, yet it was neither Cannon nor St Laurent who defeated him but the premier himself. Taschereau publicly, if not officially, defended the Quebec Power Company's interests. His deputies on the committee, except those from Quebec City, obediently cast their votes in favour of renewing the power company's charter.[20]

As head of the federal Liberal wing in Quebec, it was incumbent upon Lapointe to work hand in glove with the Liberal premier. But it was getting increasingly difficult for him to support the reactionary and corrupt Taschereau regime. Female suffrage in Quebec was a case in point. As he declared in the House of Commons in March 1931, Lapointe favoured full voting rights for the women of his province; but it was clear that as long as Taschereau was in office female suffrage was a lost cause. Thérèse Casgrain, whom Lapointe respected and admired, had been trying for years to obtain the vote for women in provincial elections. Each session of the legislature, she and her band of dedicated suffragists would ask a friendly member to sponsor the bill, and every time the bill went down to defeat in a barrage of gross, misogynistic humour. In 1932 the bill was coming up for the sixth time (the sponsor that session was Dr Anatole Plante, who also supported a bill to outlaw anti-Semitic hate literature), and Madame Casgrain asked Ernest and Odette to be present. Seated on the floor behind the MLAs, father and daughter were shocked by the vulgarity of the proceedings. At every tasteless joke the usually dignified premier slapped his knee and laughed uproariously. Disgusted beyond measure, Lapointe got up and walked out.[21]

It was also very difficult for Lapointe to accept the favouritism and rampant nepotism of the Taschereau regime. According to Chubby Power, there was 'a well founded suspicion that only two classes may expect favours from the present government – (a) relatives of the Premier, and (b) the big interests, trusts, banks, paper companies, and power companies.' Lapointe sympathized with the young, nationalistic Liberals who were beginning to break away from the Taschereau administration.[22]

In contrast to his souring relationship with Taschereau, Lapointe was even closer to King than when they were in office. King's diary is sprinkled with references to 'Lapointe and myself.' They acted as a duo on almost everything, even to refusing an invitation from Bennett, which, King gloated, 'must have been a blow to his pride.' Together they attempted to obstruct Bennett's uncapped federal relief grants in 1932, calling it a usurpation of Parliament's power of the purse. With half a million people unemployed and the prairies punished by another drought their stand was politically dangerous, but for King and Lapointe it was a matter of principle that 'Parliament must decide.'

In the summer of 1932 King suggested that the two of them take a motor trip through eastern Quebec and the Gaspé to stir up a little enthusiasm for the party. 'Quebec is not too strongly Liberal at present,' King noted in his diary after mixed by-election results. 'Lapointe is the only one who really can do much, and he, like myself, is becoming too much of a "home man" and not enough out and about.'[23] On a beautiful July day, they set out in a car lent to them by a Quebec hotel-keeper. At every stage of their journey they were wined and dined by local Liberal politicians, who then brought in their constituents to pay their respects. Much of it was a nostalgic trip for Lapointe, and he took great pleasure in introducing King to the places and people of his youth. From the simple Gaspésian hospitality, they moved on to the resort town of St Andrews in New Brunswick, where they stayed at 'Clibrig,' the magnificent summer home of Senator Wilson and her husband. After much partying with the rich and titled, they started back, arriving on 12 July at the Lapointes' rented cottage at St Patrice just outside Rivière-du-Loup.[24]

'Lapointe and I had a most delightful trip,' King reported to Senator Dandurand. They returned to Ottawa just in time for the Imperial Economic Conference that Bennett convened in July 1932 to push through his plan for an imperial trading bloc. King and Lapointe's opposition to Bennett's plan was already on record: 'As French and English Liberal leaders we stood together for action on the eve of the conference,' King had written proudly in his diary in May.[25] After the conference, again working in tandem, King and Lapointe managed to convince an apprehensive Liberal caucus to oppose the Ottawa agreements that Bennett had forced upon Britain.

There was a feeling in the press gallery that in opposition King was overshadowed by Lapointe. The latter's enduring popularity in Quebec and his prestige in the West made him, according to *Maclean's*, 'the most influential figure in the Liberal party.' But, added the columnist, 'he does not allow anyone to say so.' Lapointe's loyalty to King was total, and he discouraged any talk of dethroning the leader.[26]

CHAPTER EIGHTEEN

Back in Power

The devastating effect of the depression was threatening the two-party system in Canada, which had been re-established with the demise of the Progressives. The inability of the governing Conservatives to relieve the widespread misery created a cynical, anti-government sentiment. In the privacy of his diary, Mackenzie King expressed the fear that the public did not regard the Liberals as much better. Both old parties were believed to be in the pockets of the 'trusts' who bankrolled their campaigns. In King's opinion, this was the real impetus for a socialist movement that was spreading on the prairies.[1] Headed by J.S. Woodsworth, the Co-operative Commonwealth Federation (CCF) had just issued a radical manifesto at an inaugural conference in Regina.

In the province of Quebec, a similar urge for reform had fostered a revolt against the seemingly impregnable Taschereau regime. A group of young Montreal Liberals were openly repudiating the premier for his alliance with the 'rapacious' capitalists of St James Street, in particular his protection of the 'power trust.' By the late summer of 1933 the revolt had coalesced into a political movement. The leader was Paul Gouin, the younger son of the late Sir Lomer Gouin.

Paul Gouin was an unlikely candidate for the role. In the first place, he was devoted to the memory of his father, who as premier had been as much a friend of big business as Taschereau. Second, he seemed to be temperamentally unfitted for the rough-and-tumble of political activism. Formal and reserved, he avoided the familiar form of address even with his closest associates. Gouin was a pioneer collector of Quebec arts and crafts and a distinguished writer and lecturer on the subject. There were those who suspected that if Taschereau had given him the museum curatorship he wanted, Gouin's interest in reform might have remained theoretical. But this was perhaps the cynicism of the times because Gouin, as one of his disciples put it, was an 'impenitent ideal-ist,' a man of uncompromising principles and deep convictions.[2] A dedicated Quebec nationalist of the Abbé Groulx school, his aim was to reverse the flight to the cities and send unemployed Quebeckers back to the land, notwithstanding the dismal failure of previous colonization efforts in unsettled parts of the province. The development of small local industries and rural electrification were the other pillars in his utopia. With Taschereau doing nothing to relieve unemployment, ex-cept for family members, several of Lapointe's staunchest followers had joined with Gouin and his Young Turks in what was still a reform movement within the provincial party. In this brewing revolution, Thérèse Casgrain's 'Monday nights' became a political salon for the clique of reformers.[3]

Lapointe supported the rebels in these early days. Though Gouin spoke bitterly of the treatment his father had received from the Quebec federal ministers,[4] he did not seem to hold it against Lapointe. It would have been against his interests to do so. Gouin's supporters looked to Lapointe as their mentor. He was regarded as a true liberal, as opposed to a false one like Taschereau, and he affirmed his liberal-mindedness with a much-praised speech on social justice at Trois-Pistoles that sum-mer. As Chubby Power informed a reporter for the *Vancouver Sun*, Lapointe enjoyed 'overwhelming prestige' in the province of Quebec.[5] Indeed, his prestige had increased immeasurably as French Canadians compared his influence in the King administration with the puppet role played by the two French ministers in Bennett's cabinet who had little or no patronage to hand out. As for English Quebeckers, most would have agreed with a newspaperman who in 1934 described Lapointe as the spirit of enlightened Liberalism in Quebec.[6]

Chubby Power, who shared Lapointe's opinion of Taschereau as a hopeless reactionary, acknowledged that Lapointe's sympathy for the rebels had brought about 'a dangerous coolness between the federal and provincial wings of the Liberal Party.'[7] Lapointe and Taschereau had had their jurisdictional disputes in the past, most openly at the 1927 Dominion-Provincial Conference, but encouraging the premier's opponents in his own party was something different. It had created what King described to a correspondent as 'a cleavage' between Lapointe (and by extension himself) and Taschereau.[8] The situation had so dete-riorated that Lapointe sent a message to an office seeker that he was 'labouring under a fanciful delusion when [he] thinks that my influence with the provincial authorities could help him.'[9]

Because of the split in the provincial Liberal party, Lapointe was most reluctant to speak at the summer conference arranged by Vincent Massey, the president of the National Liberal Federation. The conference was to take place at the beginning of September at an elite boarding school for boys near Massey's country estate at Port Hope, Ontario. A kind of brainstorming session, it was intended to come up with new policies as an alternative to the socialist agenda. The roster of speakers included left-wing professors and one of Roosevelt's New Dealers. Extremely anxious to have a French-Canadian speaker, Massey urged Lapointe to come, but in vain. Lapointe told Massey that the situation was 'so difficult' in Quebec that he did not want 'to lay himself open to an attack as the result of anything he might say in Port Hope.' Massey thought Lapointe was being 'unduly apprehensive.' He turned to King for help. If Lapointe would only take the chair at one of the meetings, 'it would bring a French Canadian into the picture and relieve us of criticism which we are otherwise certain to get.'[10] King immediately wired Lapointe, urging him to speak and assuring him that 'nothing more than a few formal remarks would be expected.'[11] At this point fate stepped in. Lapointe was involved in a motor accident, which, though not serious, excused him from attending the conference.[12]

Notwithstanding similar misgivings, that autumn Lapointe accepted an invitation to become president of the League of Nations Society of Canada. The Society was looking for a new president, and the executive believed the time had come for a French Canadian. Lapointe was first approached by an executive member named C.G. Cowan. 'We need above all a national figure for President and one who understands and has sympathy with the League and the collective system generally,' Cowan wrote. A formal invitation followed from the current president, Dr Henry Marshall Tory, head of the National Research Council. Lapointe replied that if he could be convinced that it was his duty he would not shirk it; but he expressed several doubts about his fitness for the post, particularly the fact that 'my province has not given the Society the support I would have liked ... and this might be a consideration with the members.' At this Dr Tory backed off, but Senator Cairine Wilson assured Lapointe that he would be a most tremendous advantage to the Society, 'for you hold such a wonderful place in the opinion of English-speaking Canadians as well as amongst your own people, and your previous experience as delegate at Geneva will be of great value.' She ended with a cordial invitation to him and his wife to stay at the 'Manor House,' her Rockcliffe mansion, before the opening of Parliament.[13]

Despite his honest reservations, Lapointe accepted the presidency. It was a misjudgment on his part because, despite what Cowan thought, Lapointe was no advocate of collective security and was to become increasingly isolationist as the decade proceeded. The League of Nations was proving toothless. Japan's invasion of Manchuria in 1931–2 had gone unchecked, and this gave the go-ahead to European dictators, in particular Italy's Benito Mussolini and Germany's Adolf Hitler. First Japan and then Germany withdrew from the League in 1933.

Shortly after becoming president of the League of Nations Society of Canada, Lapointe showed his uneasiness about taking a hard line against aggressor states. On the eve of the 1934 parliamentary session, the Liberals' chief organizer, Norman Lambert, suggested that 'in view of the fact that we are still supposed to have faith in the League of Nations,' the party should introduce a motion calling for Canada to put on record its support for 'an economic and financial boycott of any power which may resort to war or used armed forces in contravention of the covenant of the League of Nations.' Lambert sent his draft resolution to King, who told him to send it to Lapointe.[14] Lapointe did not introduce Lambert's sanctions resolution. As he had indicated to Cairine Wilson, getting involved in the League's affairs was highly unpopular in Quebec.

During that parliamentary session Lapointe espoused a very popular cause with Quebeckers – bilingual currency. The Bennett government had introduced a bill to establish a central bank. Ultimately all legal tender would be issued by the Bank of Canada, and this renewed French-Canadian demands for a bilingual currency. Lapointe insisted on introducing an amendment to the Bank of Canada bill that would require all currency to be in the two languages. Although King did not approve of bilingual currency any more than he did of bilingual stamps, he supported Lapointe's amendment. The most Bennett would do was to allow a separate issue of French-language banknotes for Quebec province, and this led to a headline-making 'clash' with Lapointe. The prime minister accused the former minister of justice of playing politics 'pure and simple.' For nine years as a minister of the Crown, shouted Bennett, Mr Lapointe had never suggested printing money in both languages; in fact, just before leaving office, the Liberals contracted for a five-year supply of paper money – in English. The prime minister resumed his seat triumphantly. In high dudgeon, Lapointe denied any political motive: 'I send it back in your teeth,' he shouted across the floor. Lapointe's amendment was defeated, but his vigorous demand for bilingual currency (the 'tense scene in the Commons' was well reported) reinforced his position as the champion of his people.[15]

Meanwhile, in Quebec Gouin and the Liberal rebels had moved out of the official Liberal party and formed a party of their own – the Action Libérale. The ALN (the party soon added 'Nationale' to its name) was attracting tremendous support from the nationalist and Catholic press, from youth groups and the Catholic unions, and from politicians who favoured public ownership of electricity. An invaluable convert to the reform movement was Edward Lacroix, a millionaire lumberman and MP for Saint-Georges de Beauce. Lacroix was an 'ardent admirer' of Lapointe. He informed Gouin that he would support him financially as long as he maintained solidarity with Lapointe and the federal wing of the Liberal party. On 12 August 1934 Gouin unveiled the party's platform at Saint-Georges de Beauce before an estimated seven thousand people. The crowd was at its most enthusiastic when Gouin promised to end the electricity trust. In contrast to the refined Gouin, Lacroix was a self-educated rough diamond, and he roused the audience with cries of 'Down with the trusts! Down with Taschereau!' Bobby Lapointe, now studying law at Laval, was among those who attended the inaugural rally.[16]

A few days after the rally, Chubby Power met with Taschereau. Though he had served notice on Taschereau that he would not act as organizer in the next provincial campaign, Power offered his help to mend the breach with Lapointe and the federal wing. He left the meeting convinced that there was little hope of reconciliation. Power sent Lapointe a letter reporting on his meeting with Taschereau – as usual, the Lapointes were spending the summer at St Patrice on the St Lawrence. He was convinced, Chubby told Ernest, that the premier had 'no intention whatsoever of taking either of us into his confidence, nor of using our services, except for the purpose of showing to the Public that the Federal and Provincial Parties are united.'[17]

Power proved a poor prophet because within a matter of days Taschereau offered Lapointe the chairmanship of a commission of inquiry on hydroelectric power and Lapointe accepted.[18] Thérèse Casgrain, for one, thought Lapointe had sold out to Taschereau. When Lapointe asked her if she was going to congratulate him, she replied, to her husband's great embarrassment, 'No, because when you start by giving

way in small things, you are soon giving way in big things.'[19] No doubt
Lapointe was influenced to some extent by the $6,000 stipend that went
with the appointment – he was having a hard time financially, as he
admitted to Mackenzie King. But he may also have wished to mend
fences with the premier. The provincial Liberal machine was important
to him.

By setting up the commission Taschereau showed that he was finally
taking the ALN seriously. He had not changed his mind in the slightest
about privately owned utilities, but he realized that a seal of approval
from an impartial body was needed to restore public confidence. He
had no compunction about trying to influence Lapointe's decision.
While Lapointe and his side members (an accountant named McDonald
and Augustin Frigon, the director of Montreal's Polytechnic) toured the
province holding hearings, the premier deluged him with a steady
stream of articles, investment service circulars, and opinion letters in
favour of private ownership of utilities.[20]

At the beginning of October Lapointe interrupted his commission
work to go on an unexpected holiday with King. For several months
King had been thinking about taking a trip to England 'to get a complete rest and change before the beginning of the session.'[21] At the last
minute he invited Lapointe to accompany him. Lapointe was dying to
go, but he wired back that there were 'difficulties.' The commission
hearings were not the problem; it was his personal finances.[22] King
acted with alacrity, buying him a round-trip ticket at the advantageous
rate of $435.75 and arranging for his passport. On 29 September the two
sailed for Europe on the *Empress of Britain*.[23]

London was, of course, the perfect backdrop for this pair of Pickwic-
kian travellers. They visited all the tourist sights and sampled the
famous roast beef of England at Simpsons in the Strand. They ordered
suits and coats from Savile Row tailors. In the West End theatre district
they saw a play about Clive of India. On Lapointe's birthday – his fifty-
eighth – King took him to the Cheshire Cheese for lunch, where they sat
at a table facing Samuel Johnson's favourite seat. In Westminster Abbey
they knelt together in silent prayer. King was deeply moved that here
they were, 'Lapointe Roman Catholic & French, myself Protestant &
English – both pretty much of one mind in our faith & outlook.'

King started phoning around to activate their political contacts. Because Britain was now governed by the National Coalition under Ramsay
MacDonald, they met with politicians of all parties. L.S. Amery, secretary of state for the Dominions in the Baldwin administration, gave

them a guided tour of the Houses of Parliament. They had tea at Gray's Inn with Lord and Lady Hamar Greenwood – the former Canadian had left the British Liberal party and was now treasurer of the Conservative party. They lunched at the National Liberal Club where a cabinet minister told King that there were Conservatives, 'very high up in Britain, who would be mighty thankful when I defeated Bennett.' On another occasion, King introduced Lapointe to Lloyd George. Seemingly confused about Canadian party politics, the former prime minister opened the conversation by asking, 'Where's Bennett?' (The Canadian prime minister was also visiting England at this time.) No doubt amused, Lapointe replied that Bennett was 'fishing in other waters.'[24]

After a delightful two weeks in the 'mother country,' and a short sojourn in Paris, Lapointe returned to his duties on the electricity commission. In January 1935 he submitted his report. Typically, he stopped short of recommending public ownership. Instead, he advised the premier to set up a hydroelectric commission to regulate the private power companies. The halfway measures met with considerable criticism from some of Lapointe's most devoted followers, including Edward Lacroix and Oscar Drouin.[25]

At this time, Lapointe began pulling back from the role of Dutch uncle to Gouin and his followers. Not only had the ALN slammed his electricity report, but he heard rumours of an alliance between the former Liberals and Duplessis's Conservatives to defeat Taschereau in the next provincial election. To keep Lapointe on side, in January Gouin publicly offered him the leadership of the ALN. Lapointe refused, and during the winter and spring he made several speeches disavowing third parties. Seeking to end the fissioning that had begun with the ALN, he told young Liberals at the Club Lapointe in Quebec City, 'Preach reforms, demand them, but demand them in the ranks of the Liberal party which alone can accomplish them, and not from outside, in new groups which can only divide the liberal forces.' In March, on the same platform as Taschereau, he pointedly announced, 'I am a man of my party.' In fact, Lapointe and Taschereau had reached a rapprochement. Chubby Power called it 'an armed truce.'[26]

Still, Lapointe did not break with the ALN. Gouin was speaking throughout the province and gaining important adherents. In May Oscar Drouin, the MLA for Quebec East whom Lapointe counted on to run his campaign for re-election, declared himself a member of the new party and became its organizer. With a federal election in the offing, Lapointe needed the ALN. The need was reciprocal. When Gouin mused that he might have to attack Lapointe, Edward Lacroix asked for advance notice so he could quit the ALN.[27] When the election was finally announced in the late summer, Lapointe had ensured the support of both the establishment Liberals and the breakaway ALN.

With a Liberal victory certain in the province, the biggest problem was the host of candidates who wanted to get on the bandwagon. The federal Conservatives were anathema in Quebec. Bennett had ignored the French Canadians to the point of showing scorn for them. At the Ottawa Conference in 1932 he could find no place for French civil servants above the secretarial level. He had refused to have bilingual currency. His few French ministers were powerless. And the number of unemployed in Quebec was among the highest in the country.

Bennett himself was a casualty of the depression. It had been humanly impossible for him to keep the promises he had made to the electorate in 1930 to bring back prosperity. In January 1935 he took to the radio to promise unemployment insurance, health insurance, an eight-hour day, and other social legislation. His attempt to ape Roosevelt's New Deal did not convince the working classes of a better world, and he alienated the Conservatives' traditional supporters with his proposals for higher taxes on investment income and anti-monopolistic measures. But the worst blow for Bennett came when his minister of trade and commerce, H.H. Stevens, left to form his own party.

Stevens's Reconstruction party was one of three new parties running candidates in the 1935 federal election. There was the CCF, J.S. Woodsworth's new socialist party. Moreover, the success of the Social Credit party in Alberta had spurred its founder, William Aberhart, a radio evangelist with peculiar monetarist ideas, to enter the national arena. But these were special interest groups and regional parties, and none of them posed a threat to the Liberals – the party of national unity.

As well as the depression, the threat of war was an issue in the campaign. Following the failure of arbitration sponsored by the League of Nations, Mussolini was massing troops for the invasion of Ethiopia, a League member. Given the strong isolationist sentiment in Quebec, all parties outdid themselves promising that their party would not let Canada be drawn into war. Lapointe declared before a large audience in Quebec City that Ethiopia was not worth the life of a single Canadian citizen: 'No consideration could justify Canada's participation in such a war, and I am unalterably opposed to it.'[28] King, on the same platform, endorsed Lapointe's sentiments. There would be no foreign wars without Parliament's consent or even a plebiscite, he reassured his listeners.

But as the campaign went on, Lapointe informed King that the war issue was minor. He was being heckled on the hustings because of the Liberals' pledge to repeal Section 98 of the Criminal Code. The 1931 conviction and imprisonment of Tim Buck and other leaders of the Communist Party of Canada under Section 98 – a peacetime version of arbitrary wartime regulations – had been popular in Quebec. Indeed, it was one of the few times Bennett received kudos from the francophone press. Lapointe was closely associated with the move for repeal. As minister of justice he had repeatedly introduced bills for this purpose only to have them killed in the Senate. In opposition he had supported Woodsworth's attempts to strike out Section 98. Because of this, he found himself dogged by a smear campaign throughout the election. He complained that rabid nationalists, funded by the Conservative party, 'insulted and disparaged' him as a 'Communist and non-believer.' He would later tell the House that during the election campaign 'my leader and I were described as the friends of the men who want to pull down the steeples, the men who protect those who walk on crucifixes, and so on.'[29] (His opponents may have seen divine intervention in a freak accident that happened to Lapointe at a rally in a Quebec town hall. A slab of plaster fell from the ceiling on him and thirteen others. Rendered unconscious for ten minutes, he revived and delivered an hour-long speech. Mackenzie King read about it in the *Prince Albert Daily Herald* and immediately sent a wire expressing great concern.)[30]

On 14 October 1935 the Liberals were swept back into power with the largest majority of any party since Confederation. Lapointe was in the parish hall at Limoilou with the Casgrains and Louis Letourneau when he heard that his majority had doubled.[31] Good news kept pouring in. After losing 24 seats to the Conservatives in 1930, the Liberals had stormed back with 60 of the 65 Quebec seats. Lapointe was particularly proud that not a single French-Canadian Tory was elected.

In what had now become a tradition, Lapointe was the first to be called in by King. He was greeted warmly, not only by the prime minister but by Pat, King's beloved terrier. Despite the 'calumny' of their opponents, Lapointe told King that the campaign had cost him less anxiety and effort than any previous one. After reviewing the campaign, they began to go over the names of possible cabinet ministers. King was not really surprised to find that Lapointe wanted to keep Cardin and Rinfret, although Lapointe himself had no high opinion of them: 'With Lapointe, it is who the boys want, for example regarding

Montreal he would have Cardin and Rinfret just because if the Montreal members were polled, they would name these men, though he knows there is a feeling that Cardin is co-operating with Simard and other Tories in working out contracts, and admits Rinfret is not much help in the government nor of the best judgment in parliament or in the country.'[32]

One thing, though – King was determined to have no drinkers. 'You will have a pretty difficult time,' Lapointe replied sceptically. This, of course, brought up the case of Chubby Power. While recognizing his 'ability, friendship and loyalty,' King was afraid to give him a cabinet post because of his drinking. But Lapointe was quite insistent. He did not see how they could ignore Power without all kinds of trouble in Quebec. He kept repeating that Power would be able to smooth out other members: otherwise there could be 'a combination' against King and himself. King formed the opinion that Lapointe would not care 'to battle the situation' without Power. 'He has not the strength or knowledge to do so,' King wrote in his diary. A superb judge of people (as his new cabinet would show), King had long recognized an inherent weakness in Lapointe. He would need propping up, but King knew he could find no better Quebec lieutenant.

Though Lapointe had succeeded in getting a cabinet post for Power – he was to become minister of pensions and health – he did not get the post he wanted for himself. Several months before the election he had indicated to King that he would like external affairs, but King did not think him suitable. 'English Canada would not welcome his having control of External Affairs while war is on,' he wrote in his diary, 'also, he, himself has not stood up for the League of Nations as I think he should have, having been President of the Ottawa Society, and having been its strongest advocate in Canada.'[33] King would keep the rudder of external affairs in the stormy waters ahead, with the invaluable Skelton as his first mate. Lapointe agreed to return to Justice, which King embellished by adding the secretary of state department. But as time would tell, Lapointe would be very involved in foreign affairs and would be instrumental in shaping King's views and government policy.

King confided his reservations about Lapointe to no one but his diary. Lapointe entered upon the second King administration at the height of his prestige and popularity. The *Ottawa Journal* (a Conservative paper at that) expressed the general opinion of Ernest Lapointe in 1935: 'The first man to be summoned to Ottawa by Mr. Mackenzie King was Mr. Ernest Lapointe. He could have beckoned no truer nor more loyal Captain, no finer Canadian. In this son of old Quebec, great-hearted, generous and lovable, Mr. King has an adviser who is an asset to more than Mr. King and his party, an asset to his Province and to Canada, at once a proud possession and vindication of our democracy.'[34]

CHAPTER NINETEEN

The Ethiopian Crisis

Glancing around the table at the first meeting of the new cabinet on 25 October 1935, Lapointe saw a number of fresh faces. He had agreed with King that these were the best men available, taking into consideration the usual regional factors. James Ilsley, a Nova Scotia lawyer, had sat in Parliament during the last Liberal administration. A Rhodes scholar, he had a brilliant mind, and the fact that he was a poor speaker would be no drawback in the post of minister of national revenue. Clarence Howe from the Lakehead in northern Ontario was a new recruit and a novelty in this or any other Canadian cabinet. An American-born civil engineer, he had constructed millions of dollars worth of grain elevators, pulp mills, coal docks, and other heavy engineering projects all over the world. As minister of transport he would make the trains run on time (as they said about Mussolini). Jimmy Gardiner, former premier of Saskatchewan, was another potential strong man, as Lapointe knew from his negotiations with him on the separate schools question. Gardiner had taken on Agriculture. He had wanted Finance, but that went to Dunning, his arch rival. King and Lapointe expected sparks to fly between those two. The new minister of labour was Norman Rogers, King's former secretary and protégé. Barely forty, his appointment was sure to please the young people, Lapointe had told King.

The French-Canadian contingent was basically the same as in the earlier administrations – Lapointe, Cardin, Rinfret, and Dandurand, with the addition of Michaud from New Brunswick. Chubby Power was in a manner of speaking an honorary French Canadian.[1] Certainly he was a Quebecker first and foremost. Just a glance at Power's smiling Irish face, with the cigarette plugged into it, was enough to cheer up Lapointe.

Paul Martin, a rookie MP from Windsor, Ontario, assessed the cabinet as a fairly conservative lot aside from Norman Rogers. The finance minister, Charles Dunning, was 'the voice of big business and economic orthodoxy.' Euler and Howe were two more of the same kind. As for T.A. Crerar, he was back in the nineteenth century, 'blind to the problems of industrial society.' Although Lapointe also was 'far from a radical,' Martin admired him immensely 'for his efforts to build a country where two cultures could coexist happily.'[2] The example of the 'great Lapointe' would have helped the young Franco-Ontarian bury old feelings of racial inferiority that, according to the warden of Hart House, had made Martin prickly and defensive as a university student.[3]

Foreign affairs were at the top of the agenda. At the beginning of October Italy had invaded Ethiopia and was declared an aggressor by the League of Nations. It was at this serious turn of events that the change of government in Canada occurred. Howard Ferguson, Bennett's appointee to the League, immediately resigned, leaving a career diplomat, Dr W.A. Riddell, to speak for Canada. With King fully occupied in forming his new cabinet, Riddell was left without instructions and took it upon himself to play a leading role on the Committee of Eighteen discussing sanctions against Italy.[4]

King found his new cabinet divided on this question of sanctions. While all present were against military sanctions, Ilsley and Rogers wanted the government to emphatically support the League and economic sanctions, and the rest of the English ministers went along with them. But Lapointe, Cardin, and Power 'were all in the other direction.' The Quebec ministers knew their province. Habitually distrustful of the League and of British imperialism, Quebec was adamantly opposed to intervention in the Italo-Ethiopian war. Not only was Lapointe bound to take a non-interventionist position because of public opinion in his province, but he himself had distrusted the League's collective security mandate from the beginning. And how could he recant his much-quoted statement in the recent election campaign that Ethiopia was not worth a single Canadian life? Indeed, a few days before the cabinet meeting he had told King bluntly that 'there would be no going into war by Canada.' King was no more ready to go to war over Ethiopia than Lapointe, but he recognized that Canada could be dragged in if Britain got involved. The net result of the cabinet discussion was a shaky consensus to support economic, but not military, sanctions.

After the meeting King drafted a press release and reviewed it with Lapointe. In the back of both their minds was the possibility that

economic sanctions would lead to military involvement. If the government ever decided on military sanctions, Lapointe warned King, he
would resign at once. Under this threat, King admitted to himself that
his statement to the press on 29 October was a little more cautious than
the majority of his cabinet would have liked. It stated that the Canadian
government would comply with the economic sanctions recommended
by the League committee to date, but 'at the same time desires to make
it clear that it does not recognize any commitment binding Canada to
adopt military sanctions, and that no such commitment could be made
without the prior approval of the Canadian Parliament.' Moreover,
approval of economic sanctions should 'not be regarded as necessarily
establishing a precedent for future action.'[5]

In Geneva Riddell chose to interpret King's press release (External
Affairs wired him a summary) as the green light to expand economic
sanctions. On the morning of 2 November he introduced a motion at
the Committee of Eighteen to include oil, iron, and steel and their
derivatives on the list of prohibited exports to Italy. Lester Pearson,
then secretary and adviser to the Canadian delegation, confirms in his
memoirs that Riddell had received no reply to his 'urgent' telegrams to
Ottawa when he walked into the fateful meeting.[6] That afternoon a
cable arrived from Ottawa instructing Riddell not to initiate any further
sanctions but simply to support the majority view, whatever it may be.
It was too late.[7] The next day newspaper headlines announced 'Canada
Urges Wider Embargo ... Dominion Insists Boycott of Italy Must Be
Airtight ... Riddell at League Meetings Demands full Sanctions.'[8]
Riddell's unauthorized proposal of oil sanctions was adopted by the
Committee of Eighteen. From there it was circulated to the member
nations for approval. Oil supplies were crucial to Italy's war effort, and
Mussolini was shaking his sabre at the western powers. The French-
Canadian press pulled out all stops in its condemnation of Riddell's
initiative.

On 8 November King left for Washington to negotiate a trade treaty
with Roosevelt. With King went Dr O.D. Skelton, who had remained
under-secretary of state for external affairs throughout the Bennett
regime. Lapointe, now acting prime minister, was left in charge of
external affairs, but during November Quebec politics claimed his attention. Hoping to return to power on the coat-tails of the federal
Liberals, Taschereau had called an election for 25 November. For the
first time in his sixteen years as premier he was faced with real competition. The Liberal rebels in the ALN had teamed up with the Duplessis

Conservatives, and in an accord signed at the Ritz Carlton Hotel in Montreal on 7 November they had agreed to field one candidate only in each riding. If the alliance triumphed, Gouin would cede the premiership to Duplessis but would have the right to name the majority of the cabinet members.

Gouin's alliance with Duplessis ended any sympathy Lapointe had for his erstwhile protégés. Taschereau's flawed Liberalism was infinitely preferable to a Duplessis-led government in Quebec. Lapointe felt that his fiefdom was in jeopardy. Putting his prestige on the line, he spoke at a large rally in Quebec City on behalf of Taschereau. He was observed to be uncomfortable backing the politician whose big business affiliations he was known to disapprove. His speech was essentially a plea for party solidarity despite differences of opinion.[9] Even with gross fraud at the ballot box,[10] Taschereau was only able to secure a narrow victory – six more seats than the combined Duplessis-Gouin forces. It was clear to Lapointe, and to Taschereau himself, that a change of leadership was necessary if the Liberals were to stay in power.

During the campaign, Lapointe was reminded (if he needed reminding) of the downright hostility in Quebec to sanctions against Italy. Mussolini was threatening to go to war against Britain if the League imposed an oil embargo. The worst of it was that the proposed oil sanctions continued to be referred to in the international press as 'the Canadian proposal.' Lapointe was deeply concerned that Canada would be blamed if war resulted from the imposition of sanctions. The consequences for himself in his home province were unthinkable.

Lapointe's fears were fed by Laurent Beaudry, the acting undersecretary of external affairs. Skelton's department was a nest of isolationists,[11] and towards the end of November Beaudry sent Lapointe an alarmist memo. 'In view of the fact that Canada through the unauthorized action of Dr. Riddell, has initiated the proposal for the oil embargo,' Beaudry wrote, 'the responsibility thus assumed by Canada is very great, and the consequences for Canada herself may be still greater under the circumstances.' To avoid 'armed conflict,' Beaudry advised that 'the most careful consideration should at once be given to the position officially taken by our representative.'[12] Beaudry's memo no doubt played a part in Lapointe's decision to take action.

On 28 November Beaudry wired Dr Skelton, who was holidaying with King at Sea Island, Georgia, that 'Mr. Lapointe is disturbed by headlines in the press emphasizing the initiative taken by Canadians and is wondering whether some course of action could be adopted to counteract this effect.' Up to this time, King and Skelton had kept their disapproval of Riddell private, simply instructing Beaudry to keep a rein on the headstrong diplomat. Moreover, King's diary gives no hint that Canada's unwanted prominence over sanctions was disturbing his walks on the seashore with Skelton until Lapointe urged action. On 29 November Skelton wired Beaudry that the 'Prime Minister agrees with Mr. Lapointe as to serious effect of press emphasis on alleged Canadian initiative.' Lapointe was authorized to give a statement to the press declaring that the Canadian government had taken no initiative to extend the embargo and that the 'opinion expressed by Canadian member of Committee of Eighteen represented only his opinion as member of Committee.'

Strangely enough, Skelton had argued against disavowing Riddell, telling King that it would weaken the hands of Britain and France and the other League members, and would look like 'we were backing down in the face of Mussolini's threats of European war.' But King went to bed easy in his mind and woke up next morning convinced that he had made 'a wise and true decision.'[13] On 2 December Lapointe issued a press release repudiating Riddell. It bluntly stated that Riddell put forward the resolution to extend the embargo on his own and that the government had no knowledge of it:

The suggestion which has appeared in the press from time to time, that the Canadian Government has taken the initiative in the extension of the embargo upon exportation of key commodities to Italy, and particularly in the placing of a ban upon shipments of coal, oil, iron and steel, is due to a misunderstanding. The Canadian Government has not and does not propose to take the initiative in any such action; and the opinion which was expressed by the Canadian member of the Committee – and which has led to the reference to the proposal as a Canadian proposal – represented only his personal opinion, and his views as a member of the Committee – and not the views of the Canadian Government.'[14]

Lapointe's press release was page-one news in Canada and around the world. The headline in the *Montreal Gazette* was typical: 'Lapointe Declares Canada Not Taking the Initiative in Drive for Oil Sanction ... States suggestion to League was from Riddell Personally.' The *New York Times* informed the American reading public that 'Canada Disclaims Proposing Oil Ban ... Backs Pacific Steps Only.' In Europe Lapointe's statement created a sensation. It was seen as a repudiation of the whole idea of oil sanctions. The *Osservatore Romano* rejoiced that sanctions would now certainly fail.[15]

Riddell was banished to a conference in Chile, although Lapointe denied that his reassignment had anything to do with what had passed at Geneva.[16] But Riddell later wrote: 'The Italian consul-general and his Quebec friends must have thought that Providence had smiled upon them when the Department was left in the hands of two French Canadians – Lapointe and Beaudry.'[17] Many in Canada thought the same. The day after Lapointe's statement, Newton Rowell commiserated with Riddell from Toronto: 'Your friends in Canada feel that you have been sacrificed to some political exigencies.'[18]

Rowell, a true believer in collective security, did not hide his disapproval from Lapointe. He sent Lapointe a highly critical wire, which somehow got leaked to the press. At the same time Rowell issued a statement intended for publication. Citing the relevant articles of the League Covenant, Rowell asserted that it was the 'clear and inescapable duty of every member of the League to impose the prohibition on the export of oil and other key materials.' To Lapointe he expressed his regret that Canada did not deserve credit after all for proposing an oil embargo that would have stopped Italy's aggression.

Lapointe immediately sent Rowell a conciliatory letter. He explained that the press statement had been released because the government believed it politically necessary to correct the erroneous impression that Canada was taking the lead in urging more severe sanctions. He assured Rowell that Canada would continue 'loyally cooperating in the application of economic and financial sanctions which have the general support of the League against a Covenant-breaking state.'[19]

As past president of the League of Nations Society of Canada, Lapointe felt the need to justify his actions to the Society: 'My attitude is far from being one of no cooperation with the other members of the League, but I claim that on any question which involves the question of peace and war the Canadian representative at Geneva must first secure the authorization of the Canadian government before making such a momentous proposal.'[20] Lapointe received some cold comfort from Senator Dandurand in Paris: 'Your communiqué has rejoiced the numerous friends of Italy here, who see a disavowal not only of Riddell but of the subsequent action of the Committee [in adopting the oil sanctions proposal].'[21] As always, unconditional approval came from his old patron, H.G. Carroll. Retired and in very poor health, Quebec's former lieutenant-governor applauded Lapointe's action: it was time to put 'this Riddell' in his place, but beware of the English press, he warned.[22]

While Quebec's French-language papers (with the notable exception of *La Presse*) praised Lapointe, the English press was divided on the subject.[23] And so was anglophone public opinion. The Irish-Catholic chief justice of Ontario, F.R. Latchford, congratulated Lapointe 'warmly' on his 'courage and wisdom in dealing with the ill-inspired declaration of Dr Riddell at Geneva.' 'Rest assured,' the judge told him, 'that all Canadians worthy of the name are with you heart and soul.' Letters pro and con poured into Lapointe's office. His private secretary, Philippe Picard, claimed that his boss got more praise than criticism, but one cynical correspondent from Manitoba, highly critical of Lapointe, anticipated that 'a pussy-footing secretary would not trouble his employer with the brain wave of an obscure voter in the distant town of Winnipeg.'[24]

An irate Saskatchewan merchant expressed the wish that the prime minister would do unto Lapointe what Lapointe had done unto Riddell, and on his return 'state that you were only voicing your own personal opinion.' When King returned he did in fact give a press conference in an attempt to counteract the impression left by Lapointe's statement that Canada was opposed to sanctions. Canada simply did not want to take the initiative, he told the press. The government had already implemented all sanctions so far approved by the League and would consider further sanctions if brought forward by other nations.[25] Lapointe felt 'very much abused for having stated what was, after all, the truth with regard to the position of Canada.' 'It was not properly a repudiation of any man,' he would later tell the House. 'It was the repudiation of what was being stated everywhere in the world, that it was Canada that was proposing this oil sanction.'[26]

The journalist Bruce Hutchison found Lapointe in a foul mood in late December when he came to interview the prime minister. Nothing was said about the Ethiopian affair until Lapointe suddenly strode in without knocking. Instead of his 'friendly, jovial, Gallic' self, the minister was 'scowling, sullen, and obviously under strain.' Casting his usual prudence to the wind, he launched into a 'fierce attack' on Riddell right in front of the journalist. The Hoare-Laval deal had made sanctions impossible he growled, before stalking off as abruptly as he had arrived.[27]

On 9 December the world had been shocked to learn that the British and French foreign ministers, Sir Samuel Hoare and Pierre Laval, had signed a secret agreement in Paris two days earlier recognizing Mussolini's territorial demands and effectively selling out Ethiopia. Although public indignation in Britain was so strong that the Baldwin government disavowed the agreement and Hoare resigned (repudiation of diplomats was becoming a habit in the Ethiopian affair), the revelation of Britain and France's dirty work made sanctions against Italy a lost cause. Hoare-Laval seems to have turned King as isolationist as Lapointe. 'It all shows, I think,' he wrote in his diary, 'the absurdity of Canada trying to deal in European or other world situations of which she has no knowledge and with respect to the decisions upon which she will have no voice. I agree with Lapointe that the League of Nations, as an agency for world peace, cannot contemplate action which necessarily means war.'[28]

Lapointe, meanwhile, was worrying about the fracturing of the Quebec Liberal party. The Gouin-Duplessis forces had refused to accept the thin Liberal victory in November; they continued with their public meetings and radio broadcasts as if the election had not taken place. To notch up the attack on Taschereau, Duplessis fathered an organization of rabidly nationalistic youth, the Jeunesses Patriotes, whom he let loose at Liberal rallies.[29] Quebec Liberals were insisting that Lapointe obtain some kind of accord with Gouin. 'You have all the necessary prestige to reestablish peace,' one correspondent told him, adding that all the Liberals he talked to thought it was 'high time you put your hand to it.' Some people urged Lapointe to take over the leadership of the provincial party – just for a short period to reunite the Liberal forces. Others urged against it, saying that he was needed in Ottawa.

Actually, Lapointe had no intention of taking over the mess in Quebec. On 15 December he dispatched Chubby Power as his emissary to Paul Gouin to see if the ALN leader would consider some sort of coalition with the Taschereau government. This started rumblings against Lapointe by the Jeunesses Patriotes who, as Duplessis's boys, were out to sabotage any revitalization of the provincial Liberal party. In any event, Gouin would have nothing to do with the old regime. Lapointe next thought of the MP Edward Lacroix for the leadership of the provincial Liberals. Taschereau gave his blessing, but the plan fell through when Lacroix told King, Lapointe, and Power that it was too late for the Liberals, no matter who the leader was – Duplessis would inevitably become the premier.[30] Right after the unproductive meeting with Lacroix in King's office, Lapointe left for a golfing vacation in

Bermuda with Jack Elliott. King found it 'very singular that with a crisis such as this in Quebec, Lapointe should go off on a trip to Bermuda.'[31]

King himself was in a state of nervous exhaustion. At the first cabinet meeting of the new year, feeling overworked and underserved, he lashed out at his colleagues. Rhyming off his numerous responsibilities, he was even more incensed when Euler suggested matter of factly that the prime minister give up a portfolio. Obviously fuming, King said he would gladly give external affairs to Lapointe (who was absent), but did they think anyone other than the prime minister could handle it if there was a war in Europe? Everyone took the cue and agreed it would not be wise, including Chubby Power who tactfully shook his head.[32] King left his dazed ministers under the impression that he was abdicating the task of leading the House. That evening at a dinner party at the Country Club, Charles Dunning took Dr Skelton aside for a long talk about the scene in cabinet. Who could they get to lead the House if King would not do it? he asked the number one mandarin. In Dunning's opinion, Lapointe was too indolent, Crerar had no gumption, and if he himself took it on it would make Jimmy Gardiner and others think he was trying to oust King. Skelton assured him that he did not have to worry. King would be fine now that he had got it all out of his system.[33]

In calling Lapointe indolent Dunning expressed the opinion of his colleagues. Chubby Power would later comment (though not in his memoirs) that Lapointe had the reputation of being lazy: 'It was almost like pulling teeth to get him to go and make speeches'[34] – a surprising revelation about the renowned French-Canadian orator. In fact, Lapointe left more and more to Power, who became his mainstay in the third King administration.

CHAPTER TWENTY

The Curse of Patronage

Five years of R.B. Bennett's neglect had created a pent-up demand in Quebec for patronage. After the election that returned the Liberals to power, their 'famished supporters,'[1] as Henri Bourassa remarked humorously to King, descended upon Lapointe. Both Taschereau's and Gouin's people had campaigned for the federal Liberals; now they were clamouring for their reward.

Lapointe's riding of Quebec East was a microcosm of the provincial situation, with rival groups fighting for control of patronage. The Club Mercier, long a centre of Liberal influence in Quebec East, had been taken over by ALN supporters. Strangely enough, these bolters still claimed to be Liberals, calling themselves National Liberals and demanding patronage from the federal party. The reaction of 'orthodox' Liberals to the ALN takeover of the Club Mercier was to start a new political club. The former MLA for Quebec East, Louis Letourneau, was active in its formation. Presuming on their long friendship, Letourneau warned Lapointe that the ALN people were using his name to get patronage for their own friends and to 'ruin your true friends.' Lapointe replied that Letourneau was asking him to take sides against people who had always supported him.

In the hope of extricating himself from the tug of war between the orthodox Liberals and ALN 'Liberals,' Lapointe set up a committee of two from each ward to deal with patronage.[2] Nevertheless, the pressures on him continued. One good Liberal infuriated Lapointe by holding up Rodolphe Lemieux as a model for what a Quebec politician could get out of Ottawa. Lapointe defended himself vigorously: 'It will surprise you to learn that I got three times more millions for Quebec harbour in nine years than Lemieux got for the Gaspé in thirty. Moreover, it was I as Minister for Quebec District who persuaded the government to acquire the Gaspé railway, which is perhaps not an act I should boast of because of the deficit of the national railways which increases every year.'[3] He also informed his friendly critic that a large sum of money had just been allocated for work on Quebec's ramparts.

To add to his problems, French-Canadian youth organizations, fired up by ultra-nationalist priests, were even spouting separation from Canada. The fountainhead of clerical nationalism was Abbé Groulx at the University of Montreal. Through lectures, books, and articles in L'Action Nationale, Groulx propagated the idea of a separate French Catholic state, which he called 'Laurentia.' The Laurentide ideal held immense appeal for young people who had little hope of finding jobs. The most incendiary belonged to Groulx's junior auxiliary, Jeune Canada, or to Jeunesses Patriotes, the organization started by Duplessis to break up Liberal rallies. Since the raison d'être of these young nationalistes was to tear down Confederation, nothing the federalist Lapointe could do would satisfy them.

That Lapointe regarded Abbé Groulx as a genuine threat to national unity is clear from a letter he wrote to Charles Dunning on 20 February 1936: 'You may have read reports of lectures by such a man as Abbé Groulx who openly advocates the creation of a distinct state of Quebec because of the alleged unfairness with which our Province has been treated under the present system of Confederation. This I am afraid makes a strong appeal to the young men of Quebec and I hope my friends will strengthen my hands and the hands of those who are fighting and will fight against any such doctrine.'[4]

Lapointe was certainly intimidated by these extremist nationalist youths. He did his best to appease them and their clerical mentors. A case in point was his careful handling of Father Thomas Mignault, a teacher at the Jesuit College Sainte-Marie. Mignault was an open separatist. His every lecture, be it history, geology, literature, or economics, was directed at inspiring a belief in the desirability and inevitability of 'Laurentia.' Early in the new year he wrote Lapointe an insulting letter informing him that he was losing popularity in Montreal and was being held up to scorn. After this inauspicious beginning, Mignault proceeded to ask Lapointe to stay the deportation of 'a distinguished Frenchman,' an engineer who unfortunately had not filled out the proper papers.[5] Immigration fell within Crerar's department of mines and resources, and Lapointe wrote to his old friend vouching for the deportee: 'I have been given to understand through reliable sources

First Session of the 13th Parliament, held in the Victoria Museum, 1918. The museum was Parliament's temporary home after fire destroyed the original building in 1916. The first session in the present building was held in February 1920.

Ernest Lapointe, Mackenzie King, and Vincent Massey returning from the Imperial Conference of 1926 on the SS *Majestic*. The gentleman on Lapointe's right is Senator W.L. McDougald, subsequently a principal figure in the Beauharnois Power scandal.

Emma 'Mimy' Lapointe in the 1920s.

Ernest Lapointe with sixteen-year-old Hugues (right) and secretary Philippe
Picard in Egypt en route to Geneva from Canberra in 1927.

The Canadian delegation bound for the ODL Conference in London in 1929, on the *Empress of Australia*. Behind Lapointe, wearing a cap, is the self-effacing under-secretary of state, Dr O.D. Skelton.

Ernest and Emma Lapointe on shipboard in the 1930s.

Ernest Lapointe with King Edward VIII at the unveiling of the Vimy Ridge Memorial, 26 July 1936. This was one of the few public ceremonies King Edward attended before his abdication.

Mackenzie King and Ernest Lapointe, photograph by Horsdal, 1938.

Mackenzie King and Ernest Lapointe, in Windsor uniforms, greeting King George VI and Queen Elizabeth on their arrival at Quebec City for the royal tour in May 1939.

Ernest Lapointe leading cheers for Mackenzie King at the banquet celebrating the prime minister's twenty years as Liberal leader, Toronto, 8 August 1939.

Emma Lapointe was as keen on bridge as her husband was on golf.

Senators A. Blais, F. Fafard, J.H. King, and Ernest Lapointe playing golf at Harrison Hot Springs, British Columbia, 1941.

Funeral cortège of Ernest Lapointe in Quebec City, 29 November 1941.

On the occasion of his thirty-fifth anniversary as a member of Parliament, Lapointe was honoured at a banquet in Quebec City on 18 February 1939. This page from the program sums up his career pictorially.

that this gentleman would not be a charge to the community, that he is perfectly reliable and that if he broke our regulations in any way he was not aware of them when he first entered Canada.'

Crerar replied that the man had entered from the United States in 1928 without complying with the Immigration Act and had been on relief for three and a half years. The deportation was properly ordered, but (clearly to oblige Lapointe) the man would be allowed to remain in Canada on condition that he cease to be a public charge. This was as far as he could go, Crerar told Lapointe.[6] It was not far enough to suit Mignault, who protested that the minister of immigration had given financial assistance to a great number of less desirable foreigners. He claimed that the father prefect of the Society of Jesus was 'scandalized.' Lapointe tried again, instructing his secretary, Philippe Picard, to 'build' another letter to Crerar. (In the end his advocacy was successful. This man and his wife continued to draw unemployment relief, and on the fall of France in 1940 Lapointe obtained an order-in-council allowing their daughter to immigrate to Canada.)[7]

By the end of March Lapointe was on the verge of a nervous breakdown. He was suffering terrible insomnia, and he confided to King that he could not control his nerves. 'I strongly urged Lapointe to take a trip overseas, as he is planning to do,' King wrote in his diary on 28 March; 'It means an absence of three weeks, but I feel that unless he gets away he is apt to incur a breakdown, through worry, patronage and pressure of one kind or another.'[8] Their cabinet colleagues would have been surprised to learn the real nature of Lapointe's illness, which necessitated his leave of absence during this extraordinarily busy session. They probably assumed it was a recurrence of his physical ailments, which had now been diagnosed as diabetes. With his boyish smile and twinkling eyes, his wit and good humour, Lapointe would have seemed the last one among them to have a nervous breakdown.

He spent a quiet April at the Paris legation with the Roys. Not only were Philippe and Hélène devoted to him, but it is not without significance that Philippe was a physician. On the 17th Lapointe wrote King that he was gradually feeling better. 'I am trying to acquire a new spirit under which I will do my best in every way, and cease to worry so much about unfair, unreasonable, ungrateful and crazy people.' Reluctant to meet people, he did make one call on a law professor from the University of Paris. Lapointe was sponsoring the repeal of Section 98 of the Criminal Code, and he wanted to hear the distinguished jurist's opinion on unlawful associations. Introduced in 1919 to incriminate the leaders of the Winnipeg General Strike, Section 98 made it a criminal offence, with a maximum penalty of twenty years, to be a member of, or even to attend a meeting of, an organization that allegedly advocated the use of force to bring about governmental or economic change. When the professor read the provision with its restrictions on the basic freedoms, he told his visitor in no uncertain terms that it was 'a blot on the statutes of any land.' 'People here,' Lapointe wrote King, 'cannot understand that any citizen could be prosecuted for a crime just because he holds certain views, however nefarious they might be, if he never translates them into action.'

Coming from Canada where Tim Buck and the communist leadership had been sentenced to seven years in jail in 1931 simply for belonging to the party, Lapointe was amazed to see that French communists were treated like any other politicians. France was going to the polls, and communist rallies proceeded unhampered by the police. Lapointe noted that the French party attracted a higher class of followers than the Canadian: 'Here the Communists are gentlemen,' he informed King.[9]

Lapointe was back in his place at the cabinet table on 2 May. King thought he looked well and rested and was extremely glad to see him. More than ever, King regarded Lapointe as his right-hand man. Symbolically, when a photographer came to take pictures of the new cabinet, King also had him take a photograph of just himself and Lapointe.[10] On 19 June Lapointe moved second reading of the bill to repeal Section 98 of the Criminal Code. His sponsorship of this measure greatly enhanced his reputation for liberal-mindedness. Freedom of speech was the gospel in English Canada; public opinion, except in Quebec, was strongly in favour of repeal.

Drawing attention to the fact that Section 98 duplicated the War Measures Act word for word, Lapointe declared that wartime measures in peacetime infringed upon the citizens' liberties and created a dangerous precedent for setting aside the rule of law. He called it indefensible that, under this provision, the police could enter a home on mere suspicion that they might find objectionable literature. He pointed out that even possessing revolutionary literature could put a person in jail for twenty years. He attacked the underlying presumption of guilt whereby a person was presumed guilty just for attending a meeting of 'a so-called illegal association.' Besides, Lapointe asserted, this kind of law was useless; it made martyrs of men like Tim Buck. Public sympathy had secured his release when he had served half his sentence, and the first thing he did was to hold meetings challenging the authorities to rearrest him.

Lapointe knew that some people were saying he was a friend of the communists for taking this position. 'Those who say that know that I am not. I abhor, I hate the teachings and ideals of communism. But I want to fight them in a successful way.' That way was by providing social justice. There was a flash of his old antagonism towards 'the interests': 'Conditions which permit a small group of men to get together with a little sum of money which with the help of privileges and of protective laws and insufficient social legislation became $15,000,000 after a few years, are productive of communism.' Like all Canadian civil libertarians of his generation, Lapointe looked to Britain as the exemplar. Citing English court decisions and the nineteenth-century Whig writers, he concluded that some overt act of incitement was required; simply holding an opinion was not enough to prove danger to the state.

Lapointe's speech that morning was the testament of a liberal – but a cautious 'King Liberal.' After stating that the Criminal Code provided sufficient protection against sedition, he announced in an offhand way that he proposed 'to add a few words to Section 133.' The proposed subsection (4) would make it unlawful to teach or advocate the use of force to bring about governmental change. For Woodsworth, this was simply shuffling the restrictions on freedom of speech from Section 98 to Section 133. The CCF leader observed dryly: 'The minister has taken the responsibility of urging the repeal of this section, but unfortunately, in my judgment, what he gives with one hand he partly takes away with the other.'[11]

Oscar Boulanger, a Liberal MP, interpreted Lapointe's addition to the Code the same way, although he heartily approved of it. In the past the Senate had defeated attempts to repeal Section 98; yet this time the bill sailed through the upper house. In September Boulanger wrote a worried Cardinal Villeneuve that the reason repeal passed the Senate so quickly was because of the amendment to Section 133. 'The government,' he soothed the prelate, 'abrogates with the one hand and takes it back with the other.'[12]

Lapointe piloted another important resolution through the House before Parliament prorogued at the end of June. The Liberals were proposing an amendment to Bennett's Bank of Canada Act, and the Quebec caucus insisted that Lapointe reintroduce his motion for bilingual currency that had been defeated in 1934. Bennett's grudging policy of separate French banknotes for Quebec was totally unacceptable. Backed by King, Lapointe inserted a clause in the government bill requiring bilingual banknotes. Appropriate to his subject, Lapointe began in French and then switched over to English. He emphasized that private Canadian banks had always issued bilingual currency and that this was the practice in all countries with more than one official language. Furthermore, he warned the House that failure to have bilingual banknotes would provide ammunition for the separatist movement that was gaining ground among young Quebeckers. In a pointed reply to the former prime minister who had opposed any more 'concessions' to the French, Lapointe declared, 'We do not want any concessions. We do not ask even privileges, we ask simply the right to live as we have lived ... There are nine generations of my family buried in this country. I do not need concessions in Canada or anywhere else.'[13]

The sincerity and dignity with which Lapointe defended his people's language rights carried the day. King was relieved when not a single Liberal voted against the bilingual banknotes clause. Rumour had it that some anglophone Conservatives rebuked Bennett for his 'concessions' speech.[14] Lapointe never hesitated when it came to promoting bilingualism in the federal government. With the death of George V on 20 January 1936, civil servants were required to take an oath of allegiance to King Edward VIII. At the request of numerous francophone organizations, Lapointe arranged for the oath to be taken in French. The St Jean-Baptiste Society expressed its thanks: 'We know that you do not let any occasion pass for affirming the principle of official bilingualism in the federal government.'[15]

Appreciation from the leading nationalist organization offset to some degree the very unpleasant 'veiled threats' he was receiving from ultra-nationalist youth groups. Accustomed to adulation from Quebec's young people, Lapointe was unprepared for the insolence of the Jeunesses Patriotes. In June they wrote two letters that displayed utter contempt for King and himself. The one to Lapointe came from Réal Denis, one of Duplessis's plants in the youth organization. On the surface a complaint about C.D. Howe's disrespect for the French language, the letter was really more about federal patronage – or the lack of it. In March Howe had introduced a bill to consolidate the seven corruption-ridden federal harbour boards into a single national board. Four of these boards were in Quebec, and the new policy would eliminate most local contracts. The Jeunesses Patriotes sent a letter of protest about the bill to Howe claiming that the government had betrayed the French Canadians. Howe's reply (basically advising them to read the bill before they judged it) came to them in a rather ungrammatical French translation. Enclosing a copy of the offending translation, Denis wrote an outraged letter to Lapointe – 'You will judge yourself the massacre of the French language.' He warned the minister of justice that if he did not take action, the Jeunesses Patriotes would be 'forced to use the same means with our representatives at Ottawa that we've used in Quebec.' Lapointe recognized this as a threat to pillory him and the other federal ministers from Quebec, as they had done to Taschereau.

Lapointe's initial response was to instruct Picard to chastise Denis for the tone of his letter, but the original draft was not sent. Instead, a conciliatory reply went out, advising Denis and his group that 'Mr. Lapointe has made personal representations to his colleague about this translation and can assure them there will be improvement on that side.' Lapointe did send a personal note to Howe, telling him that his letter had been widely published in the Quebec papers and that he agreed with these young men that the French translation was 'horrible.' Howe replied that the translation branch was in the process of reorganization.[16]

King received an even more outrageous letter from the president of the Jeunesses Patriotes. Writing in French, Walter O'Leary berated the prime minister: 'You have imposed the law centralizing the four big Quebec ports, and, against principles of liberty, have imposed silence on French Canadian MPs who opposed it.' There followed a denunciation of the Liberals' centralizing policy in banking, radio, and transportation, which the writer charged 'attacks the autonomy of our province.' The young people of Quebec 'warn you publicly and loyally that we will frustrate the plan for total centralization prepared by the enemies of our nationality.' Needless to say, this distasteful communication moved out of King's office swiftly and landed on Lapointe's desk.[17]

Meanwhile, events were transpiring in Quebec that would further bedevil Lapointe's relations with his home province. On 11 June Taschereau resigned with his entire cabinet, hounded out of office by Duplessis's obstructionism and character assassination. Lapointe may have played his part in Taschereau's political tragedy by refusing to bail him out with a federal loan when the provincial legislature would not grant supply. But the death blow for Taschereau came with Duplessis's vicious and sustained attack in the legislature for corruption in his government, irreparably soiling the sixty-nine-year-old premier's reputation. Throughout the turbulent session, Paul Gouin had remained silent. In fact, he had faded out of the picture. Duplessis had co-opted ALN members by paying off their campaign debts, and the June announcement that the Gouin-Duplessis alliance was at an end came as no surprise to anyone. Before departing, Taschereau had announced an election for 15 August, which Duplessis's Union Nationale was widely expected to win.

Lapointe and Power had to find a successor to Taschereau quickly. The man they selected to lead the provincial Liberals for the remainder of their term was Adélard Godbout. An unimposing person, Godbout nonetheless was a good speaker and had a reputation for honesty. Though he had been Taschereau's minister of agriculture, he was untainted by the corruption that had brought down the government. Godbout and Lapointe were closely connected. They both came from St Eloi, and Godbout's brother was married to Lapointe's sister. An agronomist with a farm that was more of a hobby than a livelihood, Godbout had little money of his own. To be out of office was an undoubted hardship for him, but the caretaker premiership was hardly a prospect for long-term employment. Nevertheless, pressed by Taschereau and Lapointe, he accepted. Perhaps because he liked the man, Lapointe insisted that Godbout had a good chance to win the election. But Chubby Power's more realistic assessment was that the Liberals had little prospect of winning with a leader who was 'not a good drawing card.'[18]

Neither Lapointe nor Power was on hand to help Godbout and the tattered provincial Liberal party. Prior to the announcement of the provincial election, King had delegated them, along with the minister of defence, to represent Canada at the dedication of the Vimy Memorial to Canada's war dead. Before leaving for France in early July, Lapointe issued a press release expressing confidence in Godbout. With an ocean between him and the Quebec nationalists, Lapointe, speaking at an official luncheon in Paris, held up Canada as an example of racial unity that European nations might well emulate. He worked the same message into his speech at the dedication ceremony at Vimy Ridge.

On 26 July 1936, on the battlefield of Vimy Ridge in northern France, a quarter of a million people, including 6,000 Canadians, thronged the slope where in April 1917 the four divisions of the Canadian Corps had swept up to take the ridge. Soaring above the crowd was the memorial of white stone pylons bearing the figure of the cross, designed by Canadian sculptor Walter Allward. As squadrons of British and French planes dipped their wings in an aerial salute and military bands played

'God Save the King,' Edward VIII ascended the monument escorted by Ernest Lapointe. Speaker followed speaker – the official chaplains, the king, the president of France, Lapointe, and the Canadian minister of defence. Mackenzie King's message, a plodding appeal for peace, was read by the Honourable C.D. Power. (Listening to the ceremony over the radio, King 'could have cried with agony' at Chubby's delivery. He felt certain that 'delivered by myself, with the sympathy I felt, [it] would have made an impression.')[19]

On 11 August Lapointe sailed back to Canada with a hungover Chubby Power. Bad news about the Quebec election campaign greeted them even before they stepped ashore at Quebec. Bobby Lapointe and Chubby Power's son, Pen, who had come out on the pilot boat, reported to their fathers that solid Liberal constituencies were defecting to the Union Nationale. Chubby noticed that Ernest was 'shocked' to hear that his old riding of Kamouraska would probably elect the Union Nationale candidate René Chaloult, a radical nationalist lawyer from Quebec City.[20] With only a few days to go, Ernest and Chubby tried to stem the Union Nationale tide. The day of their arrival in Quebec City, they spoke at an enormous rally for Godbout on the Esplanade, where Lapointe encountered heckling from rebellious young Liberals. Over the next few days they addressed dozens of meetings, but to no avail. The Union Nationale was elected in a landslide, and not even Godbout saved his seat. In Kamouraska René Chaloult defeated the Liberal incumbent. In his victory speech he denounced Lapointe and Power for mixing into the provincial election. If the Ottawa Liberals continued their meddling, he prophesied that a Quebec nationalist party would enter the federal arena. *Le Devoir* reported loud applause. In Quebec East, where Oscar Drouin won the seat for the Union Nationale, feeling against Lapointe personally ran so high that a UN supporter dared to state publicly that he could 'spit on' him.[21] (Sensing how the election would go, King had prudently stayed out of it. On 14 August he issued instructions forbidding the use of his name in the provincial election.)[22]

After forty years, the Liberal grip on the province of Quebec was broken. Utterly disheartened, Lapointe returned to Ottawa. Without preamble, he told King he was going to resign his seat: 'If those fellows don't want me, they can elect someone else.' King gathered from the distraught Lapointe that people were saying the Quebec result was a non-confidence vote in the federal ministers. King could see that his pride and vanity were hurt. ('It is the French temperament,' King wrote sententiously in his diary. 'They cannot stand defeat.') He was also shocked by Lapointe's appearance. Lapointe had put on weight, especially around the stomach, and looked completely 'knocked out.' After King's sympathy and his advice not to make a hasty decision, Lapointe sufficiently collected himself to attend the afternoon cabinet meeting.[23]

A few days later they had another personal talk. Lapointe was deeply hurt by the criticism he was getting in *Le Devoir*, especially from the editor, Georges Pelletier, who pretended friendship for him. Pelletier had written that Lapointe would have been better advised to do something about Howe's harbour bill than to interfere in the provincial campaign. Lapointe told King that he did not think he could win another election. Another of his worries was that he would be left without Chubby Power, who, he admitted to King, had fallen off the wagon pretty badly at the Vimy ceremonials. He complained bitterly of the harassment he suffered from people who wanted contracts and jobs.[24]

The new businesslike ministers displayed little appreciation of Lapointe's difficulties. Ilsley, for instance, continued to send unilingual English revenue officers into Montreal. Lapointe was not blind to the lack of technically trained French personnel. Mines and Resources was being moved to Howe's department, and Lapointe was aware that among the present staff no French Canadian would qualify for a senior position after the reorganization. To counter the anticipated absence of French branch directors, he urged Fernand Rinfret, the secretary of state, to appoint Gustave Lanctot as chief archivist without delay. Otherwise, as he told his confrère, they would certainly face bitter criticism from their province.[25]

'I notice that the Quebec ministers have become very insistent on increasing the French representation on Boards,' King wrote in his diary.[26] Lapointe's best efforts, however, fell short of expectations in his home province. 'THE MINISTER OF JUSTICE!!! WHAT JUSTICE!!!!' exclaimed *L'Action Catholique*; the organ of the Catholic Church in Quebec complained that out of thirty-two positions on the boards of the Bank of Canada, the Canadian Broadcasting Corporation, and the CNR, only six went to French Canadians. *Le Devoir*, a Duplessis supporter, sneered that bilingual currency did not make up for under-representation on government committees, and concluded on the ominous note that if the Liberal MPs did not do more for French Canadians they would be replaced. Even the appointment of Ernest Chevrier to the Ontario Court of Appeal did not earn Lapointe any thanks in *Le Devoir*, which harped on the twenty-five years it had taken to get a Franco-Ontarian appointed.[27] (The demand for more French Canadians on government boards took a nasty turn in the case of the CBC. Quebec nationalism of the Groulx school was virulently anti-Semitic. The appointment of the Ontario movie-theatre mogul N.L. Nathanson to the CBC board was condemned by *Le Devoir* as a sop to the Jewish minority, which it claimed deprived the French minority of an extra seat.)[28]

Lapointe was still undecided about his future in September when King went off to Geneva to attend a session at the League of Nations, leaving him as acting prime minister. While King was away Lapointe received a body blow that all but decided him to quit public life. The Quebec MPs, previously full of respect for their spokesman and leader, turned on him. Unfortunately, Chubby Power, who might have put down the revolt, was in the hospital. Claiming to speak for all French-Canadian members, a Quebec MP sent Lapointe a letter reproaching him in the strongest terms for not securing more federal appointments for French Canadians. He stated that he and the other Quebec MPs had to answer for the lack of patronage. The abolition of the regional harbour commissions was a particular grievance. The writer also alluded to the unhappy results of the provincial election and seemed to hold Lapointe responsible. The gist of the letter was that Lapointe was not representing the Quebec caucus adequately.

Lapointe did not hide his hurt and anger. He felt the charge was completely unjustified, particularly since he had just announced the appointment of a Franco-Ontarian to the Ontario Court of Appeal, something French Quebeckers had been pressing for for years. In a letter circulated to all the members of the Quebec caucus, he defended himself and the government. He accused the MPs of not knowing how to present the facts to their constituents. They needed to publicize the fact that after last year's election, Ontario had almost as many MPs as did Quebec and Quebec no longer held the overwhelming balance of power. While he regretted as much as they did that French Canadians were not among the ten officers in the new departments, they could not expect incumbent officers to be dismissed in favour of less senior or less experienced francophones. He also reminded them that appointments to government agencies had to be representative of the country as a whole. Then in a *cri du coeur*, he asked why were they uniting with his critics instead of standing behind him.

The revolt against Lapointe broke in the press. First reported in Quebec City's *Le Soleil*, it was then picked up by the *Montreal Gazette*. How painful it was for him to see the front-page headline: 'Disgruntled

Liberals in Quebec May Cause Lapointe Retirement.' (The subhead read: 'Members Feel Patronage Scarce for French-Canadians, Blame Situation on Present Leader of Party's Federal Arm in Province.') The article speculated that he might go to the Supreme Court to replace the ailing Arthur Cannon or perhaps to Paris to succeed Philippe Roy as Canadian minister to France. From the *Gazette* the story moved on to the pages of *Le Devoir*, where new revelations appeared. It seemed that for some time there had been an underhand campaign in the corridors of Parliament to oust Lapointe as minister of justice. Often so critical of Lapointe, Pelletier in this instance was supportive, declaring that there was nobody in the Quebec delegation of a calibre to replace him. Moreover, said Pelletier, Lapointe could not be blamed for the defeat of the provincial Liberals; he had entered the fray at the last moment, at the urgent request of federal and provincial Liberals, when the cause was irremediably lost.[29]

Rumours of his resignation were growing daily. The secretary of the Club Lapointe urged him to deny them. Lapointe's response showed that he had made his decision. He would stay at his post, he told his well-wisher, as long as he had the confidence of the voters.[30] In fact, the whole brouhaha was subsiding. On 10 October the MPs for Quebec district issued a press release stating they had informed the Honourable Minister of Justice that, contrary to rumours in the press, they wanted him to keep his post as head of the French Canadians in Parliament. Behind the scenes, however, they presented him with a list of demands: absolute and exclusive control of patronage (they couldn't get elected without it); more public works in Quebec – for example, the transcontinental highway then under construction; all ice-breakers to be put in service the next winter to provide jobs; and the English directors in the post office to be replaced by French.[31] All very well for the MPs to claim they could choose qualified people better than the Civil Service Commission, Lapointe thought, but as he told one Quebec district Liberal, 'No government could succeed in reestablishing patronage in permanent employment.'[32]

Like the Quebec MPs, his constituents did not understand that he had to fit their demands into government policy. Lapointe's old problem with the boot and shoe manufacturers' lobby was as bad as ever. King was determined to lower tariffs. Lapointe agreed in principle, but when it came up in cabinet that the duty on footwear was to be reduced from 25 to 20 per cent, he put up a fierce resistance. 'They're saying that I'm no good and can't protect my constituency,' he told his colleagues morosely. 'I will have to defend a defense programme, and I cannot see how I can face my electors if I allow any change.'[33] His colleagues agreed that he was in an 'untenable' position, but sympathy was all he got. At the next meeting, however, with prodding from King, cabinet only moderately lowered the tariff on footwear.

Lapointe could not shake his depression. From Paris Philippe Roy prescribed a long rest before the next session. Roy urged King to let Lapointe come over for a month's holiday 'to recover his strength and energy.' Otherwise he felt that their 'dear friend' would resign, and this would create 'a panic' in French Canada 'at this present moment.' King's reply was suave. 'I agree,' he wrote Roy, 'that he has been worried a great deal by patronage seekers who are the curse to all of us.' But 'I doubt if it would be in his own interests to plan another trip to Europe in the interval. He has, as you know already had two visits to France this year.'[34] To save his sanity, Lapointe deputized Oscar Bouchard to deal with the hordes of patronage seekers. Various government personnel were told to consult with Bouchard, who operated out of the Quebec City post office, before proceeding on patronage requests. Nevertheless, the Simard shipyards continued to receive rich contracts, cooked well in advance of tenders.[35]

At cabinet meetings Lapointe was a Cassandra, trying to awaken his English colleagues to the hostility developing in Duplessis's Quebec towards the federal government. At year's end he presented King with translations of some articles from L'Action Catholique, Le Devoir, and Le Droit so he could see 'what many of our Newspaper Editors think of us.'[36] The papers denounced the federal Liberal party for failing to give Quebec its due and demanded more patronage and more bilingualism in the government. Since these papers represented nationalist opinion, Lapointe's sample was one-sided. It was a different story in Quebec's most widely read newspaper, La Presse, and in the Liberal organ, Le Soleil. But it was clerical nationalism, harnessed to Duplessis's triumphant chariot, that was giving Lapointe such cause for concern.

King thought Lapointe was overreacting. A good dose of liberalism administered to his own people would cure them of this unhealthy sectionalism. With Anglo-Saxon phlegm, he commented in his diary: 'No one can convince me that if he, himself, and a few others would begin to expound the doctrines of Liberalism to the younger generation of Quebec, it would not take long to free them from clerical or political intolerance.'[37] But King would not interfere. Quebec was Lapointe's business.

CHAPTER TWENTY-ONE

The Padlock Act

On 5 January 1937 Mackenzie King was having tea with the apostolic delegate's secretary at Laurier House. Monsignor Mossoni had spent the holidays in Quebec. Over the teacups he confided to his host that Ernest Lapointe was losing his hold on the province, even among the clergy. King was surprised to hear this, though Lapointe had been telling him the same thing for months.[1] King did not seem to understand what had happened in Quebec. He even expressed the opinion that it might be easier to deal with an opposition government than the provincial Liberals. Lapointe knew better. In the past he had locked horns with Taschereau over waterpower and constitutional reform, but now he was confronted by a premier satisfied with nothing less than complete provincial autonomy and with whom he would have no influence. It was worse than that. According to Chubby Power, the Union Nationale and Duplessis detested Lapointe and 'conducted a kind of whispering campaign against him.'[2]

Unlike Taschereau, whom the hierarchy had cordially disliked for his periodic musings about taxing church property, the new premier was manifestly a devoted son of the church. Despite his drinking and vulgarity, the craggy-faced bachelor enjoyed a special rapport with Cardinal Villeneuve. Both were obsessed with communism; indeed, church and state had an implicit concordat to eradicate any Red presence in the province. There was no real communist threat, however. The Catholic province was an inhospitable place for anyone on the left. Church-led French Canadians were a deeply conservative people. Every Sunday they heard their curés damn the pernicious doctrine from the pulpit. In all seriousness, one monsignor wrote Lapointe in February 1937 that the Reds were about to make a violent attack upon Quebec City – 'the innocent blood will be in large part your responsibility,' Lapointe was told, for his part in repealing Section 98.[3]

The proposed visit to Canada of three Spanish republicans in October 1936 illustrates Quebec's intolerance of anything that smacked of communism. Civil war had broken out in Spain in July 1936. The leader of the revolt against the republican government was a general of the extreme Catholic right, Francisco Franco. Franco was kept well supplied with arms by the German and Italian dictators while the republican government – a coalition of the left ranging from socialists to anarchists – had little beyond some antiquated guns from the Soviet Union. Quebec was strongly on Franco's side against the Soviet-backed, anticlerical republicans whose anarchist allies, over whom it had no control, were burning churches and murdering priests and nuns. When word of the visit of the Spanish republicans reached Quebec City, a mob of stick-wielding students threatened to riot if the visitors were allowed to hold a meeting. The mayor cancelled the permit, and Duplessis and Cardinal Villeneuve commended the students publicly.[4]

In December the RCMP advised cabinet that another delegation of Spanish republicans, two men and two women, might be coming to Canada to raise money for the government forces. Lapointe urged cabinet to deny them entry. 'Lapointe seemed to think that if they were allowed to come into Canada at all, it might only lead to secession of the Province of Quebec from the rest of the Dominion,' King wrote in his diary. Though the two other French ministers present supported Lapointe, the English ministers refused to bar the representatives of the duly elected government of Spain. They told Lapointe that it would bring into question the very right of freedom of speech in Canada. That evening King delivered a stirring address on liberty to his diary: 'I would rather go out of office and out of life itself, if need be, fighting to maintain the liberties we have and which have been bought so dearly, than to be a party to losing them through fear and prejudice however strong.' He added that 'Lapointe's fear of the Cardinal and Duplessis amounts to absolute terror.' The end result was a typical King compromise. The Spanish republicans were to be informed that if they came to Canada they must stay away from Quebec.[5]

Germany and Italy were using the Spanish civil war to test their new bombers and fighter planes. Encouraged by the League of Nations' inaction when Mussolini invaded Ethiopia, in March 1936 Hitler had marched into the demilitarized zone of the Rhineland. Although this was a violation of the Versailles Treaty and the Locarno Pact, England

and France did nothing to stop Hitler. At the time, King wrote in his diary: 'If League decided to support France as I believe the Council will, I feel Canada will have to support the League to the extent of sanctions, as imposed against Italy, but with the same limitations, namely economic sanctions only and not military as well.' Lapointe agreed wholeheartedly. The international situation was still tense when he was in Paris in April 1936, and he had written King that 'it would be almost an act of criminal stupidity on the part of Canada to espouse any European quarrel just because of our constitutional and international status.'[6]

At Geneva in September 1936 King delivered a lecture that effectively consigned the League to a debating society. (Lapointe cabled him congratulations on behalf of the cabinet.) When asked by the British on his way home what Canada was prepared to do in the event of war, King said in effect, 'Don't count on us.' In a discussion with the secretary of state for Dominion affairs, he pointed out the 'nationalistic feeling in Quebec and the feeling that many had of sympathy with the United States' point of view, that as a North American continent we should not be drawn into the Old World situation.'[7]

As he confided to his diary, however, King was convinced that if there was a world war, Canada could not escape. Britain and the other Dominions were beginning to arm; Canada would have to increase its defence spending too. Before leaving for Geneva he had set up a cabinet defence committee composed of Lapointe, Dunning, and the defence minister Ian Mackenzie, with himself as chairman. At the first meeting, the chiefs-of-staff made it plain that Canada's defence capability was completely inadequate. The country had to be prepared with something more than several unseaworthy destroyers and the few dozen obsolete planes that comprised its air force. 'All the French members, with the exception of Lapointe,' King noted, 'were pretty well content to leave matters as they were.' Lapointe was amenable to a bigger defence budget so long as there was no build-up of the army, as this would trigger Quebec's fear of an expeditionary force. King went along with Lapointe since this meshed with his own thinking that the money would best be spent on aircraft, which could be justified in terms of coastal defence.

Lapointe had rallied to the chief, but he was nervous. When the 1937 defence estimates came up in cabinet, King noted that 'Lapointe seemed greatly concerned about Quebec, fearing the nationalistic party will soon become a solid block in Parliament against any expenditures for defense purposes.'[8] Despite his fears, Lapointe loyally supported King in facing down resistance from their English as well as French colleagues. The French ministers were not alone in opposing an increase in defence spending – King was 'amazed' at how isolationist the cabinet was. The minister of defence was allotted a budget of $35 million, a sizeable increase over the $20 million for 1936 but a far cry from the $65 million asked for by the chiefs-of-staff.[9] To sell the estimates to Parliament and the country, the government would promise that the money would be used for the defence of Canada only.

Lapointe defended the rearmament policy in caucus. As he expected, he met with outspoken resistance from the Quebec MPs. King had hoped to have Mackenzie's departmental estimates slip by the House with little debate, but as soon as they were tabled Woodsworth introduced an amendment that 'in the event of war Canada should remain strictly neutral regardless of who the belligerents may be.' King replied emphatically that he could not have his hands tied in that manner; when and if war came, Parliament would decide Canada's role. On 4 February 1937 Lapointe rose to speak against Woodsworth's neutrality motion. Everyone could see that he was not his usual calmly confident self. Since the end of the Great War he had categorically denied the possibility of Canada participating in another war. Now he was taking the first step on an unfamiliar path that could be hazardous.

He began by saying that he hoped Canada would be able to remain outside any conflict, but 'if international chiefs or gangsters ever come to assail us on a mad impulse – because the world is mad at the present time – we cannot meet them with a declaration of neutrality. Canada must be ready to defend itself.' Emphasizing that participation would go no further than defending Canada from invasion, he maintained that his present position was consistent with the position he had taken in the fight against conscription in 1917. He had said then that French Canadians would be ready to defend Canada when the time came, and that statement still held good, he assured his listeners. Lapointe had the satisfaction of seeing only three Quebec Liberals vote for the Woodsworth amendment, which was handily defeated. When the debate on the main motion came, sixteen Quebec backbenchers, who were rarely heard from, rose one after another and, speaking in French, put on record their opposition to overseas involvement. Having got this off their chests, they fell in line, and to Lapointe's immense relief the French MPs without exception voted in favour of the defence estimates. Despite his anxiety about a nationalist revolt, Lapointe had carried the entire Quebec bloc with him through what King had viewed with foreboding as 'the most dangerous of all divisions of the session.' 'We have kept the unity of the party,' King exulted. He could thank his Quebec lieutenant for it.

Lapointe had little time to savour his victory before Maurice Duplessis sprang an unpleasant surprise on him. On 17 March 1937 the Quebec premier introduced a bill empowering the attorney general (Duplessis himself) to padlock any premises allegedly used for the propagation of communism. When a member ventured to ask how communism could be recognized without a definition in the Act, Duplessis replied smugly that it could be 'felt.' Unless they were ready to be branded as 'pinks,' the Liberal opposition had no choice but to vote for the bill. It sailed through three readings in half an hour and was passed unanimously by both chambers of the Quebec legislature. Duplessis hinted broadly that the anti-communist legislation had been proposed by the cardinal himself.

The bill was, in fact, instigated by Villeneuve. The cardinal had formed a secret committee to study and counter the greatly inflated problem of communism in Quebec. Composed of five ultra-nationalist clerics and laymen, the committee had enlisted the provincial police chief to supply it with information. The cardinal used this committee to orchestrate a write-in campaign to the minister of justice calling for the reintroduction of Section 98. When that appeared unlikely, His Eminence encouraged his friend, Premier Duplessis, to pass legislation outlawing communism.[10] Duplessis needed little encouragement. The public at large knew only that the cardinal gave the Padlock bill his unequivocal blessing.

As was his habit, Lapointe read the English-language press thoroughly, and he saw that the Quebec legislation was 'universally condemned.'[11] Even the *Financial Post* defended the right of the communists 'to present their point of view to the public.' The *Ottawa Journal* called it 'a vicious law' aimed not against lawlessness but against liberty. The *Winnipeg Free Press* went further, denouncing it as 'one of the most savage assaults upon freedom which Canada has ever seen.'

The so-called Padlock Act was Duplessis's answer to the repeal of Section 98. He had left no doubt of that during the debate in the legislature. The provincial legislation clearly invaded the federal field of criminal law. As minister of justice Lapointe had the option of disallowing it (with a year to make up his mind) or of referring it to the courts where it would likely be found *ultra vires* of the province's powers. But if he quashed the bill Duplessis would accuse the federal government of interfering in provincial affairs. It could start an open war between Quebec and Ottawa.

On 30 March Woodsworth raised the matter of the Padlock Act in the House. Would the government disallow the legislation or, in the alternative, refer it to the courts? He appealed to Lapointe to protect the civil rights of all Canadian citizens, 'even in Quebec': 'I feel that I am appealing to a minister who fundamentally is a Liberal at heart and to whom an appeal of this kind could not be made in vain but must meet with a favourable response.' Lapointe sought the politician's customary refuge by saying that he had not seen the bill as yet. When Woodsworth offered to pass it over to him, Lapointe was truculent: 'When the bill comes to me it will come in an official and regular way, not through the agency of the hon. member for Winnipeg North Centre.'

While acknowledging that the federal government was empowered to disallow provincial legislation, Lapointe asserted that it had not exercised that power for years. He said that if the bill was *ultra vires*, the courts would so rule. But wishing to avoid a confrontation with Duplessis and showing his usual deference to Quebec public opinion, Lapointe would not undertake to refer the bill to the courts. Still, it was clear that he personally disapproved of the bill. It was a denial of freedom of speech. The way to combat communism was not by 'arbitrary methods, which are not strictly according to the British practice.' Those ways 'do not appeal to me,' he declared. 'I would rather adopt the Hyde Park method than force conspiracies in cellars.' He asserted that the sedition laws and the RCMP (which he praised as 'the best police force that exists') were sufficient to combat any threat to law and order.

Most of Lapointe's forty minutes of debating time were devoted to denying that he was soft on communism. He expressed his abhorrence of the doctrine, but the way to fight it was not by laws but by according justice to all, the poor as well as the rich, the humble as well as the powerful. 'We should endeavour to eliminate the grievances and abuses which now exist in our system. But while that system may need reforming, we still want to keep it.' If he could find support for the idea, he would like to organize 'a league of Canadian citizens' whose aim would be 'to preserve the democratic state in Canada; to combat communism and fascism and to counteract the activities of all subversive and revolutionary forces which seek to overthrow the democratic state by force and violence, to guard the religious heritage of Canada from the protagonists of foreign and atheistic doctrines and to assist the state in every lawful way to the end that Canada may remain a place of safety ... and that peace, order and good government may be maintained in our dominion.'

King thought it 'a first-rate speech against Communism and Fascism.' What was more important, 'it greatly pleased the Quebec members.' But to civil libertarians in the affected province, Lapointe's hypothetical educational league was hardly an answer to the present danger of confiscation and arrest posed by the Padlock Act. Consequently, a Montreal branch of the Canadian Civil Liberties Union was formed to fight Duplessis's bill.

Although Lapointe took an anti-liberal stance against his will in dealing with the Padlock Act, on his own volition he adopted a right-wing stance during the Oshawa strike in April 1937. Following up on a successful sit-down strike at the main Géneral Motors plant in Flint, Michigan, the CIO (the industrial union started by John L. Lewis in the steel industry) had come into Canada to organize the auto workers at the General Motors plant in Oshawa. The Liberal premier of Ontario, the erratic Mitchell Hepburn, was determined to keep industrial unionism out of the province. Although the Oshawa strikers had not staged a sit-down strike in the plant, and in fact the company appeared willing to sit down with them at the bargaining table, Hepburn claimed the union leaders were communists and subversives, and he demanded the assistance of the RCMP.[12] Lapointe sent one detachment to Toronto and would have sent a second had King and the cabinet not stopped him. 'I was astonished,' King wrote in his diary, 'in finding Lapointe ready to use every means to prevent a C.I.O. getting any recognition in Canada.' Indeed, it was obvious that Lapointe's 'whole sympathies [were] against the men because they were associated with Lewis's organization.'[13]

King was probably correct in attributing Lapointe's attitude to the Oshawa strike as another concession to Quebec opinion. Quebec was intolerant of international unions, which competed with the Catholic unions sponsored by the church. (In the House Woodsworth referred more in sorrow than in anger to the alacrity with which the minister of justice had sent in the RCMP. He could not help but contrast it in his own mind with Lapointe's outspoken support for industrial unionism at the time of the Winnipeg Strike in 1919.)

Crossed in his desire for more Mounties, Hepburn threw a public tantrum, announcing in the press that he would order the federal government to remove the detachment standing by in Toronto. King was quick to seize upon Hepburn's irrationality. With cabinet 'solidly behind' him, he instructed Lapointe to send a wire recalling his police. Lapointe told his colleagues frankly that it was against his judgment, but he would carry out their wishes. The Ontario premier set up his own strike-breakers, who were soon known by the pejorative term of 'Hepburn's Hussars.' In the end the company offered to settle with the strikers on condition that the agreement made no reference to the hated United Auto Workers or the CIO.[14] Hepburn felt that the federal Liberals had let him down. While King and Lapointe were in London at the coronation in May, he issued a much publicized statement that he was 'not a Mackenzie King Liberal any longer.' Just as Duplessis was Lapointe's hair shirt, Mitchell Hepburn would henceforth be King's. The predictable result was that the two provincial premiers joined forces to fight the central government.

Canada was sending a large delegation to the coronation of George VI. In December 1936 the uncrowned Edward VIII had abdicated, saying he could not reign without the woman he loved, the American divorcée Mrs Simpson. Led by the prime minister, the delegates included five cabinet ministers, the House Speaker Pierre Casgrain, a whole coterie of government officials headed by Dr Skelton, and a group of MPs. The latter were selected by the Canadian branch of the Empire Parliamentary Association. To his great disappointment, the Montreal MP Sam Jacobs was not named to the delegation. Jacobs had long since given up hope of a cabinet appointment, and the prospect of a senatorship had vanished with the last round of appointments, but having been an active and effective Liberal member since 1917 he expected to be a delegate to the coronation. He rightly attributed his rejection to anti-Semitism. What he did not know was that Lapointe and Casgrain had gone to Arthur Beauchesne, the clerk of the House who was the Parliamentary Association secretary, and insisted that Quebec could not be represented by a Jew.[15] (In contrast to Quebec, Manitoba sent Abraham Heaps as one of its delegates.)

Meeting Mackenzie King in the halls of the Parliament Buildings, Jacobs told him of the Parliamentary Association's discrimination against him and that he had resigned from the association because of it. He informed the prime minister that anti-Semitism was growing rapidly in Quebec, adding that there was no real freedom of thought in the province any more. As usual King satisfied his liberal conscience with a few sanctimonious sentiments in his diary: 'I think it all important everything should be done to prevent the development of racial and religious feelings.'[16]

On 24 April 1937 the Canadian delegation sailed to England on the

Empress of Australia. Mimy and Odette, who was now engaged to be married, accompanied Ernest. Bobby was already in London. With the abdication crisis behind them, the British rejoiced in the ascent to the throne of a family man with a lovely consort. After the colour and excitement of the coronation, King and Lapointe attended the Imperial Conference at which the last sessions were presided over by the new prime minister, Neville Chamberlain. A Canadian external affairs officer, Lester Pearson, noted that Mackenzie King listened to reports about the dangerous developments in Europe 'without committing himself or Canada to anything.'[17] 'Lapointe and I were in entire agreement with Chamberlain and Eden over the attitude to be taken towards Abyssinia and toward the League generally,' King recorded in his diary. Anthony Eden, once the advocate of collective security, had abandoned the idea of sanctions against Italy and earnestly seconded Chamberlain's policy of non-intervention in Spain.

Never had Lapointe enjoyed more honour at the centre of empire than he did in 1937. Along with several other Commonwealth leaders, he received an honorary degree from Cambridge University, but the highlight was his appointment to the Imperial Privy Council, which carried with it the title of 'Right Honourable.' Though Lapointe may never have known this, it was his confessor, the Dominican Father Gaudrault, who put the idea in King's head. On 21 April, a few days before leaving for England, King received a letter from the priest urging him to recommend Lapointe for the Imperial Privy Council. While Gaudrault set out a dozen good reasons why Lapointe should be a 'Right Honourable,' probably his most compelling argument was Lapointe's lack of personal ambition and his utter devotion to King. Lapointe's father confessor understood the bond between the soulmates – 'You were born to work one with the other. He sees eye-to-eye with you. I know how much he appreciate [sic] you, and I also know how you reciprocate.'[18] The next day King shot off a coded cable to the British premier asking him if at all possible to make Ernest Lapointe a member of the Imperial Privy Council. 'Personally I should much welcome this recognition of the one who has been my closest friend and associate in the public life of Canada.'[19] When Skelton heard about it he thought it was 'very unwise' to ask for this recognition from the British government; he also thought that Lapointe as a Canadian nationalist might not accept.[20] King knew his soulmate better. As Lapointe's thank-you note shows, the recipient was deeply grateful.

Lapointe strongly approved King's decision to go to Germany to meet Hitler after the conference ended. But he prevailed upon King to first visit Paris with him and Pierre Casgrain on the invitation of the French government. Following the official events, the Lapointes took a short holiday before returning to Canada. In the pile of mail awaiting the now 'Right Honourable Ernest Lapointe' was a package of stickers printed with the message 'Youth Betrayed ... Beware of War Schemers, Remember 1914.' Postmarked Trois-Rivières (Duplessis's home town), the unsigned letter suggested sarcastically that 'after your eminent services to national politics, services recently rewarded by your London bosses, it will no doubt please you to use these stamps.'[21] The imperial privy councillorship had invited biting scorn from the young Quebec nationalists.

Far more disturbing for Lapointe was the way Cardinal Villeneuve lent the prestige of his office to the nationalist cause. He learned that in his absence the cardinal had given a public testimonial to Abbé Groulx. At a lecture by Groulx, the cardinal told the audience, 'I have come here this evening to manifest the friendship I have for the Abbé Groulx, to express my gratitude to him, at the risk of scandalizing the weak. Abbé Groulx is one of the masters of the hour; he is one of those to whom our race owes much.'[22] This was no sudden departure. As a young Oblate priest in Ottawa in the 1920s, Villeneuve had written an article for Groulx's review, L'Action Française, openly espousing separatism. La Nation had recently reprinted it.[23] Lapointe did not know Abbé Groulx personally, nor did he wish to. As a good Catholic and a federalist, Lapointe deeply resented the way the abbé linked French-Canadian nationalism to religion. He thought it 'monstrous' (as he told Henri Bourassa, meeting him by chance on the train) that Groulx used the French Canadians' strong faith to compromise their patriotism. Bourassa, estranged from his former disciple since the 1920s, agreed that Groulx's speeches and articles were 'grotesque declamations.'[24]

For a time Lapointe put aside his concern over Quebec nationalism and turned his full attention to family affairs. Odette's wedding was to take place on 25 September in Quebec City. Lapointe was pleased with his future son-in-law. Roger Ouimet was a Quebec City lawyer. He had been a leading light in the ALN in its early days when Lapointe approved of and encouraged these young reformers. By the provincial election in August 1936 Ouimet had returned to Liberal orthodoxy, appearing on the platform with Lapointe and Godbout at the big rally on the Esplanade in Quebec City.

King travelled to Quebec City for the wedding with Jack Elliott. His gift to the bridal couple was an engraved silver bowl accompanied by a personal note in his miniaturist script. The elderly bachelor had always been fond of his colleague's bright, attractive daughter. Odette often graced the table at Laurier House when King had to entertain important young male visitors, such as David Rockefeller or Lord Pentland. In 1929 King had hand-picked her for president of the Twentieth Century Club – the young Liberals organization he sponsored – and she had done an excellent job, organizing a big conference at the Chateau Laurier in May 1936.[25] Odette had a role model in the family friend Thérèse Casgrain. With her parents living in the Roxborough apartments in Ottawa, during her courtship Odette spent weeks at a time with Casgrain in Montreal or in the country at Malbaie. Odette was an asset to her father and to the Liberal party. A Quebec woman who heard her speak wrote Lapointe to say that his daughter was following in his footsteps.[26] In another age she might well have followed her father into politics.

The marriage ceremony took place in the beautiful Catholic church on the Grande Allée and was performed by Father Gaudrault. Odette looked lovely and very happy. After the service there was a large reception at the Lapointes' apartment. King's toast to the bride was much appreciated by the family (though, as usual, he felt he had left out 'some of the best bits'). He seems to have assumed the role of an honorary uncle at the wedding. Essentially a very lonely man, King remarked in his diary that Odette's wedding had drawn Lapointe and himself 'much together.'[27]

CHAPTER TWENTY-TWO

Aberhart's Legislation Disallowed

Canada in the 1930s was not the country envisaged by the Fathers of Confederation. The neat division of powers set out so confidently in 1867 had proved to be a jurisdictional hornets' nest. The financial relationship between the Dominion and the provinces obviously had to be revised. While Duplessis and Hepburn were straining to distance themselves from Ottawa, the western premiers were clamouring at the door, cap in hand. The price of wheat had fallen so low that it hardly paid farmers to grow it; then nature stepped in and turned the prairies into a dust bowl. Heavy spending on mechanization in the late 1920s had mired the wheat farmers in debt. Provincial finances were utterly inadequate to provide relief to the impoverished westerners. Early in 1937 the chairman of the Bank of Canada, Graham Towers, advised King that Manitoba and Saskatchewan would be bankrupt unless they received further assistance from the federal government.

When King first suggested a royal commission on Dominion-provincial finances Lapointe was against it,[1] foreseeing that Duplessis would charge interference in provincial affairs. However, King brought him around to see the danger of doing nothing. Unemployment insurance, for instance, was a necessity in modern Canada, but it fell under provincial jurisdiction. The provinces could not afford it, and Duplessis was adamantly opposed to handing it over to the federal government. King and Lapointe had wiped out all Bennett's 'new deal' social legislation, including unemployment insurance, by sending it to the courts, which ruled it *ultra vires*. A Liberal program had to be put in its place, and this would require constitutional reform.

Ever since the Liberals returned to power in 1935, Lapointe had been frustrated in his attempts to find a way for Canada to amend its own constitution. The problem was how to get the provinces to agree. He had almost succeeded at the Dominion-Provincial Conference of 1935. Taschereau, docile since his near defeat, no longer objected, and had it not been for opposition from New Brunswick Lapointe's formula would have been accepted.[2] Now with Duplessis in power, Lapointe knew he had no chance of achieving provincial unanimity. In the meantime, he fended off Tory proposals for constitutional reform. As King said, Bennett wanted to have all the glory.

King and Lapointe agreed that Newton Rowell was the ideal person to head a royal commission on Dominion-provincial relations. Twenty years earlier Rowell had tried to convince Lapointe that laissez-faire liberalism was inadequate to meet the needs of the twentieth century. The depression of the 1930s had proved him right. When the ninety-two-year-old Sir William Muloch tottered down from the bench in 1936, Lapointe named Rowell chief justice of Ontario. Now he and King conscripted Rowell to undertake the enormous task of revising Confederation. Attracted by the prospect of working with Rowell, J.W. Dafoe of the *Winnipeg Free Press* agreed to be a commissioner. Lapointe was hopeful that the veteran Canadian nationalist would come up with a solution to the problem of constitutional amendment. Rowell's French counterpart was the Quebec notary Dr Joseph Sirois, who was named co-chairman after Judge Rinfret, the original appointee, retired for health reasons. Throughout the autumn the Rowell-Sirois commission held hearings in all the provincial capitals. The obstreperous premiers of Quebec, Ontario, and Alberta refused to cooperate. Wilfrid Eggleston, a junior staff member of the commission, recorded in his diary that Duplessis kept them 'cooling their heels' for an hour and then turned up drunk for the official dinner at the Chateau Frontenac, that Hepburn presented a smart-alecky brief attacking Mackenzie King, and that while they were sitting in Edmonton the legislature 'formally voted to have nothing to do with us.'[3]

Indeed, William Aberhart was at loggerheads with the federal government. There was almost no money in circulation in Alberta, and without credit available or lower interest rates the indebted farmers were being foreclosed by the hated eastern banks. After King refused Aberhart a loan in March 1936, the feisty premier decided on radical measures to combat the injustice of 'poverty in the midst of plenty.' He defaulted on some provincial bonds, arbitrarily cut the interest rate on others, and cancelled interest on farm mortgages retroactive to 1932. Crying that Aberhart's legislation would plunge the country into financial anarchy, bankers and brokers lobbied Lapointe to disallow the Alberta legislation or refer it to the courts. Corporate lawyers wrote him heart-rending letters about the loss and suffering of elderly people who lived on interest from bonds or mortgages. The leader of the Canadian bar, the Toronto lawyer W.N. Tilley, gave Lapointe his unsolicited opinion that there was a real danger Alberta's repudiation of debt would spread to other provinces. 'Don't delay action too long,' he sternly admonished Lapointe.[4] The talk in Ottawa was that the federal government was not going to disallow the legislation for fear of making a martyr out of Aberhart,[5] and in fact Lapointe took no action for over a year.

In the spring of 1937 Aberhart introduced his own banking system to free up credit and start money circulating. He passed a bill authorizing unbacked provincial scrip, and to ensure that his 'funny money' would be accepted he enacted legislation barring the chartered banks from operating in Alberta unless they agreed to be licensed by a provincial body. In the frankly named 'Act to Provide for the Restriction of the Civil Rights of Certain Persons,' bankers were denied the right of appeal to the courts. A third bill prohibited a constitutional challenge of any Alberta legislation without the permission of the Social Credit government.

At first King thought of leaving it to the banks to challenge the legality of the legislation – that would avoid a federal-provincial confrontation. But Lapointe convinced King and the cabinet that the government must disallow legislation that invaded the federal field of banking and denied Canadian citizens access to the courts.[6] Despite Lapointe's assertion during the debate on the Padlock Act that the federal power of disallowance was virtually obsolete, in August 1937 he disallowed the three Alberta bills.

On 23 September, Lapointe received word of Aberhart's reaction to the disallowance of his bills. The lieutenant-governor of Alberta, J.C. Bowen, wired Lapointe that Aberhart intended to re-enact the disallowed legislation 'in modified form.' Bowen said he expected the premier to dissolve the legislature in order to seek public approval beforehand. The lieutenant-governor was 'inclined' to refuse a request for a dissolution to thwart Aberhart.[7] Would this be a repetition of the Byng affair? With a shudder, King forbade this 'mad course' out of hand.

As he told cabinet on 28 September, Lapointe thought that the best course was to have the lieutenant-governor exercise his power to reserve on the Aberhart bills. In that way the legislation would come before the federal cabinet, which could then refer it to the Supreme Court. Mackenzie, Rogers, Power, and Gardiner disagreed; they were in favour of allowing the Alberta legislation to pass and leaving it to the banks to fight it in the courts. Dunning was undecided. Cardin agreed with Lapointe, and when King supported his lieutenant the others fell in line.[8]

Not only did Aberhart proceed to enforce the offending acts, but he introduced further controversial legislation into the Alberta legislature. On 3 October a vice-gubernatorial wire alerted Lapointe that the Alberta legislature had approved bills to tax bank holdings, regulate credit, and (a new departure) to require newspapers to reveal their sources for articles critical of the government and to print verbatim all government rebuttals. The Press Bill was aimed at the *Edmonton Journal*, which was extremely critical of the Social Credit government. In a wire to Lapointe, the lieutenant-governor proposed to reserve on two of the four bills. Lapointe wired back laconically: 'See no objection your reserving all four bills mentioned.'[9] Again the cabinet was split, but Lapointe had his way. With Aberhart's concurrence, on 2 November the Alberta bills were referred to the Supreme Court, as well as the question of the right of the federal government to disallow provincial legislation.

Meanwhile, Lapointe was keeping a weather eye on Quebec. The summer had been uncomfortably hot for Duplessis with defections by leading nationalists and a strike in the key textile industry in which his ally, Cardinal Villeneuve, had supported the Catholic Workers Union. By mid-October Lapointe and Power felt it was time 'to test the feeling in Quebec' with a federal by-election. Shortly afterwards, the incumbent Liberal in Lotbinière riding died, and the writs were issued for a by-election on 27 December. Paul Bouchard, the editor of *La Nation*, announced he would run as an independent against the Liberal candidate, J.-N. Francoeur.

Bouchard was not a man to be taken lightly. An Oxford graduate and lawyer, he was a doctrinaire separatist and had founded *La Nation* purely to spread the idea of separatism. He had initially hailed the Union Nationale victory as 'the first step towards separatism,' but when Duplessis came out in his true colours as a *bleu*, hand in glove with the electricity trust, Bouchard turned to European fascist models. He was beginning to attract a following. To keep this dangerous separatist out of the House of Commons, Lapointe and Chubby Power were obliged to take to the hustings in support of Francoeur.[10]

Bouchard and his nationalist supporters conducted a demagogic scare campaign, denouncing Ottawa's defence spending as rank imperialist militarism and telling voters that it would inevitably lead to overseas conscription. At a large rally just before the campaign closed, Lapointe and Chubby Power spiked Bouchard's guns. Speaking as a veteran Power declared, 'I went overseas in one war. I'll never go back, and I'll never send anybody else.'[11] Lapointe was even more positive. 'The government of which I am a member will never apply conscription.' This solemn pledge won the by-election for the Liberals. On 29 December, Lapointe was on his way south aboard the de luxe 'Havana Special.' He wrote King that he was 'tired and somewhat nervous but very happy at the result in Lotbinière.' 'Its significance cannot be exaggerated,' he told his chief.[12] Lapointe had won a significant victory in his struggle against ultra-nationalism in Quebec.

When the House convened after the new year, Lapointe was faced with the disturbing contrast of his failure to disallow the ill-regarded Quebec Padlock Act and the disallowance of the Alberta legislation. He had left himself open to accusations of inconsistency and favouritism to Quebec. His critics, notably Woodsworth, had plenty of ammunition. The public outside Quebec was outraged by the tactics used in enforcing the Padlock Act. Quebec police were raiding homes and shops, confiscating and destroying books and papers indiscriminately. Not only communists but trade unions and Jehovah's Witnesses (dangerous heretics according to Cardinal Villeneuve) were targeted as well. Most of the raids proved to be wild goose chases and the crestfallen police retired without padlocking the premises. Indeed, they often made laughing stocks of themselves. One woman whose home was raided wrote Woodsworth that the police had taken away a copy of *Time* magazine because it had a picture of Trotsky and a book of fairy tales in German, which they confused with Yiddish. According to the Canadian Civil Liberties Union, from 9 November 1937 to 27 January 1938 there were some fifty raids under the Padlock Act. R.L. Calder (the Conservative prosecutor in the long-forgotten *Margaret* inquiry) was making a six-weeks' speaking tour for the CCLU to alert the country to the dangers of the Act.[13]

Internal memos in the justice department reveal that at no time did Lapointe consider disallowing the Padlock Act. The law officer assigned to the file was hard-pressed to distinguish between the Padlock Act and Alberta's Press Bill in order to justify the minister's inaction. At first, on this lawyer's advice, Lapointe announced that he could not act because there had been no formal request for disallowance.[14] But this excuse evaporated when the Civil Liberties Union presented him with a petition in January 1938.

On 4 March the Supreme Court declared the Alberta legislation *ultra vires* and confirmed the validity of the federal government's power of disallowance. Written by Chief Justice Duff, the Press Bill decision provided a precedent for nullifying Quebec's Padlock Act. Foes of the Act were not slow in picking up on Duff's ringing phrase that 'the right of free public discussion of public affairs ... is the breath of life for parliamentary institutions.' On 14 March the Social Service Council of Canada sent a brief to the federal cabinet urging disallowance of the Quebec legislation. Calling the Padlock law 'dangerously vague,' the brief submitted that it was beyond the province's authority and contrary to the fundamental rights of British citizens and public policy in Canada. It asserted that much of the anti-communist agitation in Quebec was really anti-Semitism. This organization and its church affiliates could not be dismissed as a left-wing pressure group, and the CCLU petition still had to be dealt with.[15]

Encouraged by the Duff decision, the Civil Liberties Union requested a meeting with the minister of justice. Lapointe announced that he would not hear the CCLU lawyers without allowing lawyers for the Quebec government to present their case. A copy of the CCLU petition was sent to Duplessis with an invitation to debate the issue before the minister. Duplessis regarded the minister of justice's assumption of the arbitrator's role as colossal nerve and declined the invitation.[16] On 30 March Lapointe had to go ahead with the hearing for the CCLU only; he promised to respond to their petition at some future date.

Lapointe was being inundated with letters and petitions for and against the Padlock Act. Canada had cracked along its usual fault line: French versus English. A well-organized campaign was under way in Quebec to urge the minister not to disallow the Act. Form letters poured in from municipal councils, social organizations, school boards, and the Catholic unions. A pastoral letter approving the Act was read in the churches at Easter, with a flurry of copies to Lapointe. Resolutions came in from the St Jean-Baptiste Society and the Society of St Vincent de Paul, praying him not to disallow the Act (and to pass a similar law for the rest of Canada). The Knights of Columbus from his home town of

Rivière-du-Loup petitioned him 'to take all measures to prohibit communist ideas.' There were unsigned threats: 'Be assured that at the next
federal election, the population of this province will take into account
the government's decision and will vote in consequence. It is a primor-
dial law for us and we want to keep it.'[17]

Form letters and petitions from English Canada demanding disallowance were almost as plentiful. They came from trade unions,
churches, and lobby groups (many of which were communist front
organizations). But Lapointe also heard from individuals dismayed by
the Padlock Act. One English immigrant wrote that 'enactment of such
a monstrous law in England would be impossible.' A professor from
the University of Alberta urged King not to give in to Quebec: 'I trust,
Sir, that your love for liberty and your far-sightedness in Canadian
affairs will override all political considerations in this crucial matter.'[18]

During the 1938 session, through an excess of caution Lapointe lost
the chance of achieving one of his main goals on a bipartisan basis. C.H.
Cahan, a constitutional expert on the Tory side, reintroduced a motion
he had brought forward the previous year to abolish appeals to the
Privy Council. Canada was growing up. There was considerable support now for the motion. Lapointe himself freely expressed his agreement. He reminded the House that he had been pressing for this assertion
of Canadian sovereignty since the Statute of Westminster. Nevertheless,
he advised delay to 'let public opinion digest it.' He undertook to
support the motion if it was introduced next session. Cahan obligingly
withdrew his motion, hopeful that it would re-emerge as a government
bill. In 1939, however, Lapointe again put off action through the familiar tactic of a reference to the courts.[19]

Just as Quebec's fear of communism dictated Lapointe's position on
the Padlock Act, anti-Semitic sentiment in the province was doubtless
the main reason for his implacable opposition to admitting Jewish
refugees. French-Canadian politicians, the St Jean-Baptiste Society, and
the nationalist press vociferously protested against allowing in the
victims of Nazi persecution. Official anti-Semitism in Germany had
begun with Hitler's accession to power. The Nuremburg laws of 1935
deprived Germany's 550,000 Jews of their citizenship rights, excluding
them from the professions and government and prohibiting marriage
to non-Jews. Under daily threat of arbitrary confiscation of their property and deportation to concentration camps, many had left Germany.
The problem was to find sanctuary. The western countries had closed
their doors to immigrants during the depression, and Britain, the man-

datory power in Palestine, was bent on keeping them out of the national home that the Balfour Declaration had promised the Jewish
people. In 1936 A.J. Freiman, the president of the Canadian Zionist
Organization and a neighbour of King's at Meech Lake, had tried to
prevail upon the prime minister to intervene with the British. But King
told Freiman it would only 'create an issue in Canada without helping
his friends.'[20] Hitler's annexation of Austria in March 1938 augmented
the Jewish exodus – and strengthened the determination of other countries to keep their doors closed. If anything, Canada tightened its restrictive immigration policy and was wilfully blind to the difference
between refugees and immigrants. King had already cautioned his
delegates to the Evian Conference on the Jewish refugee problem,
scheduled for July, not to make any commitments.[21]

On 17 May 1938 the three Jewish MPs – Jacobs, Heaps, and Factor –
accompanied by J.S. Woodsworth and a Montreal MP, Thomas Vien,
waited upon King with a proposal they hoped he could not refuse. This
was to admit 1,000 Jewish refugee families over the next five years with
a guarantee from the Jewish community that they would not become a
public charge. King readily expressed sympathy for the persecuted
Jews but worried aloud that letting them in could stir up anti-Semitism
in Canada. In any event, he promised to set up a cabinet subcommittee
to meet with the delegation. His suggestion that they should also meet
separately with the Quebec ministers on the committee was tacit admission that the real stumbling block was anti-Jewish sentiment in
Quebec. When the others had left, Sam Jacobs remained for a while to
try to impress upon King the peril of the European Jews. King clearly
did not wish to pursue this topic and turned the conversation to Jacobs's
obvious poor health. Seizing upon Jacobs's passing reference to trouble
with his teeth, King enlarged upon his own dental problems, explained
the value of X-rays, and advised Jacobs to take Krushen salts.[22] This
vignette typifies King's technique of detouring uncomfortable conver-
sations.

As promised, King appointed a cabinet committee to meet with the
delegation. Tom Crerar, the minister of immigration, was the informal
chairman; the others were Lapointe, Rinfret, Ilsley, and Mackenzie.
King's Quebec lieutenant failed to show up at the meeting, and his
conspicuous absence dashed the hopes of the Jewish MPs. Despondent
and angry, Jacobs and Heaps sent a message to the prime minister
informing him that Lapointe had failed to attend the meeting. The
result was that at the cabinet meeting of 7 June Crerar reported that it

was impossible to get an agreement from his colleagues on the committee regarding the admission of Jewish refugees.[23]

In this, as in other things, Lapointe was constrained by his compatriots' prejudices. But to what extent did he share their anti-Semitism? Throughout his career he preached tolerance and minority rights – Jewish Canadians praised him for this very virtue – but as his speeches show he meant tolerance of the French Catholic minority by the English Protestant majority. Growing up in a backwoods Quebec village he may have assimilated the religious anti-Semitism preached from the pulpit. His treatment of Sam Jacobs, going back to his disregard of Kirk Cameron's suggestion of a cabinet post for the Montreal MP, and most tellingly excluding him from the coronation delegation, demonstrated that Lapointe would not 'waste' Quebec's rewards on a Jew, no matter what service had been rendered to the Liberal party.

It is also a fact that Lapointe took no effective steps to control the flood of anti-Semitic hate literature in circulation by fascist groups and the Deutsche Bund. In August 1937 H.M. Caiserman, the executive secretary of the Canadian Jewish Congress, wrote King that anti-Semitic material was distributed anonymously through the simple expedient of a post office box number. He requested that post office boxes no longer be available for this purpose. He further requested that legal measures be adopted to make distribution of such libellous material a criminal offence. Caiserman enclosed some samples, which sufficiently shocked one of King's bland secretaries into describing them as 'strongly anti-Semitic in nature and, in some cases, of a very obnoxious character.' King referred the whole matter to Lapointe and Jack Elliott, the postmaster general. Nothing was done, lending substance to Caiserman's words in his letter to King that 'without interference from federal or provincial governments, [it] creates the impression that this nefarious activity is actually approved by the government.'[24] In contrast to his lack of action on hate literature, Lapointe used his influence with King to stop the importation of an atheistic American review. 'I trust you will realize the importance this question may take in the Province of Quebec,' he told the prime minister.[25]

Lapointe at this time was having a bad attack of nerves, mainly because of the infernal 'business of patronage.' Some of the leading men in his riding had said to his face that he had not done anything for Quebec. He was so irked that he told them to get somebody else – he was leaving. 'Lapointe complains a great deal of being fatigued and exhausted and clearly is such,' King wrote in his diary on 9 May. 'He is losing interest in Quebec politics and anxious to get out of the fray, being sick of the kind of contention which comes from men like Duplessis who represent a new type in public life, as Hepburn does toward myself.'

A few weeks later Odette was in Ottawa attending the National Liberal Women's convention. In a private chat with King, she confided that she was worried about her father, and that he was worried about himself. He was hesitant to bring it up, she said, but he had deputized her to ask the prime minister to let him go. King made something of a joke of it. 'Would you let Roger go?' he asked the newly married young woman.[26] But Odette was serious. Her father wanted to give up his seat in the Commons, she told the prime minister. What he would really like was to go to the Senate as government leader. King promised to speak to her father immediately, and a day or so later he had Lapointe come to his office.

'I had assumed,' King told his soulmate with visible emotion, 'that you would know that any wish of yours would be carried out so far as I am concerned. Supreme Court, Lieutenant Governorship of Quebec, a senatorship – take any one you please!' Lapointe was extremely appreciative. 'I would not think of suggesting a change if I did not want to escape a complete breakdown which I feel is coming,' he said. The two agreed that the best post for him was government leader in the Senate. 'Your experience ought to be reserved for parliament,' King said.[27] Ten years before, Lapointe would have liked to go to the Supreme Court, but no longer. He had lost much of his interest in legal and constitutional argument and, it seems, did not regard himself as a very good lawyer any more.[28]

Did Lapointe leave King's office assured that he would go directly to the Senate? Not a bit of it. As usual, King euchred his loyal friend into staying on. King was in no condition to part with his right-hand man. The prime minister was so distraught from pressures at home and abroad that in an address to the Press Club he spoke of 'Sir Wilfrid Borden' and referred to Bennett as the prime minister![29] He had no intention of letting his Quebec lieutenant go before the next election – despite Lapointe's assertion that he could not tackle another campaign. At this time an ambitious young recruit to the prime minister's office was looking around official and political Ottawa 'to differentiate between those who mattered and those who did not.' 'I realized that the most important and influential minister was Ernest Lapointe,' Jack Pickersgill writes in his memoirs. 'From the gallery I saw that he was a splendid parliamentarian, effective in debate and obviously well liked on both sides of the House. He was a big man physically but even bigger politically, and the dean of the House of Commons.'[30]

In May more constitutional problems were dumped on Lapointe's lap when Aberhart passed another batch of his quixotic bills. The aim, as summed up by Lapointe, was to bring about a general clearance of mortgage debts in Alberta. Practically speaking, the legislation deprived creditors of all legal remedies. Chartered banks, insurance, trust, and loan companies, and their depositors swamped King and Lapointe with protests. On 9 June King brought up the matter of the Alberta legislation in cabinet. Much of it would have to be disallowed, he announced to his ministers. Knowing that he was not going to disallow the Padlock Act, Lapointe hesitated. He was prepared to discuss it with the minister of finance, he intoned, and if Dunning confirmed that the effect on the financial institutions would be as dire as they predicted, the department of justice would carefully consider disallowance. To the surprise of all present, King swept aside Lapointe's hesitation and declared that he himself had no doubt of the disastrous effect of the legislation and it must be disallowed. Reluctantly, Lapointe disallowed the Alberta bills.[31] In all, by June 1938 thirteen bills of the Alberta legislature had either been disallowed or referred to the courts by the federal government.

Lapointe had only three more weeks before the time for disallowing the Padlock Act expired. At the department of justice the law officer who handled the file sent a memo to his superior stating that an examination of the Padlock law would convince anyone that its unconstitutionality could be pleaded in the courts.[32] On 5 July Lapointe read his draft recommendation on the Padlock Act to cabinet. At first it sounded as if he was proposing to refer the Act to the courts, but as he read on it became evident that he was recommending that they leave it to affected individuals to test the law. Gardiner, Crerar, and Ilsley came out strongly for disallowance or a reference to the courts. They felt that if the government did not disallow the Quebec legislation after disallowing the Alberta bills, it would cause difficulties in the West. King put the contentious matter over to the next day.

At the next day's meeting, Cardin again was the only one to support Lapointe. Mackenzie, Euler, and Rogers tried in vain to get Lapointe to either disallow the Padlock Act or to refer its constitutionality to the Supreme Court. King too disapproved of the Act: 'In the circumstances, we were prepared to accept what really should not, in the name of

Liberalism, be tolerated for one moment – any interference with the freedom of speech, the freedom of the Press, freedom of religious belief, or freedom of thought.' But when it came to Quebec, King seldom overruled Lapointe, who told his colleagues that disallowance would most certainly bring on an election in Quebec that Duplessis would win. King then settled the matter, telling his ministers that they had no choice. It was a question of national unity.

Lapointe's refusal to disallow the Padlock Act was greeted with jubilation in Quebec and criticism in the rest of Canada. In a belated response to the CCLU petition, he gave his reasons: the Quebec legislation did not invade federal jurisdiction, and in that case the Dominion government could not 'pass judgment upon the wisdom or propriety of a provincial Act.' Moreover, despite the protests from all over the country, the rights of people outside of Quebec'were not affected. He advised the Civil Liberties Union to go to court to fight the Act themselves.[33]

Eugene Forsey, a McGill professor of constitutional law, responded with a withering article in the CCF organ, the *Canadian Forum*. 'When it is a matter of the liberties (and property) of banks, insurance companies and trust companies in Alberta, [King and Lapointe] are as brave as lions. But when it comes to defending the liberties of ordinary citizens in Quebec, all their courage oozes away.' Forsey flatly contradicted Lapointe's assertion that the Quebec law did not invade federal jurisdiction in criminal law. It was precisely on that ground that the Civil Liberties Union had asked for disallowance. In fact, Forsey said, Premier Duplessis boasted that the law was meant to replace Section 98 of the Criminal Code. As for Lapointe's contention that of 'recent' decades ministers of justice had been reluctant to recommend disallowance merely because the provincial legislation might be *ultra vires*, Forsey reminded him that he had exhibited no such reluctance in disallowing the Alberta legislation. And why should the CCLU have to undertake the expense of going to court when the minister did not mete out the same advice to banks and insurance companies? While Mr Lapointe was clearly afraid to buck the Quebec hierarchy by disallowing the Padlock Act, he would have been on safe ground to leave it to the courts to decide a legal question. By not pronouncing on the merits of the case himself, Mr Lapointe 'could surely have braved even the thunders of the Cardinal and the hysterical accusations of Dominion tyranny and pro-Communist tendencies which Mr. Duplessis would have hurled at him.'[34]

Lapointe did not need Forsey to tell him that he was on thin ice legally, inconsistent in his treatment of the provinces, and disloyal to the tenets of Liberalism. According to his family, allowing the Padlock Act to stand was a source of great distress to Lapointe.[35] In his handling of the Padlock Act, Lapointe was a long way off from the liberal principles he espoused in his speeches.

CHAPTER TWENTY-THREE

In the Appeasers' Camp

Lapointe's refusal to disallow the Padlock Act had as much to do with events abroad as at home. There were war clouds on the horizon. If Britain went to war, it was inevitable that the anglophone majority in Canada would insist on fighting by its side. He would then be called upon to bring in his unwilling compatriots. Under these circumstances he could ill afford to quash legislation that was so popular in the province. Meanwhile, he and King wholeheartedly endorsed Chamberlain's appeasement policy. Hitler, emboldened by his unopposed takeover of Austria, was demanding the Sudetenland from Czechoslovakia on the pretext of protecting the large German minority. The summer of 1938 had passed with Chamberlain pressuring the Czech president to make concessions to the leader of the Sudeten Germans – a Hitler puppet. King and Lapointe's great hope was that the little democracy would not provoke the bully by mobilizing.[1]

In a private conversation with King on 31 August, Chubby Power ventured to say that some of the Quebec members would leave the party if Canada declared war. King was vehement that the French cabinet ministers would have to make the French Canadians see their obligation to participate if war came. Power sounded doubtful. 'Lapointe would become so nervous and upset that he would be good for nothing,' he told the prime minister. King feared that this was only too true. Lapointe was leaving for Europe to attend the League of Nations Assembly, and King hoped that what he learned at the League and in France would cause him to feel differently – in effect, stiffen his backbone.[2]

On 2 September the Canadian delegation to the League Assembly boarded the *Empress of Britain* in Montreal. Lapointe was the senior delegate and his wife, of course, was with him. As caught by a photographer on deck, they were a staid-looking, elderly couple; an unsmiling Ernest holding a cane and Mimy in a tailored suit, brimmed hat, and sensible shoes. Other delegates were the Liberal MPs Paul Martin and J.T. Thorson, and (a breakthrough for women) Nellie McClung, the guiding force in the 'Persons' case. The permanent representative to the League, Hume Wrong, and several other external affairs officers completed the official party.

Lapointe's first dinner aboard was spoilt by Joe Thorson, who kept bringing up complicated legal questions. After dinner Lapointe summoned Paul Martin to his cabin. 'Now, Paul,' Lapointe cautioned, 'we have seven days together on this boat, and it could be very pleasant. But if that man Thorson talks at me every time he sees me, I will not leave my cabin. It may be an interesting academic exercise for him to discuss constitutional law, but it makes me tired.'[3] As tactfully as possible Martin let Thorson know that the minister of justice did not want to talk shop. Thorson did not take the hint, however, and after a few days Lapointe and his wife took their meals in their cabin. Upon their arrival at Geneva Lapointe was honoured to find himself unanimously elected chairman of the League's Third Commission, whose terms of reference were to study and report on arms reduction. Under the circumstances, the commission's deliberations were bound to be a waste of time.

The League Assembly convened on 12 September in an atmosphere of crisis. The sessions in the new 'huge, modern, white, dignified, lavish, empty' Palais des Nations had an air of unreality. The world stood on the brink of war, yet the Czechoslovakian situation was not on the agenda.[4] Instead, earnest discussions on economic and social programs were the order of the day. Outside in the halls the delegates expressed their feelings of helplessness. Lapointe was holding private talks with various European statesmen to get their views on the crisis. One evening he and Paul Martin were invited to Eamon De Valera's hotel suite to discuss an urgent matter. The prime minister of the Irish Free State had just received a telegram from Neville Chamberlain. The British prime minister wanted to know what the attitude of the Commonwealth leaders would be if he bypassed diplomatic channels and met with Hitler personally. Lapointe told De Valera that Mackenzie King would strongly endorse such an approach.[5]

Hopes rose and fell during Chamberlain's shuttle diplomacy. At Berchtesgaden on 15 September, England and France gave in to Hitler's demand for self-determination for the heavily German parts of the

Sudetenland, afterwards twisting Czechoslovakia's arm to agree. Still, Hitler's ravenous appetite for conquest was unsated, and at Godesburg on 22 September he expanded his original demands. Now he was insisting on annexing the Sudetenland as he had Austria. The delegates at Geneva heard that in London they were handing out gas masks, piling up sandbags, and digging trenches in the parks.

In Canada, King was bedridden with an excruciating attack of sciatica brought on by worry. Lying on his bed of pain he had no illusions that Canada could remain neutral if Britain went to war, and he was prepared to announce his own version of Laurier's 'Ready, aye ready.' Skelton was trying to calm what he called King's 'exalted imperial cum democracy and freedom mood.' As isolationist as ever, Skelton could see no reason why Canada, five thousand miles away, should stick its neck out. Indeed, in the Czechoslovakian crisis of 1938 the under-secretary of state for external affairs was fighting a rearguard action to keep Canada neutral; if Canada went to war 'my 14 years here wasted,' he wrote in his diary.[6]

At Geneva, Lapointe reaffirmed Canada's position that sanctions must be non-obligatory in character.[7] His address on 23 September completed his personal contribution to the disempowerment of the League of Nations, which began with his proposed amendments to Article X in 1922. He met with no argument from his fellow delegates. Article XVI of the Covenant, the enforcement article, had been a dead letter since the League had stood by helplessly during the Manchurian and Ethiopian crises. The day after his Geneva speech, Lapointe received a 'Most Secret' telegram from King that greatly perturbed him. He had it in mind, he said, to issue the following public statement if it became evident that France and England would be involved in a war: 'The world might as well know at once that Canada will not stand idly by and see modern civilization ruthlessly destroyed if we can by cooperation with others help save mankind from such a fate.'[8] He asked for Lapointe's opinion.

Lapointe rejected the idea of any official statement prior to the outbreak of war. Only yesterday, he said, he had delivered a speech at the League 'based on our previous stand and constantly expressed policy' that any decision to go to war would have to be made by the Canadian Parliament. He spelled out the problems that such a precipitous statement from the prime minister would create for him in Quebec: 'I do not see how I could advise any course of action that would not only be opposed to personal convictions and sacred pledges to my own people but would destroy all their confidence and prevent me from carrying weight and influence with them for what might be essential future actions. Please consider these views and submit them to colleagues before reaching final decision. God help you. I still strongly feel that conflagration shall be avoided.'[9]

Skelton was overjoyed by Lapointe's wire: 'Good old Ernest came across with an emphatic rejection of any pre-war statement,' he exulted in his diary. King seemed surprised, but Norman Rogers was not. Rogers told Skelton confidentially that Lapointe was unwilling to take any decision.[10] Though Skelton thought the prime minister became 'a bit less belligerent' after Lapointe's telegram, King nevertheless held a press conference where he intimated that Canada would intervene in the event of war.

A declaration of war was expected at any minute. The French army and the British fleet were mobilizing; Czechoslovakian troops were manning the fortifications on the German border. On 26 September Lapointe received a wire from King calling him home. His colleagues, 'and the country,' would appreciate his returning as soon as possible 'so that we might all be able to consult together at this time.' Lapointe immediately booked a cabin on the *Queen Mary* and that night was driven to the railway station through a blacked-out city.[11] None of the passengers who boarded the British luxury liner with Lapointe on 28 September doubted that war with Germany would be declared by the time they disembarked at New York. But in mid-ocean news arrived that set the champagne bottles popping. At the blackest hour, Chamberlain had returned from Munich with a piece of paper signed by Hitler guaranteeing peace between their countries. In a four-party pact with Germany and Italy, England and France handed the Sudetenland to Hitler without so much as asking Czechoslovakia. Lapointe received a jubilant cable from King: 'Great rejoicing Canada today. Welcome home.'[12]

Munich was a reprieve for the soulmates. Lapointe shared King's 'unbounded admiration' for Chamberlain who had bought peace by dismembering Czechoslovakia. But joy over the Munich pact turned to doubt when, within a matter of weeks, the Nazi dictator, whom England and France had so shamefully appeased, revealed the true nature of his regime. On 9 November 1938 the Nazis unleashed a pogrom of unprecedented proportions. Ostensibly a groundswell of popular indignation at the shooting of a junior German diplomat by a young Polish Jew, the pogrom was in fact orchestrated by the Nazi leaders who had been waiting for just such a pretext. 'Crystal Night,' so-called because of the smashed glass from Jewish businesses and homes that littered the streets of Berlin, shocked the world. It seemed incomprehensible that a civilized country was capable of such barbarity.

The *Globe and Mail* headlines on 11 November were typical of what Canadians were reading in their local papers and hearing on the radio: 'Reich Swept by Anti-Jew Terrorism, Destruction, Looting and Burnings throughout the Country Unequalled since Red Revolution.' 'Police Stay Hands while Huge Silent Crowds look on.' It was obvious that the wreckers worked under police protection. Indeed, the German government had dropped all pretence that the attack on the Jews was not officially sanctioned. On 12 November the *Globe* reported more Nazi horrors: 'Fleeing Jews Crawl across Czech Border, Women and Children Many Badly Injured, Loaded in Reich army Trucks and dumped at Sudeten Line ... Beatings and Tortures in Nazi Detention.' On 14 November the paper reported that the German government had levied a $400 million fine on the country's half a million Jews, who were seeking desperately to raise the money.

Mackenzie King recorded his outrage in his diary. After a tearful interview with Mrs Freiman he wrote that 'the sorrows which the Jews have to bear at this time are almost beyond comprehension.' A few days later: 'I feel Canada must do her part in admitting some of the Jewish refugees. It is going to be difficult politically, and I may not be able to get the Cabinet to consent, but will fight for it as right and just, and Christian.'[13] In the interval he made no public statement, and a *Globe* editorial on 18 November castigated the government for 'Canada's Silent Voice.' While King said nothing, the new Conservative leader, Dr Robert Manion, came out against Jewish immigration. Speaking in Quebec, where he hoped his Catholicism and French-Canadian wife might win him votes, he opposed the admission of refugees, citing the current unemployment. Only the CCF called for admission of a fair quota of refugees.

On 20 November huge rallies protesting the German treatment of Jewish citizens were held all across Canada. Though organized and paid for by the Canadian Jewish Congress, they were co-sponsored by Protestant churches and labour unions, addressed by community leaders, and attended by thousands of non-Jews. In Toronto 20,000 people turned out for the rally at Maple Leaf Gardens; among the notables on the platform was the retired chief justice of Ontario, Sir William Mulock. To enthusiastic applause, speakers urged an open-door policy for Hitler's victims. The English-language press gave abundant favourable coverage to the rallies, the *Globe* calling them an example of 'the brotherhood of man.'

Traditionally anti-immigration, French Canada was vociferously opposed to allowing in any Jewish refugees whatsoever. *Le Devoir* saw the anti-Hitler demonstrations as the work of 'a group, relatively small in numbers, but solid, compact, marvellously active in stirring up the public with their own anger and indignation.' While granting that the Jews of Germany were to be pitied, for *Le Devoir* that was no reason to admit them: 'If Germany has become the Jewish hell, is that a good reason for making Canada the Jewish paradise?'[14] The St Jean-Baptiste Society was circulating a petition 'protesting vigorously against immigration of any kind whatever and especially against Jewish immigration.' Ultimately, 127,364 people signed the petition, which Wilfrid Lacroix, the member for Quebec-Montmorency, presented to Parliament in January 1939.

The day after the rallies, King brought up the refugee question again in cabinet. 'I told the Cabinet I did not think we could afford to be indifferent to humanitarian considerations, that we would have to make some provision for those who had been obliged to flee from their countries.' Rogers and Crerar strongly seconded him, and Gardiner had indicated his support the previous day. But King could see from their 'gloomy' expressions that Rinfret, Cardin, and Lapointe were opposed. Lapointe seemed to 'wilt' in the discussion, leaving it mainly to the other two to argue the Quebec position. Easily put off by the Quebec ministers' objections, King hastened to add that the whole question of Jewish immigration would have to be very carefully studied.

Later in King's office, Lapointe again brought up the refugee problem, perhaps conscious that he had not sufficiently impressed King with the strength of his own opposition to Jewish immigration. He kept looking at King in a way that reminded King of a dream he had had that morning. In his dream Canada was at war – there was a barracks with soldiers marching about – and he and Lapointe were sitting side by side anticipating an invasion. Lapointe was completely prostrated, seemingly overcome by the feeling that he was going to die, and he handed King a memorandum to give to his wife after his death. He leaned over, bringing his face close to King's: it was that same baleful expression that King saw on his friend's face in the office. That look reminded King of Lapointe's 'complete prostration' when they were out west in 1921 and word came that his son was gravely ill.[15]

Lapointe may have been troubled by what he thought was the political necessity of refusing sanctuary to Hitler's victims. Nevertheless, it was Lapointe, speaking for Quebec, who influenced King the most and shaped government policy on the refugee question. Later that day King, ever cautious, told reporters at a press conference that the question of admitting German refugees required further study. He said that, at most, the government would extend about a hundred visitors' permits to German Jews who were already in Canada, and that each case would be considered on humanitarian grounds.

The next day King and Crerar received a delegation of Jewish community leaders accompanied by the MPs Heaps and Factor – Sam Jacobs had passed away in September. They had hoped that the tremendous public support displayed at the rallies would influence the prime minister to loosen up the strict immigration rules. Disheartened by King's statement to the press, they nevertheless pleaded for the admission of 10,000 refugees over the next five years and, as they had in May, assured the prime minister that there would be absolutely no cost to the country since the Jewish community would care for them. King's reply dashed their hopes. 'As long as there are unemployed, we have to consider them first,' he told the delegation, and he made oblique reference to Quebec's opposition to Jewish immigration. While the government ministers felt sympathy with the Jews in their plight, they 'had to consider the constituencies and the views of those who are supporting the Government.'[16]

By early December it was clear that Quebec was not the only 'constituency' that was resistant to taking in refugees. Though English Canada was awash with sympathy, the prevailing opinion was that the country should not open its doors; the usual reason given was unemployment, but anti-Semitism was a large factor. Canada was no different from the other democracies. World leaders were anxious to find homes for refugees, but like King, 'in some land other than our own.' *Le Devoir* sneered: 'None of the European nations whose press groans under the fate of these exiles appears eager to receive them.'[17]

At the same time the Canadian government was secretly planning to admit several thousand anti-Nazi Sudeten Germans, though most possessed no more farming experience than the Jewish refugees – a point acknowledged by the Sudeten representative in Ottawa.[18] The discriminatory immigration policy was not the fault of the immigration minister. In fact, Crerar recommended admitting 10,000 Jewish refugees, but his Quebec colleagues, who remained 'strongly against any admission,'[19] and his rabidly anti-Semitic deputy minister, F.C. Blair, stymied him. Senator Cairine Wilson proved to be the Jewish refugees' strong advocate. She had succeeded Lapointe as president of the League of Nations Society in Canada and had injected new purpose into the languishing organization with the formation of the Canadian National Committee on Refugees and Victims of Persecution. Yet even her eminent committee could not swim against the tide of public opinion, and the CNCR's efforts on behalf of the Jewish refugees were largely fruitless.

Lapointe and Chubby Power had made their presence little felt in Quebec since the provincial Liberals' defeat in 1936. Power's explanation was that Lapointe, as minister of justice and King's right-hand man, was taken up with the international situation while he himself was occupied with his department of pensions and national health. Although it was a thankless task to try to maintain a federal Liberal organization with Godbout's Liberals thoroughly 'routed,' at the end of 1938 Lapointe made several important speeches in Quebec because King was talking of a federal election in the spring.

In a speech to the Reform Club in Quebec City on 28 November, Lapointe announced the government's intention to introduce an unemployment insurance law in the next parliamentary session.[20] This was a direct challenge to Duplessis who, despite extraordinarily high unemployment in the province, repelled the federal initiative as an invasion of provincial jurisdiction and opposed amendment of the constitution to permit it. Lapointe also addressed a capacity audience at the parish hall in Limoilou in his Quebec East riding. The timing was significant. On the previous day, a nationalist organization had staged a large rally in Montreal to celebrate the anniversary of the Statute of Westminster. Abbé Groulx was the keynote speaker at the rally – Lapointe, of course, had not been invited. In his speech Lapointe reminded the audience of the part he had played in the passing of the Westminster Statute, which had brought about Canadian autonomy, stating categorically that the statute made Canada equal to England in the Commonwealth.

He quoted facts and figure to show that during his years as their representative, the Liberal government had done a good deal for the province and for Quebec City in particular. He announced several government policies bound to appeal to his working-class audience and gave his 'solemn word' that changes to the British North America Act would respect and fortify minority rights. To dispel rumours that he was retiring from public life or going to the Supreme Court, he told his constituents that he would continue to represent them. 'My character has been tempered in the steel of battle and conflict,' he declared. 'I still have something to accomplish and I want to accomplish it before disappearing. If God lends me life and health, I am going to accomplish it.' It was the kind of old-fashioned oratory that brought his audience to its feet. Lapointe had never lost his Québécois accent, and he spoke to the working class in their own idiom. Léopold Richer, *Le Devoir*'s Ottawa correspondent, said of him that although he had risen to the highest level in public life he had not changed. 'He is not like his master, Sir Wilfrid Laurier. He has stayed close to us.'

Lapointe then went on the attack against what he called 'the enemies of liberalism.' The first of these was the Union Nationale premier. Alluding to Duplessis's alliance with Hepburn to oust King, Lapointe launched into an encomium to the prime minister: 'His beautiful soul, his patriotism, his love of country, will triumph in all the battles waged against him, be they out in the open or dark conspiracies. King's loyalty will triumph over all treason, take my word for it.'

His next target was Quebec's fascist movement. Lapointe obviously took Adrien Arcand and his shirt movement more seriously than he let on in the House of Commons. He was aware from reports of the RCMP's secret agents in Quebec that fascists were infiltrating factories and government bureaus – employees at the customs department in Montreal distributed hate propaganda and gave the Nazi salute quite openly. Frankly worried by the spread of subversive ideas among Quebec workers, he warned his audience that the same people who abused freedom of speech to incite race hatred and undermine democratic government also conducted 'hateful campaigns' against organized labour: 'These exploiters of racial and religious prejudice would not have so much latitude if they lived under a fascist or nazi regime. But in fomenting unhealthy agitation, they work to destroy respect for all authority ... They seek to prepare a revolution in a country where, in the opinion of foreign visitors, conditions are better than anywhere else in the world.' He carefully distinguished between the fascists and 'young ambitious people who, discontented with their condition, believe they can improve their fate by denigrating their elders.' Although the young ultra-nationalists were a thorn in his side, Lapointe – the consummate politician – knew that his audience would not take kindly to any criticism in that direction.

Lapointe tackled the touchy subject of defence spending. He assured his constituents that the increase in armaments was strictly for the protection of the country in the event of invasion, nothing more. To a cheering crowd, he uttered a quotable statement that would come back to haunt him: 'Instead of waging war in a foreign land, we shall remain at home and defend the Canada we love.' He and the other speakers steered clear of the refugee question. When a member of the audience called out, 'What about Jewish immigration?' Chubby Power, who was then at the microphone, simply ignored the interruption.[21]

Broadcast throughout the province, the Limoilou speech was a personal triumph for Lapointe. One ardent admirer wrote him that he was 'the glory of our race.' Alexandre Taschereau, in political exile in his mansion on the Grande Allée, dropped Lapointe a note that 'everyone in Quebec is talking about your speech.' (The former premier added sadly, 'I am far from the smoke of battle but I still permit myself to sit at the window and see who passes by.')[22]

The speech – especially his guarantee that Canada's role in any conflict would be limited to home defence – revived Lapointe's prestige and popularity in his home province. Nevertheless, the thought of spending the Christmas recess in Quebec depressed him infinitely. The threat of war had unleashed strident anti-imperialist, anti-war sentiment in the province. Groulx's separatist doctrine had never been more popular or openly espoused. And a new nationalist movement calling for neutrality in any foreign wars had been launched in Montreal by the editor of *La Nation*, Paul Bouchard – the quasi-fascist whose federal ambitions Lapointe had killed in the 1937 Lotbinière by-election. A version of Social Credit, tailored to Quebec nationalism, had also recently come on the scene.

Moreover, on their home soil some of the Quebec MPs sounded like separatists in Liberal clothing. Particularly disturbing to Lapointe were public statements by Maxime Raymond, the leader of the Quebec nationalists in the House and the smartest of the lot in Lapointe's opinion. At the Montreal rally Raymond had implicitly criticized King and Lapointe for continuing 'to pay tribute to Great Britain,' pointing out that in the negotiations leading up to the Statute of Westminster 'Canada never asked or wished for the right not to participate in Britain's wars.'[23] As it happened, Raymond was nursing a grievance against Lapointe and King at the moment. He was angling to succeed Philippe Roy as minister in Paris, but in spite of heavy lobbying by his brother, the Liberal bagman Senator Donat Raymond, Maxime Raymond was not going to get the appointment.[24] Understandably, King and Lapointe would not have a Quebec nationalist representing Canada in France at this juncture.

Fleeing more than Quebec's cold weather, Lapointe left for Florida on Christmas Day, dropping King a line en route: 'I was so tired and nervous that I finally made up my mind to go South for ten days, play golf, and forget things, in order to be in a better condition for the Session. A stay in Quebec under present circumstances is worse than the ordinary work.'[25]

CHAPTER TWENTY-FOUR

Neutrality Abandoned

At the opening of Parliament on 16 January 1939, Mackenzie King enunciated Laurier's famous dictum, 'When Britain is at war, Canada is at war.' Lapointe was horrified. Afterwards he reminded the prime minister that since the Statute of Westminster, Canada was no longer a colony that would automatically be at war alongside Britain. Canada would be at war only if the Canadian cabinet, and not the British ministers, so advised. Sir Wilfrid's statement had been made in 1910 and was completely out of date, he told King.[1]

At caucus two days later, however, the anglophone MPs and senators showered praise on King. Lapointe was then called upon to speak. He was in a quandary. He totally disapproved of King's statement, yet his loyalty to his leader was unshakeable. Carefully avoiding any direct reference to King's speech, he dwelt on their 'intimate association over many years,' saying that the only thing stopping him from retiring to make way for younger men was his personal friendship for the prime minister.

Lapointe was able to head off an incipient revolt among the francophone MPs. He knew what ammunition King's ill-advised statement would provide for Quebec nationalists, and he cautioned the backbenchers who were thinking of straying from their obedience to the prime minister. 'I could get the widest publicity possible were I to announce to the public that I am against my leader today,' he said. 'But in the course of my time, I have followed the careers of men and have noticed that those who separated from their leaders were big men for the first few hours and days. But it has invariably been found that these men, as time went on, were left behind by the party or were out altogether.'[2] Lapointe managed the situation with finesse. He had not publicly confronted King and had shown the wisdom of supporting the leader even when differing from him. The anti-war group – Maxime Raymond, Liguori Lacombe, Wilfrid Gariepy, Jean-François Pouliot – spoke out strongly but did not bolt.

By the time cabinet met on 27 January, King was on the defensive. His young secretary, Jack Pickersgill, had told him frankly that his speech was 'appalling,' and King had not even dared to discuss it with Skelton because he 'knew what his attitude would be.'[3] To justify his contentious remark, King attempted to alarm his cabinet colleagues by quoting freely, if selectively, from British Foreign Office dispatches. One dispatch stated that, according to information received, Hitler might make a sudden air attack without pretext on England and follow up with land and sea operations against western powers. King queried whether anyone could say that Canadian ports were not vulnerable to attack. The guileful King had failed to mention that the dispatch acknowledged that the information came from unverified, anonymous sources. King's self-justification continued. He wished to remind his colleagues that at the cabinet meeting prior to the opening of Parliament, he had told them what he proposed to say, and he thought they were all agreed. 'Was I there?' Lapointe asked. 'Oh yes,' answered King. 'Then I must have been asleep,' was his lieutenant's wry response.

King's next argument was that the government could not appear less loyal to the empire than Sir Wilfrid was in his day. This won general acceptance from the anglophone ministers but not from Lapointe and a glowering Cardin. Lapointe objected in the strongest terms to 'rushing into a statement of where we stood until we had to.' Although he agreed with King that Canada would have to go to war if Britain were attacked by Germany, he stuck to his guns that Canada should not commit itself in advance. Unable to overcome Lapointe's opposition, King resorted to a subtle form of blackmail. They all knew how sick he had been with sciatica, and he said he could feel the pain starting up again in his right leg. 'I can be put out of business altogether, especially at a period of great strain and emergency.' If anyone doubted it they could call his doctor. Lapointe then introduced his own form of blackmail. Perhaps he and Cardin would be better out of cabinet. He indicated that staying in a cabinet that endorsed policies unpopular in Quebec made them suspect with their own people. Outside cabinet, they could help to explain the situation and to 'steady' their people.

Lapointe's threat worked. For King the French ministers walking out was unthinkable. National unity would be shattered and he would be forced to give in to Mitch Hepburn, who was agitating for a union government like Borden's in 1917. 'We all understand the difficulties our French Canadian colleagues face,' King soothed Lapointe and Cardin, but surely they all knew each other well enough that the differing views could be accommodated so that no one would have to leave. As gracefully as he could, King retreated to a compromise position. He proposed, and all agreed, that should Britain declare war Canada would not jump in but would 'take time to study our home course.' For the benefit of the French members he said he would make perfectly clear in debate that 'we were not irrevocably tied' to Britain.

Under pressure from Lapointe and Cardin, King had docilely returned to the 'no commitments in advance' policy. The gentlemanly contest between King and his Quebec lieutenant had taken a good two hours. Afterwards King instructed Skelton to draft a public statement that would explain his 'When Britain is at war' speech in a way that Lapointe would accept. Skelton remarked that it would not be easy to reconcile what he had said in Parliament with what he was saying today.[4]

Skelton was in his office on 2 February working on a policy statement to soften King's battle cry when Lapointe's large silhouette loomed in the doorway. 'How can we prevent the prime minister from making any more breaks?' he asked Skelton. Skelton replied that it was hard for him to do it if fifteen colleagues in cabinet could not curb him. 'Unfortunately, some of the fifteen are worse than he is,' Lapointe said. 'The prime minister is fooling himself,' he went on, 'if he thinks that Cardin and I agreed with his statement. I told him that whatever the government as a whole agreed, individual members would have to decide what stand they would take and I made no commitment on that point.'[5] Lapointe had acknowledged in cabinet that Canada would be drawn into a British war; however, his conversation with Skelton reveals that in February 1939 he was not ready personally to support participation. The logical conclusion is that he was seriously considering resignation. Lapointe left the office with Skelton promising to let him see the draft before it went to King.

At this psychological moment, Lapointe's powerful position as the political leader of French Canada and the prime minister's closest collaborator received due recognition at a banquet in Quebec City on 18 February 1939 to celebrate his thirty-five years in Parliament. Chubby Power had organized the event with King's enthusiastic support. The ballroom and the dining room at the Chateau Frontenac were thronged with guests – 1,500 seated and almost as many in the gallery. There were delegations from Quebec East and from his old constituency of Kamouraska. Indeed, people from all over the province had come to pay tribute to their renowned native son. With the exception of Dunning who was in ill health, the cabinet was all present along with most of the Liberal MPs. Many of Lapointe's former colleagues had come as well. As King looked around, he thought that he had never seen as distinguished a political gathering even in Sir Wilfrid's day.

Jack Pickersgill, who had hitched a ride in King's private railway car, records that the banquet was 'a feast of oratory.' There were in all twenty speeches, yet never a dull moment according to King. He himself was cheered to the rafters, especially his banter that if Lapointe had gone into the church he would probably be a cardinal. In a more serious vein, he told the audience that Lapointe was practically co-premier of the country. Lapointe gave a moving address exclusively in French, closing his remarks with a quotation from the Provençal poet Mistral: 'The builders are dead, but the temple is built. I would like these lines to apply, even in a small way, to the career you have so kindly recalled tonight,' he told the audience with visible emotion. Thérèse Casgrain, the only female speaker (she would later entitle her memoirs *A Woman in a Man's World*) spoke beautifully. Cardin, co-chairman of the evening with Chubby Power, outdid himself. But the unprepossessing Adélard Godbout won the palm as the best speaker of the evening. A conspicuous omission from the roster of speakers was Taschereau, and King's sympathy went out to him: 'Knowing his proud nature and the power he has exerted in Quebec for so many years, to see him obliged to sit at the end of the table and not be called upon to speak. It made one feel how cruel public life is in some of its aspects.' But this was a night to rejoice in the political life and the inspiring example of the close working friendship between the English Mackenzie King and the French Ernest Lapointe.[6]

The wonderful evening seemed to rekindle Lapointe's interest in politics. He made a definite decision to stay on, and even his health improved. Resplendent in his Windsor uniform, he started sitting for his portrait by Charles Maillard, the director of l'École des Beaux-Arts in Montreal. The presentation portrait was a gift from his friends and admirers – again Chubby Power was the organizer. King gladly contributed a hundred dollars and asked Power to get a price from the artist for a copy. 'A painting of Lapointe should find its place in our Houses of Parliament, as well as in his own home, or that of his children.'[7]

Tributes to the French-Canadian statesman poured in from across the country. In an editorial headed 'Great in Heart and Mind,' the *Toronto Star* praised Lapointe for promoting 'harmony, tolerance and moderation,' calling him an inspiration to all Canadians and applauding his decision to remain in public life as King's principal colleague. 'This combined leadership follows the pattern of Canadian government at its best: Baldwin-Lafontaine, Macdonald-Cartier.' Not all English Canada shared the *Star*'s admiration for Ernest Lapointe. The impending royal visit had brought imperialist sentiment to the boil. Unprecedented for a ruling monarch, King George VI was coming to Canada with Queen Elizabeth in May. In 1937 Mackenzie King had tentatively suggested a royal tour, but the timing indicates that with England teetering on the brink of war in 1939 the British government was sending the royal couple to strengthen the Dominion's allegiance.

Particularly at such a time, Canadian monarchists strongly resented the coddling of Quebec that Lapointe represented. Their antagonism came to the fore when early in March Lapointe spoke out publicly for still greater independence from Britain. He told the House of Commons that the Westminster Statute was 'a great step' but not the final one. First and foremost, Canada could not amend its own constitution. He asked how Canada could be accepted internationally as a sovereign nation 'when we have to resort to the Parliament of another country to change our constitution.' It was the same with appeals to the Privy Council of the British House of Lords. 'We can abolish them but we have not done so and litigants have to go outside of the country to get final decisions.' Finally – and here he sounded like a Quebec nationalist – Canada should have its own flag. He denied that taking these steps would lead to separation from the Commonwealth. 'I believe the best way to keep the Dominion in the British Commonwealth – and I hope to God it stays there – is to have a Canada free in every respect.'

A few days later King received an irate letter from a prominent member of the Ontario Liberal Women's Association. According to this woman, English-speaking Liberals were highly indignant that 'at this critical time' a cabinet minister would sponsor the changes that Lapointe had publicly favoured in Parliament. If the prime minister hoped to be re-elected with a firm majority, the writer asserted, he had better banish Ernest Lapointe to the Senate. 'At this time of national tension, as well as Canada being enthusiastic over the visit of the King and Queen, loyalty will be at its peak.' Lapointe's untimely suggestions 'would not save Quebec for the Liberal Party in the coming election, but they most certainly will unite ... the Women of every Party, the Veterans, the Loyalists against you and your government.'[9] It was precisely this loyalist element that King had in mind when he made his statement, 'When Britain is at war, Canada is at war.'

On 15 March 1939 the German army rolled into Prague, and from its historic castle Hitler theatrically proclaimed the annexation of Czechoslovakia. Even the most determined appeaser could not excuse this incursion as the reclaiming of German lands. Hitler had guaranteed the Czech frontier in the four-party agreement. On 17 March Chamberlain denounced Hitler for breaking the Munich pact, effectively ending the failed appeasement policy. On 20 March Mackenzie King announced in the House of Commons that if London were bombarded, 'we would regard it as an act of aggression, menacing freedom in all parts of the British Commonwealth.' In other words, Canada would definitely go to war. This time Lapointe did not demur. 'There will be hell to pay for it but it cannot be helped,' he told his soulmate.[10]

Isolationism foamed up immediately in his home province; anti-war rallies were organized in Montreal and Quebec City, and Le Devoir stated ominously that with such open talk of participation French Canadians would withdraw their support from the government. Lapointe received abusive letters from extreme nationalists and pleading letters from ordinary Quebec citizens to keep Canada out of war.[11] Predictably, he became very discouraged. It would help somewhat, he said to King, if he could promise his constituency some public works. A few days later he informed King that the Quebec situation was 'getting out of hand.'[12] The notorious rabble-rouser René Chaloult had introduced a resolution in the provincial legislature, calling on the Duplessis government to inform Ottawa that 'the overwhelming majority in the Province of Quebec is opposed to any participation in any war whatever, save for the defense of Canadian soil.' When Duplessis blocked the motion on the ground that it impinged on federal jurisdiction, noisy students invaded the legislature and protest meetings sprang up throughout the province.[13]

Notwithstanding the anti-war sentiment on his home front, Lapointe felt he could no longer postpone the moment he had dreaded for years. The German invasion of Czechoslovakia had made it abundantly clear that war could not be avoided. He knew that the Anglo-Canadian majority, with its umbilical attachment to the mother country, would insist on participating in England's war. Virtually alone among French-

Canadian politicians, he was at home in the rest of Canada and understood the English. He was stating no more than the simple truth when he told the House that 'there are not many who know the mentality and feelings of their fellow-citizens in all parts of Canada better than I do.'[14] The minority would have to bow to the wishes of the majority. The time had come to tell his compatriots that Canada could not stay out of the coming conflict.

What made it so much more difficult was that he would have to do a complete about-face. For decades he had promised his people that Canada would never become embroiled in a foreign war again. He and King had campaigned on this promise in 1935. He had used it to defeat the separatist, Paul Bouchard, in the Lotbinière by-election in 1937. There was his much-quoted isolationist statement at Limoilou in December 1938. As recently as the past January, he had told the confederation of Catholic trade unions that he agreed with the non-participation statement in their brief.[15] King was to deliver a major speech in Parliament on the international crisis on 30 March, and Lapointe would follow him. When King outlined at cabinet what he proposed to say, Lapointe amazed him by remarking that he intended to 'go very much further.'[16]

The prime minister's two-hour address revealed the restraining hand of Skelton, who wrote the initial draft. Supposedly a foreign policy statement, it contained no commitment and left its listeners in the dark as to the government's intentions. Woodsworth told the House that after listening to the prime minister for two hours, 'I really do not know, in the event of war, what action the government would take ... The Canadian nationalist, the imperialist, the League of Nations collectivist, the pacifist, the North American, the belligerent militarist – each will find some crumb of comfort in the Prime Minister's speech.'[17]

Lapointe's speech the next day dispersed the clouds. He declared that it was impossible for Canada to remain neutral if Britain became involved in a war. 'The citizens of Quebec would have to close the port of Quebec to the *Empress of Britain* if she carries guns during a war, and even fight her if she wanted to come in against their will.' Canadians would not be able to enlist in the British forces; British sailors who sought refuge in Canadian ports would be interned. Turning to the Quebec backbenchers he asked if they could 'believe seriously that this could be done without a civil war in Canada.' Though Canada 'had gone far ahead in the march towards nationhood,' neutrality was possible only for sovereign states, and Canada was still tied to Britain.

Realistically, the right to remain neutral was 'meaningless.' He exposed the inconsistency of the anti-war *nationalistes*. 'May I say that in my own province those who are most eager to declare that we would have nothing to do with any war of Britain or of the Commonwealth are those who refuse peremptorily to have the right to amend their constitution or to abolish appeals to the privy council.'

He then appealed to English Canada to understand 'the feelings, the mentality, the views' of French Canada. He said that unlike English Canadians, French Canadians have 'only one country, one home.' They would fight to defend that home, but they 'will never agree that any government has the right to force them to military service on the other side of the ocean.' Lapointe asserted that he had opposed conscription in 1917 as a frightful blunder, and he had never altered his view. He declared that he would not be a member of a government that would enact conscription, and he would oppose any government that would enforce it.[18]

It was a pivotal moment in his life. Lapointe had abandoned the 'home defence only' position and retreated to a second line of defence – participation in the war but no overseas conscription. In this penultimate speech of his career (a greater one was still to come), he summed up his lifelong commitment to national unity: 'The best way, the most effective way of helping is not the way that would divide our country and tear it asunder.' His address so electrified the members that when his forty minutes were up the House rang with cries to continue.

After it was over, King raved about the speech. 'It was really the crowning speech of your career,' he congratulated his lieutenant. 'It will give you a real place as a world statesman.' 'I hope it will help to prepare the way for Canada to play her part, should war come,' Lapointe replied.[19] King's praise was not unmixed with a little envy, stirred up by the press gallery's consensus that Lapointe had 'stolen the show.'[20] He admitted to himself that he had lost something by being so vague. He had told Skelton that the speech needed 'pointing up' to bring out the obvious – that Canada could not stay out of the coming conflict. 'I feel that my own position, this year, will suffer as it did last year from an impression of aloofness so far as relations between Canada and Britain are concerned.' He shuddered to think what an impression he would have left if he had not made many changes to Skelton's draft.

By the evening session, however, he had come to the conclusion that it was just as well he had spoken with reserve. 'If I had made the speech Lapointe made, the party might have held its own with Jingos in

Ontario, but would have lost Quebec more or less entirely.' Lapointe could reject neutrality; he, King, could not. King perfectly expressed their symbiotic relationship in his diary: 'Together, our speeches constituted a sort of trestle sustaining the structure which would serve to unite divergent parts of Canada, thereby making for a united country.'[21] King knew Lapointe as no one else did, and he realized what this act of patriotism cost him. Cautious to a fault, even timid, and certainly not a betting man, Lapointe had risked his influence in French Canada to tell his compatriots that neutrality was out of the question because it would break the country apart. *Saturday Night* hailed Lapointe for 'the most courageous utterance ever made by a French Canadian.' The headline read: 'Lapointe Canada's Number One Statesman.'

Lapointe's speech made 'a very profound impression' both in English and French Canada, an Ottawa family court judge told Picard some time later. Lapointe's private secretary did not need to be told; for weeks he was busy answering the mail that came in. The anglophone establishment was delighted with Lapointe. Even the expatriate millionaire Sir James Dunn sent congratulations from his fashionable address in London. Few letters of praise, however, topped the one from a wealthy Toronto businessman and future Tory cabinet minister who wrote, 'Thank God for Ernest Lapointe!'[22]

While English Canadians were reassured by Lapointe's rejection of neutrality, French Canadians could take comfort in his promise that there would be no conscription. Nevertheless, Maxime Raymond and his coterie of nationalist MPs continued to oppose participation in a European war, cautioning that they would go no further than home defence. Speaking in the House in April, Raymond held Lapointe to his now famous promise: 'Instead of waging war in a foreign land, we shall remain at home and defend the Canada we love.' But Lapointe was much less intimidated by Maxime Raymond and the anti-war MPs. Overcoming his habitual indecision had given him new strength.

The very day of Lapointe's speech, Chamberlain had announced that if Germany invaded Poland, Britain and its Allies would go to war. However, the stiffening attitude of the western powers did not stop the dictators. Hitler responded to the Anglo-Polish mutual assistance pact by demanding a corridor through Poland to East Prussia and the return of Danzig, a free state since the war. Mussolini invaded Albania. The Spanish civil war ended in the victory of the fascist Franco. If his diary is any indication, the black news from Europe hardly penetrated King's thoughts that spring. He was obsessed with the impending royal visit, planning it down to the most minute detail. Lapointe did not share King's delirious excitement. According to his daughter, he was a 'tepid' monarchist at best, which is borne out by the fact that he later declined with thanks King's invitation to join the royal train at Rivière-du-Loup.[23] But he did his part to ensure a good reception for the royal couple in Quebec. He and Rinfret enlisted the aid of Cardinal Villeneuve. The cardinal, who relished pomp and ceremony and envisaged a gratifying role for himself, issued a pastoral letter to all parish priests to urge their flocks to welcome the king and queen when they landed at Quebec City on 17 May.[24]

When King George VI and Queen Elizabeth arrived on the *Empress of Australia*, Mackenzie King and Ernest Lapointe were standing on the wharf waiting to greet them officially. 'In their identical Windsor garb of cocked hat and gold braid' they reminded Bruce Hutchison of 'a tiny Tweedledum and giant Tweedledee.' Although lukewarm about royalty, his proudly erect, portly figure indicated that it was a thrilling moment for Lapointe. And he need not have worried about the royal couple's reception from Quebeckers. A cheering mass crowded the lower town, clung to the trail that Wolfe's army had clambered up, and blanketed the Plains of Abraham on the bluff, forgetful of historic humiliation. From Quebec the royal couple travelled to the capital. Here too Lapointe had an official role as host when the queen opened the new Supreme Court building. Deviously disposing of the governor general's claim to precedence, Mackenzie King accompanied the royal couple on their tour, leaving a furious, red-faced Tweedsmuir steaming in Government House. As always during the prime minister's absence, Lapointe took over for him.

Jack Pickersgill, the only secretary left in the prime minister's office, got to know Lapointe well, and the latter became 'something of a hero' to him. Pickersgill found he could discuss everything with Lapointe whereas with King he had little or no discussion regarding public affairs. Besides, he felt that Lapointe liked him while King always gave him the feeling that he regarded him as 'impudent.' The ambitious young secretary would later say that he learned more about the real functioning of cabinet government from Lapointe than from his usual boss. He also said that he 'began to see how the process of keeping French- and English-speaking Canadians together in a single political party actually worked.'[25] Pickersgill makes no mention of it, but a chilling instance of how King and Lapointe kept the nation together occurred at this time.

King was on the royal train bound for Washington when he received a telegram signed by sixty very important Torontonians headed by George M. Wrong, an eminent professor emeritus and the father of Hume Wrong, counsellor at the Canadian legation in Washington. The telegram was a plea to King to offer sanctuary to a shipload of Jewish refugees aboard a liner, the *St Louis*, lying at anchor off Halifax. The 907 passengers, all German Jews of the professional classes, had sailed from Hamburg with Cuban visas, but arriving at Havana they had been refused entry. A nightmare voyage had then begun. None of the Latin American countries would allow them to disembark, and the United States had ordered the coast guard to see that the *St Louis* stayed well away from its shores. Canada was the refugees' last hope. The telegram from the concerned humanitarians was nothing less than an SOS:

> As a mark of gratitude to Almighty God for the pleasure and gratification which has been vouchsafed the Canadian people through the visit of their Gracious Majesties King George and Queen Elizabeth and as evidence of the true Christian charity of the people of this most fortunate and blessed country, we, the undersigned as Christian citizens of Canada respectfully suggest that under the powers vested in you as Premier of our country you forthwith offer to the 907 homeless exiles on board the Hamburg American ship St. Louis sanctuary in Canada.

King wired Skelton a verbatim copy and told him to show it to the acting prime minister and the director of immigration.[26] Unfortunately for the desperate people on the *St Louis*, the immigration director was F.C. Blair and the acting prime minister was Ernest Lapointe. Over luncheon at the White House, the subject of the refugee ship came up. As King records it in his diary, President Roosevelt 'explained' the situation to King George, adding that he thought Canada also placed certain restrictions on immigration. The U.S. secretary of state, Cordell Hull, murmured something about 'a fraudulent transaction which accounted in part for the situation.' King said nothing about Professor Wrong's wire.[27]

Right after lunch King received a secret and confidential telegram from Skelton. Skelton reported that as far as Blair was concerned, the *St Louis* passengers did not fit within the classifications of admissible immigrants. They were not farmers, they did not have relatives in Canada, they did not have investment capital (having been stripped by Hitler of all their assets), and Blair could not see how their admission would be beneficial to the country. Blair also wished to remind the prime minister that some 720 Jews had been admitted by order-in-council since January. But the definitive factor for King was Skelton's report that the minister of justice was 'personally emphatically opposed' to the admission of the *St Louis* passengers.[28] Accordingly, they were not allowed to land and the ship turned back to Europe carrying many of its passengers to their doom.

King would probably have made the same decision had he been in his office in the East Block. Before leaving on the royal tour, he had informed Abraham Heaps, with a frankness unusual for him, that Canada was not prepared to do anything more than exchange information with other countries regarding the Jews seeking sanctuary.[29] The *St Louis* incident proved the truth of a remark by Secretary of State Rinfret a few months earlier that had embarrassed King and Lapointe. Speaking in Montreal in January, Rinfret had stated that 'despite all sentiments of humanity, so long as Canada has an unemployment problem there will be no "open door" for political refugees here.' King and Lapointe had hastened to deny that this was official policy.[30] The White House luncheon reveals Roosevelt and Cordell Hull as devoid of humanitarian feelings as King and Lapointe.

CHAPTER TWENTY-FIVE

Canada Goes to War

After the *St Louis* incident, Lapointe concentrated on the domestic political situation. A federal election would likely take place in 1939, and his job was to deliver Quebec. When Duplessis became premier in 1936, Lapointe had become extremely pessimistic about the federal Liberals' chances in Quebec in the next election. But in the summer of 1939 he changed his mind. Duplessis had lost much of his popularity. The provincial debt was up substantially, and so were taxes. Unemployment continued to be high. Quebec's new hours of work legislation had actually led to less take-home pay for the employed.

Many Quebec nationalists had deserted Duplessis and were back in Lapointe's camp. And Lapointe believed that he had won over the cohort of young nationalists who took their lead from *L'Action Nationale*'s brilliant young editor, André Laurendeau. Moreover, he was convinced that Duplessis's provincial supporters would vote Liberal federally. War was almost a certainty, and the curse of 1917 still hung over the Tories. Lapointe knew that Quebeckers trusted him rather than Robert Manion, the Conservative leader, to avoid conscription. On 28 June Grant Dexter of the *Winnipeg Free Press* found Lapointe 'happy and enthusiastic.' He strode around his office, gesturing animatedly, full of confidence. 'My friend, Quebec is all right. There is no trouble there. People say we will lose seats in Quebec. My friend, we will not lose seats.' Lapointe did not say why he was so optimistic. His monologue was mainly a denunciation of Duplessis, whom he clearly detested.[1]

At a private interview in the Lapointes' apartment at the Roxborough, *Le Devoir*'s Ottawa correspondent, Léopold Richer, also found the minister of justice 'jovial and optimistic.' Lapointe had come back visibly tired from a long cabinet meeting. Sinking gratefully into a familiar arm chair, he reminisced about men he had known and told anecdotes about those who were still around. Little by little his fatigue disappeared. He answered Richer's questions frankly. He was sure of himself. Richer sketched a word portrait: 'His face is open, made for easy and frank laughter. There is nothing stiff or affected about him. His manners are affable and welcoming, though a little paternal. He scrutinizes faces with a keen eye. He remains typically French Canadian, with the sly, cunning air of the peasant and the speech of a *Quebeçois*.'[2]

As this home interview suggests, Lapointe made an effort to cultivate *Le Devoir*'s Ottawa correspondent. While Richer admired Lapointe as a man he did not like his politics. In his opinion, Lapointe accepted King's centralist views without question and then imposed them on Quebec. Richer preferred to interview nationalist MPs such as Wilfrid Gariepy, who had recently referred to Lapointe in the House as King's 'Siamese twin.' Around the beginning of June Richer wrote an article criticizing Lapointe for killing an amendment to the Companies Act put forward by Maxime Raymond. The amendment required disclosure of records from Dominion Textiles and other companies enjoying tariff protection, which, Raymond claimed, were 'making exorbitant profits and distributing scandalous dividends and bonuses to their shareholders while paying workers less than living wages.' Richer implied that Lapointe was protecting the companies. Lapointe was incensed. Richer should know how hostile St James Street was to him. When more critical articles followed, Lapointe was sufficiently offended to complain to *Le Devoir*'s editor, Georges Pelletier.

Lapointe had a friendship of sorts with Pelletier that went back to their early days in Rivière-du-Loup. They addressed each other familiarly, dropped in to each other's offices, and on occasion Lapointe would send Pelletier internal departmental documents. Because of their 'personal relations,' he wrote Pelletier, he felt he should bring to his attention the unjust and ill-natured remarks Richer had been making about him for some time. This was the thanks he got for giving Richer special briefings to oblige Pelletier. Pelletier replied that he would not countenance any injustice to Lapointe and he would talk to Richer.

However, an even more critical article appeared, and Lapointe complained again. This evoked a long, unsatisfactory letter from Pelletier who supported his correspondent. Pelletier suggested that Lapointe was sometimes blinded by his loyalty and friendship with King and did not see things that others saw more clearly. Pelletier did not disguise the fact that *Le Devoir* shared the thinking of the nationalist MPs.[3]

Under Pelletier's direction, the paper leaned towards Quebec separatism as it never had in Bourassa's day. And it was influential well beyond its 12,000 subscribers.

In mid-July of 1939, King polled his ministers about election prospects in their provinces. Lapointe's optimism had become somewhat tempered after sounding out some key Quebec Liberals. Still, he strongly advocated a general election at the earliest possible time. Though certain of a Liberal victory in Quebec, he predicted that it would be 'a pretty difficult campaign and probably a dirty one in which I will be the main target.' Their adversaries, he told King, would concentrate on the repeal of Section 98 and the federal government's refusal to put something like Duplessis's Padlock Act in the Criminal Code.[4]

Lapointe had a foretaste of the Conservatives' dirty campaign in a speech by Sam Gobeil, a former minister in Bennett's cabinet. At a public meeting at Ste Hyacinthe on 9 July, Gobeil told his devoutly Catholic audience that Lapointe was the kind of anticlerical liberal that the papacy anathematized. He smeared Lapointe as the friend and patron of communists for repealing Section 98 and for granting passports to allow Tim Buck to go to Russia and 2,000 Canadians to fight with the Spanish Reds. In a vicious anti-Semitic harangue, Gobeil also accused Lapointe and the Liberal government of favouring Jewish immigration, which would have struck Abe Heaps as the height of irony.[5]

By August Lapointe was not so sure that an election should be called. His change of mind had nothing to do with the sniping of Tories and nationalists. The international situation was deteriorating by the minute, and on 11 August Lapointe told his cabinet colleagues that, in his opinion, it would be impossible to have an election if there was any real chance of war. King noted in his diary that Lapointe 'swayed' the cabinet. In any event, the election had to be put off when the Russians astonished the world by signing a non-aggression pact with Germany. Invasion of Poland seemed a certainty. In England Chamberlain called an emergency session of Parliament. He was expected to announce momentarily that England would honour its pledge to Poland. King immediately met with his cabinet, deferring any serious discussion until Lapointe arrived on the noon train.

Lapointe preferred to hear what the others said before expressing his own opinion; however, when Ilsley pressed King to issue a statement that Canada would stand with Britain if Germany invaded Poland, Lapointe broke in to say that he saw no purpose in that. Yes, Canada would have to go to war, but they should stick to their policy of saying nothing in advance that would divide the country. Most of the ministers agreed with Lapointe that there should be no advance statement; Rogers offered a half-way measure; the defence minister, Ian Mackenzie, sided with Ilsley. Only Michaud, the minister of fisheries from New Brunswick, tried to hold King to his oft-repeated position that military action would be limited to the defence of Canada. Ignoring Michaud, King expressed gratification that all his colleagues were in agreement that Canada would participate if Britain were drawn into war – it was simply a matter of timing the announcement. He said Parliament would be summoned the moment Britain declared war. For years King and Lapointe's slogan had been 'Parliament will decide,' but the decision to go to war was taken by the executive and Parliament would merely be asked to rubber-stamp it. In the meantime, if questioned by the press King would answer obliquely that 'the government's position had been fully stated in Parliament last session by Mr. Lapointe and myself.'[6]

As war drew nearer, King would not take a step without clearing it with Lapointe. Cabinet colleagues were used to hearing the prime minister preface his remarks by saying, 'I have already talked the matter over with Lapointe.' The day after the Russo-German pact, King conceived the idea of making a last-minute appeal to Hitler. With a draft in hand, he went over to the new justice building to get Lapointe's views. (The sight of Lapointe's 'magnificent' office with its 'wonderful' view stirred up a little of the old rivalry: 'It is as far ahead of the prime minister's office as day is ahead of night,' he wrote in his diary.) Lapointe instantly approved the draft as 'wholly in accord with our policy ... We as a party have always been for settling international differences by peaceful means, if possible.'[7]

The cabinet was less than enthusiastic. Ilsley and Rogers, the most hawkish of the ministers, took a strong stand against any communication with Hitler, asserting vehemently that the time for appeasement was past. At this, Lapointe 'jumped in' with 'a passionate plea' for sending the appeal, and the telegram went off. Lapointe had correctly gauged Quebec public opinion. The French-Canadian press unanimously approved King's eleventh-hour attempt to avert war, *Le Devoir* declaring that 'this time Mr. King acted as the head of a free nation.' Chamberlain, Roosevelt, and Daladier also dispatched similar pleas for peace to Berlin. But for some reason, King heeded the German consul general's advice to send an identical telegram to the Polish president, who was understandably offended. The Polish president replied sourly that it was not Poland that was making aggressive demands and provoking the international crisis.[8]

Early on the morning of September the first, King was awakened with the news that Hitler had invaded Poland. He sped over to the East Block to confer with his staff. It was King's businesslike principal secretary, Arnold Heeney, rather than Dr Skelton, who took matters in hand. Skelton was despondent. Totally opposed to Canada's entry into the war and his arguments for remaining neutral having failed with King, he offered his resignation. King refused to accept it. Only Lapointe knew about this behind-the-scenes drama. No doubt he helped convince Skelton to stay on in spite of his principles.[9]

At 9:00 a.m. the cabinet convened and King briskly read out the order-in-council summoning Parliament for a special session on 7 September. He announced that a state of apprehended war existed and cabinet listened sombrely as Lapointe read out the proclamation reviving the War Measures Act of 1914. It was decided to backdate the proclamation to 25 August to cover appropriations under governor general's warrants, which had been used to purchase American planes. The United States had passed a Neutrality Act, but as long as Canada was not technically at war its friendly neighbour could sell it war materiel. Under the authority of the War Measures Act, orders-in-council were passed to call up the militia and place the tiny permanent forces on active duty. The important thing was how to present these wartime measures to the country before war was actually declared. The press was waiting for a statement.

King had been working on a statement for days with Lapointe. On 31 August Lapointe sent over some suggested language to Laurier House: 'Our co-operation is going to Britain and her allies in this hour of great sacrifice, not only because she is a sister nation, the senior partner in the Commonwealth, but because she is fighting for the cause of freedom and democracy, and Canada, in the interest of its own security must help to maintain the present world order.' King incorporated some of Lapointe's wording into his draft, but after several vettings by cabinet and staff the statement was stripped to the bare essentials. 'In the event of the United Kingdom becoming engaged in war in the effort to resist aggression,' it read, 'the Government of Canada has unanimously decided, as soon as Parliament meets, to seek its authority for effective cooperation by Canada at the side of Great Britain. Meanwhile necessary measures will be taken for the defence of Canada.' Lapointe said he was satisfied. King then called in the reporters.[10]

Wilfrid Eggleston was one of the newsmen attending the press conference. On his way into the prime minister's office, he passed Dr
Skelton slumped in a chair, 'looking more exhausted and strained than
I had ever seen him.' The prime minister himself looked 'older, his wisp
of hair thinner, his face lined.' In a 'grave, low, firm' voice he read out
the statement to the press. Though Eggleston thought it cautious and
non-committal, even ambiguous, it meant that Canada would go to
war. When the prime minister finished talking, the reporters rushed to
the phones. Dr Skelton was 'still slumped in courageous despair.'[11]

On 3 September Britain and France declared war on Germany. King
summoned his ministers – there would be no time for church or recov-
ering from a hangover this Sunday morning! The first business was
Lapointe's order-in-council to put into effect the Defence of Canada
Regulations, which would come under his jurisdiction. Based on the
recommendations of Commissioner S.T. Wood of the RCMP, they called
for full censorship of press and radio, preventive detention of potential
enemy aliens and suspected spies, surveillance of lesser suspects, and
prohibitions on any statements that could hinder recruitment or prejudice the war effort. Colonel Wood had also wanted to outlaw a long list
of organizations, including left-wing labour unions, but Lapointe had
put that on hold. King would later say that cabinet approved these
draconian regulations 'almost unread and unconsidered' because there
was no time to deal with things thoroughly. The Defence of Canada
Regulations were proclaimed that same day.[12]

King was scheduled to broadcast a message to the country in the
afternoon, and he took it for granted that Ernest would read the French
translation. Lapointe tried to get out of it. Why did he always have to be
the one speaking for participation? he asked King. It did him no good
in his own province. King convinced him that only he had the necessary prestige to issue the call to war to French Canada. Put like that
Lapointe accepted his duty 'nicely.' He would have been even more
reluctant if he could have foreseen the crisis at the broadcasting studio.
Not only was a page of text missing from the English version, but half
the French translation was not there. The anxiety was terrible. With just
minutes to spare, the errant pages arrived and the country heard, in
English and in French, that Canada would voluntarily enter the war
pending parliamentary sanction of the government's recommendation.[13]
Canadian families, clustered around their radios, understood that war
was a foregone conclusion.

With one voice the French-Canadian nationalist press condemned the government for presenting Parliament with a fait accompli. King and Lapointe were castigated for having caved in to Britain. *L'Action Catholique* asked why Canada should get involved when the United States and fourteen European countries, to whom Hitlerism was much more of a threat, remained neutral. *Le Devoir* urged Parliament to adopt a policy of home defence only and benevolent neutrality towards England.

Protest meetings erupted at once in Montreal and Quebec City. On 4 September Paul Gouin's resurrected ALN drew a crowd of several thousand to Montreal's Maisonneuve market. On the podium with Gouin were some of the most extreme nationalists. Gouin delivered a fiery anti-war speech; waving a newspaper before his audience, he quoted 1935 statements by King and Lapointe that Ottawa did not have the right to take Canada into war without a plebiscite. At the mention of their names, the crowd booed and someone called out 'Kill them!' Paul Bouchard appealed to the crowd's anti-Semitism: 'We don't want to see thousands of young Canadians die overseas to save international Jewry's finances.' Thunderous applause greeted René Chaloult's thinly disguised incitement to open rebellion – if conventional methods of protest were exhausted, he shouted, 'French Canadians would rather fight in the streets of Montreal than in Europe.'

The next day the Comité de Défense Nationale held a rally at the Monument Nationale in Montreal. Organized in haste by André Laurendeau, the committee united the intellectual nationalists of the reviews and the Catholic unions. In an orchestrated protest the crowd chanted 'We won't go' at fifteen-minute intervals – this would become the war cry at a series of protest rallies. A resolution was put to the crowd, which roared its approval, demanding that the federal Members of Parliament express the opinion of the overwhelming majority of French Canadians by voting against participation in the war. Laurendeau telegraphed the resolution to the sixty Quebec MPs in Ottawa.[14] To what degree did this isolationist outpouring reflect French-Canadian public opinion? In retrospect André Laurendeau judged it 'a surface reaction, not a ground swell.' But Chubby Power had no doubt then or later that 'the predominant sentiment in Quebec was reluctance to embark upon war, and in many cases an absolute antagonism to doing so.'[15]

Shortly before Parliament was to meet, panicky MPs descended upon Lapointe. They told him they were being deluged with anti-war messages. They said they would have to vote against the party. 'You're going to kill yourself,' they said, 'and you're going to kill us.' Calmly and authoritatively, Lapointe explained that if the Quebec bloc voted against Canada's entry into the war it would kill the party in the rest of Canada. He himself would have no option but to resign, and King would be forced to give way to a union government controlled by jingoes who would soon bring in conscription. Having alarmed them with the consequences of isolationism, he then reassured them that their constituents would accept participation so long as there was no overseas conscription. As they were well aware, he said, he and King were pledged to that. He sent them away with a promise that if they would stay solidly behind him, he would look after them.[16]

Grumbling and reluctant, most of them agreed to support their chief, but they wanted to avoid a division and a recorded vote. Cardin, never a conciliator, insisted that the members would have to stand up and be counted so the party would know who its friends were. When King heard what was going on, he tactfully discouraged Cardin's attempts to drum the dissidents out of the party. Canada must enter the war with a semblance of unity.[17] There would be no recorded vote, only a voice vote, which would drown out any members opposing participation.

In cabinet Lapointe was disquieted to hear his English colleagues talk about the inevitability of conscription. He would have to speak out against *that* when the time came, he told them. King leapt in to second his soulmate. There would be no conscription during his administration; before allowing overseas conscription he would submit the resignation of his entire cabinet.[18] This silenced the hawks. Nevertheless, the 'all-out war' side had got a boost with the appointment of Colonel J.L. Ralston to replace the ailing Dunning as finance minister. Not that Lapointe objected to Ralston. When King told him he was thinking of putting Ralston back in the defence portfolio he had held in the 1920s, Lapointe readily agreed that he was the best man for the job in wartime. As it happened, Ralston did not want to displace his friend, Ian Mackenzie, so Norman Rogers was shortly moved up to National Defence from the junior department of labour.

On 7 September Lapointe took his customary place in the House at the desk he shared with King. He was acutely conscious of the Quebec contingent on the benches behind him. Had he convinced them to support him? He anticipated opposition from the half-dozen diehard ultra-nationalists. Lapointe was aware that Maxime Raymond was going to present an anti-war petition. Circulated by Paul Gouin and the ALN, it was said to have 100,000 signatures and read in part, 'We refuse to sacrifice our most vital interest to the petty interests and exigencies of international high finance and manufacturers of armaments.'[19]

The Address from the Throne said little more than that the government was seeking authority to implement the necessary measures for the defence of Canada and 'for co-operation in the determined effort to resist further aggression.' Adoption of the address would be followed by a declaration of war. The debate on the throne speech was the crucial test for King's Quebec lieutenant. The typed text of his speech lay at hand; he had poured his heart and soul into it. King too recognized that his reply to the address was 'the most important speech of my life.' Faced with the greatest threat to national unity since the conscription crisis of 1917, King and Lapointe prepared to work in tandem, as they had done so many times over the past twenty years, to hold the two Canadas together.

On behalf of the government King formally recommended war against Germany. He was as bland and King-like as possible. Ruling out conscription as unnecessary, he stressed the need to defend Canada, particularly on the Atlantic side, and indicated that Canada's wartime role would be that of an arsenal and food depot for the Allies. Measures would be taken to avoid the mistakes of the first war, especially profiteering. The speech was characteristically uninspiring and interminable. Despite the awesome importance of the occasion, bored opposition members began to drift out. Nevertheless, King soldiered on doggedly to put on record the entire account of the government's actions over the past five years and its reasons for leading the country into a second world war so soon after the first. He did not care what impression he was leaving, he later told his diary, 'knowing the importance of having the case well set forth.' And, indeed, Bruce Hutchison likened the speech to a lawyer's brief.[20] It would be up to Lapointe to win over the Quebec isolationists.

Before Lapointe spoke, the House heard Maxime Raymond. The nationalist spokesman made no comment on the petition that he had previously tabled, but he warned that 'interior divisions' would be the consequence of Canadian participation in the European war. The French Canadians in Quebec felt obliged only to defend their own soil, he told the English members. He submitted that Parliament had no mandate to decide whether Canada should participate in Britain's war; that was a decision for the people through a referendum. He reminded Lapointe of his Limoilou speech in December where he stated that 'we will stay here and defend the Canada we love.' Raymond prophesied that intervention in the war would inevitably lead to conscription.

On 9 September Lapointe rose to give the most important speech of his life. He did not address the opposite benches. With the exception of

J.S. Woodsworth, whose pacifism cost him the CCF leadership, the opposition parties were behind the government to a man. The real opposition was the French members of his own party, and Lapointe turned to face them. Anger at Maxime Raymond lent fire to his opening remarks. 'With massive shoulders heaving, huge hands clenched, and dark face contorted' (as he appeared to Hutchison in the gallery), Lapointe reminded Raymond that it was the tradition of British freedom of speech that allowed him to voice his objection to aiding Britain in its justified fight against Hitler. England had worked for peace, and it was 'base calumny' to suggest that it was in any way responsible for the present conflict. He and the prime minister had also worked for peace and supported the League of Nations. 'I hate war with all my heart and conscience but devotion to peace does not mean ignorance or blindness.' He argued that neutrality was impossible from a practical and legal standpoint. Canada was linked with Britain not only through a shared monarchy but in many other ways. Notwithstanding the Statute of Westminster, the power of amending the constitution remained with the British Parliament: this was because Canadians wanted it that way, though he himself did not necessarily share that view. Canada used the diplomatic and consular functions of Britain throughout the world, Canadian ships sailed under British registry, and Britain had naval bases at Halifax and Esquimault. Of course, all these things could be cancelled or repealed, but, he asked his compatriots, did they honestly think the majority of Canadians would stand for it?

He would go further, he declared. Canada could not be neutral without providing aid and comfort to the enemy. 'I say to every member of this House that by doing nothing, by being neutral, we actually would be taking the side of Adolf Hitler.' As to the suggestion in some Quebec papers that Canadians who wished to do so could join the British forces, 'if Canadians go to the front line of battle, they will go voluntarily, as Canadians under the control of Canada, commanded by Canadians, and maintained by the Dominion of Canada.' Lapointe squarely faced the possibility of an expeditionary force, warning that any government that ignored the wishes of the majority could not stay in power. In the cause of national unity, he urged his compatriots to support the war.

Then turning around, he addressed the House as a whole. There were extremists on both sides, he said. Those who were shouting for conscription (and here he pointed the finger at the *Ottawa Citizen*) would split the nation just as surely as those of his compatriots who were campaigning for neutrality. With grave seriousness he told the English members:

Quebec will never agree to accept compulsory service or conscription outside of Canada. I will go further than that. When I say the whole province of Quebec, I mean that I personally agree with them. I am authorized by my colleagues in the Cabinet from the Province of Quebec, Senator Dandurand, my good friend and colleague, the Minister of Public Works, Mr. Cardin, my friend and fellow townsman and colleague, the Minister of Pensions and National Health, Mr. Power, to say that we will never agree to conscription and never be members or supporters of a government that will enforce it.

'Is that clear enough?' he asked.

Lapointe had given his pledge to his people and made a pact on their behalf with the rest of Canada. No one who heard him could doubt his sincerity. There was thunderous applause when he declared, 'I believe the majority in my Province trust me. I have never deceived them and I will not deceive them now.' 'I have been told,' he said, 'that my present stand means my political death. Well, at least it would not be a dishonorable end and I am ready to make sacrifices for the sake of being right ... if only I can keep my physical strength, fall I shall not; and my friends shall not fall either.' His dramatic peroration stirred the House in a way that King could only envy and never achieve. Openly in tears, Lapointe quoted the queen's bilingual parting remark, 'Que Dieu bénisse le Canada, God bless Canada.'

Yes, God bless Canada. God save Canada, God Save Canada's honour, Canada's soul, Canada's dignity, Canada's conscience. God give Canadians the light which will indicate to them where their duty lies in this hour of trial so that our children and our children's children may inherit a land where freedom and peace shall prevail and where our social, political and religious institutions may be secure and from which the tyrannical doctrines of Nazism and Communism are forever banished. Yes, God bless Canada, God bless our Queen, God bless our King.[21]

Lapointe sat down amid an ovation from all parts of the House. The delighted Mackenzie King clasped his hand warmly. 'It was a very noble utterance throughout, very brave and truly patriotic,' he later recorded in his diary.

The French-Canadian isolationists then had their chance to dissent from their party's war policy. After Lapointe spoke, Liguori Lacombe introduced a non-participation amendment to the Address from the Throne. It was seconded by Wilfrid Lacroix. But no other member, not even Raymond, supported the amendment.[22] The threatened revolt had collapsed. The throne speech was adopted by a voice vote with a few faint negatives. The Quebec MPs had fallen in line behind their chief. Lapointe had risked his political life and won. Listening to the speech from the gallery, J.W. Dafoe, who had thought himself 'too old and hardened' for such a reaction, was 'stirred to the depths of my emotions.'[23]

Following the unanimous support in the Senate, the cabinet gathered in the prime minister's office for the signing of the declaration of war with the German Reich, which would then be cabled to King George for ratification. The office was dim, lit by a single ceiling light. King signed and then offered his chair to Lapointe. The latter shook his head and simply leaned over King's shoulder and affixed his signature.[24] Reluctantly, he had fulfilled his duty as attorney general (hitherto an honorific adjunct to his justice portfolio). Poor Lapointe! It was his name that stood out most prominently on the Proclamation of War that was reproduced on the front pages of the newspapers. Because of such unwanted prominence, he feared that he would be blamed for plunging Canada into war. He could only hope, as he wrote the associate judge of Quebec's superior court, 'that the stand I took in the House of Commons will be understood by our compatriots.'[25]

Lapointe was not surprised or particularly disturbed by Paul Gouin's dismissal of his speech as 'shameless and dishonorable.' Nor by a poisonous note from an organization in Lévis, Quebec, calling itself the Comité des droits des Canadiens Français, which read, 'Your treason is consummated. Contrary to your pretensions, the population of Quebec is not with you.'[26] More disturbing was the criticism in Le Devoir. The paper called his speech 'more imperialist' than King's and doubted his word that he would resign if conscription were imposed. But Le Devoir was the exception. The mainstream papers in Quebec were favourable, praising King and Lapointe for limiting Canada's involvement in the war. La Presse, the most widely read daily with a circulation of 142,000, accepted participation 'within the limits set by the speeches of Messrs. King and Lapointe, i.e. putting our national interests first and adhering to the voluntary principle.' La Patrie commended 'the King-Lapointe cabinet' for taking into account 'so far as is humanly possible' the feelings of both the majority and the minority. *L'Evénement-Journal* called it 'a policy of the golden mean.' *L'Action Catholique* preached that 'it is our duty to accept this decision of Parliament' – the church organ was likely under orders from Cardinal Villeneuve, who was ready and willing to cooperate in the war effort.[27]

Mackenzie King glowed with self-satisfaction at the caucus meeting on 12 September. He boasted that the country's united stand was attributable to his policy of no commitments in advance. He compared Canada's entry into the war with 'that of a vessel sailing over a smooth and sunlit lake,'[28] forgetting that Lapointe had to pull him back on course more than once. Jack Pickersgill gave Lapointe full credit for bringing Quebec into the war. Chubby Power felt that no one but Lapointe could have won over the Quebec members when the province they represented was so strongly isolationist. But for André Laurendeau and the *nationalistes*, Lapointe won the day by his solemn pledge that the government would never resort to conscription for overseas.[29]

CHAPTER TWENTY-SIX

Duplessis Beaten

Hitler's blitzkrieg made short work of Poland. Military intervention by England and France was strategically impossible, and within two weeks the country was conquered and partitioned between Germany and Russia. Recruiting had begun in Canada. Although the patriotic fervour of 1914 was missing, young Canadians, especially the British-born, answered the call, and high unemployment created a strong incentive to volunteer. On 19 September the government announced that a division of 16,000 volunteers would go overseas. At this time Norman Rogers, who had proved himself as minister of labour, replaced the inadequate Ian Mackenzie as minister of defence.[1]

Recruitment in Quebec was surprisingly good, considering that French Canadians did not feel any emotional tug to fight for 'Mother England' or for the *patrie* that had cast them adrift in 1763. 'This war is exceedingly unpopular among the French Canadians,' the Montreal lawyer Brooke Claxton wrote to a friend at the *Winnipeg Free Press*. 'The figures of recruiting really don't mean much ... The young irresponsible student element and the riff-raff of younger unemployed are inflamed to a degree they have never been before.'[2] Certainly the anti-war protests continued. On 18 September the Ligue des Patriotes, an offshoot of the Créditistes, held a rally at the Palais Montcalm in Quebec City where Dr Philippe Hamel and Ernest Gregoire, embittered proponents of nationalized electricity, denounced the dictatorship not of Hitler, but of the 'trusts.'[3] The announcement of an expeditionary force dispelled the comforting idea of limited participation, and the francophone newspapers were taking a harder line against the government. King complained that 'practically no papers in Quebec are presenting the case in its true light,' and he put funds at Lapointe's disposal 'to counter the false representation in Quebec.'[4]

Hoping to capitalize on anti-war sentiment in Quebec, on 25 September 1939, with a year and a half remaining in his term of office, Maurice Duplessis called a snap election for 25 October. He was going to the hustings on the well-worn issue of provincial autonomy. Duplessis charged that the federal government was using the war as 'a pretext' to centralize power and to assimilate the French-Canadian people. In his usual immoderate language, Duplessis condemned Lapointe and the other federal ministers from Quebec, associating them with the war-time restrictions imposed by the War Measures Act and the probability of conscription.

Duplessis's election call fell like a bolt from the blue on Lapointe. He saw it as an attempt to effectively neutralize Quebec. He had brought Quebeckers into the war, and now Duplessis was trying to take them out by the back door. Moreover, he recognized it as a direct challenge to Cardin, Power, and himself for supporting the war policy. He told King that it was 'straight sabotage, the most unpatriotic thing he knew.' King was as angry as Lapointe. It was 'a diabolical act' on Duplessis's part; the Quebec premier was using the 'gangster' tactics of 'a Hitler.'[5] If he should win he would embarrass the federal government throughout the war. On 25 September – the very day of the thunderbolt – Lapointe told King that he and Chubby Power felt they would have no option but to resign from the cabinet if Duplessis was re-elected. As Power put it, Duplessis had declared war on the federal government and on the Quebec ministers. His re-election would amount to a lack of confidence in them on the part of their constituents. How could they claim to represent Quebec opinion at Ottawa if Quebeckers voted for Duplessis's anti-war policy?

King was all for his Quebec ministers getting into the election campaign, but he was strongly opposed to their quitting the cabinet if they lost. Lapointe explained that this was their trump card. While they were in the cabinet Quebeckers knew there would be no conscription. If they threatened to resign if Duplessis were elected, people would vote against him for fear of a conscription cabinet in Ottawa. King could see their point, but he pleaded with them not to commit themselves to resign. They might hint at it, he said, but they should not say or do anything irrevocable. Not good enough, Lapointe told him. Only by threatening to quit could they be sure of defeating Duplessis, who was going into the election with an overwhelming majority.

King was very nervous about the idea, but he was filled with admiration for Lapointe. Lapointe was ready to lay his tremendous prestige on the line, to risk everything to ensure national unity in wartime. The timid, indecisive Lapointe of the past was the strong man of the present. If he succeeded in beating Duplessis, King wrote in his diary, 'it would give Lapointe a position even higher if that is possible than that held by Laurier in the esteem of Canada.' Indeed, he would become 'a world hero.'[6]

The next day Lapointe and Power conferred with Cardin and Adélard Godbout – the provincial Liberal leader had rushed to Ottawa to discuss the situation with the federal ministers.[7] After some hesitation, Cardin said he would go along with his colleagues. Godbout was only too happy to have the federal ministers intervene on his behalf. He looked on Lapointe as his patron. Following the 1936 provincial election when he lost his seat, Lapointe had used his influence to ensure that he was not replaced. Besides, Godbout knew that his only chance of defeating Duplessis was to yield precedence to the federal ministers.

On 29 September Lapointe issued a press statement the purport of which was that the federal ministers from Quebec would take part in the Quebec election, and if Duplessis was re-elected they would resign. By precipitating a fight on constitutional questions, it stated, Duplessis was 'sowing the seeds of discord at a time when national unity was a sacred duty.' The election should have remained strictly provincial, but Mr Duplessis had made criticism of the federal government and the federal ministers an election issue. 'Under such circumstances, we cannot remain indifferent and our duty is to take up this unprovoked challenge.' A verdict in Duplessis's favour 'would be a verdict against us.'[8]

Duplessis was taken by surprise. He had not anticipated a contest with Ernest Lapointe. His real motive for the premature election call had been to get a new mandate before the electorate learned how he had mismanaged the province's finances. The provincial debt had soared, and he could not get credit. He had gone to Ottawa and come back empty handed. He was reduced to borrowing in New York at exorbitant rates, and now with the U.S. Neutrality Act that source was cut off. Adélard Godbout alone would have posed no obstacle to his re-election, but Mackenzie King's Quebec lieutenant was a formidable adversary. Le Devoir decried Lapointe's threat to resign. 'The Liberal candidates will present Lapointe's resignation as a national disaster,' wrote his persistent critic, Léopold Richer. 'For two years these arguments have been used to render docile members of Parliament who do not like government policy.'9

Despite the entry of the federal heavyweights into the campaign, the consensus in Ottawa as well as in Quebec was that Duplessis would win. Chubby Power had taken over the organization of the campaign, and he felt he was in for the fight of his life. 'The view of Power and the boys,' one journalist reported to his editor, 'is that Duplessis will win hands down.'10 The *Montreal Gazette*, looking at the Union Nationale's 77 seats against the Liberals' 16, declared that Lapointe, Power, and Cardin were 'staking their ministeral status on what appears to be a political and mathematical impossibility.' The strongly isolationist André Laurendeau saw the election as 'a kind of plebiscite' on participation, and he predicted 'a negative reply.'11 One hopeful thing for the Liberals was that Paul Gouin had revived his moribund ALN party and was fielding some fifty candidates. That could syphon off some of the nationalist vote from Duplessis.

It was perhaps the first time that the outcome of a Quebec election affected the country as a whole. The *Ottawa Citizen* found it 'scarcely believable' that the Quebec premier would inject 'sectional dissension into a war program that has to be national in every respect.'12 That the election was of vital interest far beyond Quebec's boundaries is apparent from the fact that Jimmy Gardiner lent Chubby Power $25,000 from the Saskatchewan campaign chest.13 In a letter to Arnold Heeney meant for Mackenzie King's eyes, the Montreal lawyer Brooke Claxton warned that the Quebec election could be 'the first shot in a Canadian civil war, or the break-up of Confederation.' Claxton did not think much of Lapointe's threat to resign: 'Unless Mr. Lapointe intended to come down here and fight as he has never fought before in his life, he should not have said a word.'14

But Lapointe intended to fight as he had never fought before. While Chubby Power usually found it 'like pulling teeth' to get Lapointe to make speeches, this time he was 'willing and able to go anywhere to speak at any meeting, and he covered the province thoroughly.' Initially, the federal ministers met with heckling and anger for supporting Canada's participation in the war.15 Lapointe even heard himself blamed for bringing Canada into the war because his name and signature were so prominently displayed on the widely reproduced proclamation. Ridiculous as the charge was it caused him considerable anguish, and he turned to his deputy minister for advice on how to counter it. Edwards replied somewhat brusquely that it had been his duty as attorney general to sign, and 'any suggestion that you personally plunged Canada into war is childish.'[16]

Early in the campaign Duplessis obliged his opponents by putting his foot in it. Speaking before a crowd of some 50,000 people on his home ground at Trois-Rivières, he was in an unbuttoned mood ('roaring drunk' according to his biographer). Much of the speech was a rabble-rousing attack on Lapointe – 'Quebec would never be the creature of any Ottawa minister,' Duplessis proclaimed. Carried away by liquor and the enthusiasm of his audience, he shouted that a vote for Lapointe was 'a vote for participation and conscription.'[17] King and Lapointe had realized from the start that Duplessis was making a subliminal appeal to Quebeckers to vote against participation in the war. Now he had said it outright. While the crowd loved it, an English cabinet minister, shocked by his party chief's disloyalty, stalked off the platform, later resigning from the Union Nationale along with another English MLA. Reported in the Montreal Gazette, Duplessis's apparent stand against participation sounded like sabotage. It cost him the support of the anglophone press and of English Quebeckers, who represented 20 per cent of the population.

This hitherto crafty politician proceeded to cut off his nose to spite his face. Under the wartime regulations, all radio addresses had to be submitted for approval to the censors. Duplessis refused, branding the regulation a further example of the federal government's restraints on personal liberty.[18] By so doing he deprived himself of the most efficient and effective method of electioneering. Lapointe, Cardin, and Godbout made full use of the airwaves, as did Gouin.

In a radio broadcast on 9 October, Lapointe launched a hard-hitting attack on Duplessis, charging him with national sabotage for calling an election at a time when Allied forces were engaged in a 'crusade for civilization.' He scoffed at Duplessis's contention that he and King were out to centralize power: 'The people of Quebec know that during all my parliamentary life I have always been an upholder and an advocate of provincial autonomy.' The real reason for the election, he said, was 'the unfortunate financial situation' in which Duplessis and his ministers found themselves: they had spent money 'like drunken sailors.' As to radio censorship, the regulations applied to everybody; the radio address they were hearing had been submitted to the censors. Then came his solemn pledge that there would be no conscription so long as he and his colleagues were in the cabinet. 'We are the rampart between you and conscription.' The speech culminated in a threat to resign. 'Je ne resterai pas là malgré vous' – 'I will not stay on if you do not want me.'

In this radio broadcast he summed up his thirty-five-year career: 'I have worked all my life to bring about Canadian unity. I have succeeded in staunching the wounds. I have held the Canadian banner high and steady, convinced that the sacred interest of my province lay in the preservation of the Canadian ideal. Canada must stay unified. Any attempt to break this union is fratricidal and criminal.'[19] From the sidelines his soulmate cheered. Lapointe's sixty-third birthday came in the midst of the campaign and King sent him birthday greetings:

> It seems to me that Providence has reserved for you this particular year as the highest peak in your great career. It is my firm conviction that no man in the history of Canada will hold a higher place than yourself – not even our beloved chief, Sir Wilfrid, for none has ever had quite so significant a part to play as is yours at the moment.
>
> May God grant you the strength necessary to your great task, and preserve you in health and abundantly bless you through many years to come.[20]

Despite this encomium, King continued to remonstrate with the Quebec ministers over their intention to resign. At cabinet on 10 October he made a last stab to dissuade them. Neither he nor their English colleagues approved, he said, as heads nodded around the table. Lapointe replied that their decision stood, but he assured the English ministers that they would win the fight against Duplessis. King was doubtful. While he felt Duplessis would be cut down considerably, he was far from certain he would be defeated. Le Devoir's Ottawa correspondent, Léopold Richer, tapped his inside sources to report, on 11 October, that Duplessis's victory was conceded in Ottawa.

On the campaign front Lapointe was pounded by Duplessis and Gouin for his change of heart on Canadian involvement in a European war. Reminding listeners of Lapointe's anti-participation speech at Limoilou in December 1938, Gouin told a radio audience on 13 October that 'never in such a short time has a politician made such a disconcerting volte-face; never has a statesman blackened his entire political career with such a sweeping lie.'[21] Duplessis hammered away at Lapointe on the conscription theme. The federal minister would send young men overseas, he told his audiences: 'A vote for Godbout and Lapointe is a vote for conscription, assimilation, and centralization.' ('Participation' was discreetly omitted from the list of evils.)

By sticking to their guns that they were the rampart against conscription, the federal ministers began to win over their audiences. Cleverly, they turned Duplessis's rallying cry on its head. A vote for Duplessis was in fact a vote for conscription, they asserted, because if he won and they quit there would be nobody in Ottawa to protect Quebec's young men. What could Duplessis do to save his province from conscription? Lapointe asked a spillover crowd at the Sherbrooke arena on 15 October. Lapointe and Cardin flogged the 'no conscription pact' in every speech. At Sherbrooke Lapointe stated categorically that Parliament had accepted his terms and was bound by its promise not to impose conscription. In any event, he said, conscription was 'a phantom of bygone days.'[22] Meanwhile, Godbout, on a whirlwind tour of the province, concentrated on provincial issues, asking voters rhetorically 'whether the administration of ruinous waste, scandal and deception, headed by Premier Maurice Duplessis shall continue.'[23]

Lapointe, Cardin, and Power were growing more optimistic every day. Oscar Drouin was once again running as a Liberal in Quebec East, and Lapointe, who had maintained his personal friendship with him throughout his defection to the ALN, welcomed him back like the prodigal son. The nationalists were flocking to the Liberal standard, including, incredibly enough, the rabid nationalist René Chaloult. (This was too much for Chubby Power, who withheld campaign funds from Chaloult.)[24] Several strong Quebec Liberals resigned their seats in Parliament to run provincially. Shortly before the close of nominations, the popular mayor of Montreal, Camillien Houde, threw his cap in the ring as an independent with Liberal backing.

Lapointe dominated the election. Godbout was variously described as his echo, shadow, or messenger. From his editorial pulpit, Georges Pelletier preached to the converted that with Godbout as premier, Quebec would be a branch plant of Ottawa.[25] Although Godbout was a first-rate orator in his own right, one observer wrote that 'beside the great Lapointe, the provincial leader disappeared, even physically. He could slip in between his legs; he could almost curl up in his pocket.'[26] Cardin had never been more eloquent, but he did not capture his audience as Lapointe did. In fact, speaking in Quebec City on 15 October he was drowned out by a hostile crowd – 'a damned well organized opposition,' was Chubby Power's caustic comment.[27] In contrast,

Lapointe enjoyed one personal triumph after another. He touched the hearts of his listeners even in unfriendly territory. '[Quebec] heard from Lapointe a passion of oratory which Laurier had never excelled. It saw a towering black figure whose soul was poured nakedly into his pleading, whose outstretched arms seemed to embrace the province and the nation, whose face was knotted in pain, whose eyes often gushed tears. Soon the audiences in the cities and the little towns were crying with him. He had touched an ultimate stratum of French Canadian feeling which the pinpricks of Duplessis could never penetrate.'28

One unfriendly critic who followed Lapointe's campaign with intense interest, and involuntary admiration, was André Laurendeau. Laurendeau was in the audience when Lapointe spoke at the Montreal Forum towards the end of the campaign. Anticipating trouble from hotheaded nationalists, Power had arranged for tight security, and hundreds of police were stationed throughout the auditorium. Such precautions proved utterly unnecessary. The crowd went wild for Lapointe. Who would not believe this 'debonair giant,' Laurendeau acknowledged grudgingly, when he declared in his rich accent from the lower St Lawrence that 'between conscription and you, we are the barrier, we are the rampart'? When he punned that 'Union Nazionale' was a better name for Duplessis's party than 'Union Nationale' the crowd loved it. And when he spoke of the thrilling hockey games he had witnessed in the Forum they cheered him to the rafters. Laurendeau left the rally, 'cursing and secretly admiring him.'29

It was the same when he addressed an enormous crowd in the Quebec City arena. Introduced as the greatest Canadian since Laurier, Lapointe, switching effortlessly between English and French, made a passionate plea for national unity. He warned that a Duplessis victory would not only isolate Quebec but would rejoice Berlin. He had the audience in the palm of his hand. With every charge against Duplessis the crowd roared its approval. At one point the ovation lasted a full two minutes. Brushing aside tears, Lapointe thanked his compatriots 'for the greatest reward you can give me.' When he sat down the prolonged applause brought him to his feet again, and 'Il a gagné ses épaulettes' rang out from approximately 15,000 throats. Many felt it was the best speech of his long political career.30

Duplessis too was getting ovations and earning his epaulettes in song. Nevertheless, in the final hours of the campaign, the federal ministers and Godbout were reasonably certain of victory. Lapointe was in a buoyant mood and virtually unstoppable. The night before the election he addressed three separate meetings. The last was at St Sauveur, a lower-class district known as 'the Hell's Kitchen of Quebec politics.' Warned beforehand to expect trouble, Lapointe (according to the *Montreal Gazette*) 'gritted his teeth, stuck out his jaw, and said, "Lead me to it."'[31] Chubby Power need not have worried about a disturbance. At St Sauveur as elsewhere, there was delirium. Lapointe was a consummate psychologist who knew how to reach his audience. The *Gazette* reported that he 'gave the St Sauveur crowd what they wanted – gestures, table-thumping and the most pithy style of oratory he has yet uttered in the present campaign.'

Results on 25 October vindicated Lapointe, Cardin, and Power. They had been right and King had been wrong. It was a Liberal landslide – 70 seats (including Chaloult and Houde) against 14 for the Union Nationale. Gouin and all the ALN candidates lost their deposits. Godbout recovered his seat with a comfortable majority of 566 votes; as was generally acknowledged, however, it was not he but Lapointe who had defeated Duplessis. In Ottawa King was ecstatic. Forgetting that he had forecast a Duplessis minority government, he congratulated himself on having been right all along: 'As I said to Lapointe at the outset, I thought we would score a great victory.' He shuddered to think what would have happened if results had gone the other way. Germany would have thought that the dismemberment of the British Empire had already begun.

Lapointe and Power returned to Ottawa next morning as conquering heroes. Stepping off the train they found King, Ralston, Howe, Euler, Mackenzie, and numerous Liberal senators and MPs had all come out in a heavy rain to welcome them. (Cardin missed the hero's welcome by motoring up from Montreal.) It was a happy group of Liberals assembled at the station, and King outdid himself in flowery praise. Although Lapointe looked 'tremendously pleased and relieved,' Chubby Power was beetle-browed and glowering. Smelling of whisky, Power asked to meet with King before the afternoon cabinet meeting.

Power was feeling very sorry for himself and was in revolt against Lapointe. As he told King in his office, he had done all the dirty work of the campaign while 'others' had made speeches. He felt he had earned the right to have some say in Quebec matters. He demanded that King immediately appoint General Fiset as Quebec lieutenant-governor and Fernand Fafard as senator. Lapointe wanted to delay the appointments, he said, and furthermore Lapointe would not agree with him on the timing of by-elections. Power insisted that King overrule Lapointe, otherwise he would resign. King 'humoured' him, but at the cabinet meeting Power made a scene. In a voice loud enough for everyone to hear, he told Lapointe that while he made the speeches, he, Power, had really won the election. Obviously under the influence, he pounded the table, yelling that Fiset and Fafard must be appointed at once. Lapointe stayed cool. It would be a mistake, he said, to appoint a new lieutenant-governor until Godbout was installed as premier, and as for Fafard, he was in no hurry to go to the Senate. In fact, he and Fafard were leaving on a golfing holiday the next day. Power struggled to his feet, announced he was resigning, and slammed out of the room.[32] The real reason for his outburst, Lapointe and King knew, was the lack of personal recognition. Power had outstanding ability and was shamefully underemployed as postmaster general. But his drinking problem made it impossible to entrust him with a key portfolio such as Defence.

The Quebec election of 1939 was Lapointe's finest hour. 'I venture to say,' King enthused in his diary, 'that Lapointe's place today is as far in esteem as that of Sir Wilfrid in the best of his days. He will have a place second to none in Canadian history, and well merited as a patriot.'[33] Expressions of praise and gratitude came in from all over the country. He was regarded as the saviour of national unity. A Saskatchewan court of appeal judge suggested that a practical way to show appreciation was to set up a publicly subscribed fund for Lapointe.[34] King agreed heartily, knowing that finances were a perennial problem for his soulmate. Lapointe was lionized in the press. 'If he were to die tomorrow,' declared the *Winnipeg Tribune*, 'he would be ranked along with Laurier among the greatest of Canadians.' Even *Le Droit* acknowledged that national unity had been preserved. Lapointe's triumph made *Time* magazine. Millions of Americans read about Canada's 'spectacular Minister of Justice' who could have been prime minister 'if he were British.'[35]

There were sour notes, of course. Gouin charged that Lapointe had betrayed Quebec, and he predicted conscription in two years. Duplessis looked into his crystal ball and announced: 'We shall have conscription in Quebec and I will be back.' Pelletier in *Le Devoir* and Professor Frank Scott in the *Canadian Forum* advised the Liberals not to take their victory as Quebec's endorsement of the war: it was simply fear of conscription that led to Duplessis's defeat.[36] Not surprisingly, the Conservative leader, Dr Manion, downplayed Lapointe's success. In a private letter he sneered that 'the people of Quebec ... allowed themselves to be hoodwinked once again into thinking that Lapointe is such a great Canadian.' In his view Lapointe was bound to win either way: if the

Liberals carried the election he would get kudos, if they lost he would step into the Senate or onto the bench. Looking ahead to a federal election, Manion complained that intervention in the provincial campaign had given 'Lapointe and his gang a chance to get their filthy machine back in power down there.'[37]

As it happened, Lapointe was not revelling in his success as Manion supposed. Granted, he had overcome Duplessis and the nationalists and carried the federalist flag to victory, but at the same time he had given his people to understand that he would see they received their fair share of wartime appointments. At the beginning of December, the announcement was made of appointments to the war services boards and commissions, and of 138 appointees only 12 were French Canadians. The worst of it was that this had a trickle-down effect. Lapointe had a list drawn up of the personnel employed by the various commissions and, as he told King, he was 'deeply distressed' at 'the scarcity of French names among those employees. The percentage was infinitesimal.' The cause of the problem was obvious, he said: 'The various presidents and directors of those Commissions bring the men they know as directors or managers or secretaries, and those in turn appoint people they know or who are recommended to them by people they know and they do not care about anything else. Of course this cannot do.'[38] When he spoke to directors on these boards, they shifted the blame to the Civil Service Commission, but the commission denied any responsibility other than setting salaries.

Above all, Lapointe blamed the cabinet ministers because it was they who appointed the boards. He felt that his colleagues had undermined him and given aid and comfort to his nationalist enemies at home. At the next cabinet meeting he voiced his displeasure strongly about the disproportionate number of English appointments over French. He warned that the list, which had just been published in the *Financial Post*, could prejudice the successful continuation of the war effort in Quebec. In fact, it could be 'disastrous.' The next day he sent a personal and confidential letter to all the ministers requesting them to issue instructions to the heads of the various commissions to rectify the situation. There were qualified francophones, he told King, and it should be easy enough if his colleagues had 'good will.'[39]

He did receive some show of goodwill. Norman Rogers replied that he would attempt to redress any wrong that had been done inadvertently.[40] And Jimmie Gardiner said he would instruct the new chairman of the (all anglophone) three-man Bacon Board to consult with Premier

Godbout to see that Quebec was properly represented on any advisory committee or among any new staff, but he added that the prairies were also neglected when these boards chose personnel.[41] King seconded Lapointe's plea. In a letter to all his cabinet ministers he said he would be obliged if they would review with their deputy ministers and the heads of boards and agencies 'the existing personnel with a view to seeing what adjustments should be made in order that a fair share of the positions in the agencies related to our war effort will be held by French-speaking Canadians.'[42] But the prime minister set up no formal mechanism, and to the end of his days Lapointe would complain with good reason about the lack of appointments for French Canadians in wartime Ottawa.[43]

CHAPTER TWENTY-SEVEN

Wartime Election

In King's opinion, Lapointe had always been overly influenced by the RCMP.[1] Now with the war on, he seemed to adopt Commissioner Wood's repressive anti-subversion measures without question. In fact, when the Defence of Canada Regulations were being drafted, Lapointe instructed John MacNeil of his department to defer to the RCMP: they should be 'the guiding light' because they were 'closer to the facts than we are.'[2] As originally issued, the defence regulations applied only to individuals suspected of subversive activity. By November 1939 there were some three to four hundred internees – mainly German nationals and Bundists.[3] But Wood felt hampered in his task of cleaning out subversion because fascist and communist organizations could still operate legally. In particular, he wanted to eradicate the Communist Party of Canada, although Adrien Arcand's Nazi party was no less active in spreading anti-war propaganda.

There was pressure on Lapointe from sources other than the RCMP to institute stronger measures in the interest of security. G.D. Conant, Ontario's attorney general, was demanding the re-enactment of Section 98 of the Criminal Code, but Lapointe was not ready to bring back that notorious legislation even in wartime. Besides, as he told the attorney general, he did not think it was necessary since Section 133(4) of the Code, in conjunction with the War Measures Act, accomplished the same end.[4] So J.S. Woodsworth had not been far wrong when he told the House in 1936 that the justice minister had simply moved the restrictions on individual freedom from Section 98 to Section 133.

On 16 November Lapointe arrived at cabinet with an order-in-council to expand police power and to outlaw organizations suspected of subversion. Under his proposed amendments to the Defence of Canada

Regulations, the prohibition on statements by an individual 'which would or might be prejudicial to the safety of the state or the efficient prosecution of the war' would be broadened to apply to publications and to organizations. It was not the suppression of radical organizations such as the Communist Party of Canada that disturbed his colleagues; it was his proposal to give greater powers to the police. As it was, Regulation 21 permitted the RCMP, in the name of the minister of justice, to arrest a person without laying a charge and to keep that person in custody indefinitely on suspicion alone. Furthermore, they could search any premises they chose without a warrant. King was uncharacteristically blunt. 'I do not trust the judgment of the Mounted Police on these matters,' he told Lapointe. 'They are apt to go too far when given power of investigation, searching, etc.' Lapointe gave him an argument. Canada was at war after all, and he was ready to put the issue before Parliament. King shook his head. They must not give the CCF an excuse for claiming that the government was suppressing freedom and liberty. (The November issue of the *Canadian Forum* provided a preview of what the debate would be like. The CCF organ called the regulations 'unnecessary and dangerous' and pointed out that in Ontario people were being arrested for 'silly remarks in beer parlours.') To control Lapointe's zeal, King set up a committee composed of Euler, Mackenzie, Ilsley, and McLarty to review the order-in-council. He himself, he said, would go over it with Dr Skelton.[5]

Skelton and his Oxbridge-educated coterie in External Affairs were 'appalled' by the rigours of the original defence regulations, let alone Lapointe's proposed amendments. Though fighting a losing battle, Skelton continued to argue for freedom of speech and association in wartime Canada. In a memo to King, he took aim at Lapointe's proposed amendments:

Nothing should be done that would prohibit criticism of war policy ... or the right to differ with the majority. Sedition is one thing, criticism is entirely another. A good many people in Canada are prone to think that anyone who differs from their convictions or prejudices should be suppressed. The real ground for dealing with Communist or Nazi sympathizers, individually or as an organization, should be that they are acting not as Canadians but as tools of foreign and unfriendly governments.[6]

In cabinet Lapointe continued to take a drubbing from his colleagues. In particular, the lawyers among them objected to the fact that detainees' appeals were heard by an appointed tribunal rather than the courts. The most vociferous criticism came from Euler and Power, who argued that when Canadians were fighting for liberty abroad it should not be repressed at home. Power had all but shed his allegiance to his long-time friend and mentor because he felt that Lapointe was completely 'under the influence of the police mentality of some of the officers of his department [who] had been pressing for this kind of restrictive legislation.'[7] But he was nurturing a personal grudge as well. He was 'fed up' with being treated like 'a handyman ... doing odd jobs,' and he blamed Lapointe for his lack of an important war job. Lapointe told King that Power was not even speaking to him.

Just how far the RCMP should be allowed to go in suppressing civil liberty caused 'one of the rare differences' between the soulmates – as Jack Pickersgill noted from his vantage spot in the prime minister's office. In his diary King expressed surprise 'at how fearful Lapointe is in these matters, and how reactionary he is prepared to become during the war period.' He added charitably, 'perhaps it is in part a nervous strain and less power of resisting demands of his officials.'[8] A meeting with Lapointe and Commissioner Wood a few days later failed to convince the prime minister that extra police powers were called for. Existing legislation was quite sufficient, he told them. However, he agreed that the defence regulations should be amended to apply to organizations as well as individuals.

The Communist Party of Canada was the main target for Wood and Lapointe. King shared their phobic anti-communism to a lesser extent, but it was also good politics. An election was coming. To outlaw the party would be popular throughout the country – hatred of Russia was running at an all-time high following the invasion of Finland by Soviet troops in November. Beefing up the defence regulations would also take the wind out of the sails of Conant and Mitch Hepburn who, to further their campaign for a national government, charged that King was not fighting subversion sufficiently. In December Lapointe came back to cabinet with a modified version of his amendments to the defence regulations. He felt that he had met his colleagues' main objections. 'The features which were so strongly objected to are being eliminated,' he told King, 'for instance the power given to the Police Heads or to persons authorized by the Minister to permit searching houses or premises, and in every case it will have to be by virtue of a search-warrant granted by a Justice of the Peace.'[9]

Skelton's fears were not allayed. He urged King to follow the British example. The ancient freedoms of expression and association were so ingrained in England that the Chamberlain government had been forced to substantially soften the Defence of the Realm regulations. Though still strongly opposed to the order-in-council, 'out of regard for Lapointe' King pushed it through cabinet at the first meeting of the new year. Deploring the weakening of parliamentary control over government, Chubby Power nearly resigned. He drafted a letter of resignation but was mollified after a heart-to-heart talk with King at Laurier House. Walking out into the cold, snowy evening, he was convinced that King felt as he did but could not 'vigorously oppose Lapointe, who had been his right-hand man ever since he became prime minister.'[10]

To the disillusioned Power, Lapointe, the 'philosophical radical' of yesteryear, had become an authoritarian. But the truth was that Lapointe was uncomfortable with the draconian measures issued in his name. He sometimes felt like a prisoner of his departmental officials. In January the *Winnipeg Free Press* ran a series of articles by Grant Dexter showing how freedom was being eroded by unnecessarily harsh defence regulations. Calling John MacNeil into his office, Lapointe waved the articles at him and said they exactly expressed his own sentiments – he was 'glad to see that there were some Liberals left in the country.' Complaining that the law officers had got him into this 'mess,' he instructed MacNeil to draft a response to the criticism. In due course MacNeil presented his chief with a memo 'to explain and justify the Defence of Canada Regulations.'[11]

Lapointe was torn between his liberal principles and reluctance to oppose the RCMP recommendations for internal security. The RCMP was cracking down on communists. Off the record, Lapointe expressed his disapproval. But as Grant Dexter said, 'Is it any use for ministers, privately, to disavow their public acts; to pose as ardent advocates of freedom to their friends and in the privacy of their cabinets, while they knock the stuffing out of the common folk?'[12] However, Lapointe encountered little personal criticism. The consensus at this stage was that the wartime restrictions on liberty were in safe hands because Ernest Lapointe was 'a democrat and a gentleman.'[13]

Actually, the dictatorial powers given to the minister of justice were more apparent than real. The minister was bound to act on police information, and as the *Canadian Forum* put it, 'Police interpretation of "communism" and "subversive" are notoriously all-inclusive.' Moreover, the easily abused regulation prohibiting statements or publications 'likely to be prejudicial to the safety of the state or the efficient prosecution of the war' was out of Lapointe's hands; the provincial attorneys general – men such as Gordon Conant of Ontario – enforced it, on information provided by the RCMP. In spite of his reservations, Lapointe implemented all the RCMP's recommendations, interning hundreds of people and outlawing among other organizations the harmless Jehovah's Witnesses. There is nothing to indicate that he made any attempt to restrain Commissioner Wood and his Mounties. He satisfied his conscience by privately deprecating their extreme measures. Like King he resorted to self-deception.

The proscription of the Jehovah's Witnesses, however, was Lapointe's doing, and it was not because the Witnesses' children refused to salute the flag at school. The Catholic hierarchy and the priesthood were incensed by this sect, which went from door to door distributing anti-Catholic tracts. To add insult to injury, their magazine *The Watchtower* was published in a French translation. In the *Tour de Garde* French Canadians read that papal infallibility was a false doctrine, that the Catholic Church was venal and provided no help for suffering humanity. Truth, said the Witnesses, was to be found only in the Bible, and they themselves were 'message bearers from the Lord.' Inundated with complaints from Catholics across the country that these tracts were subversive, Lapointe referred the matter to the press censors, Wilfrid Eggleston and Fulgence Charpentier. They advised him that while the literature was 'undesirable,' it was not such that they could recommend action against the Jehovah's Witnesses under the Defence of Canada Regulations.[14] Meanwhile, the parliamentary committee set up to recommend which organizations should be outlawed had not yet reported as to the Jehovah's Witnesses. Nevertheless, Lapointe pre-empted the work of the committee, ignored the advice of the censors, and on 4 July 1940 tabled an order-in-council in the House declaring the Witnesses an illegal organization.

The fact is that Lapointe banned the Jehovah's Witnesses to oblige Cardinal Villeneuve. At the end of June 1940 Lapointe's secretary received a letter from the cardinal's chancellor, asking him to convey to the minister the cardinal's great displeasure with the Jehovah's Witnesses, whom he called the most destructive and demoralizing force in the country. On 4 July Lapointe instructed his secretary to telephone the chancellor to let him know confidentially that the Jehovah's Witnesses would be declared illegal 'even that very day.' In a letter of thanks, Cardinal Villeneuve expressed his satisfaction with the 'ministerial decree' – 'such a prompt and happy solution merits our felicitations and gratitude.'[15]

E.J. McMurray had tried to head off the ban. Retained by some Manitoba Witnesses, he had written to Tom Crerar in the hope that Crerar could influence Lapointe. Far from being radicals or subversives, McMurray wrote, the Witnesses were a group of 'good-living, God-fearing people, of sound middle-class Canadianism,' who simply preached the gospel. He maintained that they had no more political significance than the Anglican Church, the Salvation Army, or the Quakers.[16] Crerar had passed McMurray's letter on to Lapointe, but the civil libertarian lawyer had little hope of influencing Lapointe in light of the cardinal's intervention.

Lapointe was more of a moderate when it came to censorship. Perhaps it was because he was dealing with journalists predisposed to freedom of the press instead of overzealous RCMP officers. Wilfrid Eggleston, the deputy English-language censor, characterized both King and Lapointe as 'small-l' liberals and in retrospect wrote that 'so long as men like O.D. Skelton and Ernest Lapointe were powerful figures in government, so long as a man of Mackenzie King's temperament was chief of state, we could ward off demands that certain papers should be shut down.'[17] However, Eggleston had to ward off Lapointe's demands with respect to the American magazines that were flooding across the undefended border. Some of them carried articles less than friendly to the Allied cause. Lapointe even wanted to ban the *Saturday Evening Post* – the family magazine with Norman Rockwell covers. (It must be acknowledged that he was being pushed by right-wing Tories such as Dr Herbert Bruce, a former lieutenant-governor of Ontario.) Eggleston was able to persuade Lapointe that none of the American articles contained matter that was prohibited under the defence regulations.[18]

Although Lapointe was relatively moderate when it came to censorship, his views were much stricter than those of the prime minister. At a press conference in January 1940, King called much of the censoring of news reports 'nonsense,' which would 'inevitably undermine the confidence of the people in their newspapers and greatly increase the circulation of U.S. papers in Canada.'[19] While he was playing to his audience of journalists, King was expressing his personal opinion (at least in the early months of the war). King and Lapointe's differences regarding censorship came to the fore during the federal election in March 1940. Presiding at a cabinet session, Lapointe was 'obdurate' about censoring radio speeches of the opposition leaders. Only the next day when King was present and overruled him did he give in – 'glumly.'[20] None of these differences of opinion altered the close relationship between King and his Quebec lieutenant. In war as in peace, and even with the rising importance of wartime ministers such as Ralston, Howe, and Rogers, Lapointe was King's closest confidant, consulted on virtually everything (though sometimes simply as a sounding board). Lapointe had input into every public statement King made, and with each new development King's first impulse was to call him.

On 18 January Lapointe received an agitated call from the prime minister. King had just learned that his *bête noire*, Ontario premier Mitch Hepburn, had joined with the opposition leader, George Drew, to pass a resolution in the Ontario legislature condemning the federal government for a poor war effort. King was fully aware that the Toronto cabal of Hepburn, McCullagh of the *Globe and Mail*, and George Drew was determined to replace him with a coalition government. Nevertheless, he was shocked that provincial Liberals would publicly censure him. It was some consolation that ten of Hepburn's Liberals had voted against the resolution. Lapointe was 'amazed and most indignant' when King called him. He agreed that it meant a general election at once.[21] Actually Hepburn had helpfully provided a *casus belli* for the federal Liberals. Although the government still had five months to run, they could go to the polls now in defence of national unity – their tried-and-true platform. It was extremely desirable to get the election over with before serious fighting began that would bring with it the loss of Canadian lives. The government had just announced that a second division was going overseas.

Parliament was not in session but was scheduled to open on Thursday, 25 January 1940. King wanted to call an election without delay. He could have immediately asked the governor general to dissolve Parliament, but he had promised Dr Manion, the Conservative leader, that he would not call an election before first holding a parliamentary session. At the last minute, King inserted an announcement of the dissolution into the throne speech. He then told Parliament that his government's ability had been challenged by the Ontario legislature and he proposed to let the electorate decide between him and his critics. Before the astonished assembly, he moved that Parliament adjourn. He then hurried over to Rideau Hall and advised the governor general to dissolve Parliament at once. The wily King had kept his promise to Manion. There had been a parliamentary session, albeit a brief one. The opposition had been given no opportunity to debate the throne speech, let alone press for a wartime coalition government.

King had kept his colleagues in the dark. In the days preceding the opening of Parliament, he had told cabinet that an election was imminent. But none of his colleagues, not even Lapointe, knew how imminent. On Wednesday, the day before the opening, King had read Lapointe a draft of the throne speech over the phone, and it made no reference to a dissolution. As far as Lapointe knew, King was planning to announce the dissolution the following Monday, which would have allowed some time for debate on the Address. It was not until Thursday morning, minutes before the House assembled, that he received a startling call from King, who said he felt they should not wait until Monday but should announce a dissolution in the throne speech. Lapointe offered a few words of caution – there would be an uproar in the House and some protest over springing an election – but this time he was just a sounding board. King had definitely made up his mind to dissolve the House at once, and he left Lapointe the task of informing their colleagues.[22]

The prospect of fighting another election was almost too much for Lapointe to bear. His health was worse than ever, and (as he told King) he was 'afraid of a breakdown which might mean going around as an invalid, half paralyzed.'[23] He was thinking of men such as Fielding and Rowell who had overtaxed their strength and ended up stroke victims. In fact, he felt it was time now to hold King to his promise to release him from his heavy duties and to let him retire gracefully to the Senate. Considering King's awareness of Lapointe's medical history and his present condition, the prime minister's reaction was unfeeling and almost heartless. Though dripping compassion, he pressured Lapointe to stay on and fight the election. King promised Lapointe that this would be the last time he would ask him to do so and that after the election Lapointe would go to his reward as government leader in the Senate. Lapointe's loyalty to King and the party was paramount. Having received his marching orders, the Quebec lieutenant wearily entered the fray.

Lapointe was not the only one who wanted a senatorship. So many cabinet ministers wished to exchange front-line politics for the safe ground of the upper house that King issued a diktat: the cabinet would remain intact until the campaign was over. Surprisingly, the combative Chubby Power, always game for an electoral fight, was one of those looking for a Senate seat. But it was security, not retirement, he had in

mind; he wanted to bring with him a ministerial portfolio or alterna-
tively to be Senate leader. Anxious to have Power's superb organiza-
tional ability in the election campaign, King humoured him; but, as he
reported to Lapointe, he had told Chubby that leadership of the Senate
was reserved for Ernest. Never personally ambitious and doubtlessly
grateful to Power for his decades of support, Lapointe said he would
step aside in his favour. King regarded such unselfishness as 'very like
Lapointe' but would not hear of it. Besides, Power's drinking sprees
disqualified him for the top Senate post.[24]

Although he would not be appointed to the Senate himself, Lapointe
was deeply involved in the usual pre-election flurry of filling vacancies
in the upper house. King suggested former Quebec premier Alexandre
Taschereau for one of the four Quebec vacancies. While agreeing it was
well deserved, Lapointe sided with the other Quebec ministers in turning thumbs down on the ground that Taschereau's ultra-conservative
views expressed in the Senate could prove an embarrassment to the
party. Lapointe compensated Taschereau by appointing his son Robert
to the Supreme Court.

One controversial Senate appointee King was considering was A.J.
Freiman. He liked Mr and Mrs Freiman – he regarded them as acceptable Jewish neighbours at Kingsmere. (King had bought adjacent land
to keep out other Jews.) The Freimans were the royal family of the
Jewish community in Canada. Moreover, their philanthropy included
donations to the Liberal party. King had been putting Freiman off for
years, explaining that the climate of opinion in the country was not
propitious (in other words, anti-Semitism was rife). King sounded out
Lapointe on the appointment. After some hesitation, the latter agreed,
provided that Freiman would fill an Ontario vacancy and not a Quebec
one. (Freiman was eligible for a Quebec vacancy because of his country
house on the Quebec side of the Ottawa River.) Freiman was not appointed, apparently because of opposition from English Canada.[25]

It was, however, Lapointe and the French ministers who saw to it that
Sam Factor was not brought into the cabinet. The Jewish member from
Toronto was serving as an officer at the air force base at Trenton,
Ontario, and King was ready to appoint him. 'I could see however there
would be difficulties with Quebec colleagues if he were taken in ...
French colleagues seemed afraid of the prejudice against Jews.'[26] Preju-
dice against women on the part of the Quebec ministers also killed
Thérèse Casgrain's chances of becoming a senator. When Howe sug-
gested her at a cabinet meeting, Power and Cardin in unison shouted

'no!' King had a very high regard for her – he kept Pierre on 'mostly on Thérèse's account as the ability lies with her.'[27] In the pre-election discussions in cabinet King expressed the view that women should be brought into public life. Interestingly enough, Manion was secretly planning to take a woman into his cabinet if he were elected.[28]

The appointment of deputy ministers was an ongoing problem for Lapointe. Unlike Dandurand, who was militant about francophone appointments, Lapointe acknowledged the dearth of qualified French candidates. When King asked his French ministers to nominate a deputy minister for Fisheries, none of them could think of a name. Unless they had a French Canadian to recommend, King told them flatly, they should 'forever after hold their peace.'[29]

The biggest vacancy of all occurred when the governor general, Lord Tweedsmuir, had a stroke and died during the campaign. Lapointe tentatively suggested a Canadian governor general, but King had made up his mind to recommend Queen Mary's brother, the Earl of Athlone. He would have recommended Sir Lyman Duff, he told Ernest, if the chief justice had a wife (he was a widower), but there was no other appropriate Canadian. Then realizing that he may have offended Lapointe he hurried to make up for his blunder: 'If you want the job when the Athlones leave, you can have it.' In all probability, Lapointe was too modest to have ever thought of the vice-regal post for himself (though others had suggested him to King). In any event, Lapointe readily agreed that, in wartime, Athlone, with his fraternal tie to the dowager queen, would be particularly appropriate.[30]

Though bone-tired of politics himself, Lapointe had the satisfaction of launching his son and his devoted private secretary, Philippe Picard, on their political careers. Bobby was running in Lotbinière to replace the troublesome nationalist, Liguori Lacombe, and Picard was the Liberal candidate in Bellechasse. As in past elections, Lapointe also made a swing through the West with King. When they parted Lapointe was joined by Chubby Power. Everywhere he and Power spoke, they were received with great enthusiasm for their part in defeating Duplessis and keeping Quebec in the war. In Regina a crowd of 3,000 would not let Lapointe go but 'howled for more' every time he indicated an intention of concluding his speech.[31] Lapointe was 'delighted' with his reception in western Canada. He was less happy with the situation in his own riding.

Lapointe was being opposed in Quebec East by the separatist Paul Bouchard, who was running a virulent campaign the likes of which

Lapointe had never encountered. Bouchard called Lapointe a trickster and liar who had 'freely and voluntarily' plunged the country into a ruinous war that it had no business getting into. As he had in the recent provincial election, Lapointe was making conscription the main issue in his Quebec campaign. 'The maintenance of national unity,' he stated in a province-wide radio broadcast, 'demands that our military effort be and remain voluntary.' Bouchard turned this to his own advantage: How could voters believe the man who had promised them in December 1938 that Canada would not go to war on foreign soil, and in March 1939 that the time was past for expeditionary forces, when this same man on 10 September 1939 signed the declaration of war on Germany and on 17 December sent the first Canadian Expeditionary Force overseas? 'Lapointe lies when he declares that enrollment will be voluntary. When there are no more volunteers do you think he will stop the war?' Bouchard's second line of attack was to discredit Lapointe's performance as the senior Quebec minister: 'Five thousand new functionaries since the war and Lapointe has not been able to name 200 French Canadians!' As for Lapointe himself, Bouchard charged, he was preparing to go to the Senate, but before going he had looked after his son, his son-in-law, and his secretary. Bouchard had no chance of beating the great Lapointe, but he was certainly attracting a lot of voter interest. Moreover, he had shortened the odds by getting the Conservatives to put up a straw man to split the federalist, pro-war vote. Bouchard was backed by the like-minded Créditistes. With their leader, Louis Even, Bouchard stumped the riding, warning voters that if the war continued the Liberals would inevitably impose conscription.[32]

Bouchard's campaign probably inspired the unpleasant incident that occurred the day before the election. Lapointe was returning from a broadcasting station to his hotel in Quebec City when his car was attacked and damaged by a hostile crowd. Luckily he was not hurt, but the shock was immense. Never in his long career had he been subjected to physical violence, and that it should happen in his own riding made it even more disturbing. Ottawa was buzzing with the story, and when King heard of it he dashed off a wire to Power asking for full details: 'Disturbed by stories here this morning that Lapointe attacked by hoodlums in Quebec City ... Sincerely trust Lapointe has not suffered any ill effects but do not wish to disturb him if this rumour is groundless.'[33]

The next day was a happier one for Lapointe. The Liberals were swept back in with the largest majority since Confederation. Quebec voted for them as a bloc, giving them 64 of its 65 seats (including independent Liberals). Quebec voters obviously felt they had a better chance of avoiding conscription with a King-Lapointe government than with Manion, who had also promised no conscription. Even *Le Devoir* and the isolationist MPs had supported Lapointe as the lesser evil. Nevertheless, the results in Quebec East were a surprise to many. Lapointe won handily with 17,900 votes, but Bouchard showed surprising strength with 12,300.[34] Any distress this caused Lapointe was offset by his son's and Philippe Picard's victories in their ridings. The expected kudos came in, but they came with a rider. Quebec would hold him to his promise to save them from conscription, Senator Parent warned Lapointe on his departure for Ottawa.[35]

King and Lapointe savoured the election victory together in a quiet dinner at Laurier House, just the two of them. 'Your efforts have contributed as nothing else has to the sweeping victory,' King said. He could see that Lapointe was extraordinarily fatigued, and he knew that he had undergone 'a rather dirty campaign.' Nevertheless, forgetful of his promise of a Senate seat, King manoeuvred the faithful Lapointe into agreeing to continue his onerous wartime duties at least for a while. Soothed by the balm of King's flattery and charm, Lapointe conceded that he was in no hurry to go to the Senate. Thus he missed the opportunity to press for the appointment that was supposed to be his immediately after the election. Indeed, he took the occasion to further Ralston's ambitions rather than his own, passing on the information that the minister of finance had 'his heart set' on becoming chief justice when Duff retired. 'Lapointe himself might have pressed for that post had he been other than the unselfish man that he is,' King told his diary.[36] Indeed, King had been taking advantage of that unselfishness for twenty years.

Ironically, it was Lapointe's very success as the Quebec lieutenant that deprived him of the desired Senate seat. Only mediocrities were appointed senators, or those whom King no longer had use for. Lapointe tried to recover his health and spirits by a Florida golfing vacation, but the cure did not work and he ended up in an Ottawa hospital. King was very concerned when he visited him. Lapointe looked terrible, and he complained of stomach pain, misdiagnosed as intestinal flu. Incredibly blind to his own part in keeping Lapointe on the treadmill, King wrote in his diary that Ernest had 'tried to jump into work too quickly on his return.'[37]

On 11 May King received a confidential phone call from Lapointe's physician, Dr Mohr. The doctor told him that he was discharging his patient but that his condition was not good. Lapointe had suffered a nervous breakdown on his return from the States and would never be quite the same after that. As well, he was diabetic and overwork increased his blood sugar level. He would have to take it easy. After hearing the medical prognosis, King commiserated with himself that he would not be able to count on Lapointe in future as he had in the past. Lapointe would probably have to go to the Senate but not as government leader. Even before he heard from the doctor King had reached the conclusion that Lapointe was no longer up to the demanding job of winning Senate approval of government policies, and he had taken the precaution of exacting a promise from the nominated Speaker to step aside for Lapointe if need be. Certainly, Lapointe would be 'a distinguished figure as Speaker.'[38]

But by tacit agreement, when Lapointe got out of the hospital there was no further talk of the Senate. The phoney war was over. Following a lightning conquest of Denmark and Norway, on 10 May Hitler invaded the Netherlands, Belgium, and Luxembourg. On 14 May the Netherlands capitulated, and German tanks were rolling towards France. A British expeditionary force had been sent over to aid the Belgians, but the combined efforts of British, French, and Belgian forces were proving incapable of stopping Hitler's blitzkrieg. In Britain Chamberlain was forced to resign and was replaced by Winston Churchill and a coalition cabinet. King feared that the same thing would happen to him, and he looked to Lapointe for help.

As the war worsened for the Allies, the demand for a coalition government in Canada gained momentum. King's worst nightmare was an all-party administration in which he would be superseded by Arthur Meighen, who was lying in wait in the Senate, poised to make a comeback as Conservative leader. Since the beginning of the war Lapointe greatly assisted King in fighting off demands in English Canada for a coalition. As well as being loyal to King, Lapointe was expressing Quebec opinion that bringing Tories into the government would lead to immediate conscription. King needed Quebec's support to counter the lack of it in Ontario. At this juncture, he was not likely to part with his Quebec lieutenant no matter the cost to the latter.

When the House opened on 17 May, Lapointe was in his accustomed seat to the right of the prime minister. He looked ill. As a compliment to him, King had chosen 'young Hugues Lapointe' to move acceptance of the Address. While his son was speaking, Lapointe was visibly under strain. He need not have worried. The twenty-eight-year-old freshman

MP did his father proud – as well as his mother, sister, and wife sitting in the gallery. With barely a glance at his notes, he gave a finished performance in French and English worthy of his father. King was delighted by 'his beautiful reference to the association of his father and myself.'

At this first wartime session of Parliament, the government announced that a committee of the House would be appointed to review the Defence of Canada Regulations. During the months of the phoney war, the defence regulations had come in for a good deal of criticism because of their anti-democratic nature. As early as January King had mused about the need to set up a parliamentary committee in order to satisfy these critics. Lapointe had observed morosely at the time that this would just increase trouble in the end. Nevertheless, King had pursued the idea, and at the opening of the May session Lapointe announced that a Commons committee would be set up 'for the purpose of considering the Defence of Canada regulations.'

However, Canadian public opinion had changed radically by late May when mechanized units of the German army were cutting through the defences of western Europe as easily as a knife through butter. The public outcry now was for more internments and more rigorous censorship. Norway's capitulation, believed to be the work of traitors, introduced a new word into the Canadian vocabulary – 'quisling,' after a Norwegian collaborator. In the prevailing hysteria about a fifth column, citizens of German descent were automatically taken for spies. The climate was such that when soldiers ran riot in Regina, attacking a Ukrainian Labour Temple, a German social club, and a restaurant with the unfortunate name of Austrian Kitchen, they were egged on by a crowd of civilians. In Saskatoon a rampaging party of soldiers got their enemy aliens mixed up and vandalized a Chinese café.[39] As Lapointe told the House on 20 May, up to a few days ago the criticism he heard was that the regulations were too arbitrary and severe. Now the criticism was all the other way. Dryly, he observed that 'the original intention in appointing the committee was to give an opportunity of expression to those who criticized the regulations because they were too drastic. Apparently now the committee will hear instead those who find the regulations not drastic enough.'

On 23 May Lapointe rose to report on the government's handling of subversion. The gist of his speech was that the RCMP had everything well in hand. In any event, he said, the security measures would be submitted to the committee of the House 'for consideration and recommendation as to any changes that may appear to be desirable.' Though a report on the defence regulations and order-in-council government might have been expected to cause fireworks in the House, it occasioned very little debate and no real controversy. The parliamentary committee was already taking the heat off the government.

The war news was graver by the day. France was like a house of cards, with one city after another falling to the Germans. The French army was collapsing (as a last faint hope, the elderly General Weygand was appointed to replace the doddering General Gamelin). In what was regarded as a dastardly act, King Leopold of the Belgians ordered his army to capitulate, and the British expeditionary force was retreating as fast as it could to the coast. Thanks to a miraculous rescue operation on the beaches at Dunkirk, the bulk of the army was brought back to England, leaving 30,000 dead or prisoners of war and all its equipment jettisoned. On 4 June – the final day of the evacuation at Dunkirk – Lapointe issued an order-in-council declaring sixteen organizations illegal, most of them communist front groups. And the RCMP finally took action against the Canadian Nazis, rounding up Adrien Arcand and his chief aides who had been publishing and distributing German propaganda for years. When Lapointe later announced their internment to the House, M.J. Coldwell, the CCF leader, commented that it was long overdue.[40]

If the demand for a harder line against the enemy within was on the rise, so was the demand for a coalition government. Many Canadians felt that Mackenzie King, with his bland, conciliatory ways, was not the right wartime leader. Certainly, he suffered by comparison with the dynamic Winston Churchill. King began to suspect that demand for a coalition government, which would include the viper Meighen, had seeped into his very cabinet. On 29 May he disingenuously announced to his colleagues that he was quite prepared to step out if that was what they wanted. 'Naturally' his first choice of a successor was Lapointe, but he knew that Lapointe only stayed on to be at his side. His next choice, he announced, was Ralston, who as an ex-soldier would be most suitable. However, while he would gladly serve under Ralston, he was far from sure that Lapointe would serve under anyone else but him.[41] King counted on every minister around the table recognizing that Ernest Lapointe was essential to the war effort. The trust and loyalty that he inspired in Quebec, and consequently his ability to keep Quebec in the war, made him indispensable even if King was not. But they could not have Lapointe without King! The master of self-abnegation then went on to describe himself as the irreplaceable linch-pin between Churchill and Roosevelt. The upshot was that Ralston, a true believer in King, fell over himself in rejecting the greatness King had feigned to thrust upon him. And the cabinet meeting ended with a consensus that there was no alternative to King. In an off-the-record interview with Grant Dexter, Ralston stressed King's ability to hold the country together, 'Quebec-wise.'[42]

CHAPTER TWENTY-EIGHT

The National Resources Mobilization Act

Lapointe had promised French Canada over and over again that participation in the war would be voluntary and moderate. By June 1940 he realized that it would be impossible to keep that promise. France was about to fall, and Britain was stoically preparing for the possibility of invasion. With the Allied cause going from bad to worse, Churchill introduced an Emergency Powers Act giving the government control over manpower and production. In English Canada a growing clamour arose for the King government to follow suit. At the Liberal caucus meeting on 5 June 1940 a Toronto MP raised the subject of national registration. Lapointe was leery. Registration had been the forerunner to conscription for overseas in the last war; he shuddered to think of 'the devilment' registration would cause in Quebec. King backed him up.[1]

June was a very bad month. On 10 June Mussolini, certain that Germany would win, declared war on the Allies. There was very bad news at home that day as well. The bright young minister of defence, Norman Rogers, was killed in an airplane accident on a domestic flight. Chubby Power, recently named minister for air, became acting defence minister until Ralston took over early in July. On 17 June the Reynaud government resigned in France. The revered Marshal Henri Pétain, the hero of Verdun, became premier with the obvious mandate of negotiating an armistice with Germany. On 14 June Paris fell, and two days later the French government under Marshal Pétain capitulated.

Lapointe was profoundly affected by the fall of France. France was Lapointe's cultural home as it was for other members of the French-Canadian elite. He had hobnobbed with the leading figures of the Third Republic. At Vimy Ridge in 1936, Marshal Pétain had presented him with three commemorative medals, which he treasured.[2] He enjoyed the friendship of General Maxime Weygand who, at the eleventh hour, had taken over as commander-in-chief of the retreating French forces. In the dark days before the French surrender, Weygand sent Lapointe a message pleading for Canada's help to bring the United States into the war. Lapointe was told that the French did not have the guns or airplanes to withstand the German onslaught, and without the Americans France was lost. Lapointe could do nothing but weep. According to people near him, he frequently broke down in tears.[3]

With France gone, Canada became Britain's chief ally. There was concern that if England fell Canada would be invaded. Lapointe was now convinced that the country had to move towards compulsory service for home defence. So were Power and Cardin. At cabinet that evening King was surprised to hear his Quebec ministers come out for a national call-up of manpower. Lapointe added the caveat – as long as it was for the defence of Canada only. Skelton, present at the cabinet meeting, made the same qualification. The English ministers, in particular Howe and Crerar, were predictably gung-ho.[4]

Buttressed by cabinet solidarity, King introduced the National Resources Mobilization Act (NRMA) on 18 June 1940, and Lapointe seconded it. The bill gave the government 'special emergency powers' to mobilize manpower and material resources. Men between nineteen and forty-five were to be called up for a thirty-day training period, and everyone over sixteen, female as well as male, would be required to present themselves for national registration. But the NRMA contained the Quebec caveat: Section 3 of the Act stated that no one would be required to serve in the military forces outside Canada. Nevertheless, two maverick Liberal MPs, Liguori Lacombe and Wilfrid Lacroix, attempted to lead a revolt. They put forward an amendment to kill the bill on first reading and substitute a statement that Canadian participation must remain free, voluntary, and moderate. In other words, they simply mimicked the former statements of Lapointe, Cardin, and Power.

Lapointe and Cardin made powerful rebuttals. Speaking in French, Lapointe insisted that the purpose of the bill was to put Canada 'in a position to defend herself in a tragic emergency.' Home defence was the end-all and be-all of the bill, as Lapointe characterized it. He told the House that he was convinced Canada was threatened with invasion, and 'its very possibility compels us to take those precautions which worthy sons of a country must take to defend their mothers, their parents, their families and their territory.' In top form, he lashed out at the two nationalists. Surely they did not wish to suggest that Canada could resist invasion by a 'voluntary and moderate' effort: 'The monsters who at this time want to destroy civilization and who are drawing nearer to us, must not expect that we are going to repel their attacks with moderation. We are going to defend ourselves with all the strength we can find in our hearts and souls and to the utmost of our capacity.' He denied that he had reneged on his promise when war was declared to keep service voluntary and insisted that there was no conflict between what he said then and what he was saying now. Overseas service would remain voluntary, 'as I have always said.'[5]

King also guaranteed no overseas conscription. He declared that it was not the purpose of the upcoming national registration to recruit for overseas. Lacombe's amendment found no support. Even the nationalist leader in Parliament, Maxime Raymond, announced he would vote for the bill because it was limited to the defence of Canada on Canadian soil. The following day the mobilization bill passed without a division. Lapointe and Cardin had effectively worked the back corridors to reassure timorous Quebec MPs worried about anti-conscription sentiment back home. King attributed the bill's easy passage to the stand he and Lapointe had taken 'so strongly on no conscription overseas.' He was undoubtedly right.

Once again Lapointe had 'steadied' the Quebec contingent. This time he was helped rather than hindered by the provincial government. During the second day of debate in the House a telegram arrived from Premier Godbout reporting that the Quebec legislature had overwhelmingly rejected a motion by René Chaloult that the province oppose the federal law on the ground that it would be used to bring in overseas conscription. Recalling the Quebec election that saw Duplessis defeated, King wrote in his diary: 'No one will ever be able to say what service Lapointe, Power and Cardin rendered in that Province, and what it has meant to Canada having a Liberal Government in office at this time.' Only Le Devoir dared the censors' wrath by declaring that conscription had been 'imposed' on the country and represented the repudiation of the government's promise that participation would be voluntary.[6] The rest of the francophone press expressed confidence that Lapointe and the other Quebec ministers would protect French Canadians from enforced overseas service.

But Lapointe wanted to speak directly to the people of Quebec to provide reassurance. In a radio broadcast on St Jean-Baptiste Day, he stressed that conscription under the National Resources Mobilization

Act 'is restricted and confined to the defence of Canada and of her territory, and that *never* [spoken with emphasis] can it be availed of for overseas service.' His obvious sincerity was enough to reassure his listeners.[7] It was a source of strength and comfort to Lapointe that Cardinal Villeneuve was outspokenly behind the war effort as well. Indeed, it was said in nationalist circles that Villeneuve could refuse Lapointe nothing.[8] The cardinal instructed the parish priests to explain the NRMA and to preach obedience in the upcoming national registration. In his radio address on 23 June, Lapointe emphasized Cardinal Villeneuve's approval of the mobilization act.

Meanwhile, Lapointe was deteriorating visibly under the strain. Léopold Richer describes a luncheon at the Dominicans' residence in Ottawa where those attending were shocked by the change in Lapointe. There was an animated discussion about the latest war news, but the minister, who usually dominated the conversation, just stood with his shoulders bowed and a downcast expression on his face. He greeted newcomers with a weary gesture. At the table he hardly spoke. The person sitting beside Richer whispered in his ear, 'He doesn't say anything.'[9]

King had used Lapointe's failing health to deny him leadership of the Senate, but he did not hesitate to shift on to him the daily grind of leading a wartime House of Commons. He himself was too busy acting as the linchpin between Churchill and Roosevelt to spare time for the parliamentary debates. Lapointe was desperate to be relieved of his duties. He suggested to King that Cardin replace him as minister of justice. King shot down the idea. While Cardin might be acceptable to Quebec, he was not a sufficiently commanding figure nationwide and was not likely to be acceptable to members of the bench and bar. King sugar-coated his refusal of Lapointe's request with an appeal to their long and close relationship. 'I need someone at my side in Justice,' he told him, 'whose judgment I can absolutely rely upon, and with whom I could be in close and immediate touch.' He found Lapointe 'as always, very considerate.'[10]

Lapointe tried another avenue of escape. Through Chubby Power he let King know that he would like the presidency of the Privy Council. Though this was essentially an honorary position with few actual duties, King held on to it himself. He had refused to give it to Sir Lomer Gouin in 1921, seeing it as an attempt to set up a rival premiership, but to withold it from the loyal and devoted Lapointe was an act of unmitigated selfishness. As always King managed to rationalize the situation to his own satisfaction. Divesting himself of the presidency of the council, he told Ralston and Howe (who apparently were pleading Lapointe's cause) would deprive him of the services of Arnold Heeney, the clerk of the council. If Ralston and Howe could persuade Heeney to return to the prime minister's office, then it might by possible for him to give up the council presidency. Heeney had no intention of coming back to be King's office boy – and King knew it.[11]

The upshot was that on a sweltering day early in July Lapointe went to pieces in King's office. He was a shadow of his former vibrant and powerful self, having lost twenty-seven pounds in two and a half months. He told King that he could not sleep, and he was afraid he was having a complete nervous breakdown. He then 'began to cry like a child.' King went over and sat beside him. He tried to reassure him that it was just the strain of the war: 'Naturally, the fall of France and of changed conditions would have this effect.' Patting Lapointe's shoulder, King told him to go away immediately for a complete rest and not to bother with the remainder of the session. Lapointe said he would go down to Rivière-du-Loup with his family, but knowing how much he was needed in Ottawa he could not go with an easy mind. 'In his characteristically generous way,' King wrote in his diary, 'he said he hoped that he was not leaving too much to me and that I would be able to get along without him.'[12]

Lapointe spent the next month resting at St Patrice in the family's rented summer home on the St Lawrence. Odette was there with her husband and baby. She was so accustomed to her father's reserve within the family that she was not fully aware he had suffered a nervous breakdown.[13] Enjoying the first grandchild with Mimy, playing golf at the country club, and relaxing with neighbours such as the corporate lawyer Louis St Laurent, Lapointe gradually recovered his spirits. During his stay at St Patrice the national registration was announced for mid-August. It was to be handled by volunteers, and Odette put her name down to take registrations at the country club. Interviewed at his country home on 31 July by a reporter for the *Toronto Star*, Lapointe stated emphatically that Quebec had accepted national registration and compulsory service for home defence 'as loyally and warmly as the rest of Canada.'

Actually, the reason why he interrupted his convalescence to give an interview was to scotch a rumour circulating around Ottawa that his sick leave was really to camouflage a break with King over national registration.[14] Sitting in a lawn chair overlooking the river, he snapped at the reporter that it was all lies. 'Hell! I was there when the registration policy was decided upon. I approved it fully then and I approve it now.' He maintained that he had no intention of going to the Senate or resigning his ministerial post. Unless his health completely failed him, he would stay by King's side to the end.

Lapointe was planning to return to Ottawa in about a week, but an unforeseen event forced him to hurry back early. On Friday, 2 August, he received a call from Cardin, who was spelling him as justice minister. Cardin informed him that at a press conference that day Camillien Houde had denounced national registration as a step towards overseas conscription and had declared his intention not to register. The worst of it was that he urged his fellow citizens to defy the law as well. Lapointe agreed with Cardin that this was a serious matter. Although regarded as a clown by some, Houde was beloved by the working classes, and as mayor of Montreal he spoke with authority.

Lapointe and Cardin agreed that something must be done. Houde's statement could have a serious effect on registration in Quebec. They decided to impose censorship. But before they could act, an editorial in an early edition of Saturday's *Montreal Gazette* carried Houde's statement.[15] Although the press censors ordered suppression of the editorial in later editions of the *Gazette*, Houde's statement was public knowledge. When the House opened, a gleeful leader of the opposition not only raised Houde's defiance of the government but also the government's bungled attempt to hush it up. King gave the only reply he could – the justice minister was studying the subversive statement.[16]

When cabinet met at noon, all the ministers agreed that action should be taken against Houde. Some wanted to leave it to the provincial government, but Cardin insisted that the federal government take responsibility. The next question was internment or court proceedings. The consensus was that the RCMP should intern Houde at once, preferably in the dead of night to avoid press photographers. Cardin was afraid to sign the arrest warrant because of the mayor's popularity in Cardin's own Montreal district riding. When Lapointe arrived on Monday he signed the warrant without hesitation. Afterwards the venerable Senator Dandurand embraced him. There is no doubt that it took courage on Lapointe's part, but perhaps it eased his conscience for letting Duplessis get away with the Padlock Act.[17]

Once the warrant was signed, the RCMP apprehended Houde as he stepped out of Montreal City Hall and whisked him off to a detention camp in Ontario. King and Lapointe immediately received a letter protesting Houde's internment without trial from René Chaloult, Paul Bouchard, Philippe Hamel, and the Créditistes Ernest Gregoire and Louis Even. 'This summary proceeding against the first Magistrate of the metropolis is of a nature to astound our fellow citizens,' they wrote. 'Your record since the beginning of the war is in such evident contradiction with your solemn declarations of 1938 and 1939 that you should admit in all honesty that our fellow citizens justifiably doubt your word.' They warned of civil disobedience if King and Lapointe did not declare unequivocally that 'this registration will never be used under any circumstances to send one single man to fight outside of Canada.'[18]

King instructed Pickersgill to draft a reply to the effect that Houde was arrested by the police and that the government had nothing to do with it at all. It was to come from the justice department. In due course a bureaucratic type of letter went out to Dr Hamel over Lapointe's signature.[19] Lapointe also derailed an attempt by the independent Liberal MP Liguori Lacombe to help Houde. Lacombe wrote to say that he had been retained by Madame Houde to represent her husband, and he requested permission to visit his client at the internment camp.[20] Lapointe shunted him off to Pierre Casgrain, the secretary of state, who in turn referred him to the commandant of the camp. Tied up in governmental red tape, Lacombe eventually gave up.

Lapointe had judged Quebec public opinion correctly. A petition circulated by Hamel and the other four nationalists found few signers. In fact, there was no groundswell of protest against the government's draconian treatment of Houde. Even Le Devoir pronounced that Houde had acted like a fool and deserved what he got.[21] A hard law was nonetheless the law, Georges Pelletier acknowledged. André Laurendeau was not ready to stand up and be counted either. Privately, he would say that Houde was 'the only one among us to be perfectly logical,' but publicly he knuckled under, and 'like everyone else' the idealistic young nationalist went and registered.[22]

How much Quebec's total compliance with registration was due to an extremely tough and even intimidating radio address by Lapointe on the French-language CBC is hard to gauge. On the eve of registration, primarily to counter any influence Houde may have had, he made a last-ditch appeal to French Canadians to comply with the law. National registration was simply to provide an inventory of both sexes for the eventual protection of Canada, he told his listeners. Those who spread rumours that registration was the first step towards conscription of 'our young people' for service in Europe were nothing less than 'abominable traitors' giving aid and comfort to the enemy. To deny that the mobilization act was for any other reason than the defence of Canada was either ignorance or sabotage. Compliance was not enough. He demanded that citizens place their complete confidence and faith in the government: 'Those who are not with us are against us.' Having harangued his listeners as if they were on the verge of revolt, he assumed his more familiar, avuncular style, expressing his confidence that 'Quebec, always loyal, patriotic and proud, always conscious of its best interests ... would disappoint those "fishers in troubled waters."' He concluded with a solemn promise on behalf of the government that national registration would serve exclusively for the defence of Canada, and he invoked Cardinal Villeneuve's 'wise advice' to the clergy to facilitate registration. *Le Devoir*'s Léopold Richer saw the speech as an attempt to bully French Canadians into submission, and in his opinion it was completely unnecessary. French Canadians were a law-abiding people, and there had been no incidents of intention to flaunt the law. 'The shouting, the intimidations and the rest' were 'useless,' Richer wrote in a critical analysis of Lapointe's radio address.[23]

Lapointe had mustered all his strength to make this broadcast as forceful as possible. He knew his people, and he was well aware of the resentment simmering under the surface against compulsory registration of manpower. Although he had insisted to the *Toronto Star* reporter that Quebec had accepted national registration willingly, he did not underestimate the spreading nationalist movement fanned by the war. He may also have overreacted to a write-in campaign orchestrated by a handful of young communists in Quebec. Until the summer of 1941 when Hitler invaded Russia, the party line of Canadian communists was to denounce the war as an imperialist, capitalist machination and to demand that Canada get out of it. The Ligue des Jeunesses Communistes de Québec, in conjunction with several front organizations, was circulating mimeographed flyers denouncing 'Judas Lapointe' and Cardin for their strong endorsement of the war after getting elected on a peace platform. The leftists supported Houde, and they encouraged the youth of Quebec to boycott the training camps, which they dubbed 'the antichamber to the massacre.'[24] These anonymous attacks clearly got under Lapointe's skin – which despite all his years in politics remained thin.

For King it was 'a great satisfaction' to have Lapointe back in Ottawa. He and Ernest saw eye to eye on almost everything. After a discordant meeting of the War Committee, King wrote in his diary, 'I see how fatal it would be were others than Lapointe and myself to have the shaping and direction of some of the policies which bear so tremendously on the future.'[25] However, King was worried about Lapointe's sticking power. He was sinking into depression again, and though he had shown great fortitude in the Houde affair King was afraid he would have a relapse. Knowing that Madame Lapointe was still at St Patrice, King detailed Tom Crerar to look after his old friend, not to leave him alone and to get him out-of-doors 'to take his mind off things.'[26]

One thing troubling Lapointe was that Howe's department of munitions and supply was not giving French Canadians a fair share of war contracts or appointments. An air battle had been raging over Britain all summer and the department was going at full blast supplying planes and guns. Lapointe told Howe frankly that there was 'a virtual exclusion' of French Canadians in his department.[27] Howe claimed that he repeatedly asked his French colleagues for recommendations, but they did not come up with any names.[28] The fact was, however, that under current Civil Service Commission regulations the deputy minister could have requisitioned bilingual personnel but did not.[29]

At the same time, Lapointe was being inundated with demands for war contracts from Quebec businessmen who claimed their reward for supporting the Liberal party through the years. Since all war contracts had to be put out to tender, every supplicant received a standard reply from Lapointe's private secretaries: the minister would be happy to oblige if he could, but as for war contracts all political influence was strictly forbidden. All he could do was to submit their names to the minister of munitions and supply so that they would receive 'the best consideration.'[30] Nevertheless, during the March election campaign, Lapointe and Power had told a Montreal audience that Quebec had received more than $46 million in war contracts alone, exclusive of other contracts.[31] Some of this, at any rate, must be charged to patronage because francophone contractors did not usually tender bids.[32]

At a private meeting with King on 5 September, Lapointe aired his grievances against Howe's department. King was most solicitous, agreeing with Lapointe that English-speaking appointees drew upon their English-speaking circles. He declared it was quite wrong politically and otherwise. He then sidestepped the issue by moving on to something that was troubling him. Dandurand was too old and frail to properly lead the Senate. What did Lapointe think about having Senator Hugessen take over as leader? 'What about me?' Lapointe asked. Thrown off balance by Lapointe's unusual bluntness, King replied, 'Of course you can go to the Senate any moment you want, it's just for you to say and the appointment will be made at once. But I hope that you will stay in the Commons for the present.' 'I cannot go through another election,' Lapointe told him. King responded quickly: 'I would never expect or permit that.' Then he extended a juicy carrot. After the war, they would go to Europe together to ensure that Canada played a great part in the peace negotiations. Lapointe nodded his head. He would stay on, but King read in his silence that he had not relished the carrot.

Later in September there was another 'painful' discussion in cabinet about French Canadians not getting a fair share of government contracts. Lapointe took these matters far too personally, King thought. Meeting him in the hall afterwards, King tried to smooth things over, but Lapointe replied abruptly, 'I am tired and sick of it all.'[33] He had in fact reached the breaking point. After a depressed, sleepless night, he wrote King a note asking to be relieved of his ministerial duties. 'I am really not well enough to be able to stand the blows that seem to increasingly come my way.' He was obviously deeply hurt by Howe's lack of understanding of the pressure he was under from his compatriots. 'I had hoped to retain the esteem, the consideration and confidence of all my colleagues,' he wrote. 'I may be unduly sensitive, but I feel I am losing some of that.'[34] King was 'disheartened'[35] by Lapointe's letter, but he had no real fear that he would lose his indispensable Quebec lieutenant. He was confident that the loyal Lapointe would not quit the field until he himself released him.

Lapointe stayed on, but his ill health and depression were evident. Crerar, who was seeing a lot of him, felt that he was 'haunted' by his isolationist stand during the 1930s. Grant Dexter certainly got this impression from an interview he had with Lapointe on 25 October. The London blitz was into its second month; night after night firebombs rained down on a patient and courageous people; every day brought news of losses at sea. Lapointe looked dreadful. He had lost a lot of weight and his face was sagging. There was 'a hurt look in his big brown eyes.' Indeed, Dexter sensed 'an aura of sadness about Lapointe which is quite out of character.' According to Dexter, Lapointe was sincerely remorseful about his isolationism in the years leading up to the war. He seemed to be 'stricken' by the thought that he had been dead wrong about appeasement and felt 'a frightful responsibility' for its terrible consequences. He lay awake at night, he told Dexter, 'thinking and thinking.' He spoke of 'the sunshine having gone out of his life, of the blood that is being shed, of the peoples who are being crushed, of

the terrible things that have happened and must happen in the future.'
At times the stream of consciousness was 'close to poetry.'

Dexter clearly touched a 'tender spot' when he mentioned the League
of Nations. Lapointe insisted that he had always been for the League,
and he blamed its failure on the member nations for not working
together: How could the League function without the United States
and with its members unwilling to enforce peace if necessary by arms?
'We had been all wrong in our conception of world peace. We must be
prepared to fight for peace. We must keep up our arms and our ability
to make war and use them in the cause of peace.' Too late Lapointe had
become a convert to collective security. He was so overwrought that
Dexter did not remind him of his remark in the 1935 campaign that
Ethiopia was not worth the life of a single Canadian soldier.

Lapointe spoke bitterly of his colleagues. He said that he had been
compelled to make difficult decisions over the last two years, and
instead of understanding and cooperation he had met with opposition
in cabinet. Harkening back to the 1939 Quebec election, he remarked
that only his colleagues from Quebec had supported him when he
accepted Duplessis's challenge. King had opposed him at the time but
'quite happily' shared in the credit that followed his victory. It was the
first time Dexter had ever heard Lapointe 'take a dig' at King.[36]

King was also suffering pangs of guilt and regret about his isolationism in the 1930s, though he did not show it as much as Lapointe. At one
dark moment in the spring of 1940 he confided to his diary that he felt
guilty because he had not studied what was going on in Europe and
had not spoken up. This feeling intensified as the international situation deteriorated. 'He seems continually to be thinking of 1935 and 1936
and of what he did,' Grant Dexter reported to Dafoe in October, 'and he
seems to admit, to himself if not to others, that he has a share of
responsibility for what happened.'[37] Even in remorse, King and Lapointe
were soulmates. Reconciling Quebec to total war had placed Lapointe
under almost unbearable strain. Through his impassioned speeches in
Parliament and on the radio he had brought Quebec to accept, albeit
reluctantly, mobilization of manpower and national registration. No
one else could have done it, Chubby Power maintained: no one else
could speak with the same authority.[38] But the cost to Lapointe personally was tremendous. Hearing of Lapointe's regrets from Dexter, John
Dafoe, whose anti-appeasement views had been more than vindicated,
replied that 'penitence undoubtedly becomes both King and Lapointe ...
[They] may have made a larger contribution to the disaster than we

know. The Riddell incident may have been a decisive factor in halting the further applications of sanctions.' But he was sorry to hear that Lapointe was taking it so hard. 'His only way of making amends is to keep on doing what he has done so admirably since the outbreak of war.'[39]

CHAPTER TWENTY-NINE

Vichy

While German troops occupied most of France, Hitler devised the fiction of a free French state in the southern part of the country and administered under Marshal Pétain from the spa city of Vichy. The establishment of Vichy caused a rift between English and French Canada. English Canada regarded Vichy France as Hitler's puppet state, pure and simple. French Canada, largely because of Marshal Pétain's enormous prestige, accepted Vichy as the legitimate government of France and an improvement over the anticlerical Third Republic.

Lapointe venerated Pétain and could not believe that the old marshal and General Weygand were traitors, as the English press portrayed them. At a cabinet meeting in September he informed his colleagues that Quebec bitterly resented 'the violent attacks which have been made upon Pétain and Weygand since the capitulation.'[1] On the other hand, Lapointe had no use for Charles de Gaulle, who established a government-in-exile calling itself the Free French. A hitherto little-known French general, de Gaulle had set up a base in England and was committed to continuing the fight against Hitler and to keeping the French colonies in North Africa out of his grasp. Lapointe knew de Gaulle and, like many others, could not stomach his 'intolerable swagger and conceit.'[2]

Lapointe actively opposed government support for de Gaulle. He was highly displeased when the general broadcast an appeal to French Canadians to solicit their support. Lapointe remarked to Ralston, the new minister of defence, that it was 'fortunate' the de Gaulle broadcast received little publicity. He informed cabinet that General de Gaulle had no prestige in Quebec and that his broadcast was considered an 'insult.'[3] There would be few occasions for French Canadians to hear de

Gaulle. Auguste Frigon, the director of Radio-Canada, remained a Vichyite throughout the war and Gaullists were kept away from the microphones.[4]

At the end of September Lapointe learned from Ralston that a French-Canadian officer was promoting the idea of a committee under government auspices 'to further General de Gaulle's aims in Canada.' Lapointe quickly scotched the idea. 'It would be a great mistake and nothing would be more dangerous,' he told the defence minister, 'than to start a controversy in Quebec as between Pétain and de Gaulle.'[5] It was not just personal dislike on Lapointe's part. As he wrote a supporter of the general, it would be most inopportune to encourage a movement that would 'divide French Canadians into partisans of de Gaulle and partisans of the Pétain government.'[6]

As always, King took his reading on Quebec from Lapointe. From the first, his Quebec lieutenant had made him aware of the strong pro-Pétain sentiment in Quebec. Led by the nationalist press, in particular Le Devoir, French-Canadian opinion tended to blame France's defeat on the lax morals of the Third Republic – Pétain's campaign to purify France through a 'National Revolution' was in tune with French-Canadian traditional values of family, work, and the church. Lapointe impressed upon King how essential it was for the preservation of national unity not to offend this almost visceral affinity. At one point he even took the apostolic delegate with him to warn the prime minister of the 'negative impact' of any show of hostility towards the Vichy regime.[7] Left to himself, King would no doubt have shared Britain's and English Canada's antipathy towards Pétain; but thus tutored he was extremely sensitive to Quebec's Pétainist leanings.

Both King and Lapointe dreaded the thought of Vichy becoming an enemy. They fervently hoped that nothing would happen that would drive Vichy to declare war on the Allies. 'How would French Canada react to the war if France were the enemy?' King worried. He even went so far as to record in his diary that he was 'not sorry' when de Gaulle, at the head of a large British force, failed miserably in an attack on Vichy forces at Dakar in North Africa. He had in fact forewarned Churchill that such an attack would be 'serious' for the United Kingdom and 'disastrous' for Canada.[8]

Canada's position on Vichy brought it into conflict with Britain on a number of occasions in 1940. For example, in October the British authorities asked the Canadian government to seize twelve French fishing trawlers that were about to depart from the French islands of St Pierre and Miquelon. 'For the life of me, I cannot see how we can do what they ask,' Lapointe told Skelton. 'This is an act of war and we are not at war with France.'[9] King, in Halifax at the time, also thought seizure unjustified. The trawlers were permitted to sail away. King was pleased to hear later that Lapointe's reaction had been the same as his.

Like his 'chiefs,' Skelton regarded the Free French as a potentially divisive force in Quebec and did not want to see them make headway. Also in October 1940, when de Gaulle requested permission to send a recruiter to Canada (who would be very discreet, wear civilian clothes, etc.), Skelton put the matter far down on the agenda and after many weeks informed de Gaulle that the cabinet had turned down his request.[10] Though Britain had severed diplomatic relations with Vichy, Canada did not. Vichy maintained a representative in Ottawa, and King appointed Pierre Dupuy as Canadian minister to Pétain's headquarters. Actually this was done with Churchill's approval. The British prime minister intended to use Dupuy as a contact with Pétain.

Churchill, however, had no doubt that Pétain was merely Hitler's pawn. The old marshal was now sharing power with Pierre Laval, an out-and-out Nazi collaborator. Churchill received information that Pétain had agreed to hand over the French fleet to Hitler. In a broadcast Churchill urged Vichy not to yield to German demands. At the same time he begged Roosevelt to put some pressure on Pétain to stop him from committing 'another act of shame.' 'If the French fleet and French bases in the African shore are betrayed to Germany, our task will become vastly more difficult and your danger will grow.' Roosevelt responded with a stern warning to Pétain that the United States would cut off all relief to France if the French fleet was surrendered to Germany.

On rumours that Vichy would participate in a Nazi invasion of Britain, the suggestion came forth that Ernest Lapointe should broadcast an appeal to the French people. Lapointe agreed at once. To help him draft his radio talk, the British high commissioner, Sir Gerald Campbell, made available a copy of Churchill's telegram to Roosevelt, as well as a message from King George to Pétain appealing to his honour as a soldier. Skelton passed them on to Lapointe: 'I do not assume it would make any difference in what you were proposing to say.'[11]

It did not. Lapointe chose to speak to Vichy France in an uncritical and sympathetic manner, 'as a brotherly voice recalling to you that, on the other side of the ocean, there live four million men and women of your own blood who share your anguishes and your hopes.' He spoke of a future 'common victory,' a term he used 'advisedly,' he said, 'for in our eyes you are still our allies, not only on Europe's far-flung battle-fields, but here, on this American continent, where a common soul and a common language cause us to share your reverses and your tri-umphs.' He made respectful reference to Marshal Pétain, recalling the Vimy Ridge memorial ceremony in 1936. 'Let us remember Vimy and hold fast to each other.'[12] In short, he dwelt upon the glorious memory of Vimy rather than the shameful present of Vichy. Lapointe poured his heart into this address. The collapse of France had been a personal tragedy for him, and France as an enemy was unthinkable. He had sent a draft of his speech over to Laurier House. King endorsed it enthusias-tically. It was 'a first-rate statement as an appeal to the French.'[13]

Lapointe's speech to the French was carried worldwide by short wave and rebroadcast in both languages in Canada. For once Le Devoir could find nothing to criticize. Far from belittling Lapointe as was his wont, Léopold Richer compared his address favourably to Churchill's appeal to the French. Richer derived great satisfaction from the British Empire calling upon a French Canadian to intervene in the present world crisis. According to Richer, this was an answer to those Anglo-Canadians who wanted to force assimilation on the French: 'Mr. Lapointe would not have been able to speak, he would not have been able to count on a single French Canadian if the holders of the formula: "One flag, one language, one religion" ... had succeeded in stifling everything French in the country.'[14] French Canada at large was well satisfied with its spokesman at Ottawa. According to a survey of the Quebec press conducted at this time, French Canadians accepted the escalating war effort because of their faith in King and Lapointe. According to the researcher, national unity had been achieved by 'the wise consideration shown French-Canadian sentiments and prejudices by Mr. Mackenzie King, ably seconded and no doubt advised by his Minister of Justice, Ernest Lapointe.'[15]

Censure was not lacking, however. In the debate on the throne speech in early December, Sasseville Roy, the member for Gaspé and the only French-Canadian Tory, introduced an amendment that was in effect a vote of non-confidence in Lapointe, Cardin, and Power. Roy calmly declared that as the ministers had been elected on the strength of their pledge that Canada 'would participate in the war in a moderate, free and voluntary manner,' they had 'no mandate to carry this war effort to the ultimate limit.' Having broken their promises, they should resign.

An embarrassment to his own party, Roy found no seconder, but he had certainly struck a chord with the French-Canadian MPs on the government benches. Though King thought Lapointe responded splendidly, particularly in referring to Quebec as solidly British, he was obviously rattled and it was painful to watch. *Le Devoir's* Léopold Richer sneered that Lapointe simply blustered, resorting to personal insults against Roy while failing to address Roy's charge that he had no mandate to speak for French Canada.[16]

This was not the opinion of Tom Crerar, who confided to reporter Grant Dexter that since the outbreak of war Lapointe had 'followed the line that nothing must be done to hurt Quebec, to diminish morale there, to give a handle to the very active nationalist and anti-war elements.' Breaching cabinet confidentiality, Crerar cited a recent threat by Lapointe to resign if the tariff on British boots and shoes was reduced. The cost of the war had beggared Britain, and cabinet favoured lowering the duty to help British exports. Lapointe told his colleagues that if they did they would have to find a new minister of justice. A contretemps took place. 'Surely you don't mean it,' King stated. Lapointe, looking pale, replied, 'On the contrary, I have never been more serious.' Shortly afterwards he left the room, and King told the cabinet members that a boot and shoe tariff reduction would certainly be included in the budget. Lapointe would come around, he remarked in an offhand way.[17]

Actually it was King who came round. 'On Lapointe's account we did not touch the tariff on boots and shoes,' King noted in his diary. 'He is terribly sensitive on anything that affects his own constituency.'[18] Representing Quebec's footwear industry forced Lapointe into the unhappy role of protectionist. King was satisfied to make whatever concessions to Quebec Lapointe thought necessary. Canada's 'magnificent' war effort would not have been possible without national unity. Howe's conversion from a peacetime to a wartime economy was 'a colossal achievement.' Ilsley's handling of wartime finances and taxation was outstanding. 'Lapointe and I were remarking,' King wrote in his diary on 21 November 1940, 'that since Confederation there has been no government comparable to the present in the ability it has demonstrated.' Their pride was justifiable. And King no doubt felt justified in exacting continued service from his ailing minister of justice who longed to retire.

At about the same time as France fell, the Rowell-Sirois commission issued its highly centralist report. It recommended that the federal government take over the large provincial debts bequeathed by the depression. It also recommended that the federal government assume the entire cost of unemployment insurance. In return the provinces would yield their right to collect income tax, corporation tax, and succession duties. To ensure equal government services across the country, the federal government would make grants to the provinces. The net result would be greater taxing power for the federal government and equalization payments to the provinces.

Ilsley, the finance minister, insisted that a Dominion-provincial conference be held to approve the report. Lapointe and King were opposed. They knew that such a conference would stir up the old controversy with Ontario and Quebec over provincial rights. While Godbout would probably be open to federal demands, he would encounter strong opposition from nationalists in the province. As for Hepburn, the champion of provincial rights, the conference would simply provide a battleground for his war on King. Interestingly enough, Lapointe and Hepburn got on well. They had recently campaigned together in a provincial by-election for Lapointe's protégé, Laurier's nephew Robert. After the successful campaign, the jocular Hepburn wrote 'Sir Ernest' to thank him for speaking in the Ottawa East by-election and to say how it was 'like old times' being with him again. Lapointe wrote back just as amiably that he was 'pleased to be with you on the platform ... and happy at the result.'[19]

Against their better judgment, King and Lapointe gave in to Ilsley. The conference, which began on 14 January 1941, turned out to be a fiasco. Hepburn had scuttled it in advance by announcing that he was irrevocably opposed to the Rowell-Sirois report as an invasion of provincial rights. He was joined by Aberhart of Alberta and Pattullo of British Columbia. Only Bracken of Manitoba was wholly in favour of the report. As for Godbout, in the words of Le Devoir he was 'neither fish nor fowl.' Patently angry, Lapointe told the assembly that never in all his experience had he seen a report treated more unjustly and with as many false interpretations. An Ontario paper claimed it favoured Quebec, yet his desk was piled with French-Canadian petitions denouncing it as a machination to wreck Quebec's autonomy. Accusing Hepburn of being the main spoiler, Lapointe told the premiers that their opposition would not kill the report; even if it was put aside today it would not perish. At the least, the conference had focused attention on the report, and he predicted that Canadians would in future study it and express their views.

Unlike Lapointe, King attempted to distance himself from the report in an attempt to paper over the gulf that separated the provinces from each other and from the federal government. In his closing remarks, he said that he had not been in favour of convening the conference in wartime and laid the blame on Ilsley, his finance minister.[20] As if to symbolize the conference's failure, the co-author of the report, Joseph Sirois, died two days after the conference ended. The whole thing had been a setback for the King-Lapointe administration. King took it out on Skelton. The under-secretary of external affairs had been a party to forcing the conference on the government 'when both Lapointe and I were ... absolutely opposed to anything of the kind at this time.'[21] It was King's last opportunity to blame the senior civil servant for the failure of the politicians. Less than two weeks later, Skelton suffered a fatal heart attack at the wheel of his car. Lapointe did not attend the funeral because he was in bed with the flu at the time. The flu was apparently severe enough to stop him from visiting his beloved Mimy, who was in the hospital in Quebec City. King felt that his condition was worsened by Madame Lapointe's illness. 'Any family trouble knocks Lapointe out completely.'[22]

However, by 9 February, Lapointe felt well enough to travel to Montreal to attend a special Sunday mass in Notre Dame cathedral to pray for an Allied victory. The day of prayer was Lapointe's suggestion. In December he had written Quebec's lieutenant-governor, Sir Eugène Fiset, that it would provide an opportunity for all French Canadians 'to dedicate themselves to the war effort and to doing their utmost for victory.' Fiset broached the idea to Cardinal Villeneuve, who embraced it enthusiastically.[23] It was just the kind of religious extravaganza the cardinal loved; a magnifico by inclination, Villeneuve would have made an ideal Renaissance pope. All traces of his nationalist/ separatist past had vanished, and he was completely behind the war effort, flogging Victory Bonds and urging young men to enlist. His close working relationship with Lapointe had made him very unpopular in nationalist circles. The day of prayer was intended by its sponsors not only to cement French-Canadian loyalty but to put that loyalty front and centre in English Canada. Villeneuve's official announcement appeared in the *Gazette* and other English-language papers: 'French Canada will solemnly swear never to set down arms nor relax efforts on the internal front until the triumph of the democratic ideal over the Axis powers is secure.'

A crowd of 4,000 filled the beautiful old cathedral, modelled on Notre Dame in Paris, to hear Cardinal Villeneuve celebrate the mass. Lapointe read a prayer for victory and peace. It was all too much for Lieutenant-Governor Fiset who fainted. Following the religious ceremony, the congregation moved out into the Place d'Armes to view a march past by the army, air force, and navy.[24] Fifty thousand young *Canadiens* were now in uniform.[25] On a proportional basis, enlistment figures were comparable with English Canada. French Canadian youth had dutifully accepted the call-up for home defence. It was a radically different picture from the 1914–18 war when conscripts took to the bush in northern Quebec and riots erupted in Quebec City. If all was relatively quiet on the Quebec front, King and Lapointe found themselves under fire by ultra-loyalists in English Canada. The campaign for national government was heating up once more. The leading newspapers of the country were demanding a non-partisan war cabinet (Colonel Ralston, known to be a proponent of conscription, was most often mentioned to head it). The leader of the opposition, R.B. Hanson, was pushing for it in the House and so was Arthur Meighen in the Senate. King thought it would be 'little less than a miracle if we get through this year with our government remaining intact.'[26]

On 24 February 1941, after an unpleasant and highly unsatisfactory meeting with the Tory leaders that left King extremely upset, Lapointe told him that he was going to speak that afternoon in the House on this business of national government. He did not indicate what he was going to say. All he would tell King was that he thought it would be of assistance to him. Sick and exhausted as he was, that afternoon Ernest Lapointe delivered a fiery defence of the prime minister and a categorical rejection of national government, which, according to the *Ottawa Citizen*'s parliamentary correspondent, Charles Bishop, was 'quite the most notable speech this session.' 'There have been suggestions from some members and certain newspapers that we should change the complexion of this government and make what is glorified under the name of "national government,"' Lapointe told the House. However, not only did Prime Minister Mackenzie King receive a mandate from the people to carry on during the war, 'he has a definite mandate against forming a national government.' Lapointe reminded his listeners that only a few months earlier the entire King ministry had been re-elected while veteran Conservatives who favoured national government had been defeated. He himself could not sit in a coalition cabinet and represent his province because Quebec was definitely opposed to national government. The very name brought back most painful memories of the last war.

He 'implored the promoters of this scheme' not to undermine the people's confidence in their elected leaders, and he implied none too subtly that their criticism amounted to sabotage. Now as he began his thirty-eighth year in the House of Commons, he pledged himself 'to fight any diabolical conspiracy of malicious, narrow and despicable microbes which should seek to destroy the work of beauty which is Canada.'[27] (Lapointe was speaking of anti-war propaganda sheets, but if the shoe fit the mainstream newspapers could wear it.) King was filled with gratitude to Lapointe for fending off national government and at the next caucus meeting thanked him profusely for his 'chivalrous speech.' But Lapointe had gone too far and had left himself vulnerable to the wrath of the press, as he was about to find out.

Early in January an editorial had appeared in the *Ottawa Citizen* headed 'At the Business End of the Bren.' It read in part: 'When the lads come home from overseas, after some years of service at the real business end of the Bren gun, they may know better where to shoot than Canadian veterans did in the years of debt and privation after the last war.'[28] Although the *Citizen*'s editor, Charles Bowman, would later explain that he meant 'shoot with ballots' not bullets, it was a shocking statement that, taken at face value, was a clear incitement to violence. Nevertheless, until M.J. Coldwell, the acting leader of the CCF, raised it in the House on 27 February, the government took no action. Coldwell inquired why the *Canadian Tribune*, a communist paper, was closed down for weeks while the *Ottawa Citizen* was allowed to publish a subversive article with impunity. Lapointe's reply, approved by Opposition Leader Hanson, was that the Bren gun editorial was indeed subversive and that the *Citizen* would be made to answer for it in the courts.[29]

The *Globe and Mail*, which incidentally was leading the newspaper campaign for national government, seized the opportunity to pillory Lapointe. Appearing on the first of March 1941, the *Globe* editorial was the most damning comment Lapointe had ever received in his thirty-seven years in government. Headed 'Why a Minister of Justice?' it questioned his competence and ability to fill that position:

Right Hon. Ernest Lapointe has lately been providing an illuminating demonstration of the urgent need for a drastic reorganization of the Ministry to which he belongs. In its councils he is the second most important personage, and within the past week he has supplied more than one piece of disquieting evidence of a sad poverty of judgment and intelligence, which must fill all reasonable minded people with alarm at the prospect that he may continue to have an influential voice in the formulation of this country's policies.

The editorial attacked Lapointe for his 'audacity to proclaim on behalf of the Province of Quebec a categorical veto upon any plan for a National Government.' It then proceeded to denounce him for promising legal action against the *Ottawa Citizen* for subversion. With heavy sarcasm the editorial inquired whether the minister had noticed that Quebec papers were writing of conscription as 'a damnable law, an infamous tyranny' and stating that sending a contingent to Europe would ruin the country. Piling sin upon sin, it castigated the justice minister for overriding a judge's recommendation to release certain interned individuals. The editorial dismissed Lapointe as the champion of national unity, stating that in the last war he was 'the leader of the antagonists in Quebec who incited the French Canadians against conscription.' It ended with the very serious charge that as acting prime minister at the time of the Ethiopian crisis he had undermined the use of sanctions against Italy, 'which if enforced with courage might have prevented the series of events leading to war.'

John Dafoe was so 'disturbed by the war which the *Globe* has declared upon Lapointe' that he stepped out of retirement temporarily to write an editorial in the *Winnipeg Free Press* defending him. As he told Grant Dexter, 'Lapointe is our most hopeful safeguard against the development of intransigency in Quebec.' The *Globe* article was 'malicious in motive and mischievous in intent.' Dredging up the Riddell incident of 1935 was 'an artificial trumped up charge' to damage Lapointe since Dafoe could not recall any criticism from the *Globe* at the time.[30] Undeterred by the *Globe* editorial, Lapointe prosecuted the *Citizen's* editor for subversion. Charles Bowman saw himself as the victim of a witch-hunt. However, he felt that Lapointe, with whom he had travelled and who shared his concept of liberalism, had been 'needled' into filing the charge by Coldwell.[31] When the case came before Ottawa magistrate Glenn Strike, it was summarily dismissed. Doubtless the magistrate would have decided differently had the charge been brought against the *Canadian Tribune*.

In spite of Lapointe's action against the *Citizen*, civil libertarians continued to accuse him of mainly using the Defence of Canada Regulations against 'radicals and others in humble positions.'[32] There is no doubt that Lapointe shared the views of Commissioner Wood, who had written that 'it is not the Nazi nor the fascist but the radical who constitutes our most troublesome problem.' In the House Coldwell scathingly attacked the RCMP commissioner:

> To say that communist activities are more dangerous to democratic institutions than those of fascist and nazi sympathizers is surely to fly in the face of recent history. It was this attitude of mind which brought about the arrest of the communist leaders in France but let the fascist sympathizers obtain power and then betray her. The views expressed by Commissioner Wood in that regard are the views which destroyed collective security, encouraged the rise of Hitler, and through the long period of appeasement, brought us to the present crisis in our history.[33]

Under the regulations a detainee's case was reviewed by an individual (later a three-person advisory committee), who then recommended to the minister continued detention or release. Lapointe was empowered to reject the recommendation. If the RCMP was opposed to a release, Lapointe frequently overruled the committee. When Coldwell taxed him with this in the House, Lapointe countered that he was not a rubber stamp and was 'merely doing the work that has been entrusted to me by parliament.'[34] Coldwell agreed that restrictions were necessary in wartime, but he wanted to know why these wartime restrictions fell more heavily on communists than on fascists and Nazis.

One example was the case of a trade unionist charged by the RCMP with being a member of the Communist Party of Canada. He was acquitted by a county court judge but was immediately arrested by the RCMP and interned under Regulation 21 by order of the minister of justice. The Winnipeg lawyer E.J. McMurray, who defended the trade unionist, wrote his former colleague that 'I cannot help but feel that all the facts were not made known to you when the Police re-arrested McNeill,' but having little hope that Lapointe would reconsider and order the detainee's release, McMurray sent a copy of his letter to King.[35] King, who was mouthing liberal sentiments in cabinet, backed Lapointe to the hilt in the latter's wholesale internments of left-wing labour leaders. At this same time Lapointe showed that he was not against unions, just those he thought were red-tinged. On 25 July he and King talked a reluctant cabinet into passing an order-in-council that would facilitate collective bargaining in government-controlled industries.[36]

Meanwhile, Lapointe was relaxing his prohibition on Gaullist activity in French Canada. Though Quebeckers as a whole still venerated Marshal Pétain, by the winter of 1941 admiration was growing for General de Gaulle's determination to fight on in the name of France. Sensing the subtle change in public opinion in the province, Lapointe concluded that barring the Free French would be divisive in itself. Thus when Norman Robertson, Skelton's successor as under-secretary of state for external affairs, asked for his approval of an official visit from a Free French representative, Lapointe agreed on condition that the visitor made no public speeches.[37]

De Gaulle had made an excellent choice. His envoy, Commander Georges Thierry d'Argenlieu, impressed King and Lapointe immensely when they met with him on 20 March 1941. D'Argenlieu was a 'soldier-monk' in peacetime, the provincial of a Carmelite order, and in wartime a ship's captain who had served with distinction in the ill-fated Dakar expedition. Obviously a blue blood, he struck King as a 'thoughtful, cultured, earnest person – as fine a type of man as I have [seen] in many a day.'[38] (As always when confronted with a superior Frenchman, King 'regretted deeply not being able to speak French.') For an hour, King and Lapointe quizzed him on the relationship between de Gaulle and Vichy. D'Argenlieu was the soul of tact, saying only nice things about Pétain and blaming the men around him such as Admiral Darlan and Pierre Laval.

At the meeting King and Lapointe agreed that d'Argenlieu could name a liaison officer to deal with the federal authorities. In effect, this person would have status not unlike Vichy's minister. In addition, the Canadian government would recognize identity cards issued by the Free French.[39] D'Argenlieu won many friends for the Free French during his two-month stay in Canada. On his return to London, he reported to de Gaulle, who was at Brazzaville in the French Congo, that 'Mr. Lapointe, minister of Justice at Ottawa, and morally the alter-ego of Mr. Mackenzie King, asked me to tell England that my mission had rendered a very great service to the federal government. Breaking off relations with the government of Vichy, which had been impossible in June 1940 without resulting in a grave internal crisis because of the French-Canadian minority, becomes realizable after the change of opinion created by my mission.'[40]

CHAPTER THIRTY

Last Days

By the spring of 1941 Hitler had conquered all of western Europe and the Balkans. In North Africa the British had been forced out of Libya and had retreated to Egypt. On the Atlantic the loss of Allied shipping from German submarines had reached astronomical proportions. Cabinet renewed discussion of the conscription issue. The two Canadian divisions had not as yet seen action; however, defence minister Ralston advised that replacement troops would be needed when the Canadians were released from their holding pens in British camps and sent into battle. But King remained adamant. On 30 April he told his colleagues that he would never agree to conscription for overseas service under any circumstances. 'I wanted to make my position clear before both Lapointe and Ralston,' he wrote in his diary.

In private King admitted that conscription was the fairest way of dealing with the manpower problem, but like Lapointe he believed it was anti-conscription promises that kept Quebec on side. At the War Committee meeting on 9 May, Ralston asked that conscription not be ruled out; Lapointe threatened to resign if it was introduced. Lapointe stated categorically that he would never accept conscription for overseas, not only because of his public record on the subject but because it would 'wreck the Canadian war effort, destroy the national unity, and might even mean civil conflict.'[1]

To forestall the conscriptionists, King initiated a Canada-wide recruitment campaign. Desperately anxious to have more Quebeckers sign up for active service, Lapointe supported the campaign to the limit of his strength. In a radio broadcast on 15 May 1941 he launched the drive in Quebec. The duty of all able-bodied young men, he told his listeners, was to 'swell the ranks of our army.' Appealing to their pride ('the honour of the race'), he pleaded with them not to 'shirk their duty.' Sacrifice was necessary for their own security. Military service, offered on a voluntary basis today, would be brutally imposed if the Nazis were victorious.

Lapointe used this broadcast to lash out at Maxime Raymond, the leader of the small cohort of ultra-nationalist MPs. Henri Bourassa had been Laurier's cross to bear in the First World War; Raymond was Lapointe's in the Second. According to Raymond, the war was no more than an attempt by Britain to maintain its commercial and military ascendancy. He scoffed at what he regarded as the government's exaggerated 'threat' of a German invasion of Canada and did not hesitate to suggest that Lapointe had overplayed the danger to win support for the NRMA and national registration. On 7 May 1941 Raymond launched another attack on the government's war policy. Canada, he said, was expending its limited strength and resources in the interest of Britain, which after the war would probably make friends with Germany. He reminded the House that Quebec was unanimously opposed to conscription.[2]

In his radio talk on 15 May Lapointe urged his compatriots not to be taken in by anti-war propaganda:

Those whom through spite, mean personal grudges or any other less avowable motives, attempt to place their own small view above the country's sacred cause, those who have only destructive criticism to offer, and more or less imaginary grievances to voice are, whether they realize it or not, allies of the enemy. They wantonly stab us in the back, for you may be sure that the Nazis would not give them any credit for their cowardice or their stupidity, and that if opportunity arose they also would fare no better than we would. Even the 'boches' despise traitors.[3]

Quebec's major paper, *La Presse*, asserted that Lapointe spoke for most French Canadians when he repudiated Raymond's anti-war position. *La Patrie* admiringly trotted out the familiar comparison with Laurier. There were numerous personal letters commending his stand. Senator Léon-Mercier Gouin told Lapointe that he was right to be so brutally frank. 'Those who fight you merit only scorn and it is time to make them feel ashamed of themselves.' *Le Devoir*'s Léopold Richer interpreted Lapointe's attack on the nationalists differently. In his opinion, Lapointe was profoundly worried about the inevitability of conscription and hid his apprehension 'under a mask of certitude.'[4]

The recruiting drive had mixed results. Quebec City, Lapointe's own bailiwick, exceeded its quota, though Montreal, with its anglophone and francophone population, was under quota. The thoroughly English cities of London, Ontario, and Victoria, British Columbia, also failed to meet their objectives; this may have been due in part to a whispering campaign that a successful recruiting drive would eliminate the need for overseas conscription.[5]

Animosity against Lapointe in conscriptionist circles was one reason why King felt he must refuse Churchill's urgent invitation to attend a conference of prime ministers in London. If he left the country, King reasoned in his diary, he would have to ask Lapointe to be acting prime minister, and should relations between France and Britain worsen, or should overseas conscription become more of an issue, the conscriptionists would go on the offensive against Quebec and Lapointe would become the main target of abuse. The resulting racial tensions would certainly unsettle Quebec's cooperation in the war effort. On the other hand, if he did not appoint Lapointe, Quebec would feel slighted and the consequences would be similar. Besides, King doubted if any other cabinet minister could handle wartime Canada. As he wrote his high commissioner in London, Vincent Massey, 'it is only by the two of us [Lapointe and himself] working so closely together that Canada's national unity has remained up to the present what it is.'[6]

Lapointe was just as opposed to King's going to England. As soon as he heard of the possibility, he cabled Massey in the strongest terms:

Please convey my views to Churchill that King is one national leader who cannot must not leave own country. Canada now united. Some politicians here who dislike unity are behind suggestion that King leave Canada for England. Is as necessary here as Churchill is in Britain. As far as Quebec concerned King is the leader who they will trust exclusive of all others. I beseech British friends not suggest even short absence from Canada as the suggestion rather weakens the Canadian front.[7]

People expected that the long-postponed invasion of England was only days away. Instead, Hitler turned eastwards and on 22 June 1941 invaded Soviet Russia, with whom he had signed a non-aggression treaty. Although the opening of the Russian front relieved fears of an immediate invasion of Britain, it placed yet another weight on Lapointe's bowed shoulders. Overnight the godless Reds had become 'our gallant allies.' How could he combat the ingrained anti-communism in traditional, Catholic French Canada? As usual, King was looking to his Quebec lieutenant to keep the French province 'steady' in the face of this extraordinary development.

Considering the Vatican's implacable enmity towards Soviet Russia, it was ironic that Lapointe's most invaluable ally in keeping Quebec behind the war effort was the head of the Roman Catholic Church in Canada. Cardinal Villeneuve used the prestige of his office to make French Canada swallow the alliance with the Soviet Union. In his St Jean-Baptiste Day sermon in the Quebec basilica two days after the Nazi invasion of Russia, the cardinal commanded the faithful to shun nationalism and to do their utmost for an Allied victory. However, a month later Villeneuve informed Lapointe that he was picking up disquieting signals. People were complaining more and more bitterly that 'despite Quebec's sacrifices, despite the multiple proofs of our loyalty, despite my own pronouncements, the French-Canadian element is more or less betrayed, under-estimated, and unconsidered.'[8]

In this atmosphere Lapointe showed real courage by interning Georges Raphael Gillet, the president of the ultra-nationalist Ligue des Patriotes, for 'fostering disunity and hampering the war effort.' Gillet had been openly organizing anti-war meetings and spreading subversive propaganda. Many important people including Cardinal Villeneuve pressed Lapointe to release Gillet. The cardinal told Lapointe that Gillet's internment was 'causing a scandal in certain quarters'; people were saying that it was a politically inspired persecution. The subtle prelate intimated that if his intervention on behalf of Gillet was successful, his prestige and authority in nationalist circles would be enhanced and they would be more receptive to his win-the-war preaching. 'The thing could be done, in my opinion, without noise.'

Lapointe replied that he had shown great restraint in restricting internment to Gillet. The RCMP had wanted to intern the Créditistes Louis Even, Ernest Gregoire, and Abbé Lavergne, but he had overruled them although those people warranted internment. He was not disturbed, he said, by their diatribes against him, but they had no right to make statements that were 'absolutely subversive and of a kind to harm the supreme war effort in which Canada was engaged.'[9] In the end Cardinal Villeneuve took care of Abbé Lavergne for Lapointe, removing the troublesome priest from his Quebec City parish and banishing him to a monastery.[10] Lapointe was saved further pressure from on high when the advisory committee hearing Gillet's appeal recommended his release. He did not override the recommendation.[11]

By the summer of 1941 Pétain was collaborating openly with the Nazis, allowing them bases in Syria and North Africa. When the Pétainiste review, *La Droite* of Quebec City, devoted a full issue to praising the Vichy regime and criticizing Britain, Lapointe did not hesitate to close it down.[12]

Ignoring his failing health, Lapointe spoke at recruitment rallies both in and out of Quebec. An admiring journalist commented that he would 'roar like a lion in either French or English, and hold his audience ... with strong and convincing words.' His message was simple: 'We are at war. We must work, fight, win or perish together.' A heartfelt plea for national unity would follow: 'Let there be no division of section, of race, no division of nationality or religion.'[13] Lapointe's wartime speeches won him comparison with Churchill. Certainly he was the closest thing Canada had to the great English orator. Mackenzie King's small, high-pitched voice was hardly of the timbre to inspire men to march off to war. In fact, when the diminutive prime minister with his wisp of hair and round paunch appeared in newsreels, his unlikely image as a wartime leader was greeted with good-natured boos by theatre audiences.

Bobby Lapointe had joined up as a lieutenant in the Chaudière regiment and in July embarked for overseas with the third division. Ernest and Mimy, with Bobby's wife Lucette, went to see him off at Halifax.[14] It was a bitter-sweet occasion for Lapointe. As a parent he had to stifle his tears as he saw the ship pull out, but at the same time he was proud that his son had answered the call of duty. Lapointe was far from sanguine that the less privileged French-Canadian youth, whom he was urging to sign up for active service, would get fair treatment. He complained to Ralston of discrimination against the French in the army, informing the defence minister that the anti-Quebec bias among the general staff was 'unbelievable.' Still, he was not blind to the fact that lack of fluency in English and their non-technical education also blocked French Canadians' advancement in the services.[15] Chubby Power had been suggesting for some time that the reason for the scarcity of French-Canadian officers was language. Military textbooks were in English, and (as he told Grant Dexter) 'without French texts it had been impossible for the Quebec lads to learn the business of war.'[16] The army was giving some English classes, but Lapointe thought this was no solution. The idea was gaining currency among the top brass itself of bilingual training schools.

Speaking to the Quebec City Canadian Club on 24 September 1941, Lapointe had the pleasure of announcing 'a radical reorganization' undertaken by the army's general staff, designed to improve training facilities and advancement oppportunities for French-Canadian soldiers. Military manuals hitherto available only in English were being translated, and training centres in Quebec had instituted bilingual courses. The number of French-speaking instructors would be increased as more francophone cadets entered officer training schools. Similar reforms were taking place in the air force and the navy. He told his audience that these reforms would permit 'our young compatriots ... to serve in a capacity other than that of privates and to reach posts which, up to the present, seemed reserved to their English-speaking fellow-countrymen.'[17] It was a moment of great pride for Lapointe. It also marked the end of his active career.

By October 1941 Lapointe's illness had reached the point where he could no longer carry on. Awarded an honorary degree by Queen's University, he was too ill to write his own short speech for convocation, and his secretary had to do it for him.[18] To the last, Lapointe never relaxed his efforts to secure equal treatment for French Canadians. With his days numbered, he complained to King that there was no French Canadian on the unemployment insurance commission. 'Do you not think that this came as a result of the absence of French Canadians from Quebec on the various boards which advise the Ministers?' It was his old refrain. He reminded the prime minister that he had been saying this for years with 'indifferent success.' It was 'a waste of breath' trying to convince his fellow ministers.[19]

Towards the end of October Ernest and Mimy went to Quebec City to stay with Sir Eugène and Lady Fiset in the hope that a rest would do him good. There, his baffled doctors treated him for diabetes and jaundice. Although in considerable pain, Lapointe was still hopeful that he would be able to attend some of the parliamentary session slated to open on 5 November. On 26 October he wrote King that he was planning to return to Ottawa in a week or so and would stop in at Montreal to see a specialist on the way. His mind was on the upcoming session. 'I am thinking of things I will be pleased to tell Hanson and his crowd when and if they start an offensive,' he wrote King. But on 5 November he wrote again to say that although he had succeeded in getting his doctors to delay his entrance into hospital until after the end of the session, he was sorry that he could not wait any longer. 'I am restless, suffering acute pain, and feel I would not be able physically to speak in the House.' The thought of the conscription issue coming up in Parliament without him was much on his mind.[20]

When Lapointe was admitted to Notre Dame Hospital in Montreal, he was a dying man. Unfortunately, an article by Léopold Richer appeared at this time, snidely suggesting that the minister was suffering from a 'diplomatic illness.' When *Le Devoir*'s editor learned that Lapointe had been diagnosed with inoperable pancreatic cancer, he called him and wept into the phone, begging for forgiveness.[21] On 8 November King received word of Lapointe's fatal condition. He immediately telephoned Lapointe, who sounded very glad to hear from him although a little hurt that King had not contacted him in Quebec City. King was shaken at the prospect of losing Lapointe, 'the most loyal and truest of colleagues and friends. None has ever been more so to myself.' He also realized that he would be 'in a desperate plight' if Lapointe could not at least attend cabinet. Moreover, he had just learned that Hanson was retiring and the new leader of the Conservative party would probably be Arthur Meighen, who would be strenuously pushing for national government. King's need for Lapointe was never greater. The demands of the new session kept King from rushing to Montreal. Meighen had come out flatly for overseas conscription. Before Parliament prorogued on 14 November, King made a point of stating that he would not support a policy of conscription for overseas service without consulting the people – the first intimation of a plebiscite.

On the evening of Parliament's prorogation, Roger Ouimet phoned King to say that his father-in-law was dying. A stricken King recorded in his diary that 'no loss could be greater at this time, not to myself only, but to Canada and the British Empire.' He took the train for Montreal the next day. At the hospital King tried to keep the conversation unemotional to conserve Lapointe's strength. He reported on the session and the horrifying prospect of facing Meighen across the floor next session. He explained that he had not written or phoned Lapointe in Quebec City thinking it was best for him to have a complete rest. ('I reproached myself, however, for not having done both from day to day,' he admitted in his diary.) Now, when it was too late, he offered Lapointe the presidency of the council to spare him 'worries over internments, etc.' of the justice department. Lapointe's eyes filled with tears when King told him that provision had been made in his will for he and Mimy to have Laurier House to live in until the end of their days should King predecease him. Lapointe was deeply grateful to learn that King had arranged for Bobby to come home on compassionate leave. Back in Ottawa the next day, King wrote a touching letter that revealed not only his deep attachment to Lapointe but his dependence on him:

'My chief joy in public life has been in sharing everything with you, just as my sense of security lies in having you at my side.' He would keep in touch by phone, letter, or personal visits, he assured his soulmate, 'and so long as I have your counsel and advice that is all I need to feel secure.'[22]

Three days later King returned to Lapointe's bedside. Lapointe had just come out of an oxygen tent, and it was an effort for him to talk. He had been told by his doctors that his condition was terminal, and his confessor, Father Gaudrault, was there: 'He is looking after my spiritual condition,' Lapointe said with a smile in an attempt to lighten the conversation. 'You need have no concern about the condition of your spirit,' King told him gravely. 'No man ever had a purer spirit.' Though he made light of it, Lapointe was a true believer and a good son of the church. He asked King to let Cardinal Villeneuve know how sick he was and to ask him to pray for him.

Deathly ill as he was, Lapointe had been thinking of someone to replace himself as King's Quebec lieutenant. He concluded that Godbout was the only one to take his place. Sadly King agreed and promised to sound out the Quebec premier at the Laurier centenary celebration at St Lin the next day. Then casting aside all reserve and choked up with emotion, King told Lapointe what he had meant to him. Holding the dying man's hand, he said that 'no man ever had a truer friend.' 'But for you, I would never have been Prime Minister, nor would I have been able to hold the office, as I have through the years. There was never a deeper love between brothers than existed between us. We have never had a difference all the years that we have been associated together, in thought and word alike. I am grateful to you from the bottom of my heart.' He then leaned over and kissed Lapointe on the cheek. Lapointe raised up and kissed him. They kissed each other a third time. Exhausted by the effort and the emotion, Lapointe laid his head back on his pillow and closed his eyes.

King made another visit the next morning before leaving for St Lin. Lapointe had rallied a little. They spoke of the qualities necessary for a prime minister, and they agreed that patience was the primary virtue. Lapointe summoned up the energy to quote Pitt on the subject. On the way back from the Laurier ceremony, King stopped in at the hospital even though the family had told him that Lapointe was too weak to see him. But Lapointe asked for King when he heard him whispering in the hall with Mimy and Odette. King told him how much he had been missed at the ceremony and of the tributes paid to him. 'You were quite as much in the thought of those present as Laurier himself,' King said.

As in so many other ways, the soulmates were united by a strong belief in the afterlife. 'Ernest, we will see each other again,' King said. 'There is nothing truer than that,' Lapointe replied in tears. King held his hand for some minutes, then kissed him and left the room. They never saw each other again in this world.[23] On 19 November Lapointe received the last sacraments from Father Gaudrault. That night the archbishop of Montreal visited him. Later, Cardinal Villeneuve came to his bedside. On 26 November Ernest Lapointe died. Giant black headlines announced his passing. Tributes to a great French-Canadian statesman poured in from home and abroad.

King called his departed friend 'a statesman the country could ill afford to lose at any time, and least of all in these days of crisis and stress.' He compared Lapointe to Laurier. Arthur Meighen, now officially the Conservative leader, eulogized Lapointe as 'beyond question one of our ablest parliamentarians, very forceful in either language, resolute and effective.' General de Gaulle cabled: 'His fight for the allied cause ... has earned him the esteem and admiration of all French who pursue the fight for the liberation of their country and the salvation of civilization.' Lapointe's cabinet colleagues referred to his death as 'a calamitous loss' and a 'national tragedy.' Léopold Richer, contrite over his reference to Lapointe's 'maladie diplomatique,' contributed a thoroughly sympathetic obituary to the nationalist review *L'Action Nationale*. The press variously praised Lapointe for 'his contribution to Canadian autonomy,' 'the courageous patriotism that he showed at the beginning of the war,' 'his defence of the use of French in Ontario from 1916,' and 'his loyalty to the British Crown.' Only the *Globe and Mail* struck a discordant note. While acknowledging his many virtues, the paper did not retract its March editorial: 'At heart he was a keen racialist and an inveterate champion of the special rights and privileges of the French-Canadian race. On such issues the skin of his Liberalism was apt to wear very thin and there was sometimes an unfortunate discrepancy between his moderate utterances in Parliament and his passionate appeals to racial sentiment in the rural townships of Quebec.'[24]

At King's wish a state funeral was held in Quebec City on 29 November. Thousands lined the street as the cortège moved from the railway station to the provincial legislature. King, walking beside the horse-drawn hearse, thought the crowd larger than at Laurier's funeral or even on the occasion of the royal visit. As at Laurier's funeral, it was snowing hard. Marching columns of RCMP, army, navy, and air force followed the mourners through the slushy streets. After lying in state at the legislature, the body was brought to the church of St Roch in Lapointe's own riding, where Cardinal Villeneuve officiated at the service. Ernest Lapointe was buried at Rivière-du-Loup.[25]

After the funeral Chubby Power went off on a drinking bout. King's loneliness was apparent to all. He carried Lapointe's last letter in his pocket as a shield against the cabinet's growing insistence on conscription.[26] Godbout could not be talked into replacing Lapointe. He felt that he was needed in Quebec to keep Duplessis at bay, and, besides, his English was not good enough.[27] Cardin's health was too poor for him to become the Quebec lieutenant. Drunk or sober, Power was ineligible because he was not a French Canadian. At the suggestion of the Quebec ministers, King offered the justice portfolio to the highly respected corporate lawyer Louis St Laurent, although he had no government experience. St Laurent accepted out of a sense of public duty, stipulating that he would stay no longer than the duration of the war.

Without Lapointe's support, King's opposition to conscription weakened. The European conflict had widened into a world war. On 7 December 1941, just two weeks after Lapointe's funeral, the Japanese bombed the American fleet at Pearl Harbor. The United States was now at war with the Axis powers and immediately introduced conscription. When Hong Kong fell to the Japanese on Christmas Day, Canadian troops were killed or taken prisoner. King was under terrific pressure from Ralston and other conscriptionists in his cabinet. In January 1942 King announced a plebiscite for 27 August to ask the Canadian people to release the government from its promise that there would be no conscription for service out of the country.

Virtually overnight, French-Canadian nationalists organized the Ligue pour la défense du Canada to defeat the plebiscite in Quebec. Led by André Laurendeau, Maxime Raymond, Paul Gouin, and Georges Pelletier of *Le Devoir*, the Ligue marshalled the 'no campaign,' making effective use of Lapointe's anti-conscriptionist speeches during the Quebec election in 1939.[28] Cabinet ministers in Ottawa were incensed that the Ligue had got hold of recordings of Lapointe's speeches, and his '*never* conscription' was resounding throughout the province.[29] Lapointe's reputation was badly tarnished. In the House, Maxime

Raymond argued with considerable cogency that since the no-conscription promise had been made to French Canada, only French Canada could release the government from its promise.

Quebec voted 72 per cent 'no'; the rest of Canada voted 80 per cent 'yes.' Asserting that the anti-conscription pledge had been given to the country as a whole and not to any province or section, on the strength of the majority vote King quickly introduced Bill 80 to repeal Section 3 of the NRMA, which limited conscription to home service. The bill passed, with forty French MPs voting against it.[30] Despite King's famous phrase, 'conscription if necessary but not necessarily conscription,' Cardin saw Bill 80 as an irrevocable step towards conscription. Following its passage he resigned from the cabinet. Chubby Power stayed on; as associate minister of national defence and air minister he said he recognized that conscription could be justified in a time of national crisis. Louis St Laurent, the new minister of justice and Quebec lieutenant in training, was unfettered by past promises and voted for Bill 80 with a clear conscience.

What would Lapointe have done? Though he had known him so well, Chubby Power was not sure what position Lapointe would have taken. For her part, Odette Ouimet was certain that her father would have resigned over the plebiscite.[31] Besides, she thought that it might never have happened if he had lived. In André Laurendeau's opinion, Lapointe would have made no difference because the situation was beyond his control. 'I doubt that at this stage he could himself have quelled the crisis,' Laurendeau wrote in his 1960s memoir, 'either by persuading Anglo-Canadians to moderate their demands or by once again drawing French Canadians into the wake of the King government. What is certain is that his disappearance from the political scene weakened the cause of national unity.'[32]

There is reason to believe that Lapointe would have endorsed a plebiscite or referendum on conscription providing that the voting was limited to Quebec. In a profile in the August 1941 issue of the *Christian Science Monitor*, he was quoted as saying that 'there would be no conscription for overseas service unless the question was referred back to the people who had given the present government its mandate to enter the war on a specific promise not to introduce conscription.' This was Maxime Raymond's position, not King's. In spite of his devotion to King, it is impossible to believe that Lapointe would have agreed to a Canada-wide plebiscite that would swamp the French. After the passage of Bill 80, an anti-imperialist, extremely anti-Ottawa, neonationalist movement, the Bloc Populaire, grew out of the Ligue pour la défense du Canada. Although this movement was not successful at the polls, it has been suggested that the Bloc was the genesis of modern nationalist ideology in Quebec.[33]

Reluctant to impose conscription because of Quebec, King employed dilatory tactics to hold the conscriptionists at bay. He insisted that he would honour Lapointe's pledge. In 1944 he took the drastic step of replacing Ralston with General McNaughton only to find that the latter had come to the same conclusion as his predecessor – that the voluntary system would not suffice to provide the necessary replacement troops. Fearing a cabinet revolt, King gave in. On 23 November 1944, an order-in-council was passed to send 16,000 NRMA men overseas. Chubby Power announced his resignation, claiming that conscription was unnecessary in the late stages of the war.

In the best speech of his career, King justified his action to Parliament. He quoted Lapointe (whom he called 'the closest, the truest and the most devoted friend I have had in my political life') as saying that 'no government could stay in office if it refused to do what the great majority of Canadians wanted it to do.'[34] Cardin responded dryly that while the prime minister was quoting Lapointe he should have quoted his speeches in favour of the voluntary system and his denunciation of conscription.[35] King easily won a vote of confidence, but thirty-two French Canadians from Quebec voted against him.[36]

During the conscription debate, Philippe Picard, Lapointe's former secretary, expressed his conviction that if Lapointe had lived he would have strengthened the prime minister's will to resist those who promoted the divisive policy of conscription: 'Never has a man's passing away been so sadly felt, especially when we realize that his presence might have been such an agent of cohesion and of unity.'[37] Lapointe himself had no illusions that he could halt the juggernaut of conscription. On his deathbed, he said to the lamenting King, 'My departure will be more helpful to you than if I had stayed on.'[38] He was the guarantor of the pact with French Canada; without him, King could yield to the inevitable.

Conclusion

The first Parti Québécois premier, René Lévesque, acknowledged to a journalist that Ernest Lapointe had held Quebec 'in the palm of his hand.'[1] Although Lévesque's predecessors, the *nationalistes* of the 1930s, disparaged Lapointe as a federalist 'sell-out,' the masses of French Canadians trusted Lapointe's down-to-earth assurances that he was looking after their interests in Ottawa. Throughout his long career in federal politics, Lapointe worked steadily for French Canadians to be treated as equals with the English, to receive their share of government posts and patronage, to have them feel that they were 'of Canada as well as in Canada.' He promoted bilingualism in government at a time when Canada outside of Quebec was an English-speaking country. At the same time, he was not anti-English. His objective was 'the unity of the races.' As he said in one of his last speeches, 'I have worked all my life for national unity.'

He found a soulmate in Mackenzie King, who made national unity his political credo. But whereas Lapointe championed French-Canadian rights out of love for his people and his province, the motive of the anglophone prime minister was self-preservation. Quebec was King's power base. John Herd Thompson and Allen Seager, in *Canada, 1922–1939: Decades of Discord*, put it baldly: 'Without a solid Quebec behind him he [King] could kiss the prime ministership goodbye.' Having no empathy with Quebec and no understanding of the language, King needed a francophone Quebecker to muster the province behind his administration. In Ernest Lapointe he found the perfect Quebec lieutenant – a bilingual Québécois who enjoyed tremendous popularity at home and the respect of Canadians at large. Lapointe was a charismatic orator who unfailingly carried his French-Canadian audiences with him, and he delivered the Quebec vote as regularly as clockwork. Only once, in 1930, did the Conservatives make inroads in his fiefdom, and the fact that the Liberals lost that election demonstrates King's dependence on the province.

Lapointe assumed his role as spokesman for Quebec at a time when relations between French and English Canada were at a nadir. Conscription in 1917 had left Quebec so alienated that many French Quebeckers were ready to wash their hands of federalism. Lapointe's first remarkable act in the interest of national unity was to stop the Quebec caucus from opting out of the 1919 Liberal leadership convention. In doing so he assured King's victory. The partnership thus begun (after a short Gouin interlude) remained paramount in the careers of both men until Lapointe's death in 1941. Lapointe promoted King's policies in Quebec, but he greatly influenced those policies by giving King the French-Canadian perspective. That was what King required of his Quebec lieutenant. Together they coped amazingly well with the Canadian duality.

It was a close and effective political partnership. Contemporaries saw it this way;[2] the Quebec press spoke of 'le gouvernement King-Lapointe.' King and Lapointe saw it this way. In 1927, after eight years of working together, Lapointe remarked to King that they had differed only once. Ten years later Lapointe's confessor wrote King that 'Mr. Lapointe sees eye-to-eye with you.' King never wearied of referring to their closeness and in his diary repeatedly congratulates himself on having such a loyal colleague. And so he was. Whenever there were stirrings of revolt, Lapointe stood by his chief. In 1925 and 1926, when there were serious attempts to have him replace King, Lapointe dismissed the cabalists out of hand. 'He wouldn't listen to any thought of that kind at all,' Chubby Power recalled. 'Mr. Lapointe was absolutely and intensely loyal to Mr. King.'[3]

King and Lapointe had their differences, but these were differences of degree and timing rather than divergent views. Rooted in the anti-imperialist soil of francophone Quebec, Lapointe pressed harder than King for recognition of Canada's nationhood in London and Geneva, but he no more than King ever envisaged independence from the empire/Commonwealth. It is worth noting that as minister of justice he did nothing to end that vestige of colonialism – appeals to the Privy Council. Though it was Lapointe's initiative that led to the repudiation of Riddell in the Ethiopian crisis of 1935, King, 'when pushed by his Quebec lieutenant,' was wholeheartedly in favour of disowning the diplomat. Any differences between King and Lapointe did not affect their essential agreement on Canada's place in the world or national unity or, for that matter, on how to keep the Liberal party in power.

Both men were true disciples of Laurier, believing that the only way to govern Canada was through compromise and conciliation – and an excess of caution. 'Holding the sane and safe middle course,' was the way Lapointe expressed it. Perhaps this desire 'to let sleeping dogs lie' (one of King's favourite expressions) led to what Chubby Power called Lapointe's 'standpatism.' Starting off as a populist committed to civil rights, after 1935 Lapointe turned into a conservative if not a right-winger (though he continued to be regarded by the public as a civil libertarian because he talked like one). The elder Paul Martin's comment that Lapointe was a Liberal but not a liberal was very apt. Interestingly, King followed the same trajectory from liberal democrat to small-c conservative, confiding to his diary in 1940 that even as a young man he knew this would happen.[4]

In matters pertaining strictly to Quebec, King invariably deferred to Lapointe – the notable example was allowing the Padlock Act to stand. Lapointe had the power that accompanies indispensability, and he used the threat of resignation to get his way. Indeed, the King government was perceived as showing favouritism to Quebec. King certainly catered to Lapointe. The return of the western lands was delayed four years until Lapointe was satisfied on the bilingual schools issue. Despite humanitarian soliloquies in his diary, King supported Lapointe's opposition to the admission of Jewish refugees, even children. After the fall of France, King's tolerance of the Vichy regime can be attributed to Lapointe's influence. In the last months of his life, however, Lapointe adjusted his pro-Pétainist views to reflect Quebec's growing respect for General de Gaulle. For his part, Lapointe had to cater to the priorities and prejudices of his own people if he was to continue as their spokesman at Ottawa. His lifelong adversaries were the *nationalistes*, and though still small in number they could not be ignored. There is no doubt that at times he took unfortunate positions to conciliate them.

As the Quebec lieutenant, Lapointe's brand of federalism was understandably decentralist. But he sincerely believed that recognition of provincial rights was the way to achieve a harmonious nation. He voiced this position throughout his career, declaring that the provinces were as supreme in their own constitutional fields as the Dominion was in its given areas under the British North America Act. On the bedrock issue of constitutional change, he maintained that it was impossible without provincial unanimity. Nevertheless, his respect for provincial autonomy was suspended if it would bring him into conflict with Quebec opinion. Thus unlike his master Laurier who upheld provincial rights on the Manitoba schools question, Lapointe was unwilling to allow Alberta to use its constitutional power over education to abolish bilingual separate schools. Where Dominion-provincial jurisdiction overlapped, as in the case of waterpower rights, he could be a strong centralist. And after some initial hesitation, he seconded King's intentions to introduce national unemployment insurance and to establish a royal commission that would tilt Confederation towards centralization. He was 'convinced,' he told Quebeckers in 1939, 'that the sacred interest of my province lay in the preservation of the Canadian ideal.'[5]

Lapointe was much more than the Quebec lieutenant – he was King's closest colleague. Jack Pickersgill, King's secretary in the late 1930s, confirms that King relied on Lapointe's judgment on all matters. King consulted him on every aspect of policy and rarely acted without Lapointe's approval. As well as his obvious respect for Lapointe's opinions, King had an underlying motive in making him almost his co-premier. Dependent on Quebec to stay in power, King wanted at all cost to keep Lapointe from becoming disaffected. This was King's thinking when he gave in to Lapointe on Canada's seeking a seat on the League of Nations Council. He thought it was a mistake, 'but a cleavage with Lapointe on a matter which he feels deeply would be more unfortunate in the long run.'

Lapointe wisely did not press Quebec's demands beyond what English Canada would tolerate. In 1939, knowing that English Canada would go to war beside Britain, he told his compatriots that neutrality was out of the question. It was the most important and courageous act of his career. Though Mackenzie King is credited with bringing Canada united into the war against Hitler, it would have been impossible without Ernest Lapointe. Lapointe's historic address in the House of Commons on 9 September 1939 convinced all but a couple of Quebec MPs to support the declaration of war. In this most momentous decision for the country, Lapointe injected the French-Canadian perspective with his and King's pledge that there would be no conscription for overseas.

Lapointe made an even greater contribution to national unity two weeks later when Maurice Duplessis called a snap election ostensibly on the issue of provincial rights. To King and the Quebec ministers, Duplessis was out to sabotage the war effort. Lapointe threw the full force of his magnificent oratory behind the provincial Liberals and defeated Duplessis's attempt to create disunity in the country at war. English Canada regarded him as a saviour. King thought Lapointe had surpassed Sir Wilfrid Laurier: 'He will have a place second to none in Canadian history and well merited as a patriot.'[6]

During his years as King's lieutenant, Lapointe was indisputably 'the pre-eminent spokesman and leader of French Canada.' But overseas conscription in 1944 made a liar of him posthumously. His loss of reputation was compounded by the post-war upsurge of Quebec nationalism, which he had managed to contain in his lifetime. As a federalist, he was not a hero for a Quebec that elected separatist governments. But Ernest Lapointe warrants recognition as a forerunner of the pan-Canadian bilingual and bicultural politics of the modern federal Liberal party.

ERNEST LAPOINTE
1876-1941

Homme d'État, Ministre dans le Gouvernement canadien de 1921 à 1930 et de 1935 à 1941, il joua un rôle important dans l'administration du pays et dans son évolution vers sa complète souveraineté. Sa vive intelligence, sa grande éloquence, son courage et son esprit de tolérance lui ont acquis l'admiration et la reconnaissance de ses compatriotes dont il a bien servi les intérêts tant aux conférences impériales et internationales que dans les conseils de la nation. Il naquit dans une maison située sur cet emplacement. Décédé à Montréal, il fut inhumé à Rivière-du-Loup.

Statesman and federal Cabinet Minister, 1921-30 and 1935-41, Ernest Lapointe played an important role in the administration of the country and its evolution towards autonomy. His intelligence, eloquence, courage, and spirit of tolerance gained him the admiration of his compatriots as he represented them in national, imperial, and international affairs. The house where he was born was located here. He died in Montreal and was buried in Rivière-du-Loup.

Commission des lieux et monuments historiques du Canada.
Historic Sites and Monuments Board of Canada.

Gouvernement du Canada - 1955 - Government of Canada

This historic plaque is located beside Ernest Lapointe's birthplace, St Éloi, Quebec.

Notes

Preface

1 National Archives of Canada (hereafter NAC), King Diary, 19 November 1941.
2 Bruce Hutchison, *The Incredible Canadian* (Toronto: Longmans 1952), 75.
3 *Saturday Night*, 8 April 1939.
4 NAC, Lapointe Papers, Vol. 26, Mackenzie King to Ernest Lapointe, 12 August 1940.

1: National Attention

1 Frederick Griffin, *Variety Show* (Toronto: Macmillan 1936), 27.
2 H.F. Gadsby, 'Conserving the Conservatives,' *Maclean's*, 16 November 1916.
3 NAC, Lapointe Papers, Vol. 80, article by 'Odette Montausier' [nom de plume for Mme Boisonneault of the Poets' Society of Montreal], 28 December 1926.
4 Ibid., clipping from *New World*, September 1941; interview, Odette Lapointe Ouimet, 3 March 1995.
5 Lapointe Papers, Vol. 1, F.-X. Lemieux to Lapointe, 7 September 1895.
6 Ibid., J.F. Pouliot to Lapointe, 20 July 1920. The candidate was Pouliot's father.
7 Ouimet interview, 3 March 1995.
8 J.L. Rutledge, 'The Mantle of Elijah: The Story of the Man Who May Take Laurier's Place,' *Maclean's*, 15 February 1920.
9 R.T.L., 'Mr. Lapointe,' *Maclean's*, December 1933.
10 Rutledge, 'The Mantle of Elijah.'

11 House of Commons *Debates*, 26 February 1913, 11 March 1913, 18 March 1915.

12 Lapointe Papers, Vol. 8, Sir W. Laurier to Mme Lapointe, 30 January 1916.

13 Margaret Prang, *N.W. Rowell: Ontario Nationalist* (Toronto: University of Toronto Press 1975), 166. Up to March 1918, some 15,000 French Canadians saw service at the Front, another 15,000 were in training in Canada and England, and 4,000 to 5,000 served in the navy. The total of 35,000 constitutes approximately 5 per cent of the Canadian forces. This 'represents only the most accurate possible guess, as no official figures were supplied after March 1918, in an effort to let the vexed question of French-Canadian participation lie'; Mason Wade, *The French Canadians, 1760–1967*, Vol. 2, (Toronto: Macmillan 1968), 768.

14 Peter Oliver, *G. Howard Ferguson: Ontario Tory* (Toronto: University of Toronto Press 1977), 49. Oliver states: 'In the vast majority of so-called bilingual schools in eastern and northern Ontario, French alone was the language of instruction and in many of these schools the teachers were unqualified and had slight command of the English language.'

15 Ibid., 39–50.

16 Prang, *Rowell*, Chapter 9.

17 Wade, *The French Canadians*, 2:687.

18 Ibid., 2:695.

19 *Toronto Daily Star*, 10 May 1916.

20 Ibid.; Paul Bernier, *Ernest Lapointe: Deputé de Kamouraska, 1904–1919*, Cahiers d'histoire No. 14, Société Historique de la Côte-du-Sud (La Pocatière 1979), 122.

21 NAC, Laurier Papers, Laurier to Lapointe, 29 December 1908, cited in Bernier, *Lapointe*, 62.

22 Lapointe Papers, Vol. 1, Lapointe to Sir L. Gouin, 23 April 1914; A. Stein to Gouin, 27 April 1914.

23 Ibid., Sir Robert Borden to Sir George Perley, 7 October 1916; Laurier to Lloyd George, 24 October 1916.

24 Prang, *Rowell*, 170.

2: Conscription

1 Mason Wade, *The French Canadians, 1760–1967*, Vol. 2 (Toronto: Macmillan 1968), 735, 738.

2 H.F. Gadsby, 'Who, How and Why: An Official Sunshine Maker,' *Maclean's*, May 1916; NAC, Lapointe Papers, Vol. 1, R. Lemieux to Laurier, 3 June 1917.

3 *Ottawa Journal*, 20 June 1917.
4 House of Commons *Debates*, 7 May 1917, 1160–1.
5 Lapointe Papers, Vol. 1, Laurier to Lapointe, 29 December 1917.
6 Ibid., Lapointe to Laurier, 5 October 1917.
7 Paul Bernier, *Ernest Lapointe: Deputé de Kamouraska, 1904–1919*, Cahiers d'histoire No. 14, Société Historique de la Côte-du-Sud (La Pocatière 1979), 152.
8 Ibid., 150.
9 Ibid., 148.
10 J.K. Munro, 'Why Laurier Will Wait,' *Maclean's*, January 1919; Bernier, *Lapointe*, 152.
11 John English, *Borden: His Life and World* (Toronto: McGraw-Hill 1977), 164.
12 Lapointe Papers, Vol. 1, Laurier to Lapointe, 23 December 1917.
13 Grattan O'Leary, 'Giants of Other Days,' *Maclean's*, 1 January 1926.
14 Frederick Griffin, *Variety Show* (Toronto: Macmillan 1936), 35.
15 J.K. Munro, 'The Four Factions at Ottawa,' *Maclean's*, October 1918.
16 Bernier, *Lapointe*, 158.
17 Lapointe Papers, Vol. 1, Charles Murphy to Lapointe, 9 September 1918.
18 Ibid., Lapointe to C. Robillard, 9 November 1918; Robillard to Lapointe, 12 November 1918.
19 Munro, 'Why Laurier Will Wait'; Lapointe Papers, Vol. 31, J.B. Maclean to Lapointe, 13 December 1935.
20 Lapointe Papers, Vol. 1, Laurier to Lapointe, 5 November 1918.
21 House of Commons *Debates*, 6 March 1919, 246.

3: King-Maker

1 See John W. Lederle, 'The Liberal Convention of 1919 and the Selection of Mackenzie King,' *Dalhousie Review* (April 1947), 85–92.
2 J.K. Munro, 'Ottawa Is Ready for the Worst,' *Maclean's*, December 1919.
3 John English, *Borden: His Life and World* (Toronto: McGraw-Hill 1977), 191–2.
4 House of Commons *Debates*, 6 March 1919, 247.
5 Ibid., 246.
6 Ibid.
7 Ibid., 25 April 1919, 1746.
8 R. MacGregor Dawson, *William Lyon Mackenzie King*, Vol. 1, *A Political Biography, 1874–1923* (Toronto: University of Toronto Press 1958), 304; J.K. Munro, 'The Four Factions at Ottawa,' *Maclean's*, October 1918; H.S. Ferns and B. Ostry, *The Age of Mackenzie King: The Rise of the Leader* (Toronto: Lorimer 1976), 320.

9 J.K. Munro, 'Opening the New Book,' *Maclean's*, April 1919; H.F. Gadsby, 'Ribbing Up the Liberal Party,' *Maclean's*, October 1916.

10 J.K. Munro, 'Why King Won Laurier's Mantle,' *Maclean's*, September 1919; Lederle, 'Liberal Convention,' 90.

11 Marcel Hamelin, ed., *Les mémoires du Sénateur Raoul Dandurand, 1861–1942* (Quebec: Presses de l'Université Laval 1967), 266.

12 Lederle, 'Liberal Convention,' 89.

13 Munro, 'Why King Won'; Munro, 'Ottawa Is Ready'; Paul Bernier, *Ernest Lapointe: Deputé de Kamouraska, 1904–1919*, Cahiers d'histoire No. 14, Société Historique de la Côte-du-Sud (La Pocatière 1979), 162–5.

14 Jean-Charles McGee, *Laurier, Lapointe, St Laurent* (Quebec: Belisle 1948), 164; Grattan O'Leary, *Recollections of People, Press, and Politics* (Toronto: Macmillan 1977), 34.

15 Norman Ward, ed., *A Party Politician: The Memoirs of Chubby Power* (Toronto: Macmillan 1966), 375.

16 Hamelin, ed., *Mémoires*, 266.

17 Ferns and Ostry, *Age of Mackenzie King*, 320.

18 Frederick Griffin, *Variety Show* (Toronto: Macmillan 1936), 37.

19 Dawson, *King*, 1:308.

20 NAC, King Diary, 5–9 August 1919.

21 *Le Devoir*, 23 July 1919.

22 House of Commons *Debates*, 9, 10 September 1919, 109–17, 125.

23 King Diary, 9–10 September 1919. Fielding's motion was defeated.

24 Munro, 'Ottawa Is Ready.'

25 Dawson, *King*, 1:294; King Diary, 18–22 February 1919.

26 King Diary, 25 September, 17 October 1919.

27 Munro, 'Ottawa Is Ready.'

28 Leslie Roberts, 'The Wife of a Politician,' *Chatelaine* (May 1931), 75.

29 J.L. Rutledge, 'The Mantle of Elijah: The Story of the Man Who May Take Laurier's Place,' *Maclean's*, 15 February 1920.

30 Ibid.

31 Bernier, *Lapointe*, 169; NAC, Lapointe Papers, Vol. 1, Arthur Lachance to Lapointe, 29 January, 28 August 1920.

32 Munro, 'Ottawa Is Ready'; Rutledge, 'The Mantle of Elijah'; Bernier, *Lapointe*, 170.

33 King Diary, 20 November 1919.

34 Lapointe Papers, Vol. 1, Lapointe to Charles Murphy, 9 December 1919.

35 Munro, 'Ottawa Is Ready.'

36 King Diary, 22 December 1919.

4: Cabinet Minister

1 Queen's University Archives, Grant Dexter Papers, Dexter to Sir Clifford Sifton, 21 July 1919.
2 J.L. Rutledge, 'The Mantle of Elijah: The Story of the Man Who May Take Laurier's Place,' *Maclean's*, 15 February 1920.
3 Norman Ward, ed., *A Party Politican: The Memoirs of Chubby Power* (Toronto: Macmillan 1966), 77.
4 NAC, King Diary, 27 February 1920.
5 House of Commons *Debates*, 9 March 1920, 272.
6 King Diary, 26 November 1920.
7 NAC, Lapointe Papers, Vol. 1, King to Lapointe, 16 August 1920.
8 Harry Anderson, 'Hon. Henri Béland – Prisoner of War,' *Maclean's*, February 1918.
9 Lapointe Papers, Vol. 1, Dr H. Béland to Lapointe, 1 September 1920; same to same, 6 September 1920.
10 Ibid., King to Lapointe, 13 September 1920.
11 King Diary, 27 September–19 October 1920.
12 Ibid., 18 October 1920.
13 Interview, Odette Ouimet, 3 March 1995.
14 Lapointe Papers, Vol. 1, Lapointe to Adolphe Stein, 3 November 1920.
15 Ibid., J. Archambault to Lapointe, 1 December 1920.
16 Ibid., Sir Lomer Gouin to Lapointe, 20 December 1920.
17 Interview, Odette Ouimet, 3 March 1995.
18 Bernard Weilbrenner, 'Les Idées Politiques de Lomer Gouin,' *Canadian Historical Annual Review* (1965), 49.
19 Roger Graham, *Arthur Meighen*, Vol. 2, *And Fortune Fled* (Toronto: Clarke Irwin 1963), 156.
20 King Diary, 5 September 1921.
21 Ibid., 22 September 1921.
22 Ibid., 23 September 1921.
23 NAC, King Papers, L. Cannon to King, 14 October 1922.
24 Lapointe Papers, Vol. 1, Lyon Cohen to Lapointe, 7 December 1921.
25 King Diary, 10 December 1921.
26 Ibid., 23 December 1921.
27 Lapointe Papers, Vol. 1, L.P. Brodeur to Lapointe, 13 December 1921.
28 Ibid., F.-X. Lemieux to Lapointe, 29 December 1921.
29 King Diary, 23 December 1921.
30 Ibid., 24 December 1921.

31 Lapointe Papers, Vol. 1.
32 J.W. Pickersgill, *The Mackenzie King Record*, Vol. 1, *1939–1944* (Toronto: University of Toronto Press 1960), 288.

5: Diplomat

 1 House of Commons *Debates*, 1 September 1919, 113. On 17 May 1920 Lapointe told the House: 'Anything that looks like national self-assertion, anything which advances Canada along the road of nationhood appeals to me. As General Smuts said, all countries under the British flag are sister nations.' House of Commons *Debates*, 1920, 2442.
 2 Marcel Hamelin, ed., *Les mémoires du Sénateur Raoul Dandurand, 1861–1942* (Quebec: Presses de l'Université Laval 1967), 264.
 3 NAC, King Papers; for example, King to Sir Hamar Greenwood, 16 August 1922.
 4 Ibid., L. Beaudry to Mr Measures, 17 August 1922; interview, Odette Ouimet, 3 March 1995. Others claim he called King 'Rex' in private. Bruce Hutchison, *The Incredible Canadian* (Toronto: Longmans 1952), 10.
 5 King Papers, King to Lapointe, 19 August 1922.
 6 Ibid., King to Lapointe, 6 September 1922.
 7 Ibid., Lapointe to King, 21 August 1922.
 8 R. MacGregor Dawson, *William Lyon Mackenzie King*, Vol. 1, *A Political Biography, 1874–1923* (Toronto: University of Toronto Press 1958), 428; James Eayrs, *In Defence of Canada*, Vol. 1, *From the Great War to the Great Depression* (Toronto: University of Toronto Press 1964), 8.
 9 King Papers, Fielding to King, 15 September 1922.
10 Richard Veatch, *Canada and the League of Nations* (Toronto: University of Toronto Press 1975), 82.
11 Ibid., 84; Eayrs, *In Defence of Canada*, 1:9–10.
12 *Ottawa Citizen*, 19 February 1923.
13 Fielding to King, 18 September 1922, in *Documents on Canadian External Relations (DCER)*, Vol. 3 (Ottawa 1968), 76.
14 Ibid., 3:78, Lapointe to King, 19 September 1922.
15 Ibid., 3:79; Dawson, *King*, 1:411.
16 King Papers, Lapointe to King, 10 September, 18 December 1922.
17 Eayrs, *In Defence of Canada*, 1:14; *Canadian Annual Review 1923*, 104–7.
18 King Papers, Lapointe to King, 10 September, 11 October 1922.
19 *Globe*, 5, 8 October 1922.
20 L. Prince et al., eds., *Illustrated Montreal Old and New* (Montreal: International Press Syndicate 1915), 231; C.G.D. Roberts and A.L. Tunnell, eds., *The Canadian Who's Who*, Vol. 2, 1936–7 (Toronto 1937), 286.

21 NAC, Sir Lomer Gouin Papers, L.A. Taschereau to Gouin, 6 October 1922.
22 Prince et al., eds., *Montreal Old and New*, 231.
23 NAC, J.W. Dafoe Papers, Sir Henry Thornton to J.W. Dafoe, 18 June 1924.
24 King Papers, King to Lapointe, 13 October 1922.
25 Ibid., L. Cannon to King, 9 October 1922.
26 Ibid., King to L. Cannon, 14 October 1922.
27 Ibid., Lapointe to J. Bureau, 27 November 1922, copy to King.
28 Ibid., King to Lapointe, 18 December 1922.
29 Lapointe Papers, Vol. 8, P. Roy to 'my dear friend' [Lapointe], 18 October 1922.
30 *Ottawa Citizen*, 19 February 1923.
31 Dawson, *King*, 1:403.
32 NAC, King Diary, 11 January 1923.
33 King Papers, Lapointe to King, 3 March 1923.
34 *DCER*, 3:651.
35 Ibid., 3:652–3; Dawson, *King*, 1:431–4; King Diary, 17–21 February 1923; *Canadian Annual Review 1923*, 53.
36 King Papers, R.M. Dawson to Lapointe, 27 February 1923.
37 Interview, Odette Ouimet, 3 March 1995. Lapointe's deputy minister, Alex Johnston, met him in Washington. The two stayed at the New Willard Hotel. *DCER*, 3:653.
38 King Papers, Lapointe to King, 2 March 1923; King to Lapointe, 2 March 1923.
39 *DCER*, 3:657; Dawson, *King*, 1:435; *Canadian Annual Review 1923*, 53.
40 T.M. Fraser, 'The Little Grey Man! A Personal Sketch of the Hon. W.S. Fielding,' *Maclean's*, 15 May 1923. The author cites Lapointe's signing of the Halibut Treaty as an example of government secrecy. It seems it leaked out when the American press 'carried long despatches revealing that the signing of the Convention had been attended by considerable controversy between the Canadian Government and Sir Auckland Geddes, and that it constituted a constitutional precedent.'

6: Relative Obscurity

1 J.K. Munro, 'When Fielding Came Back,' *Maclean's*, 1 March 1923.
2 Norman Ward, ed., *A Party Politician: The Memoirs of Chubby Power* (Toronto: Macmillan 1966), 378.
3 Queen's University Archives, C.G. Power Papers, Power to King, 19 January 1923.
4 *Le Devoir*, 12 February 1923; Mason Wade, *The French Canadians, 1760–1967*, Vol. 2 (Toronto: Macmillan 1968), 865.

5 Quoted in *Le Devoir*, 13 February 1923.
6 NAC, King Diary, 22 September 1922.
7 Queen's University Archives, T.A. Crerar Papers, Lapointe to Crerar, 21 August 1922. Lapointe's open opposition to Gouin came as no surprise to John Dafoe, the editor of the *Manitoba Free Press*. On 22 July 1922 Dafoe had written his publisher, Sir Clifford Sifton, that 'the feeling between Lapointe and Bureau on the one hand and Gouin on the other is reaching a point where an explosion is inevitable. Lapointe has expressed his opinion very clearly to certain Progressive members with whom he is in confidential relations, but professes himself unable as yet, however, to raise the standard of revolt as he says Gouin has the backing of all the money interests and the support of the Quebec government and the ear of the Quebec press, both French and English. He is, therefore, biding his time.' Ramsay Cook, *The Dafoe-Sifton Correspondence, 1919–1927* (Altona, MB: D.W. Freisen 1966), 120.
8 King Diary, 4 April 1923. See R. MacGregor Dawson, *William Lyon Mackenzie King*, Vol. 1, *A Political Biography, 1874–1923* (Toronto: University of Toronto Press 1958), 444.
9 *Documents on Canadian External Relations (DCER)*, Vol. 3, 533–5, Sir Joseph Pope to Secretary General, League of Nations, 26 April 1923; Lapointe to King, 12 June 1923; Pope to Secretary General, League of Nations, 19 June 1923.
10 Richard Veatch, *Canada and the League of Nations* (Toronto: University of Toronto Press 1975), 84–9.
11 James Eayrs, *In Defence of Canada*, Vol. 1, *From the Great War to the Great Depression* (Toronto: University of Toronto Press 1964), 9–10.
12 J.K. Munro, 'After the Conference Is Over,' *Maclean's*, 15 December 1923.
13 NAC, King Papers, Lapointe to King, [July 1923].
14 Ibid., King's annotations on Lapointe's letter.
15 T.A. Crerar Papers, Crerar to Kirk Cameron, 6 November 1923.
16 *Le Devoir*, 21 November 1923.
17 Robert Rumilly, *Histoire de la Province de Québec*, Vol. 27, *Rivalité Gouin-Lapointe* (Montreal: Fides 1955), 91.
18 *Le Devoir*, 6 November 1923.
19 King Diary, 7 December 1923.
20 Rumilly, *Histoire de Québec*, 27:96.
21 James G. Snell and Frederick Vaughan, *The Supreme Court of Canada: History of the Institution* (Toronto: The Osgoode Society 1985), 119.
22 King Diary, 6 January 1924.
23 Ibid., 5, 10 December 1923.

24 Ibid., 25 January 1924.
25 *Le Devoir*, 2 February 1924.
26 Ibid.

7: Minister of Justice

1 Interview, J.W. Pickersgill, 10 May 1995. Even as an adult, Hugues was called 'Bobby' by family and friends. For example, NAC, King Papers, Odette Ouimet to King, 4 August 1944; Emma Lapointe to King, 4 September 1944.
2 'Mackenzie King accepted the concept of a virtually autonomous Quebec wing with a French-speaking *chef* to lead it. King spoke no French and despite occasional guilty twinges, made no attempt to learn. Although he did not have any special understanding of Quebec, he did understand its importance to his political survival; without a solid Quebec behind him he could kiss the prime ministership goodbye. King carefully chose Ernest Lapointe as his French-Canadian lieutenant and gave him a special place in cabinet and in party councils'; John Herd Thompson and Allen Seager, *Canada, 1922–1939: Decades of Discord* (Toronto: McClelland and Stewart 1985), 115.
3 NAC, King Diary, 14 January 1924; J.K. Munro, 'After the Conference Is Over,' *Maclean's*, 15 December 1923.
4 *Globe*, 15 March 1924; *Montreal Star*, 15 March 1924.
5 King Diary, 16 April 1924, 27 February 1925.
6 Ibid., 23 February 1924; King Papers, King to Lapointe, 24 January 1924.
7 *Le Devoir*, 16, 17 November 1923, 24 January 1924.
8 King Papers, Lapointe to T.A. Low, 23 May 1924.
9 David R. Williams, *Duff: A Life in the Law* (Toronto: The Osgoode Society 1984), 120.
10 King Papers, Lapointe to King, 12 December 1924; King to Lapointe, 22 December 1924.
11 H. Blair Neatby, *William Lyon Mackenzie King*, Vol. 2, *1924–1932: The Lonely Heights* (Toronto: University of Toronto Press 1963), 64; King Diary, 20 February 1924.
12 *Globe*, 11 April 1924; *Saturday Night*, 26 April 1924.
13 E.M. Macdonald, *Recollections, Political and Personal* (Toronto: Ryerson 1938), 543.
14 King Diary, 13 December 1928; *Canadian Annual Review 1924–5*, 234–5.
15 *Canadian Annual Review 1924–5*, 234.
16 Ibid., 250.

17 King Papers, J.L. Ralston to Lapointe, 20 October 1924.
18 Ibid., King to J.L. Ralston, 30 October 1924; J.W. Reid to King, 15 December 1924.
19 Ibid., Lapointe to P.J. Veniot, 13 January 1925.
20 NAC, A.K. Cameron Papers, Cameron to T.A. Crerar, 27 December 1924.
21 King Papers, Lapointe to King, 20 August 1924.
22 Ibid., Sir Eugène Fiset to George Graham, 8 July 1925.
23 Ibid., King to Lapointe, 12 August 1924.
24 Ibid., Lapointe to King, 15 August 1924.
25 NAC, Lapointe Papers, Vol. 27, T.L. Church to Lapointe, 15 February 1939.
26 King Papers, King to Lapointe, 12 August 1924.
27 King Diary, 14 February 1924.
28 King Papers, King to Lapointe, 2, 4 September 1924.
29 Ibid., Sir Henry Thornton to Lapointe, 10 February 1925; Sir E. Fiset to Geo. Graham, 8 July 1925.
30 Ibid., Lapointe to King, 15 May [1925].
31 Lapointe Papers, Vol. 2, P.A. Choquette to Lapointe, 23 May 1925.

8: Leader of the House

1 NAC, King Diary, 17 August 1925.
2 Vernon McKenzie, 'Customs' House-Cleaning Imperative,' *Maclean's* 1 March 1926, 25; House of Commons *Debates*, 2 February 1926, 689; Lita-Rose Betcherman, 'The Customs Scandal of 1926,' *The Beaver* (April/May 2001), 14–19.
3 *Montreal Star*, 24 July 1926.
4 Stevens read part of the transcript into Hansard: House of Commons *Debates*, 2 February 1926, 688–9; McKenzie, 'Customs' House-Cleaning,' 25; Grattan O'Leary, 'The Cruise of the Barge Tremblay,' *Maclean's*, 1 June 1926, 8.
5 King Diary, 3 February 1926; *Saturday Night*, 3 July 1926.
6 NAC, King Papers, Miss E.W. Johnson to King, 14 April 1925.
7 House of Commons *Debates*, 2 February 1926, 683; McKenzie, 'Customs' House-Cleaning,' 44.
8 McKenzie, 'Customs' House-Cleaning,' 44.
9 King Papers, L.C. Moyer to Lapointe, 25 September 1925.
10 NAC, Lapointe Papers, Vol. 8, L. Cannon to Lapointe, 17 December 1925. Cannon asks Lapointe to hold King to his promise to promote him to the cabinet.
11 Ibid., Vol. 2, J. Bureau to Lapointe, 25 April 1925; Lapointe to Bureau, 27 April 1925.

12 Roger Graham, *Arthur Meighen*, Vol. 2, *And Fortune Fled* (Toronto: Clarke Irwin 1963), 341.
13 King Diary, 31 October, 2 November 1925.
14 S. Peter Regenstreif, 'A Threat to Leadership: C.A. Dunning and Mackenzie King,' *Dalhousie Review* (1964), 272–89.
15 Ibid., 280.
16 King Diary, 2 November 1925; *Le Devoir*, 8 January 1926.
17 House of Commons *Debates*, 8 January 1926, 24.
18 Lapointe Papers, Vol. 8, Charles Murphy to Lapointe, 9 January 1926.
19 Ibid., Vol. 2, Oscar Boulanger to Lapointe, 15 January 1926.
20 King Diary, 20 January 1926.
21 Ibid., 9 January 1926.
22 Ibid., 26, 28 January 1926.
23 King Papers, King to Lapointe, 1 February 1926.
24 House of Commons *Debates*, 2 February 1926, 673–4.
25 Ibid., 690, 693.
26 King Diary, 3, 5–6 February 1926.
27 E.M. Macdonald, *Recollections, Political and Personal* (Toronto: Ryerson 1938), 449.
28 *Montreal Herald*, 9 March 1926.
29 Lapointe Papers, Vol. 2, F.-X. Lemieux to Lapointe, 1926.
30 NAC, RG 37, Series B, Vol. 463, transcript, CBC broadcast prepared by Elspeth Chisholm, 'Ernest Lapointe – The Last Lieutenant,' 3 May 1964, 7. Interview with C.D. Power. Chisholm used excerpts from recorded interviews with Lapointe's contemporaries. Ramsay Cook was the historical adviser.
31 King Diary, 23, 26 March 1926.
32 Ibid., 16 February 1926; H. Blair Neatby, *William Lyon Mackenzie King*, Vol. 2, *1924–1932: The Lonely Heights* (Toronto: University of Toronto Press 1963), 203.

9: The Bilingual Schools Issue

1 H. Blair Neatby, *William Lyon Mackenzie King*, Vol. 2, *1924–1932: The Lonely Heights* (Toronto: University of Toronto Press 1963), 100–2.
2 NAC, King Diary, 13 February 1926.
3 Neatby, *King*, 2:127. For a comprehensible account of the Alberta schools question of 1905, see John W. Dafoe, *Clifford Sifton in Relation to His Times* (Toronto: Macmillan 1931), 280–95.
4 House of Commons *Debates*, 18 February 1929, 192.
5 NAC, Lapointe Papers, Vol. 2, Lapointe to Henri Bourassa, 9 March 1926.

6   Ibid., Vol. 2, J.E. Brownlee to O.M. Biggar, 7 April 1926.
7   Ibid., Vol. 2, O.M. Biggar to Brownlee, 7 April 1926.
8   King Diary, 12, 21, 26 May, 22 June 1926.
9   Ibid., 26 May 1926.
10   *Saturday Night*, 3 July 1926.
11   King Diary, 14, 15 June 1926.
12   *Saturday Night*, 26 June 1926; Roger Graham, *Arthur Meighen*, Vol. 2, *And Fortune Fled* (Toronto: Clarke Irwin 1963), 396.
13   King Diary, 7 May, 18 June 1926.
14   *Saturday Night*, 26 June 1926.
15   Neatby, *King*, 2:136–9.
16   Graham, *Meighen*, 2:410.
17   King Diary, 25 June 1926.
18   Neatby, *King*, 2:145–7.
19   Bruce Hutchison, *The Incredible Canadian* (Toronto: Longmans 1952), 119.
20   Neatby, *King*, 2:153–7; Graham, *Meighen* 2:440–1.
21   Hutchison, *Incredible Canadian*, 119.
22   Lapointe Papers, Vol. 80, clipping from *L'Evénement*, 17 July 1926; King Diary, 6 July 1926.
23   *L'Evénement*, 7 July 1926.
24   King Diary, 20 September 1927.

10: The *Margaret* Affair

1   NAC, King Diary, 6 July 1926.
2   NAC, King Papers, Lapointe to King, July 1926.
3   *Montreal Daily Star*, 24 July 1926.
4   *Ottawa Journal*, 26 July 1926.
5   NAC, Lapointe Papers, Vol. 7, clipping from *Le Quotidien*, Lévis, Quebec, 26 July 1926.
6   Norman Ward, ed., *A Party Politician: The Memoirs of Chubby Power* (Toronto: Macmillan 1966), 114.
7   Queen's University Archives, C.G. Power Papers, Power to J. Bureau, 30 July 1926.
8   *Saturday Night*, 7 August 1926.
9   *Ottawa Citizen*, 30 July, 5 August 1926.
10   Unless otherwise noted, sources for the hearing are taken from the Lapointe Papers, Vol. 2, Lemieux Report prepared for Sir Henry Drayton, 18 August 1926. Chief Justice Lemieux's appointment as a one-man commission to conduct an investigation of the customs department was a

Liberal appointment confirmed by a Conservative order-in-council on 25 July 1926. According to the *Ottawa Citizen* (30 July 1926), Sir Henry Drayton, the Conservative House leader, subsequently asked Lemieux to conduct the inquiry into the cruise of the *Margaret* 'because of repeated protests and denials from the Hon. Ernest Lapointe, former minister of justice, that he was on the ship.' In his report, Chief Justice Lemieux praises 'the magnanimity' of Sir Henry Drayton 'who, on the eve of an election, gave two political adversaries opportunity to disculpate themselves from grave and humiliating accusations.'

11 King Diary, 24 June 1926.
12 *Toronto Evening Telegram*, 6 August 1926.
13 *Saturday Night*, 14 August 1926.
14 *Toronto Star*, 7 August 1926.
15 Lapointe Papers, Vol. 2, Lapointe to Mme Lapointe, 20 August 1925.
16 Power Papers, J. Bureau to Power, 31 July 1926.
17 *Toronto Star*, 7 August 1926.
18 Lapointe Papers, Vol. 2, G. Lanctot to Lapointe, 24 August 1926.
19 *Ottawa Citizen*, 7 August 1926. After the business with the *Margaret*, it was no doubt gratifying for Lapointe to have a coast guard ice-breaker named after him. Launched in 1939, the *Ernest Lapointe* is on view at the Musée Maritime Bernier in L'Islet-sur-mer, Quebec.
20 House of Commons *Debates*, 22 June 1926, 4856.
21 King Diary, 7 August 1926.
22 Ward, ed., *Power*, 113.
23 Jean-Charles McGee, *Laurier, Lapointe, St Laurent* (Quebec: Belisle 1948), 200.
24 Lapointe Papers, Vol. 8, Sir Lomer Gouin to Lapointe, 4 September 1926.
25 NAC, Sir Lomer Gouin Papers, Vol. 67, loose page from his diary, 26 July [1926].
26 Ibid., Vol. 67, Diary, 19 August 1926, 231.
27 Lapointe Papers, Vol. 2, A.K. Cameron to Lapointe, 18 September 1926; H.G. Carroll to Lapointe, 18 September 1926.
28 NAC, A.K. Cameron Papers, Vol. 11, Cameron to C.A. Dunning, 15 September 1926; King Diary, 12 September 1926.
29 King Diary, 21 September 1926.
30 Lapointe Papers, Vol. 2, H.G. Carroll to Lapointe, 18 September 1926.
31 Ibid., A.K. Cameron to Lapointe, 18, 20 September 1926; Lapointe to Cameron, 25 September 1926. Cameron exaggerated the number of Jews in Canada as well as their influence. The Jewish population numbered approximately 150,000.
32 King Diary, 20 September 1926.

33 Cameron Papers, Vol. 11, Cameron to W.D. Euler, 9 December 1926.
34 Margaret Prang, *N.W. Rowell· Ontario Nationalist* (Toronto: University of Toronto Press 1975), 434.
35 Lapointe Papers, Vol. 2, Lapointe to Maxime Morin, 25 September 1926.
36 King Diary, 20 September 1926.
37 Sir Lomer Gouin Papers, Vol. 67, Diary, 339, 351, Index: 'French Canadian Ministers against Appointment.'
38 Lapointe Papers, Vol. 3, R. Dandurand to Lapointe, 10 January 1927; Lapointe to Dandurand, 11 January 1927.

11: The Imperial Conference of 1926

1 NAC, Sir Lomer Gouin Papers, Diary, 22 October 1926, 295.
2 NAC, Lapointe Papers, Vol. 8, file 27; NAC, King Diary, 10–16 October 1926; Charles Bowman, *Ottawa Editor* (Sidney, BC: Grays 1966), 95.
3 Susan Mann Robertson, 'Variations on a Nationalist Theme: Henri Bourassa and Abbé Groulx in the 1920s,' *Historical Papers 1970*, Canadian Historical Association, 109–19.
4 King Diary, 20 October 1926.
5 Philip Wigley, *Canada and the Transition to Commonwealth* (Cambridge: Cambridge University Press 1977), 193.
6 C.P. Stacey, *Canada and the Age of Conflict: A History of Canadian External Policies*, Vol. 2, *1921–1948: The Mackenzie King Era* (Toronto: University of Toronto Press 1981), 169.
7 King Diary, 17 October 1926; Wigley, *Transition*, 265.
8 Stacey, *Conflict*, 2:79.
9 NAC, O.D. Skelton Papers, Vol. 3, Skelton to Mrs Skelton, 4 November 1926.
10 King Diary, 18 September 1922. King's invitation to Skelton to accompany him to London in 1923 may have been triggered by a letter from J.W. Dafoe, enclosing a memo by Skelton on the Halibut Treaty. In it Dean Skelton outlined the constitutional way he felt the matter should have been handled. Dafoe sent it on to King at Sir Clifford Sifton's suggestion. It evidently strengthened King's favourable first impression of Skelton. Skelton Papers, Vol. 2, Dafoe to King, 28 March 1923.
11 L.B. Pearson, *Mike: The Memoirs of the Rt. Hon. Lester B. Pearson*, Vol. 1, *1897–1948* (Toronto: University of Toronto Press 1972), 71.
12 Skelton Papers, Vol. 3, Skelton to Mrs Skelton, 19 October 1926.
13 Ibid., Vol. 2, 8 July 1923.
14 Ibid., Vol. 3, 4 November 1926.
15 Wigley, *Transition*, 257.

16 Skelton Papers, Skelton to Mrs Skelton, 19 October 1926.

17 King Diary, 19 October 1926.

18 Ibid., 25 October 1926.

19 *Documents on Canadian External Relations (DCER)*, Vol. 4, 132. Extracts from conference minutes.

20 Skelton Papers, Skelton to Mrs Skelton, 28 October 1926.

21 *DCER*, 4:113.

22 This in the opinion of the journalist D.B. MacRae, who had been sent by the *Manitoba Free Press* to cover the conference. His letters to his editor, J.W. Dafoe, are reproduced in Ramsay Cook, 'A Canadian Account of the 1926 Imperial Conference,' in K. Robinson and W.H. Morris-Jones, eds., *Journal of Commonwealth Political Studies* 3 (1965), 50–63. It should be noted that MacRae's source of information was O.D. Skelton.

23 Skelton Papers, 10 November 1926.

24 House of Commons *Debates*, 30 March 1927, 1712.

25 Bowman, *Ottawa Editor*, 113.

26 Lapointe Papers, Vol. 36, J. Désy to Lapointe, 29 March 1939.

27 Lapointe Papers, Vol. 9, file 33. Minutes of meeting at Foreign Office, 4 November 1926; House of Commons *Debates*, 30 March 1927, 1705.

28 *DCER*, 4:123–4.

29 Ibid., 134–6.

30 For Lapointe's statement, see ibid., 135. King's statement is quoted in Stacey, *Conflict*, 2:81.

31 MacRae to Dafoe, 21 November 1926, in Cook, 'A Canadian Account,' 59. In a series of articles on the Imperial Conference in *Le Devoir*, Henri Bourassa called it a contradiction in terms to say that the Dominions were independent nations so long as they remained in the empire. 'But,' he commented, 'let us not forget that logic is the last thing that Anglo-Saxons are concerned in.' Reported in the *Toronto Star*, 4 February 1927.

32 *DCER*, 4:170.

33 Skelton Papers, Skelton to Mrs Skelton, 19 November 1926.

34 Bowman, *Ottawa Editor*, 113–14.

35 In his study of the King-Lapointe relationship, H. Blair Neatby writes: 'The two men were in agreement on the broad lines of Canada's relations with Great Britain. They were both autonomists, resentful of anything which suggested a subservient or colonial status for Canada, but at the same time accepting a special association within the Commonwealth rather than isolation or independence. Within this area of agreement, however, there was still room for different emphases'; 'Mackenzie King and French Canada,' *Journal of Canadian Studies* 11 (February 1976), 10.

36 Vincent Massey, *What's Past Is Prologue* (Toronto: Macmillan 1963), 152; Sir Lomer Gouin Papers, Diary, 11 December 1926, 345.
37 *Toronto Telegram*, 5 January 1927.
38 *Toronto Star*, 3 February 1927.
39 *Globe*, 3 February 1927.
40 Lapointe Papers, Vol. 3, L.-P. Picard to O.D. Skelton, 28 March 1927, 41. King Diary, 30 March 1927.
41 King Diary, 30 March 1927.
42 Lapointe Papers, Vol. 3, J.O. Apps to J.C. Irons, Mgr. Australasian Line, 30 March 1927; interview, Odette Ouimet, 3 March 1995.
43 Lapointe Papers, Vol. 3, Lapointe to L. Cannon and Lapointe to H. Bourassa, 5 September 1927.
44 Interview, Odette Ouimet, 3 March 1995.
45 NAC, King Papers, Lapointe to King, 29 June 1927.
46 Decoded in King Papers, Lapointe to External, 5 August 1927.
47 Clipping in Lapointe Papers, Vol. 8, file 27.
48 *Ottawa Journal*, 12 August 1927.
49 Lapointe Papers, Vol. 8, O.D. Skelton to Lapointe, 15 August 1927.
50 House of Commons *Debates*, 30 March 1927, 1715.
51 Lapointe Papers, Vol. 9, O.D. Skelton to Lapointe, 16 June 1927.
52 King Diary, 4 September 1927.
53 Lapointe Papers, Vol. 9, O.D. Skelton to King, Report on League of Nations Council Election. Skelton prefaces his report by saying, 'On Sunday, September 5, we received Désy's telegram stating that after conference with Mr. Lapointe, you had authorized Canada to seek seat on Council.'
54 Quoted in Mason Wade, *The French Canadians, 1760–1967*, Vol. 2 (Toronto: Macmillan 1968), 810.
55 Lapointe Papers, Vol. 3, Georges Pelletier to Lapointe, 29 November 1927, enclosing the proof of Bourassa's article.
56 King Diary, 18 October 1927.

12: The Dominion-Provincial Conference of 1927

1 NAC, King Papers, King to Lapointe, 28 June, 15 July 1927; Frederick Griffin, *Variety Show* (Toronto: Macmillan 1936), 208–14.
2 NAC, King Diary, 27 October 1927.
3 *Globe*, 4 November 1927. The press was not admitted, but conference news percolated out through appointed 'official percolaters.'
4 H. Blair Neatby, *William Lyon Mackenzie King*, Vol. 2, *1924–1932: The Lonely Heights* (Toronto: University of Toronto Press 1963), 226–7.

5   According to Ferguson's biographer, 'So long as Regulation 17 remained, there could be no hope of [a Ferguson-Taschereau] alliance. Peter Oliver, *G. Howard Ferguson: Ontario Tory* (Toronto: University of Toronto Press 1977), 283.
6   Ibid., 234–5; *Saturday Night*, 12 November 1927.
7   King Diary, 4 November 1927; *Globe*, 4, 5 November 1927.
8   *Globe*, 10 November 1927; Neatby, *King*, 2:238, 255.
9   R. MacGregor Dawson, *The Government of Canada*, rev. ed. (Toronto: University of Toronto Press 1963), 131.
10 See Paul Bychok, '"La muraille qui vous protège": Ernest Lapointe and French Canada, 1935–1941,' MA thesis, Queen's University, 1985, 157–8.
11 *Globe*, 10 November 1927.
12 King Papers, L.-A. Taschereau to King, 2 February 1928; King to Taschereau, 20 February 1928; Taschereau to King, 2 March 1928.
13 Bourassa article in *Le Devoir*, quoted in *Manitoba Free Press*, 29 December 1927.
14 NAC, Lapointe Papers, Vol. 3, G. Pelletier to Lapointe, 29 November 1927.
15 King Papers, King to Lapointe, 10 October 1927, letter of condolence; Odette Ouimet, telephone conversation, 4 March 1996.
16 Lapointe Papers, Vol. 80, clipping, *L'Action Catholique*, 28 January 1928.
17 Lapointe Papers, Vol. 3, Lapointe to H. Bourassa, 6 September 1927.
18 Neatby, 2:251–4; King Diary, 7 July 1928.
19 Ibid., 28 March 1928.
20 Ibid., 14 December 1928; *Toronto Star*, 13 December 1928.

13: The 'Persons' Case

1   NAC, King Diary, 2 November 1928. The matter in dispute concerned the opening up of two Quebec seats by appointing the sitting members to the bench.
2   Ibid., 29 March 1928.
3   NAC, King Papers, Lapointe to King, 28 December 1927, enclosing Dr Lacasse's letter dated 23 December 1927.
4   King Diary, 4, 9, 10 January 1928.
5   Ibid., 16, 17 November 1927.
6   Ibid., 4 January 1928.
7   NAC, Sir Lomer Gouin Papers, Vol. 67, Diary, 9.
8   NAC, Lapointe Papers, Vol. 7, file 21; *Le Droit*, 25 April 1928.
9   King Diary, 11 March 1930.
10 Interview, Odette Ouimet, 3 March 1995.

11 Thérèse Casgrain, *A Woman in a Man's World* (Toronto: McClelland and Stewart 1972), 63; *Ottawa Journal*, 12 March 1928.

12 King Diary, 6 December 1927.

13 *Ottawa Journal*, 14 March 1928.

14 *In the Matter of a Reference as to the meaning of the word 'Persons' in Section 24 of the British North America Act, 1867* [1928] SCR 276.

15 House of Commons *Debates*, 1928, 2311.

16 *Ottawa Journal*, 25 April 1928.

17 *Le Droit*, 25 April 1928.

18 Casgrain, *A Woman in a Man's World*, 65.

19 *Saturday Night*, 8 September 1928. See also *Ottawa Journal*, 19 March 1928.

20 *Ottawa Journal*, 10 March 1928.

21 Lapointe Papers, Vol. 3, L. Cannon to King, 18 April 1928.

22 House of Commons *Debates*, 6 March 1928, 1055.

23 King Diary, 9 April 1928.

24 King Papers, King to Lapointe, 12 July 1928; Lapointe to King, 18 July 1928.

25 *Ottawa Journal*, 21 March 1928.

26 NAC, A.K. Cameron Papers, Vol. 13, Cameron to P. Cardin, 12 June 1928.

27 Ibid., Lapointe to Cameron, 9 November 1928; J. Robb to Cameron, 5 November 1928.

28 King Diary, 28 December 1928.

14: Silver Anniversaries

1 NAC, King Papers, King to Peter Larkin, 11 March 1929.

2 *Ottawa Citizen*, 8 February 1929.

3 Ibid., 25 February 1929.

4 House of Commons *Debates*, 26 March 1928, 1688–9.

5 Ibid., 18 February 1929, 190–7.

6 NAC, Lapointe Papers, Vol. 3, J.E. Brownlee to Lapointe, 28 December 1928.

7 NAC, King Diary, 18 February 1929.

8 *Ottawa Citizen*, 19 February 1929.

9 House of Commons *Debates*, 19 February 1929, 262–5.

10 C.G.D. Roberts and A.L. Tunnell, eds., *The Canadian Who's Who*, Vol. 2, 1936–7 (Toronto 1937), 199–200.

11 House of Commons *Debates*, 19 February 1929, 264.

12 Lapointe Papers, Vol. 3, P.-A. Cardin to Lapointe, 25 December 1928.

13 King Diary, 14 January 1929.

14 Ibid., 19 February 1929.
15 King Papers, Lapointe to King, [24 February 1929].
16 *Ottawa Citizen*, 20 March 1929.
17 Peter Oliver, G. *Howard Ferguson: Ontario Tory* (Toronto: University of Toronto Press 1977), 355.
18 King Papers, H.R.L. Henry to King, 29 March 1929.
19 King Diary, 30 March 1929.
20 Conrad Black, *Duplessis* (Toronto: McClelland and Stewart 1977), 699. The probable source for this unattributed information is Robert Rumilly, who, Black acknowledges, gave him 'the benefit of his extensive personal experience of the Duplessis era.'
21 Bruce Hutchison, *The Incredible Canadian* (Toronto: Longmans 1952), 67.
22 'Taschereau,' *Maclean's*, 1 February 1934.
23 King Diary, 1 April 1929.
24 King Papers, Lapointe to King, 14 July 1936.
25 King Diary, 11 April 1929.
26 King Papers, P. Paradis to King, 9 August 1928.
27 H. Blair Neatby, *William Lyon Mackenzie King*, Vol. 2, *1924–1932: The Lonely Heights* (Toronto: University of Toronto Press 1963), 302; King Diary, 11 April 1929. Peter Larkin volunteered the information to several reporters that the party had provided 'moderately' for Lapointe and 'handsomely' for King; King Diary, 30 March 1930.
28 King Diary, 16 July 1929.
29 Ibid., 15 May, 27 July 1929.
30 Ibid., 17, 18 June 1929.
31 King Papers, Lapointe to King, 22 August 1929.
32 Lapointe Papers, Vol. 4, O.M. Biggar to W.S. Edwards, 16 December 1929.
33 Ibid., T.C. Davis to King, 8 July 1929.
34 Ibid., Vol. 5, J.T.M. Anderson to King, 17 February 1930; King to J.T.M. Anderson, 22 February 1930.
35 King Diary, 22 February 1930; *Canadian Annual Review 1930*, 48–51.

15: The 1929 Conference on the Operation of Dominion Legislation

1 See NAC, Lapointe Papers, Vol. 6, files 7 and 8. The conference was referred to by its acronym ODL.
2 C.G.D. Roberts and A.L. Tunnell, eds., *The Canadian Who's Who*, Vol. 3, 1938–9 (Toronto: Trans-Canada Press 1939), 565.
3 House of Commons *Debates*, 26 May 1930, 2573.
4 NAC, O.D. Skelton Papers, Vol. 3, 4 and 6 October 1929.

5 Ibid., 6 October 1929.

6 Lapointe Papers, Vol. 6, file 8.

7 Ibid., Vol. 4, R. Dandurand to Lapointe, 30 September 1929.

8 Ibid., Vol. 4; Skelton Papers, Vol. 3, Skelton to Mrs Skelton, 4 October 1929.

9 Skelton Papers, Vol. 3, Skelton to Mrs Skelton, 20 October 1929.

10 Lapointe Papers, Vol. 6, file 9, Conference on ODL and Merchant Shipping, Minutes of merchant shipping committee, 22 October 1929.

11 Ibid., Vol. 4, R. Dandurand to Lapointe, 30 September 1929.

12 Ibid., Vol. 6, file 9, ODL Conference, 22 October 1929.

13 Ibid., 25 October 1929.

14 Skelton Papers, Vol. 3, Skelton to Mrs Skelton, 10 November 1929.

15 Lapointe Papers, Vol. 6, file 9, ODL Conference Minutes, 24 October 1929.

16 Ibid., 25 October 1929.

17 Michael A. Hennessy, 'World War II and the Rebirth and Death of Canada's Merchant Marine,' *Journal of the Canadian Historical Association* (Montreal 1995), 212.

18 Lapointe Papers, Vol. 6, file 10, 'Provisional Conclusions,' 22 October 1929.

19 John MacFarlane, *Ernest Lapointe and Quebec's Influence on Canadian Foreign Policy* (Toronto: University of Toronto Press 1999), 58.

20 Lapointe Papers, Vol. 6, file 11, 'Draft of Agreement to be Adopted at Next Imperial Conference,' 9 November 1929; F.M. Beyers to Lord Passfield, 18 November 1929.

21 Skelton Papers, Vol. 4, Skelton to King, 23 December 1929, 'Confidential Memorandum to supplement Report which will be published.'

22 NAC, RG 37, Series B, Vol. 463, transcript, CBC broadcast prepared by Elspeth Chisholm, 'Ernest Lapointe – The Last Lieutenant,' 3 May 1964, 8.

23 Skelton Papers, Vol. 4, Skelton, confidential memorandum for King, 23 December 1929.

24 Lapointe Papers, Vol. 4, J.R. Clynes to Lapointe, 'Private and Personal.'

25 NAC, King Diary, 16 January and 1 March 1930.

26 *Henrietta Muir Edwards v. Attorney General for Canada* [1930] AC 124 (JCPC). Interestingly enough, at this time women could not sit in the House of Lords. In 1922 a peeress, Viscountess Rhondda, had appealed the ban unsuccessfully (*Viscountess Rhondda's Claim* [1922] 2 AC 339). Chief Justice Anglin had cited this case in his decision, but Lord Sankey rejected it as a precedent.

27 A 1927 amendment to the Supreme Court Act made retirement compulsory at seventy-five. James G. Snell and Frederick Vaughn, *The Supreme Court of Canada: History of the Institution* (Toronto: The Osgoode Society 1985), 125.

28 Lapointe Papers, Vol. 4, King to Lapointe, 4 October 1929; Lapointe to King, 7 October 1929.
29 Ibid., King to Lapointe, 29 November 1929; Lapointe to King, 30 November 1929; King to Lapointe, 3 December 1929.
30 *Montreal Star*, 23 December 1929.
31 Lapointe Papers, Vol. 4, L. Fortin to King, 6 December 1929; Lapointe to Fortin, 2 January 1930; Fortin to Lapointe, n.d.
32 At the last minute, King appointed an MP from the Eastern Townships, W.F. Kay, minister without portfolio. H. Blair Neatby, *William Lyon Mackenzie King*, Vol. 2, *1924–1932: The Lonely Heights* (Toronto: University of Toronto Press 1963), 333.

16: Defeat

1 Wilfrid Eggleston, *While I Still Remember* (Toronto: Ryerson 1968), 162.
2 NAC, Lapointe Papers, Vol. 36, file 170, Financial Statement 1940. The statement shows that Lapointe had a portfolio of stocks, probably purchased during the 1920s boom.
3 NAC, King Papers, Thomas P. King to Lapointe, 28 March 1930.
4 Ibid., H.S. Béland to King, 14 January 1930; Dr Leo Langlois to King, 25 February 1930; King to Lapointe enclosing patronage requests, 21, 30 January, 19 February, 24 July 1930; H.R.L. Henry to L.P. Picard, 24 February 1930; Picard to Henry, 26 February 1930.
5 Ibid., King to Lapointe, 19 July 1930.
6 NAC, King Diary, 2 June 1930.
7 Thérèse Casgrain, *A Woman in a Man's World* (Toronto: McClelland and Stewart 1972), 66.
8 King Diary, 15 February 1930.
9 *Globe*, 26 February 1930.
10 *Canadian Annual Review 1930*, 63.
11 Ibid., 64.
12 Ibid., 52.
13 *Le Devoir*, 20 June 1930.
14 Ibid., 11 July 1930.
15 Ibid., 12 July 1930.
16 Lapointe Papers, Vol. 4, O. Drouin to Lapointe, 27 December 1929.
17 Norman Ward, ed., *A Party Politician: The Memoirs of Chubby Power* (Toronto: Macmillan 1966), 115.
18 King Papers, Lapointe to King, 25 July 1930, quoting his telegram to Sir Henry Thornton.

19 Lapointe Papers, Vol. 5, Sir H. Thornton to Lapointe, May 1930.
20 Ward, ed., *Power*, 115.
21 King Diary, 29 July 1930.
22 King Papers, A.M. Young to King, 3 August 1930.
23 Ibid., King to A.M. Young, 21 August 1930.
24 *Le Devoir*, 5 July 1930.
25 King Diary, 5 August 1930. One of those expressing astonishment was Sir Henry Thornton.
26 Ibid., 27 July 1930.
27 King to Odette Lapointe [Ouimet], 27 August 1930. Letter in possession of Mme Ouimet.
28 King Diary, 14 December 1930; King Papers, King to Lapointe, 15 December 1930, 24 January 1931; telephone interview, Odette Ouimet, 27 November 1995.
29 King Diary, 16 December 1930; King Papers, King to Lapointe, 15 December 1930.
30 King Papers, King to Lapointe, 30 December 1930.
31 Ibid., Lapointe to King, 22 January 1931.
32 King Diary, 24 February 1931.

17: Member of the Opposition

1 Leslie Roberts, 'The Wife of a Politician,' *Chatelaine* (May 1931), 75.
2 House of Commons *Debates*, 30 June 1931, 3200.
3 Ibid., 3202.
4 Ibid., 3204.
5 James G. Snell and Frederick Vaughan, *The Supreme Court of Canada: History of the Institution* (Toronto: The Osgoode Society 1985), 186.
6 Norman Ward, ed., *A Party Politician: The Memoirs of Chubby Power* (Toronto: Macmillan 1966), 333–4.
7 House of Commons *Debates*, 1931, 323–4.
8 NAC, King Diary, 28 April, 26 May 1931.
9 Ibid., 10 June 1931.
10 NAC, King Papers, L.-A. Taschereau to King, 13 June 1931.
11 Ibid., King to T.A. Crerar, 17 June 1931.
12 King Diary, 13 July 1931.
13 Ibid., 28 July 1931. King records that nine years after the scandal, Dr McDougald told him that he had transferred some securities to Lapointe (presumably some of his own shares in Beauharnois), and King recalled that 'it was Bennett's reference to securities given to Lapointe which

caused me not to go further than I otherwise would have gone in the case of the Beauharnois matter when brought up in the House of Commons by Bennett' (King Diary, 21 August 1940).

14 Ibid., 17–31 July 1931; T.D. Regehr, *The Beauharnois Scandal: A Story of Canadian Entrepreneurship and Politics* (Toronto: University of Toronto Press 1990); T.D. Regehr, 'High Powered Lawyers, Veteran Lobbyists, Cunning Propagandists: Canadian Lawyers and the Beauharnois Scandal,' in Carol Wilton, ed., *Beyond the Law* (Toronto: The Osgoode Society 1990), 403–24.

15 Ward, ed., *Power*, 325; King Papers, C.G. Power to King, 2[?] August 1931.

16 King Papers, King to C.G. Power, 4 September 1931.

17 Interview, Odette Ouimet, 3 March 1995.

18 Bernard Vigod, *Quebec before Duplessis: The Political Career of Louis-Alexandre Taschereau* (Montreal: McGill-Queen's University Press 1986), 190–1; Conrad Black, *Duplessis* (Toronto: McClelland and Stewart 1977), 99.

19 King Diary, 21 January 1932.

20 Vigod, *Taschereau*, 190.

21 Interview, Odette Ouimet, 3 March 1995.

22 Ibid. Odette Lapointe's future husband, Roger Ouimet, was one of the young Liberal rebels and founders of L'Action Libérale Nationale.

23 King Diary, 28 June 1932.

24 Ibid., 3–14 July 1932.

25 Ibid., 24 May 1932.

26 R.T.L., 'Mr. Lapointe,' *Maclean's*, December 1933.

18: Back in Power

1 NAC, King Papers, King to Lapointe, 24 August 1933.

2 Philippe Ferland, *Paul Gouin* (Montreal: Guerin 1991), 37–8.

3 Thérèse Casgrain, *A Woman in a Man's World* (Toronto: McClelland and Stewart 1972), 77–8.

4 Ferland, *Gouin*, 52.

5 Norman Ward, ed., *A Party Politician: The Memoirs of Chubby Power* (Toronto: Macmillan 1966), 332.

6 King Papers, R.H. Babbage to King, 28 September 1934.

7 Ward, ed., *Power*, 332.

8 King Papers, King to Bernard Rose, 29 August 1934.

9 Ibid., Lapointe to King, 13 December 1933.

10 Ibid., Vincent Massey to King, 26 August 1933.

11 Ibid., King to Lapointe, 30 August 1933.

12 Ibid., Vincent Massey to King, 30 August 1933.
13 NAC, Lapointe Papers, Vol. 5, C.G. Cowan to Lapointe, 24 October 1933;
    Dr H.M. Tory to Lapointe, 25 October 1933; Lapointe to Tory, October 1933;
    Cairine Wilson to Lapointe, 25 October 1933.
14 King Papers, N.P. Lambert to Lapointe, 25 January 1934.
15 *Ottawa Citizen*, 23 June 1934.
16 Conrad Black, *Duplessis* (Toronto: McClelland and Stewart 1977), 75, 90;
    Jean-Guy Genest, *Godbout* (Sillery: Septentrion 1996), 86.
17 Queen's University Archives, C.G. Power Papers, Power to Lapointe,
    17 August 1934.
18 Lapointe Papers, Vol. 5, L.-A. Taschereau to Lapointe, 23 August 1934;
    Lapointe to Taschereau, 24 August 1934.
19 Casgrain, *A Woman in a Man's World*, 81.
20 Lapointe Papers, Vol. 5, L.-A. Taschereau to Lapointe, 31 August,
    19 September, 24 September 1934.
21 NAC, King Diary, 6 September 1934; King Papers, Lapointe to King,
    17 September 1934.
22 King Papers, King to Lapointe, 22 September 1934; Lapointe to King,
    23 September 1934.
23 Ibid., King to J.C. Patteson, General Agent, Canadian Pacific Steamships,
    25 September 1934.
24 King Diary, 5–12 October 1934.
25 Bernard Vigod, *Quebec before Duplessis: The Political Career of Louis-
    Alexandre Taschereau* (Montreal: McGill-Queen's University Press 1986),
    197; Black, *Duplessis*, 89.
26 Ward, ed., *Power*, 335; Black, *Duplessis*, 90.
27 Black, *Duplessis*, 90.
28 James Eayrs, *In Defence of Canada*, Vol. 2, *Appeasement and Rearmament*
    (Toronto: University of Toronto Press 1965), 4.
29 House of Commons *Debates*, 1936, 122.
30 King Papers, King to Lapointe, 24 September 1935.
31 Jean-Charles McGee, *Laurier, Lapointe, St Laurent* (Quebec: Belisle 1948),
    239.
32 King Diary, 17 October 1935.
33 Ibid., 17 October 1935.
34 *Ottawa Journal*, 19 October 1935.

19: The Ethiopian Crisis

1 Léopold Richer, *Silhouettes du monde politique* (Montreal: Éditions Zodiac

1940), 67–8. *Le Devoir's* parliamentary correspondent describes Power as more French than English.

2 Paul Martin, *A Very Public Life*, Vol. 1 (Ottawa: Deneau 1983), 167.

3 NAC, King Papers, J.B. Bickersteth to King, 8 December 1929.

4 Richard Veatch, *Canada and the League of Nations* (Toronto: University of Toronto Press 1975), 155–6. According to Veatch, 'although the King government had assumed office on 23 October, Riddell had received no instructions since that date regarding what position to take in the session of the Committee of Eighteen which had just resumed, although he had sent repeated requests emphasizing the urgent need for instructions.'

5 King's statement to the press is reproduced in James Eayrs, *In Defence of Canada*, Vol. 2, *Appeasement and Rearmament* (Toronto: University of Toronto Press 1965), 18–19.

6 L.B. Pearson, *Mike: The Memoirs of the Rt. Hon. Lester B. Pearson*, Vol. 1, *1897–1948* (Toronto: University of Toronto Press 1972), 98.

7 J.A. Munro, 'The Riddell Affair Reconsidered,' *External Affairs* (October 1969), sums up the situation as follows: 'An examination of the files of the Department of External Affairs suggests that, while Riddell was left, as he suggested, without thorough instructions, he was, at the same time, not authorized to act independently' (p. 367).

8 R. Bothwell and J. English, 'Dirty Work at the Crossroads: New Perspectives on the Riddell Incident,' *Journal of the Canadian Historical Association* (1972), 276; *Montreal Gazette*, 2 November 1935.

9 Bernard Vigod, *Quebec before Duplessis: The Political Career of Louis-Alexandre Taschereau* (Montreal: McGill-Queen's University Press 1986), 222.

10 Ibid., 224; Conrad Black, *Duplessis* (Toronto: McClelland and Stewart 1977), 104.

11 The Department of External Affairs in the 1930s was decidedly isolationist under O.D. Skelton, with Loring Christie and Laurent Beaudry as the seconds-in-command. See J.L. Granatstein, *The Ottawa Men: The Civil Service Mandarins, 1935–1957* (Toronto: University of Toronto Press 1982), 86–7. See also John Herd Thompson and Allen Seager, *Canada, 1922–1939: Decades of Discord* (Toronto: McClelland and Stewart 1985), at 326: 'Isolationism was so fashionable at the Department of External Affairs,' and P.B. Waite, 'French-Canadian Isolationism and English Canada: An Elliptical Foreign Policy, 1935–1939,' *Journal of Canadian Studies* 18 (1983), 137: 'important senior officers in the Department of External Affairs held the isolationist positions.'

12 Munro, 'Riddell Affair,' 374–5.

13 Ibid., 373–4; NAC, King Diary, 29 November 1935. Most historians ascribe the repudiation of Riddell primarily to King, but Lapointe would seem to have been the initiator. J.A. Munro comments: 'There is no way of knowing if he [King] would have acted without Lapointe's urging ('Riddell Affair,' p. 374). John MacFarlane states that 'a look at the views of each [King and Lapointe] throughout the crisis – from August to December – indicates that King was not as uncomfortable as Lapointe about the Canadian position and that the prime minister only acted when pushed by his Quebec lieutenant'; *Ernest Lapointe and Quebec's Influence on Canadian Foreign Policy* (Toronto: University of Toronto Press 1999), 97.

14 Lapointe's press release is reproduced in Eayrs, *Appeasement*, 24.

15 Bothwell and English, 'Dirty Work at the Crossroads,' 280.

16 *Le Droit*, 6 December 1935.

17 W.A. Riddell, *World Security by Conference* (Toronto: Ryerson 1947), 129. At a time when the most ardent French-Canadian nationalists sought no more than bilingualism, Beaudry demanded that the government service become unilingually French. Appointed to act as under-secretary of state in Skelton's absence in 1937, Beaudry wrote to King in French, demanding that all correspondence to and from External Affairs be conducted in French. Threatening to resign otherwise, he said that he was making language an issue because his race was suffering from injustice. King and Skelton concluded that Beaudry was having a nervous breakdown and sent him off on paid leave. King Diary, 22, 23 April 1937.

18 Margaret Prang, *N.W. Rowell: Ontario Nationalist* (Toronto: University of Toronto Press 1975), 482. According to C.P. Stacey, 'It is not surprising that a government as dependent on Quebec as King's should shy away from the bold sanctionist policies of Ferguson and Riddell.' C.P. Stacey, *Canada and the Age of Conflict: A History of Canadian External Policies*, Vol. 2, *1921–1948: The Mackenzie King Era* (Toronto: University of Toronto Press 1981), 186–7.

19 Prang, *Rowell*, 482–3; NAC, Lapointe Papers, Vol. 31, N.W. Rowell to Lapointe, 2 December 1935; Lapointe to Rowell, 3 December 1935.

20 Lapointe Papers, Lapointe to R.B. Inch, 5 December 1935.

21 Ibid., R. Dandurand to Lapointe, 4 December 1935.

22 Ibid., Vol. 25, H.G. Carroll to Lapointe, 2 December 1935.

23 Bothwell and English, 'Dirty Work at the Crossroads,' 280; Veatch, *Canada and the League of Nations*, 162.

24 The letters pro and con Lapointe's press release are in Vol. 25 of his papers.

25 *Ottawa Citizen*, 7 December 1935.

26 House of Commons *Debates*, 1936, 123.

27 Bruce Hutchison, *The Far Side of the Street* (Toronto: Macmillan 1976), 107–8.
28 King Diary, 11 December 1935. A recent study suggests that Canada's lack of support influenced Britain's retreat from sanctions. See Brock Millman, 'Canada, Sanctions, and the Abyssinian Crisis of 1935,' *The Historical Journal* 40 (1997), 143–68.
29 Vigod, *Taschereau*, 227.
30 Ibid., 232–3; Lapointe Papers, Vol. 30, H.R. Renault to Lapointe, 4 December 1935; J.B. Archambault to Lapointe, 8 December 1935; Lapointe to J.B. Archambault, 10 December 1935.
31 King Diary, 19 December 1935.
32 Ibid., 8 January 1936.
33 NAC, O.D. Skelton Papers, Diary, 9 January 1936.
34 Queen's University Archives, C.G. Power Papers, Box 105A, Taped interview with J. Meisel, 3/5/60.

20: The Curse of Patronage

1 NAC, King Papers, Henri Bourassa to King, 19 May 1936.
2 NAC, Lapointe Papers, Vol. 30, H.P. Drouin to Lapointe, 6 March, 25 March 1936; L. Letourneau to Lapointe, 29 February, 6 March 1936; Lapointe to Letourneau, 28 March 1936.
3 Ibid., L. Faguy to Lapointe, 26 March 1936; Lapointe to L. Faguy, 30 March 1936. Lapointe might have added that in the first year of the Liberals' return to power, 44 per cent more was spent on Quebec harbour than the average annual expenditure for the port during the Bennett administration. Louis Beaudry to Lapointe, 12 December 1938, cited in Paul Bychok, '"La muraille qui vous protège": Ernest Lapointe and French Canada, 1935–1941,' MA thesis, Queen's University, 1985, 109.
4 King Papers, Lapointe to C. Dunning, 20 February 1936.
5 Mason Wade, *The French Canadians, 1760–1967*, Vol. 2 (Toronto: Macmillan 1968), 906; Lapointe Papers, Vol. 25, Fr T. Mignault to Lapointe, 9 January 1936.
6 Lapointe Papers, Lapointe to T.A. Crerar, 21 January 1936; Crerar to Lapointe, 22 February 1936.
7 Ibid., Fr T. Mignault to Lapointe, 22 January 1936; Mme Chavanon to Lapointe, 15 July 1940.
8 NAC, King Diary, 28 March 1936.
9 King Papers, Lapointe to King, 14 April 1936.
10 King Diary, 6 May 1936.

11 House of Commons *Debates*, 19 June 1936, 3905.

12 Lapointe Papers, Vol. 16, O. Boulanger to Cardinal Villeneuve, 25 September 1936.

13 House of Commons *Debates*, 11 June 1936, 3630.

14 Lapointe Papers, Vol. 31, W. Lacroix to Lapointe, 20 June 1936.

15 Ibid., Vol. 12, President, St Jean-Baptiste Society, to Lapointe, 24 March 1936.

16 Ibid., R. Denis to Lapointe, 11 June 1936; L.-P. Picard to Denis, 20 June 1936; Lapointe to C.D. Howe, 22 June 1936. In the first draft of the letter to Denis, which was not sent, Picard says, 'You know with what devotion the Minister occupies himself with the nationalist cause ...'

17 Ibid., W. O'Leary to King, 19 June 1936.

18 See Jean-Guy Genest, *Godbout* (Sillery: Septentrion 1996); Norman Ward, ed., *A Party Politician: The Memoirs of Chubby Power* (Toronto: Macmillan 1966), 341.

19 *Ottawa Citizen*, 21, 27 July, 6 August 1936; King Diary, 26 July 1936.

20 Ward, ed., *Power*, 342.

21 *Le Devoir*, 19 August 1936; Jean-Charles McGee, *Laurier, Lapointe, St Laurent* (Quebec: Belisle 1948).

22 King Diary, 14 August 1936.

23 Ibid., 19 August 1936.

24 Ibid., 25 August 1936; *Le Devoir*, 22 August 1936.

25 King Papers, Lapointe to F. Rinfret, 25 June 1936.

26 King Diary, 15 September 1936.

27 *Le Devoir*, 16, 24 September 1936.

28 Ibid., 11 September 1936.

29 *Montreal Gazette*, 1 October 1936; *Le Devoir*, 2 October 1936. Lapointe's letter, which he circulated to the Quebec caucus, is fully discussed in Bychok, 'Ernest Lapointe,' 92–4.

30 Lapointe Papers, Vol. 27, Secretary, Club Lapointe, to Lapointe, 8 October 1936.

31 Ibid., Vol. 30, F. Fafard to L.-P. Picard, 21 October 1936.

32 Ibid., Lapointe to L. Faguy, 30 March 1936.

33 King Diary, 27 November 1936.

34 King Papers, P. Roy to King, 24 October, 7, 16 November 1936; King to P. Roy, 25 November 1936.

35 Lapointe Papers, Vol. 30, Anon. [Campeau] to Lapointe, 30 October 1936; Agent, Ministry of Transport, Branch of Ministry of Marine, to L.P. Picard, 7 December 1936.

36 King Papers, Lapointe to King, 19 December 1936.
37 King Diary, 18 December 1936.

21: The Padlock Act

1 NAC, King Diary, 5 January 1937.
2 Queen's University Archives, C.G. Power Papers, Box 105A, Taped interview with J. Meisel, 3/5/60.
3 NAC, Lapointe Papers, Vol. 16, Msg. Elias Roy to Lapointe, 3 March 1937.
4 Lita-Rose Betcherman, *The Swastika and the Maple Leaf: Fascist Movements in Canada in the Thirties* (Toronto: Fitzhenry and Whiteside 1975), 87.
5 King Diary, 18 December 1936.
6 Ibid., 13 March 1936; NAC, King Papers, Lapointe to King, 14 April 1936.
7 King Diary, 20 September 1936.
8 Ibid., 10 September, 18 December 1936.
9 H. Blair Neatby, *William Lyon Mackenzie King*, Vol. 3, *1932–1939: The Prism of Unity* (Toronto: University of Toronto Press 1976), 182–3.
10 Andrée Levesque, *Virage à Gauche Interdit: Les communistes, les socialistes et leurs ennemis au Québec, 1929–1939* (Montreal: Boréal 1984), 138.
11 Lapointe Papers, Vol. 16, Lapointe to Msg. Elias Roy, 19 April 1937.
12 King Papers, M. Hepburn to Lapointe, 8 April 1937.
13 King Diary, 14, 15 April 1937.
14 Desmond Morton with Terry Copp, *Working People: An Illustrated History of Canadian Labour* (Ottawa: Deneau 1980), 160.
15 Bernard Figler, *Sam Jacobs: Member of Parliament* (Gardenvale, PQ: Harpell's Press 1959), 217.
16 King Diary, 30 March 1937.
17 L.B. Pearson, *Mike: The Memoirs of the Rt. Hon. Lester B. Pearson*, Vol. 1, *1897–1948* (Toronto: University of Toronto Press 1972), 120. The future Liberal prime minister writes: 'In a very real sense, Mr. King was a "Canada First" isolationist, notwithstanding all his emotional speeches on the mother country and the glory of our inherited parliamentary and monarchical institutions, and his equally emotional reflections on the brotherhood of all men and the internationalism implied by this brotherhood' (p. 69).
18 King Papers, Fr P.-M. Gaudrault to King, 21 April 1937.
19 Ibid., King to Prime Minister of Great Britain [Stanley Baldwin], 22 April 1937.
20 King Diary, 23 April 1937.

21 Lapointe Papers, Vol. 30, file 126, Anon. to Lapointe, 13 May 1937.
22 Mason Wade, *The French Canadians, 1760–1967*, Vol. 2 (Toronto: Macmillan 1968), 907; *Le Devoir*, 24 April 1937.
23 J.M. Nadeau, 'Does the Province of Quebec Want Secession?' *Saturday Night*, 21 November 1936.
24 Lapointe Papers, Vol. 12, H. Bourassa to Lapointe, 26 January, 2 February 1937.
25 Ibid., Vol. 30, file 122.
26 Ibid., Mme J.E. Courrier to Lapointe, 2 March 1936; Thérèse Casgrain, *A Woman in a Man's World* (Toronto: McClelland and Stewart 1972), 79.
27 King Diary, 25 September, 1 October 1937. Despite this wistful remark, Odette Ouimet recalls that King did not visit her parents' home.

22: Aberhart's Legislation Disallowed

1 NAC, King Diary, 8 January 1937.
2 Ibid., 26 January 1937; G.V. Ferguson, *John W. Dafoe* (Toronto: Ryerson 1948), 87.
3 Wilfrid Eggleston, *While I Still Remember* (Toronto: Ryerson 1968), 233–9.
4 NAC, Lapointe Papers, Vol. 20, W.N. Tilley to Lapointe, 8 December 1936.
5 Ibid., G.W. Auxier to Lapointe, 14 September 1936.
6 King Diary, 5, 17 August 1937.
7 NAC, King Papers, J.C. Bowen to Lapointe, 23 September 1937.
8 King Diary, 28 September 1937.
9 King Papers, Lapointe to J.C. Bowen, 4 October 1937.
10 Mason Wade, *The French Canadians, 1760–1967*, Vol 2 (Toronto: Macmillan 1968), 909. Ironically, in 1918 J.N. Francoeur had tabled a motion in the provincial legislature to end 'the Confederation Pact' because of English Canada's hostility to Quebec over the war (Wade, 2:754–5).
11 Norman Ward, ed., *A Party Politician: The Memoirs of Chubby Power* (Toronto: Macmillan 1966), 122–3.
12 King Papers, Lapointe to King, 29 December 1937.
13 House of Commons *Debates*, 1 February 1937, 75.
14 NAC, Department of Justice Papers, Vol. 2559, Memorandum, P. Fontaine to Acting Deputy Minister, 6 November 1937.
15 Ibid., Social Service Council of Canada to Governor in Council, 14 March 1938; David R. Williams, *Duff: A Life in the Law* (Toronto: The Osgoode Society 1984), 198.

16 Conrad Black, *Duplessis* (Toronto: McClelland and Stewart 1977), 179–80.
17 See Lapointe Papers, Vol. 39, for letters for and against disallowance of the Padlock Act.
18 Ibid., M. Shumiatcher to King, 4 March 1938.
19 House of Commons *Debates*, 8 April 1938, 2167; 27 May 1938, 3319; 3 January 1939, 211. The purpose of the reference was to determine if Parliament had the authority to terminate appeals to the Privy Council. The Duff court answered in the affirmative. However, owing to the war the matter did not go to the Judicial Committee of the Privy Council until 1946. Although the latter upheld the Duff decision, owing to the Liberals' habitual caution the Supreme Court did not become the final court of appeal until 1949. James G. Snell and Frederick Vaughan, *The Supreme Court of Canada: History of the Institution* (Toronto: The Osgoode Society 1985), 186–90.
20 King Diary, 30 August 1936.
21 Irving Abella and Harold Troper, *None Is Too Many* (Toronto: Lester and Orpen Dennys 1982), 28.
22 King Diary, 17 May 1938.
23 King Papers, Memorandum for cabinet, 18 May 1938; E.A. Pickering to King, 2 June 1938.
24 Ibid., H.M. Caiserman to King, 25 August 1937; E.A. Pickering to King, 14 September 1937; Lita-Rose Betcherman, *The Swastika and the Maple Leaf: Fascist Movements in Canada in the Thirties* (Toronto: Fitzhenry and Whiteside 1975), 94–5.
25 King Papers, Lapointe to King, 7 June, 1 July 1938.
26 Interview, Odette Ouimet, 3 March 1995.
27 King Diary, 20 May 1938.
28 Interview, J.W. Pickersgill, 10 May 1995. This was Pickersgill's personal opinion and is open to question.
29 King Diary, 28 May 1938.
30 J.W. Pickersgill, *Seeing Canada Whole: A Memoir* (Toronto: Fitzhenry and Whiteside 1994), 166.
31 King Papers, Ernest Lapointe, Minister of Justice, to His Excellency, the Governor General in Council, 13 June 1938.
32 Department of Justice Papers, Vol. 2559, Memorandum, P. F[ontaine], 18 June 1938.
33 Ibid., Lapointe to Canadian Civil Liberties Union, 5 July 1938.
34 E. Forsey, 'Mr. Lapointe and the Padlock Act,' *Canadian Forum* (August 1938), 148–50.

35 Interview, Odette Ouimet, 3 March 1995. But according to King, Lapointe 'seemed to seek to justify the legislation itself' on jurisdictional grounds (Diary, 5 July 1938).

23: In the Appeasers' Camp

1 NAC, King Diary, 26, 31 August 1938.
2 Ibid., 31 August 1938.
3 Paul Martin, *A Very Public Life*, Vol. 1 (Ottawa: Deneau 1983), 200–1.
4 R.R. James, ed., *Chips: The Diaries of Sir Henry Channon* (London: Penguin 1967), 204; William L. Shirer, *Berlin Diary* (New York: Knopf 1941), 124.
5 Martin, *A Very Public Life*, 1:203.
6 NAC, O.D. Skelton Papers, Diary, 20 May, 23 September 1938.
7 NAC, King Papers, King to Hume Wrong, 22 September 1938; Wrong to King, 23 September 1938.
8 Ibid., King to Wrong [for Lapointe], 23 September 1938.
9 Ibid., Lapointe to King, 24 September 1938.
10 Skelton Papers, Diary, 24 September 1938.
11 King Papers, King to Lapointe, 26 September 1938; Wrong to King, 27 September 1938.
12 Ibid., King to Lapointe, 30 September 1938.
13 King Diary, 12, 13 November 1938.
14 *Le Devoir*, 18 November 1938.
15 King Diary, 18 November 1938.
16 Ibid., 23 November 1938.
17 Ibid., 24 November 1938; *Le Devoir*, 3 December 1938.
18 Gerald E. Dirks, *Canada's Refugee Policy: Indifference or Opportunism?* (Montreal: McGill-Queen's University Press 1977), 78. Both M.J. Coldwell and J.W. Pickersgill told Gerald Dirks that Lapointe and Fernand Rinfret championed the restrictive immigration policy that kept out Jewish refugees (p. 59). Lapointe was also against admitting the anti-Nazi Sudetens and (not surprisingly) Spanish loyalist refugees (King Diary, 6 March 1939).
19 King Diary, 1 December 1938.
20 *Le Devoir*, 28 November 1938.
21 Ibid., 13 December 1938.
22 NAC, Lapointe Papers, Vol. 27, S.J. Moreau to Lapointe, 13 December 1938; L.-A. Taschereau to Lapointe, 14 December 1938.
23 *Le Devoir*, 11 December 1938.

24 King Papers, D. Raymond to Lapointe, 3 December 1938.
25 Ibid., Lapointe to King, 26 December 1938.

24: Neutrality Abandoned

1 NAC, King Diary, 16, 19 January 1939.
2 Ibid., 18 January 1939.
3 Ibid., 20, 27 January 1939.
4 Ibid., 27 January 1939.
5 NAC, O.D. Skelton Papers, Diary, 2 February 1939.
6 King Diary, 18 February 1939; J.W. Pickersgill, *Seeing Canada Whole: A Memoir* (Toronto: Fitzhenry and Whiteside 1994), 166; *Toronto Star*, 21 February 1939.
7 NAC, King Papers, C. Power to King, 14 February 1939; King to Power, 15 February 1939.
8 *Toronto Evening Telegram*, 11 March 1939.
9 King Papers, Edith Macdonald to King, 13 March 1939.
10 King Diary, 21 March 1939.
11 NAC, Lapointe Papers, Vol. 23, file 79A.
12 King Diary, 28 March 1939.
13 Conrad Black, *Duplessis* (Toronto: McClelland and Stewart 1977), 195.
14 House of Commons *Debates*, 31 March 1939, 2468.
15 André Laurendeau, *Witness for Quebec*, trans. P. Stratford (Toronto: Macmillan 1973), 13.
16 King Diary, 31 March 1939.
17 House of Commons *Debates*, 30 March 1939, 2443.
18 Ibid., 31 March 1939, 2468; Elspeth Chisholm, '"Never": Ernest Lapointe and Conscription,' *Canada: An Historical Magazine*, no. 3 (March 1976), 6–9.
19 King Diary, 31 March 1939.
20 R.W. Baldwin, 'Mr. Lapointe Is the Number One Statesman,' *Saturday Night*, 8 April 1939, 5.
21 King Diary, 31 March 1939.
22 Lapointe Papers, Vol. 23, J.M. Macdonnell to Lapointe, 1 April 1939.
23 King Papers, Lapointe to King, 12 June 1939; King to Lapointe, same day.
24 Black, *Duplessis*, 196.
25 Pickersgill, *Seeing Canada Whole*, 167; interview, J.W. Pickersgill, 10 May 1995.
26 King Papers, King to Skelton, 8 June 1939; Irving Abella and Harold Troper, *None Is Too Many* (Toronto: Lester and Orpen Dennys 1982), 91–2.

27 King Diary, 8 June 1939.
28 King Papers, 'External' [O.D. Skelton] to 'Beaver' [King], 9 June 1939; Abella and Troper, *None Is Too Many*, 92.
29 Gerald E. Dirks, *Canada's Refugee Policy: Indifference or Opportunism?* (Montreal: McGill-Queen's University Press 1977), 61.
30 House of Commons *Debates*, 30 January 1939, 434.

25: Canada Goes to War

1 Queen's University Archives, Grant Dexter Papers, Memorandum of conversation with Lapointe and Picard, 28 June 1939.
2 Léopold Richer, 'Ernest Lapointe,' *L'Action Nationale* (December 1941), 272.
3 NAC, Lapointe Papers, Vol. 31, Lapointe to Georges Pelletier, 5 June 1939; Pelletier to Lapointe, 7 June 1939; Lapointe to Pelletier, 7 June 1939; Pelletier to Lapointe, 12 June 1939. At a symposium in 1922, Georges Pelletier expressed his view that a separate French-Canadian state was a viable proposition. See Mason Wade, *The French Canadians, 1760–1967*, Vol. 2 (Toronto: Macmillan 1968), 886.
4 NAC, King Papers, Lapointe to King, 19 July 1939.
5 Lapointe Papers, Vol. 39, file 17. Typescript of a speech by Sam Gobeil at St Hyacinthe, 9 July 1939.
6 NAC, King Diary, 24 August 1939.
7 Ibid., 11, 25 August 1939.
8 Ibid., 25 August 1939; James Eayrs, *In Defence of Canada*, Vol. 2, *Appeasement and Rearmament* (Toronto: University of Toronto Press 1965), 79.
9 Bruce Hutchison, *The Incredible Canadian* (Toronto: Longmans 1952), 250–1.
10 King Papers, Lapointe to King, 31 August 1939; King Diary, 1 September 1939.
11 Wilfrid Eggleston, *While I Still Remember* (Toronto: Ryerson 1968), 253–4.
12 Lapointe Papers, Vol. 50, S.T. Wood to Lapointe, 25 August 1939; Reg Whitaker, 'Official Repression of Communism during World War II,' *Labour/Le Travail* (Spring 1986), 138; Frederick W. Gibson and Barbara Robertson, eds. *Ottawa at War: The Grant Dexter Memoranda, 1939–1945* (Winnipeg: Manitoba Record Society Publications 1994), 19.
13 King Diary, 3 September 1939.
14 Lapointe Papers, Vol. 48, Resolution of the Comité de Défense Nationale; Conrad Black, *Duplessis* (Toronto: McClelland and Stewart 1977), 201–2; *Le Devoir*, 5 September 1939; *Montreal Gazette*, 5 September 1939; André Laurendeau, *Witness for Quebec*, trans. P. Stratford (Toronto: Macmillan 1973), 17–18.

15 Norman Ward, ed. *A Party Politician: The Memoirs of Chubby Power* (Toronto: Macmillan 1966), 123.
16 Robert Rumilly, *Histoire de la Province de Québec*, Vol. 38, *Ernest Lapointe* (Montreal: Fides 1968), 17.
17 King Diary, 9 September 1939.
18 Ibid., 7 September 1939.
19 *Globe and Mail*, 9 September 1939.
20 Hutchison, *Incredible Canadian*, 251–5.
21 Ibid., 257–8; *Globe and Mail*, 11 September 1939; Elspeth Chisholm, '"Never": Ernest Lapointe and Conscription,' *Canada: An Historical Magazine*, no. 3 (March 1976), 13–17. Lapointe's original notes for this speech, typed and handwritten, are to be found in his papers, Vol. 50, file 35.
22 *Globe and Mail*, 11 September 1939.
23 Lapointe Papers, Vol. 23, J.W. Dafoe to Lapointe, 10 September 1939.
24 King Diary, 9 September 1939.
25 Lapointe Papers, Vol. 23, Lapointe to Judge Albert Sevigny, 14 September 1939.
26 Ibid., Le Comité des Droits des Canadiens Français, Lévis, to Lapointe, 21 September 1939.
27 King Papers, Memorandum, A.D.P. Heeney to King, 3 October 1939.
28 King Diary, 12 September 1939.
29 Interview with J.W. Pickersgill, 10 May 1995; Ward, ed., *Power*, 123; Laurendeau, *Witness for Quebec*, 21–2.

26: Duplessis Beaten

1 J.L. Granatstein, *Canada's War: The Politics of the Mackenzie King Government, 1939–1945* (Toronto: Oxford University Press 1975), 25.
2 NAC, King Papers, Brooke Claxton to G.V. Ferguson, 3 October 1939.
3 Robert Rumilly, *Histoire de la Province de Québec*, Vol. 38, *Ernest Lapointe* (Montreal: Fides 1968), 29.
4 NAC, King Diary, 20 September 1939.
5 Ibid., 25 September 1939.
6 Ibid.; Norman Ward, ed., *A Party Politician: The Memoirs of Chubby Power* (Toronto: Macmillan 1966), 346–7.
7 Jean-Guy Genest, *Godbout* (Sillery: Septentrion 1996), 118.
8 *Montreal Gazette*, 30 September 1939.
9 *Le Devoir*, 4 October 1939.
10 Frederick W. Gibson and Barbara Robertson, eds., *Ottawa at War: The Grant Dexter Memoranda, 1939–1945* (Winnipeg: Manitoba Record Society Publications 1994), 10.

11 André Laurendeau, *Witness for Quebec*, trans. P. Stratford (Toronto: Macmillan 1973), 30.

12 *Ottawa Citizen*, 26 September 1939.

13 Ward, ed., *Power*, 349.

14 Granatstein, *Canada's War*, 31; King Papers, B. Claxton to G.V. Ferguson, 3 October 1939.

15 Bruce Hutchison, *The Incredible Canadian* (Toronto: Longmans 1952), 263.

16 NAC, Lapointe Papers, Vol. 50, W.S. Edwards to Lapointe, 13 October 1939.

17 Conrad Black, *Duplessis* (Toronto: McClelland and Stewart 1977), 209.

18 Ibid., 208.

19 *Montreal Gazette*, 10 October 1939; *Le Devoir*, 10 October 1939.

20 King Papers, King to Lapointe, 6 October 1939.

21 *Montreal Gazette*, 13 October 1939.

22 Ibid., 16 October 1939.

23 Ibid., 9 October 1939.

24 Ward, ed., *Power*, 348.

25 *Le Devoir*, 24 October 1939.

26 Rumilly, *Histoire de Québec*, 38:56.

27 *Montreal Gazette*, 16 October 1939.

28 Hutchison, *The Incredible Canadian*, 263.

29 Laurendeau, *Witness for Quebec*, 33; *Montreal Gazette*, 21 October 1939.

30 *Montreal Gazette*, 20 October 1939.

31 Ibid., 25 October 1939; Ward, ed., *Power*, 130.

32 King Diary, 26 October 1939.

33 Ibid., 25 October 1939.

34 King Papers, T.C. Davis to King, 26 October 1939.

35 *Time*, 6 November 1939, quoted in Black, *Duplessis*, 219.

36 Rumilly, *Histoire de Québec*, 38:59; Granatstein, *Canada's War*, 34.

37 Quoted in Granatstein, *Canada's War*, 32; Black, *Duplessis*, 215.

38 King Papers, Lapointe to King, 8 December 1939.

39 Ibid.

40 Lapointe Papers, Vol. 33, file 147, Norman Rogers to Lapointe, 11 December 1939.

41 King Papers, James Gardiner to Lapointe, 9 December 1939.

42 Ibid., King to Lapointe, 16 December 1939. Annotated: 'Identical letter sent to all Cabinet ministers.'

43 Paul Bychok, '"La muraille qui vous protège": Ernest Lapointe and French Canada, 1935–1941,' MA thesis, Queen's University, 1985, 230–1.

27: Wartime Election

1 NAC, King Diary, 5 May 1928.
2 J.L. Granatstein, *A Man of Influence: Norman A. Robertson and Canadian Statecraft, 1929–1968* (Ottawa: Deneau 1981), 84.
3 House of Commons *Debates*, 23 May 1940, 144; see Reg Whitaker, 'Official Repression of Communism during World War II,' *Labour/Le Travail* (Spring 1986), 135–66.
4 NAC, King Papers, Lapointe to G. Conant, 15 September 1939.
5 King Diary, 16 November 1939.
6 King Papers, O.D. Skelton to King, 13 December 1939.
7 Norman Ward, ed., *A Party Politician: The Memoirs of Chubby Power* (Toronto: Macmillan 1966), 351; King Diary, 4 January 1940.
8 King Diary, 24 November 1939.
9 King Papers, Lapointe to King, 20 December 1939.
10 King Diary, 4 January 1940; Ward, ed., *Power*, 351.
11 Frederick W. Gibson and Barbara Robertson, eds., *Ottawa at War: The Grant Dexter Memoranda, 1939–1945* (Winnipeg: Manitoba Record Society Publications 1994), 39–40; NAC, Lapointe Papers, Vol. 48, J. McNeil to Lapointe, 23 February 1940.
12 Gibson and Robertson, eds., *Dexter Memoranda*, 39–40.
13 G. Grube, 'Those Defence Regulations,' *Canadian Forum* (January 1941).
14 Lapointe Papers, Vol. 34, W. Eggleston and F. Charpentier to Lapointe, 28 June 1940.
15 Ibid., M. Bernier to Monseigneur Paul Bernier, 4 July 1940; Monseigneur Bernier to M. Bernier, 8 July 1940.
16 Ibid., E.J. McMurray to T.C. Crerar, 19 June 1940.
17 Wilfrid Eggleston, *While I Still Remember* (Toronto: Ryerson 1968), 262.
18 Ibid., 263; King Papers, H.A. Bruce to Lapointe, 11 July 1940.
19 Gibson and Robertson, eds., *Dexter Memoranda*, 33.
20 King Diary, 7 February 1940.
21 Ibid., 18 January 1940.
22 Ibid., 25 January 1940. King wrote in his diary, 'I told him [Lapointe] this was a matter I had to decide myself.'
23 Ibid., 1 February 1940.
24 Ibid.
25 Ibid., 15 February 1940.
26 Ibid., 2 July 1940.
27 Ibid., 9 February, 8 May 1940.
28 Gibson and Roberson, eds., *Dexter Memoranda*, 46.

29 King Diary, 14 February 1940.
30 Ibid., 29 March 1940.
31 King Papers, D.A. McEwen to King, 8 March 1940.
32 Lapointe Papers, Vol. 48, Paul Bouchard, election pamphlet, March 1940.
33 King Papers, King to C. Power, 25 March 1940; *Ottawa Citizen*, 26 March 1940.
34 R. Rumilly, *Histoire de la Province de Québec*, Vol. 38, *Ernest Lapointe* (Montreal: Fides 1968), 118.
35 Ibid., 119.
36 King Diary, 29 March 1940.
37 Ibid., 1 May 1940.
38 Ibid., 10, 11 May 1940.
39 House of Commons *Debates*, 23 May 1940, 143.
40 Ibid., 11 June 1940, 671.
41 King Diary, 29 May 1940.
42 Gibson and Robertson, eds., *Dexter Memoranda*, 69.

28: The National Resources Mobilization Act

1 NAC, King Diary, 5 June 1940.
2 Lapointe's BBC broadcast to the French, 26 October 1940, quoted in Elspeth Chisholm, '"Never": Ernest Lapointe and Conscription,' *Canada: An Historical Magazine*, no. 4 (June 1976), 48; *Montreal Gazette*, 28 October 1940.
3 Frederick W. Gibson and Barbara Robertson, eds., *Ottawa at War: The Grant Dexter Memoranda, 1939–1945* (Winnipeg: Manitoba Record Society Publications 1994), 76–7, 83.
4 Norman Ward, ed., *A Party Politician: The Memoirs of Chubby Power* (Toronto: Macmillan 1966), 347; King Diary, 17 June 1940.
5 Lapointe was well aware that this was not what he had always said. In a handwritten note he set out his rationale for changing his mind on compulsory service: 'How could any thinking person have been through the world's experiences of the last months without having to give honest, careful reconsideration to everything he or she has hitherto thought and believed? Are we not compelled by our sacred interest to say yes, when we would say no a few years ago?' NAC, Lapointe Papers, Vol. 48, file 22.
6 Mason Wade, *The French Canadians, 1760–1967*, Vol. 2 (Toronto: Macmillan 1968), 933.
7 Chisholm, 'Lapointe and Conscription,' 44.
8 R. Rumilly, *Histoire de la Province de Québec*, Vol. 38, *Ernest Lapointe* (Montreal: Fides 1968), 184.
9 L. Richer, 'Ernest Lapointe,' *L'Action Nationale* (December 1941), 274.
10 King Diary, 25 June 1940.

11 Ibid., 24, 25 June 1940.
12 Ibid., 11 July 1940.
13 Interview, Odette Ouimet, 3 March 1995.
14 *Toronto Star*, 1 August 1940; *Le Devoir*, 2 August 1940.
15 Chisholm, 'Lapointe and Conscription,' 45.
16 House of Commons *Debates*, 5 August 1940, 2451.
17 King Diary, 3, 5 August 1940; interview, Odette Ouimet, 3 March 1995.
18 NAC, King Papers, Philippe Hamel et al. to King and Lapointe, 8 August 1940.
19 Ibid., Lapointe to Hamel, 14 August 1940.
20 Rumilly, *Lapointe*, 38:199–200.
21 Wade, *French Canadians*, 2:933.
22 André Laurendeau, *Witness for Quebec*, trans. P. Stratford (Toronto: Macmillan 1973), 44.
23 *Le Devoir*, 16 August 1940.
24 Lapointe Papers, Vol. 48, file 22–3.
25 King Diary, 5 September 1940.
26 Gibson and Robertson, eds., *Dexter Memoranda*, 77.
27 King Papers, Lapointe to C.D. Howe, 3 December 1940.
28 King Diary, 19 September 1940.
29 The chairman of the Civil Service Commission informed Pierre Casgrain that of 155 personnel requisitions from the department of munitions and supplies in October 1940, only 14 had requested bilingual candidates. Paul Bychok, '"La muraille qui vous protège": Ernest Lapointe and French Canada, 1935–1941,' MA thesis, Queen's University, 1985, 244–5.
30 Lapointe Papers, Vol. 23, file 78.
31 Bychok, 'Ernest Lapointe,' 281.
32 Ibid., 244.
33 King Diary, 19 September 1940.
34 King Papers, Lapointe to King, [September 1940].
35 King Diary, 20 September 1940.
36 Gibson and Robertson, eds., *Dexter Memoranda*, 77, 82–4.
37 Ibid., 83.
38 Ward, ed., *Power*, 123.
39 Queen's University Archives, Grant Dexter Papers, J. Dafoe to Dexter, 16 October 1940.

29: Vichy

1 Paul M. Couture, 'The Vichy–Free French Propaganda War in Quebec, 1940–1942,' Canadian Historical Association, *Historical Papers 1978*, 210.

2 R.R. James, ed., *Chips: The Diaries of Sir Henry Channon* (London: Penguin 1967), 415.
3 Eric Amyot, *Le Québec entre Pétain et de Gaulle* (Montreal: Fides 1999), 105–6.
4 Couture, 'Vichy,' 208.
5 NAC, King Papers, Lapointe to J.L. Ralston, 30 September 1940.
6 Amyot, *Pétain et de Gaulle*, 115.
7 Ibid., 39.
8 Ibid., 38.
9 *Documents on Canadian External Relations (DCER)*, Vol. 8, 785, Skelton to King, postscript, 18 October 1940.
10 Amyot, *Pétain et de Gaulle*, 43.
11 NAC, Lapointe Papers, Vol. 27, O.D. Skelton to Lapointe, 26 October 1940, enclosing copies of Churchill's telegram to Roosevelt and King George VI's message to Marshal Pétain.
12 Elspeth Chisholm, '"Never": Ernest Lapointe and Conscription,' *Canada: An Historical Magazine*, no. 4 (June 1976), 46–88.
13 NAC, King Diary, 25 October 1940.
14 *Le Devoir*, 28 October 1940.
15 Elizabeth Armstrong, *French Canadian Opinion on the War, January 1940– June 1941* (Toronto: Ryerson 1942), 1.
16 House of Commons *Debates*, 3 December 1940, 642; *Le Devoir*, 4 December 1940.
17 Frederick W. Gibson and Barbara Robertson, eds., *Ottawa at War: The Grant Dexter Memoranda, 1939–1945* (Winnipeg: Manitoba Record Society Publications 1994), 109.
18 King Diary, 29 November 1940.
19 Lapointe Papers, Vol. 27, M. Hepburn to Lapointe, 4 December 1940; Lapointe to Hepburn, 14 December 1940.
20 *Le Devoir*, 14–16 January 1941; *Ottawa Citizen*, 14–16 January 1941.
21 King Diary, 18 January 1941.
22 Ibid., 6 February 1941; King Papers, Lapointe to King, 30 January 1941.
23 Lapointe Papers, Vol. 35, Lapointe to Sir Eugène Fiset, 5 December 1940; Jean-Guy Genest, *Godbout* (Sillery: Septentrion 1996), 199.
24 Conrad Black, *Duplessis* (Toronto: McClelland and Stewart 1977), 238–9.
25 Mason Wade, *The French Canadians, 1760–1967*, Vol. 2 (Toronto: Macmillan 1968), 935.
26 King Diary, 17 January 1941.
27 *Ottawa Citizen*, 25 February 1941.
28 Ibid., 11 January 1941.

29 House of Commons *Debates*, 1941, 1073.
30 Queen's University Archives, Grant Dexter Papers, J.W. Dafoe to Dexter, 1 March 1941. Although Dafoe had forgotten, the *Globe* had in fact criticized Lapointe's disavowal of Riddell at the time in a front-page editorial (6 December 1935).
31 Charles Bowman, *Ottawa Editor* (Sidney, BC: Grays 1966), 221–4.
32 *Ottawa Citizen*, 28 February 1941.
33 House of Commons *Debates*, 27 February 1941, 1069.
34 *Ottawa Citizen*, 28 February 1941.
35 King Papers, E.J. McMurray to Lapointe, 19 July 1941.
36 Paul Bychok, '"La muraille qui vous protège": Ernest Lapointe and French Canada, 1935–1941,' MA thesis, Queen's University, 1985, 266.
37 John MacFarlane, *Ernest Lapointe and Quebec's Influence on Canadian Foreign Policy* (Toronto: University of Toronto Press 1999), 167.
38 King Diary, 20 March 1941.
39 *DCER*, Vol. 8, Commander d'Argenlieu to Acting Under-Secretary of State for External Affairs, 30 April 1941, 611.
40 Amyot, *Pétain et de Gaulle*, 145.

30: Last Days

1 NAC, Cabinet War Committee Minutes, 9 May 1941, quoted in Paul Bychok, '"La muraille qui vous protège": Ernest Lapointe and French Canada, 1935–1941,' MA thesis, Queen's University, 1985, 260–2.
2 Mason Wade, *The French Canadians, 1760–1967*, Vol. 2 (Toronto: Macmillan 1968), 944.
3 *Toronto Star*, 16 May 1941.
4 Wade, *French Canadians*, 2:944; NAC, Lapointe Papers, Vol. 27, L.-M. Gouin to Lapointe, Leon Gray of *La Patrie* to Lapointe, May 1941.
5 J.L. Granatstein, *Canada's War: The Politics of the Mackenzie King Government, 1939–1945* (Toronto: Oxford University Press 1975), 203–4.
6 NAC, King Papers, King to Vincent Massey, 13 June 1941.
7 Ibid., Lapointe to Vincent Massey, 13 June 1941. In August King did go to England for three weeks, and Lapointe became acting prime minister without any of the repercussions both feared.
8 King Papers, Cardinal Villeneuve to Lapointe (copy to King), 21 July 1941.
9 Lapointe Papers, Vol. 23, Cardinal Villeneuve to Lapointe, 5 September 1941; Lapointe to Cardinal Villeneuve, 8 September 1941.
10 Conrad Black, *Duplessis* (Toronto: McClelland and Stewart 1977), 240.
11 Lapointe Papers, Vol. 23. Lapointe signed Gillet's release, 9 October 1941.

12 Black, *Duplessis*, 240.

13 Corolyn Cox, 'Lapointe: Bulwark against "Fifth Column,"' *Christian Science Monitor*, 2 August 1941; *Maclean's*, 1 August 1941.

14 Lapointe Papers, Vol. 36. There are three letters from Lieutenant Hugues Lapointe to his father: no date, 18 August, 25 September 1941.

15 J.L. Granatstein and J.M. Hitsman, *Broken Promises: A History of Conscription in Canada* (Toronto: Copp Clark 1985), 160; *Maclean's*, 1 August 1941.

16 Frederick W. Gibson and Barbara Robertson, eds., *Ottawa at War: The Grant Dexter Memoranda, 1939–1945* (Winnipeg: Manitoba Record Society Publications 1994), 196.

17 *Montreal Gazette*, 25 September 1941.

18 Elspeth Chisholm, '"Never": Ernest Lapointe and Conscription,' *Canada: An Historical Magazine*, no. 4 (June 1976), 48.

19 King Papers, Lapointe to King, 20 October 1941.

20 Ibid., Lapointe to King, 26 October, 5 November 1941. Pierre Casgrain visited Lapointe the day before he went into the hospital and found him very distressed about the possibility of conscription; Thérèse Casgrain, *A Woman in a Man's World* (Toronto: McClelland and Stewart 1972), 100.

21 Interview, Odette Ouimet, 3 March 1995.

22 King Papers, King to Lapointe, 16 November 1941.

23 King's account of Lapointe's death comes from the Diary, 8–19 November 1941.

24 *Globe and Mail*, 27 November 1941.

25 For example, the *Montreal Daily Star*, 27 November 1941. At St Eloi, Lapointe's birthplace, there is a commemorative plaque beside his boyhood home.

26 J.W. Pickersgill, *The Mackenzie King Record*, Vol. 1, *1939–1944* (Toronto: University of Toronto Press 1960), 303.

27 Ibid., 291.

28 Granatstein, *Canada's War*, 222.

29 King Papers, Gladstone Murray, General Manager CBC, to J.A. Hume, Private Secretary to J.T. Thorson, Minister of National War Services, 27 April 1942; J.T. Thorson to W. Turnbull, Principal Secretary to the Prime Minister, 29 April 1942.

30 Wade, *French Canadians*, 2:950, 952; J.W. Pickersgill, in a review of Granatstein's *Canada's War* in *The Beaver* (June 1976), 61.

31 Norman Ward, ed., *A Party Politician: The Memoirs of Chubby Power* (Toronto: Macmillan 1966), 133; interview, Odette Ouimet, 3 March 1995.

32 André Laurendeau, *Witness for Quebec* (Toronto: Macmillan 1973), 51.

33 See Michael D. Behiels, 'The Bloc Populaire Canadien and the Origins of French-Canadian Neo-nationalism, 1942–8,' *The Canadian Historical Review* (December 1982), 487–512.
34 Wade, *French Canadians*, 2:1036.
35 Ibid., 1052.
36 Ibid., 1068.
37 Ibid., 1048–9.
38 NAC, RG 37, Series B, Vol. 463, transcript of CBC radio broadcast presented by Elspeth Chisholm, 'Ernest Lapointe – The Last Lieutenant,' 3 May 1964, 16. Excerpt from recorded interview with Mr Justice Roger Ouimet.

Conclusion

1 NAC, RG 37, Series B, Vol. 463, transcript of CBC radio broadcast presented by Elspeth Chisholm, 'Ernest Lapointe – The Last Lieutenant,' 3 May 1964, 3. Interview with René Lévesque.
2 J.W. Pickersgill dedicated the first volume of *The Mackenzie King Record* (1960): 'To the memory of Ernest Lapointe, devoted comrade in arms in the longest and closest partnership in the political life of Canada.'
3 Transcript, Chisholm radio broadcast, 7. Interview with C.D. Power.
4 NAC, King Diary, 4 April 1940.
5 Lapointe, radio broadcast, reported in *Montreal Gazette*, 10 October 1939.
6 King Diary, 25 October 1939.

Bibliography

Manuscript Sources

National Archives of Canada
  Cabinet War Committee Minutes
  A.K. Cameron Papers
  Dandurand Papers
  Department of External Affairs Records
  Department of Justice Records
  Sir Lomer Gouin Papers
  King Diary
  King Papers
  Lapointe Papers
  Picard Papers
  O.D. Skelton Papers
Queen's University Archives
  T.A. Crerar Papers
  Grant Dexter Papers
  Charles Gavan Power Papers
  Norman Rogers Papers

Publications

Canada, House of Commons. *Debates*
Canadian Annual Review
The Canadian Who's Who. 1936–7 and 1938–9
Documents on Canadian External Affairs. Vols. 3–8

Newspapers, Magazines, and Periodicals

L'Action Nationale
Canadian Annual Review
Canadian Forum
Le Devoir
Le Droit
Globe (after 1936 *Globe and Mail*)
Maclean's Magazine
Manitoba Free Press (after 1931 *Winnipeg Free Press*)
Montreal Gazette
Ottawa Citizen
Ottawa Journal
La Presse
Saturday Night
Toronto Daily Star

Interviews

Edouard Handy, 19 November 1995 (telephone)
Odette Ouimet, 3 March 1995
J.W. Pickersgill, 10 May 1995

Books and Articles

Abella, I.M., and H. Troper. *None Is Too Many: Canada and the Jews of Europe, 1933–1948*. Toronto: Lester and Orpen Dennys 1982.

Amyot, Eric. *Le Québec entre Pétain et de Gaulle: Vichy, la France Libre et les Canadiens Français, 1940–1945*. Montreal: Fides 1999.

Armstrong, Elizabeth. *French-Canadian Opinion on the War, January 1940–June 1941*. Toronto: Ryerson 1942.

Bernier, Paul. *Ernest Lapointe: Deputé de Kamouraska, 1904–1919*. Cahiers d'histoire No. 14. Société Historique de la Côte-du-Sud. La Pocatière 1979.

Betcherman, Lita-Rose. 'The Customs Scandal of 1926.' *The Beaver* (April/May 2001), 14–19.

– *The Swastika and the Maple Leaf: Fascist Movements in Canada in the Thirties*. Toronto: Fitzhenry and Whiteside 1975.

Black, Conrad. *Duplessis*. Toronto: McClelland and Stewart 1977.

Bothwell, Robert, and John English. 'Dirty Work at the Crossroads: New Perspectives on the Riddell Incident.' *CHA Historical Papers* (1972), 263–85.

Bowman, Charles. *Ottawa Editor*. Sidney, BC: Grays 1966.

Bychok, Paul. '"La muraille qui vous protège": Ernest Lapointe and French Canada, 1935–1941.' MA thesis, Queen's University 1985.

Casgrain, Thérèse. *A Woman in a Man's World*. Translated by Joyce Marshall. Toronto: McClelland and Stewart 1972.

Chisholm, Elspeth. 'Ernest Lapointe – The Last Lieutenant.' CBC Sunday Night Broadcast (3 May 1964). Transcript in National Archives of Canada.

– '"Never": Ernest Lapointe and Conscription, 1935–1944.' *Canada: An Historical Magazine*, no. 3 (March 1976), 3–21, no. 4 (June 1976), 40–53.

Cook, Ramsay. 'A Canadian Account of the 1926 Imperial Conference.' In K. Robinson and W.H. Morris-Jones, eds., *Journal of Commonwealth Political Studies* 3 (1965), 50–63.

– *The Dafoe-Sifton Correspondence, 1919–1927*. Vol. 2. Altona, MB: D.W. Freisen 1966.

Couture, Paul M. 'The Vichy–Free French Propaganda War in Quebec, 1940–1942.' *CHA Historical Papers* (1978), 200–16.

Dafoe, John W. *Clifford Sifton in Relation to His Times*. Toronto: Macmillan 1931.

Dawson, R. MacGregor. *The Government of Canada*. Rev. ed. Toronto: University of Toronto Press 1963. First published 1947.

– *William Lyon Mackenzie King*. Vol. 1. *A Political Biography, 1874–1923*. Toronto: University of Toronto Press 1958.

Dirks, Gerald E. *Canada's Refugee Policy: Indifference or Opportunism?* Montreal: McGill-Queen's University Press 1977.

Eayrs, James. *In Defence of Canada*. Vol. 1. *From the Great War to the Great Depression*. Toronto: University of Toronto Press 1964.

– *In Defence of Canada*. Vol. 2. *Appeasement and Rearmament*. Toronto: University of Toronto Press 1965.

Eggleston, Wilfrid. *While I Still Remember: A Personal Record*. Toronto: Ryerson 1968.

English, John. *Borden: His Life and World*. Toronto: McGraw-Hill 1977.

– 'The "French Lieutenant" in Ottawa.' In R. Kenneth Carty and W. Peter Ward, eds., *National Politics and Community in Canada*. Vancouver: University of British Columbia Press 1986, 184–200.

Ferguson, G.V. *John W. Dafoe*. Toronto: Ryerson 1948.

Ferland, Philippe. *Paul Gouin*. Montreal: Guerin 1991.

Ferns, H.S., and B. Ostry. *The Age of Mackenzie King: The Rise of the Leader*. Toronto: Lorimer 1976. First published 1955.

Figler, Bernard. *Sam Jacobs: Member of Parliament*. Gardenvale, PQ: Harpell's Press 1959.

Forsey, Eugene. 'Mr. Lapointe and the Padlock Act.' *Canadian Forum* (August 1938), 148–50.

Genest, Jean-Guy. *Godbout*. Sillery: Septentrion 1996.

Gibson, Frederick W., and Barbara Robertson, eds. *Ottawa at War: The Grant Dexter Memoranda, 1939–1945*. Winnipeg: Manitoba Record Society Publications 1994.

Giesler, Patricia. *Valour Remembered: Canada and the First World War*. Ottawa: Department of Veteran Affairs 1982.

Graham, Roger. *Arthur Meighen*. Vol. 2. *And Fortune Fled*. Toronto: Clarke Irwin 1963.

Granatstein, J.L. *Canada's War: The Politics of the Mackenzie King Government, 1939–1945*. Toronto: Oxford University Press 1975.

– *A Man of Influence: Norman A. Robertson and Canadian Statecraft, 1929–1968*. Ottawa: Deneau 1981.

– *The Ottawa Men: The Civil Service Mandarins, 1935–1957*. Toronto: University of Toronto Press 1982.

Granatstein, J.L., and J.M. Hitsman. *Broken Promises: A History of Conscription in Canada*. Toronto: Copp Clark 1985. First published 1977.

Griffin, Frederick. *Variety Show*. Toronto: Macmillan 1936.

Grube, G. 'Those Defence Regulations.' *Canadian Forum* (January 1941), 304–6.

Hamelin, Marcel, ed. *Les mémoires du Sénateur Raoul Dandurand, 1861–1942*. Quebec: Presses de l'Université Laval 1967.

Hutchison, Bruce. *The Far Side of the Street*. Toronto: Macmillan 1976.

– *The Incredible Canadian*. Toronto: Longmans 1952.

James, R.R., ed. *Chips: The Diaries of Sir Henry Channon*. London: Penguin 1967.

Laurendeau, André. *Witness for Quebec*. Translated by P. Stratford. Toronto: Macmillan 1973.

Lederle, John W. 'The Liberal Convention of 1919 and the Selection of Mackenzie King.' *Dalhousie Review* (April 1947), 85–92.

Levesque, Andrée. *Virage à Gauche Interdit: Les communistes, les socialistes et leurs ennemis au Québec, 1929–1939*. Montreal: Boréal 1984.

Macdonald, E.M. *Recollections, Political and Personal*. Toronto: Ryerson 1938.

MacFarlane, John. *Ernest Lapointe and Quebec's Influence on Canadian Foreign Policy*. Toronto: University of Toronto Press 1999.

Martin, Paul. *A Very Public Life*. Vol. 1. *Far from Home*. Ottawa: Deneau 1983.

Massey, Vincent. *What's Past Is Prologue*. Toronto: Macmillan 1963.

McGee, Jean-Charles. *Laurier, Lapointe, St Laurent: Histoire politique du Québec-Est*. Quebec City: Belisle 1948.

McKenzie, Vernon. 'Customs' House-Cleaning Imperative – No Matter Whose Head Comes Off!' *Maclean's*, 1 March 1926, 24.

McNaught, Kenneth. *A Prophet in Politics: A Biography of J.S. Woodsworth*. Toronto: University of Toronto Press 1959.

Munro, J.A. 'The Riddell Incident Reconsidered.' *External Affairs* (October 1969), 366–75.

Munro, J.K. 'Ottawa Is Ready for the Worst: Will Next Premier Be a Farmer? The Rise of Lapointe.' *Maclean's*, December 1919, 24.

Neatby, H. Blair. 'Mackenzie King and French Canada.' *Journal of Canadian Studies* 11, no. 1 (February 1976), 3–13.

– *William Lyon Mackenzie King*. Vol. 2. *1924–1932: The Lonely Heights*. Toronto: University of Toronto Press 1963.

– *William Lyon Mackenzie King*. Vol. 3. *1932–1939: The Prism of Unity*. Toronto: University of Toronto Press 1976.

O'Leary, Grattan. *Recollections of People, Press, and Politics*. Toronto: Macmillan 1977.

Oliver, Peter. *G. Howard Ferguson: Ontario Tory*. Toronto: University of Toronto Press 1977.

Pearson, Lester B. *Mike: The Memoirs of the Rt. Hon. Lester B. Pearson*. Vol. 1. *1897–1948*. Toronto: University of Toronto Press 1972.

Pickersgill, J.W. *The Mackenzie King Record*. Vol. 1. *1939–1944*. Toronto: University of Toronto Press 1960.

– *Seeing Canada Whole: A Memoir*. Toronto: Fitzhenry and Whiteside 1994.

Prang, Margaret. *N.W. Rowell: Ontario Nationalist*. Toronto: University of Toronto Press 1975.

Regehr, T.D. *The Beauharnois Scandal: A Story of Canadian Entrepreneurship and Politics*. Toronto: University of Toronto Press 1990.

– 'High Powered Lawyers, Veteran Lobbyists, Cunning Propagandists: Canadian Lawyers and the Beauharnois Scandal.' In Carol Wilton, ed., *Beyond the Law*. Toronto: The Osgoode Society 1990, 403–24.

Regenstreif, Peter S. 'A Threat to Leadership: C.A. Dunning and Mackenzie King.' *Dalhousie Review* 44 (1964–5), 272–89.

Richer, Léopold. 'Ernest Lapointe.' *L'Action Nationale* (December 1941), 273–7.

– *Silhouettes du monde politique*. Montreal: Éditions Zodiac 1940.

Riddell, Walter. *World Security by Conference*. Toronto: Ryerson 1947.

Robertson, Susan Mann. 'Variations on a Nationalist Theme: Henri Bourassa and Abbé Groulx in the 1920s.' *CHA Historical Papers* (1970), 109–19.

R.T.L. 'Mr. Lapointe.' *Maclean's*, December 1933.

Rumilly, Robert. *Histoire de la Province de Québec*. Vol. 27. *Rivalité Gouin-Lapointe*. Montreal: Fides 1955.

– *Histoire de la Province de Québec*. Vol. 38. *Ernest Lapointe*. Montreal: Fides 1968.

Rutledge, J.L. 'The Mantle of Elijah: The Story of the Man Who May Take Laurier's Place.' *Maclean's*, 15 February 1920, 18.

Schull, Joseph. *Laurier: The First Canadian.* Toronto: Macmillan 1965.

Shirer, William L. *Berlin Diary.* New York: Knopf 1941.

Snell, James G., and Frederick Vaughan. *The Supreme Court of Canada: History of the Institution.* Toronto: The Osgoode Society 1985.

Stacey, C.P. *Canada and the Age of Conflict: A History of Canadian External Policies.* Vol. 2. *1921–1948: The Mackenzie King Era.* Toronto: University of Toronto Press 1981.

Thompson, John Herd, and Allen Seager. *Canada, 1922–1939: Decades of Discord.* Toronto: McClelland and Stewart 1985.

Veatch, Richard. *Canada and the League of Nations.* Toronto: University of Toronto Press 1975.

Vigod, Bernard. *Quebec before Duplessis: The Political Career of Louis-Alexandre Taschereau.* Montreal: McGill-Queen's University Press 1986.

Wade, Mason. *The French Canadians, 1760–1967.* Vol. 2. *1911–1967.* Toronto: Macmillan 1968.

Waite, P.B. 'French Canadian Isolationism and English Canada: An Elliptical Foreign Policy, 1935–1939.' *Journal of Canadian Studies* 18, no. 2 (Summer 1983), 132–48.

Ward, Norman, ed. *A Party Politician: The Memoirs of Chubby Power.* Toronto: Macmillan 1966.

Whitaker, Reg. 'Official Repression of Communism during World War II.' *Labour/Le Travail* 17 (Spring 1986), 135–66.

Wigley, Philip. *Canada and the Transition to Commonwealth: British-Canadian Relations, 1917–1926.* Cambridge: Cambridge University Press 1977.

Wilbur, Richard. *The Bennett Administration, 1930–1935.* CHA Historical Booklet No. 24. Ottawa 1969.

Williams, David Ricardo. *Duff: A Life in the Law.* Toronto: The Osgoode Society 1984.

Illustration Credits

Index

Aberhart, William, 198, 329; debt legislation, 236–9, 245; Press Bill, 238; ruled *ultra vires*, 240
Action Catholique, L', 141, 220, 223, 277, 283
Action Française, L', 233
Action Libérale Nationale (ALN), 195–8, 204–5, 209, 211, 218, 233, 277, 278, 287, 290, 292
Action Nationale, L', 212, 271
Admiralty Act, 165
Alberta Act of 1905, 100–1, 130, 154
Alberta schools question, 100–2, 141–2, 154, 351
Allward, Walter, 218
Amery, L.S., 50, 123, 196
Anderson, J.T.M., 159–60
Anglin, Frank, 78, 146–7, 167–8, 170
Anti-Semitism: in Germany, 241; Crystal Night, 251–2; in Quebec, 221, 231, 241, 242–3, 253, 277; in Canada at large, 242, 254, 304
Arcand, Adrien, 256, 296, 310
Archambault, Joseph, 41
Argenlieu, Georges Thierry d', 335
Armstrong, E.H., 81
Article X of League of Nations

Covenant, 52–4, 59, 65, 68, 134, 151, 250
Athlone, Earl of, 305
Austria: annexed by Hitler, 242
Aylesworth, Sir Allen, 27, 29, 30
Aziz, Moses, 103, 114

Baldwin, Stanley, 123, 135, 163, 196
Balfour, Lord, 123–5
Balfour Declaration, 242
Balfour report (1926), 126–7, 129, 161, 174, 179
Bank of Canada Act, 194, 215, 220, 235
Beauchesne, Arthur, 231
Beaudry, Laurent, 205–7, 380n17
Beauharnois power project, 128, 154–6, 158, 184–5, 188, 376n13
Béland, Henri, 38–9, 47
Belcourt, Napoleon, 119
Belley, L.G., 112–13
Bennett, R.B., 33, 150, 154, 156, 176, 180, 182, 183–4, 186, 187, 194, 198, 199, 211, 215–16, 236; on imperial connection, 174; prime minister, 178; Ottawa conference (1932), 190, 198; his 'new deal' ruled *ultra vires*, 235